COBOL/400

J. Ranade IBM Series

AS/400 Application Development Using COBOL/400

Gerald S. Kaplan

McGraw-Hill

New York   San Francisco   Washington, D.C.   Auckland   Bogotá
Caracas   Lisbon   London   Madrid   Mexico City   Milan
Montreal   New Delhi   San Juan   Singapore
Sydney   Tokyo   Toronto

Library of Congress Cataloging-in-Publication Data

Kaplan, Gerald S.
  AS/400 application development using COBOL/400 / Gerald S. Kaplan.
    p.   cm. — (J. Ranade IBM series)

  Includes index.
  ISBN 0-07-034080-3 (hardcover)
  1. IBM AS/400 (Computer)—Programming. 2. COBOL (Computer program
language) 3. Application software—Development. I. Title.
  II. Series.
  QA76.8.I25919K43   1996
  005.2'45—dc20   96-3249
                                                                  CIP

McGraw-Hill

*A Division of The **McGraw·Hill** Companies*

1 2 3 4 5 6 7 8 9 0 DOC/DOC 9 0 1 0 9 8 7 6

ISBN 0-07-034080-3

*The sponsoring editor for this book was Jerry Papke, the editing
supervisor was Paul R. Sobel, and the production supervisor was
Suzanne W. B. Rapcavage. It was set in Century Schoolbook by
Carol Woolverton Studio in cooperation with Spring Point
Publishing Services.*

Printed and bound by R. R. Donnelley & Sons Company.

Appendixes D and G in this book are reprinted by permission from *Languages: Systems Application Architecture AD / Cycle COBOL / 400 Reference Summary, Version 2.* Copyright (1992) by International Business
Machine Corporation.

This book is printed on recycled, acid-free paper containing a
minimum of 50% recycled de-inked fiber.

This book is dedicated first and foremost to my parents, Stanley and Marcia Kaplan, who are entirely responsible for my being here in the first place. Without the assistance of a user's guide, online help, or the Internet, they were able to raise and influence me into what I am today.

To my sister Lisa, for always being around as an ear when I needed her.

To the grandmothers who are responsible for the first dedication: Dorothy Kepke and Bessie Goldman.

To the people who have helped enhance my quality of life: Wade Corbet, Nina Newby, Ken Moir (figure skating / ice dancing pros); Keiko Shintani, Mutsuko Yanagisawa (Japanese instructors).

And to my friends who have made life worth living (in no specific order): Donald Myers, Mark Maysonet, Fred Dillon, Karen Condon-Bruce, Ray Laterner, Sherwyn Samuel, Todd Wladika, Harold Wolf, Mercedes Hennessy, Shayna Pearl, Jun Onuma, Steve Lutz, Steven Lu, Alex Santagada, [this space for rent], Joan Walters.

This book was written using Microsoft Word 6.0 on my PS / 2 Model 90 with an HP LaserJet 4 Plus. All of the sample programs were developed and tested on an AS / 400 model C04 using OS / 400 version 2.3.

Contents

Part 2   COBOL/400 Enhancements

Part 3   AS/400 File Concepts

Part 4   Command Language

Part 6   Application Development with COBOL/400

Preface

Since the time I started writing programs on my cassette tape based TRS-80 Model I, I can remember listening to others predicting the death of some "verbose" programming language called COBOL. At the time I was only 15, and in my world, there wasn't much past BASIC, so I didn't pay too much attention. More than 15 years later, I am still listening to others trash COBOL and declare its forthcoming death.

In fact, COBOL is still alive and widely used. It has undergone several major revisions to keep it aligned with structured programming practices. Compilers exist on practically every platform, from microcomputers to mainframes. Extensions even exist to integrate existing COBOL programs with such object oriented languages as Smalltalk.

COBOL/400 is one of several languages available on the IBM AS/400. It is IBM's version of the ANSI standard of COBOL/85 and includes extensions that enable it to communicate with specific objects found only on the AS/400 (such as workstations, databases, printer files, etc.).

This book is designed to take you on a guided tour through developing an application that takes advantage of the most commonly used components of the AS/400. It is broken into six parts:

Part 1 gives you an introduction to the AS/400, the tools available on it, and the world famous "Hello World" program.

Part 2 discusses enhancements made to COBOL which can help make your programs more clear and concise. It discusses scope terminators, the in-line PERFORM statement, the EVALUATE statement, as well as some other noteworthy points.

Part 3 discusses files and how they relate to COBOL programs as well as the operating system. It goes into detail about display files, subfiles, and printer files.

Part 4 introduces OS/400's Command Language (CL). CL is an integral part of all applications developed on the AS/400—in fact, entire components can be developed in CL without having to use a high level language such as COBOL. It also discusses how to write commands which can make your applications more modular and flexible. OS/400 messages and message files are also discussed.

Part 5 discusses techniques that can be used when developing applications on the AS/400.

Part 6 takes you step by step through creating a telephone directory application. The application utilizes commands, CL programs, COBOL programs, display files, printer files, subfiles, physical and logical files, OS/400 APIs and OS/400 messaging. Each chapter in Part 6 adds another component to the overall application, showing how the application can be divided into logical modules. Each module can act as a stand-alone function and can be tested without the need for any of the other modules.

Finally, a variety of appendices are provided for your reference that contain information useful during the development cycle.

There are a few points that you should note before embarking on this COBOL trip:

First, the samples in this book are just that—they are provided for illustrative purposes only. I tried to incorporate as many realistic examples as possible, but sometimes it was necessary to show how a statement works with a bogus example.

Second, the samples are not always fully optimized code. Since this book's main intent is to show *clear* examples, I have opted for clarity rather than cleverness. Variable names are often long and descriptive, as are many paragraph names. Comments have been kept to a minimum since paragraphs were kept short and their names imply what they do. I also omitted using paragraph numbers (i.e., 0100-MAIN-PARA) simply because I don't like them and I think they're ugly.

Finally, when writing the example programs, I paid particular attention to providing complete examples that are independent of each other; therefore you should be able to try out any examples in this book without any prerequisites.

There are two ways of entering commands in OS/400—by keyword and by position. For example, using keywords, a command may look like:

```
CRTPF FILE(file-name)
```

This same command can be executed with positional parameters. In the CRTPF command, the FILE parameter is the first parameter, therefore, the command can also be specified as:

```
CRTPF file-name
```

Throughout the book, I have used both the keyword format as well as the positional format of various commands in order to expose you to a variety of formats of the same command.

Finally, you may see some inconsistency in how certain actions are performed. This too is intentional, as my main intent was to illustrate that there is more than one way of accomplishing the same task.

Who this Book Is for

This book is aimed at those who will be developing applications on the AS/400 using IBM's COBOL/400. It assumes that the reader is already familiar with the COBOL language; however it does provide complete examples which are easy to follow and can help in learning COBOL. Although it is not necessary to have access to an AS/400, it certainly helps—seeing is believing.

This book contains information that would normally be found in 7 or 8 different IBM AS/400 documents ranging from the COBOL user's guide and reference to the Database Management Guide, thus it can provide a good desk reference where a set of manuals is not available.

If you are a student and are studying COBOL in an educational environment, this book will show you the rest of the big picture. Developing applications in the real world requires a knowledge of more than just COBOL. This book shows how COBOL integrates with the rest of OS/400 when creating applications.

Programmers and consultants who are already familiar with the IBM System/36 and have an interest in becoming familiar with the AS/400 will find this book useful because it will provide a reference point for comparing application development on the two platforms. An understanding of the differences between the two systems is important in order to prevent System/36 techniques from bleeding into an AS/400 development project.

The examples in this book were written on a system using OS/400 version 2 release 3 (V2R3). Upon completion of the book, IBM had released version 3. The system screens shown in this book are based on V2R3; therefore if you are using a system running V3R1 of OS/400, the screens may look slightly different.

Gerald S. Kaplan

Start Here

0

Read.Me (No Kidding)

It is most important to read this entire chapter before jumping into the rest of the book. The sections of this chapter prepare your environment for all examples in this book.

Note: You will need to have access to a command line in order to do the examples in this book. If your current user profile does not allow you to use a command line, you will need to contact the security administrator of your system.

Throughout this book, you will be presented with examples that you can perform on an IBM AS/400 computer. In order to perform them, you will need to have a library to put your work in. In simple terms, a library is an object that groups other objects together, much like that of a directory in MS-DOS or a folder on the Macintosh. Objects of various types can be placed within a library. An object can be any one of several types, including programs, data files, source files, etc. The name of an object must be unique for each object of a particular type within a library. For example, *two files* in the same library cannot have the same name, but a *file* and a *program* in the same library can have the same name.

0.1 Creating a Library for the Examples

The Create Library (CRTLIB) command is used to create a new library. Type the CRTLIB on the command entry line and press F4 to be prompted for the required information.

You must specify a name for your new library. The name you select may be up to 10 characters long. Throughout this book, this library will be referred to as YOURLIB. Whenever you see reference to YOURLIB, you should use the name of the library you are creating now. On the

```
                              Create Library (CRTLIB)

 Type choices, press Enter.

 Library  . . . . . . . . . . . .    _____    Name
 Library type . . . . . . . . . .    *PROD           *PROD, *TEST
 Text 'description' . . . . . . .    *BLANK
 _____



                                                                  Bottom
 F3=Exit    F4=Prompt   F5=Refresh   F10=Additional parameters  F12=Cancel
 F13=How to use this display         F24=More keys
```

Figure 0.1 Create library screen.

Create Library display (see Fig. 0.1), enter the library name and a text description of the library (the text description is for your reference only).

The library type can be either *PROD (production) or *TEST. OS/400 uses this indicator to prevent accidental updating of production database files when debugging programs. If the value specified for the library type is *PROD, change it to *TEST. After pressing Enter, you will receive a message indicating that your library was created.

0.2 Entering Commands and Parameters

Throughout this book, you will be given commands to enter on a command line. The examples in this book have all necessary parameters specified for you; thus you will only have to type the command exactly as it is shown.

There are several ways to enter commands on the AS/400.

- If you are unfamiliar with the parameters of a command, you can type the command on a command line, then press the F4 key to prompt you to fill in the parameters (as when you created your library in Sec. 0.1). The command prompter helps you fill in the information necessary to execute the command. It also provides you with the complete list of choices that you may have for each of the command's parameters. Additional help is available for each parameter by positioning the cursor in the field in question and then pressing the help key (or the F1 key).

- If you are familiar with the command and know its parameters, you can type the command, its parameters, and values on a command line. When you type a parameter followed by a value that is enclosed in parentheses, it is called a parameter in keyword form. For example, the CRTLIB command from the previous section would look like:

```
CRTLIB LIB(YOURNAME) TYPE(*TEST) TEXT('YOURLIB personal lib')
```

- If you know the positional form of the command, you can type a command followed by the parameter values excluding the parameter names. Parameters can only be entered in the sequence shown in the syntax diagram for the command (you can find this in the CL [Command Language] Reference book). The CRTLIB command would look like this:

```
CRTLIB YOURNAME *TEST TEXT('YOURLIB personal lib')
```

Throughout this book, commands, as well as their parameters and values, will be shown exactly as they should be typed on a command line. You always have the option of typing only the command name and then pressing the F4=Prompt key to see all possible parameters and choices.

0.3 Changing the Current Library

The current library is the library that is searched first when an object is requested. If you are familiar with MS-DOS, you can think of the current library as the current directory.

Use the Change Current Library (CHGCURLIB) command to change the current library to the new library you just created (or the one you plan to use if you already have a personal library):

```
CHGCURLIB CURLIB(YOURLIB)
```

You can verify that the CHGCURLIB command was successful by entering the Display Library List (DSPLIBL) command. Verify that YOURLIB is in the list and has a type of CURLIB in the "Type" column. Since the remaining steps in this chapter assume that the current library has been successfully changed to YOURLIB, it is important that this step be completed successfully.

0.4 Creating an Output Queue

OS/400 uses output queues to manage output destined for the printer. When a job creates printed output, it is first put into an output queue where it will be held until it is released to a printer (either manually or automatically by the system).

You should have a personal output queue so that all of your spooled output is always sent to that queue. Your system administrator may have already created a personal output queue for you. If so, you can skip to the next section.

If you do not already have a personal output queue, you can create one with the Create Output Queue (CRTOUTQ) command. Personal output queues are frequently named the same as your user profile. The following command can be used to create your personal output queue. YOUROUTQ is used as the output queue name, but you should replace it with your user profile name.

```
CRTOUTQ OUTQ(YOUROUTQ) TEXT('YOURPROFILE personal output queue')
```

Once created, you must now change your job to indicate that all spooled output should be put in this queue. This is accomplished with the Change Job (CHGJOB) command:

```
CHGJOB OUTQ(YOUROUTQ)
```

If you receive a message indicating that the output queue could not be found, you may not have successfully changed the current library to YOURLIB. It may be necessary to repeat the CHGCURLIB command as described in Sec. 0.3.

Once this command has been entered, YOUROUTQ will become the default output queue for your job.

0.5   Messages

When your user profile was first created, the system automatically generated a message queue by the same name. When messages are sent to you from either the system (i.e., compilers) or other users, the messages will be put in this queue. For example, when you submit a program to be compiled to the batch job queue, the system will send you a message to indicate whether the job was completed successfully (the compilation had no errors) or abnormally (there were errors in the source that prevented a successful compilation).

A message queue's mode determines how it notifies you when messages arrive. When you first sign on, your message queue is in notify mode. This means that when a message arrives for you, the "Message Waiting" light turns on at your workstation, but you cannot see the text of the message until you enter the Display Message (DSPMSG) command.

It is possible to change how the message queue notifies you of messages. For instance, if your message delivery mode is changed to BREAK, a message will be displayed on your workstation as soon as it arrives for you. The next section describes how to change your user profile to specify this mode.

0.6 Changing Your User Profile

Your user profile contains settings that determine how your environment is set up for you each time you sign on. As discussed earlier, you will be doing all of your work in YOURLIB; thus each time you sign on, you will need to enter the CHGCURLIB command to make YOURLIB the current library. It is possible to change your profile so that each time you sign on, YOURLIB is automatically set as your current library. You can also change your profile to use the output queue created earlier, as well as to change the message delivery mode so that when a message arrives for you, you see it immediately.

If you do not want to change your profile, then you must remember to change your current library to YOURLIB as well as to change your job to use YOUROUTQ each time you sign on to the system.

The following command will change your profile so that the current library will always be set to YOURLIB, message delivery will always be set to *BREAK, and your spooled output will default to output queue YOUROUTQ:

```
CHGPRF CURLIB(YOURLIB) DLVRY(*BREAK) OUTQ(YOUROUTQ)
```

When the command is completed, you should sign off and then sign back on again. Type the Display Library List (DSPLIBL) command to see that the correct library is now your current library (indicated by the word CUR) (see Fig. 0.2).

You can verify that your messages will arrive in break mode by typing the DSPMSG command. When the Display Messages display is shown, check that the delivery mode specifies *BREAK.

```
                         Display Library List
                                                    System:    SXXXXXXX
     Type options, press Enter.
       5=Display objects in library

     Opt  Library    Type      Text
       _   QSYS       SYS       System library
       _   QSYS2      SYS       System Library for CPI's
       _   QUSRSYS    SYS       SYSTEM LIBRARY FOR USERS
       _   QHLPSYS    SYS
       _   YOURLIB    CUR       My personal library
       _   QTEMP      USR
       _   QGPL       USR       GENERAL PURPOSE LIBRARY


                                                                Bottom
     F3=Exit   F12=Cancel   F17=Top   F18=Bottom
     (C) COPYRIGHT IBM CORP. 1980, 1993.
```

Figure 0.2 Displaying the current library list.

```
                    Display Job Definition Attributes
                                                  System:   SXXXXXXX
  Job:   DSP01

  Job description . . . . . . . . . . . . . . . . :   QDFTJOBD
    Library . . . . . . . . . . . . . . . . . . . :   QGPL
  Job queue . . . . . . . . . . . . . . . . . . . :
    Library . . . . . . . . . . . . . . . . . . . :
  Job priority (on job queue) . . . . . . . . . . :
  Output priority (on output queue) . . . . . . . :   5
  End severity  . . . . . . . . . . . . . . . . . :   30
  Message logging:
    Level . . . . . . . . . . . . . . . . . . . . :   4
    Severity  . . . . . . . . . . . . . . . . . . :   0
    Text  . . . . . . . . . . . . . . . . . . . . :   *NOLIST
  Log CL program commands . . . . . . . . . . . . :   *NO
  Printer device  . . . . . . . . . . . . . . . . :   PRT01
  Default output queue  . . . . . . . . . . . . . :   YOUROUTQ
    Library . . . . . . . . . . . . . . . . . . . :    *LIBL
                                                                More...
  Press Enter to continue.

  F3=Exit    F5=Refresh    F9=Change job    F12=Cancel    F16=Job menu
```

Figure 0.3 Displaying the current job's definition.

To determine if the output queue has been correctly changed, you can use the Work with Jobs command. Type WRKJOB on the command line and press Enter. Select option 2 (Display Job Definition Attributes; see Fig. 0.3) and then look at the *default output queue* and *Library* prompts to make sure they have been changed correctly. They should specify YOUROUTQ in YOURLIB.

0.7 Working with Spool Files

When a job creates output that is destined to be printed, the output is first accumulated in a spool file. Once the output is complete, the spool file is then held in the output queue until it is either released to a printer or deleted. In this section you will see how to preview the spool file on the display before printing it, as well as how to move the spool file to an output queue that is associated with a printer.

Before you can work with a spool file, you must create one. The following command will generate a report containing details about your current job:

```
WRKJOB OUTPUT(*PRINT)
```

After this command is executed, a spool file will be created and placed in your output queue. The spool file will be named QPDSPJOB.

The Work with Output Queue (WRKOUTQ) command is used to work with all spool files that are queued in an output queue. Enter

```
                        Work with Output Queue

   Queue:     YOUROUTQ      Library:    YOURLIB        Status:    RLS

   Type options, press Enter.
     1=Send    2=Change    3=Hold    4=Delete    5=Display    6=Release    7=Messages
     8=Attributes          9=Work with printing status

   Opt   File         User         User Data    Sts    Pages    Copies    Form Type    Pty
     _    QPDSPJOB     GERRYK                    RDY      5        1       *STD          5








                                                                         Bottom
   Parameters for options 1, 2, 3 or command
   ===> _____

   F3=Exit    F11=View 2    F12=Cancel    F22=Printers    F24=More keys
```

Figure 0.4 Working with an output queue.

the following command to work with all of the spooled files in
YOUROUTQ:

```
WRKOUTQ YOUROUTQ
```

The Work with Output Queue display is shown in Fig. 0.4. Type a 5 in
the Opt column next to the QPDSPJOB file to display it. QPDSPJOB is
the name of the printer file created by the WRKJOB command. When
you press Enter, you will be able to view the contents of the spool file as
it will be printed. When you are finished viewing the spooled file, press
Enter to return to the Work with Output Queue display.

As an alternative to using the WRKOUTQ command, you can also
use the Work with Spooled Files (WRKSPLF) command. The main difference between the two commands is that the WRKOUTQ command
works with all spool files that are in a single output queue, whereby the
WRKSPLF command works with all spool files created by your current
job (they may be located in different output queues). Entering the
WRKSPLF command with no parameters defaults to working with all
spooled files created by the current user.

0.8   Printing a Spooled File

Spool files that reside in your personal output queue will never be
printed unless you manually move them into an output queue that is
associated with a printer. Each printer on the AS/400 is associated with

exactly one output queue (which always has the same name as its associated printer). For example, if there is a printer device named PRT01, there will also be an output queue named PRT01. Moving a spool file from one output queue to another is accomplished using the same screen as you used in the preceding section when you displayed a spool file.

To print the spool file created in Sec. 0.7, perform the following actions. These actions assume that there is a printer on your system named PRT01.

Type the WRKOUTQ command as in Sec. 0.7.

Type option 2 (change) next to the spool file named QPDSPJOB; then press Enter.

The Change Spooled File Attributes screen will be shown (see Fig. 0.5). Locate the line that specifies which printer to use. Change the field from *OUTQ to PRT01; then press Enter.

The spooled file will be moved to the output queue associated with printer PRT01, and then printed (other system- maybe and/or operational-related factors that are beyond the scope of this book may prevent the spool file from immediately being printed).

```
                 Change Spooled File Attributes (CHGSPLFA)

 Type choices, press Enter.

 Spooled file . . . . . . . . . > QPDSPJOB Name, *SELECT
 Job name . . . . . . . . . . . > DSP01   Name, *
   User . . . . . . . . . . . >   GERRYK       Name
   Number . . . . . . . . . . >   025870 000000-999999
 Spooled file number  . . . . . > 1 1-9999, *ONLY, *LAST
 Printer  . . . . . . . . . . .   PRT01_____   Name, *SAME, *OUTQ
 Print sequence . . . . . . . .   *SAME     *SAME, *NEXT
 Form type  . . . . . . . . . .   *STD_____    Form type, *SAME, *STD
 Copies . . . . . . . . . . . .   1_____    1-255, *SAME
 Restart printing . . . . . . .   *STRPAGE___   Number, *SAME, *STRPAGE...

                         Additional Parameters

 Output queue . . . . . . . . .   YOUROUTQ      Name, *SAME, *DEV
   Library  . . . . . . . . . .   YOURLIB       Name, *LIBL, *CURLIB

                                                                Bottom
 F3=Exit   F4=Prompt   F5=Refresh   F10=Additional parameters   F12=Cancel
 F13=How to use this display   F24=More keys
```

Figure 0.5 Moving a spooled file to a printer's output queue.

0.9 Creating Source Physical Files

The final preparation step is to create the source physical files that you will need for entering source programs.

Program source code is kept within a "source member"; a source physical file is a special type of file that contains program source members. IBM uses standard names (introduced later in this book). For now, you should simply enter the following commands to create the appropriate source physical files for use with the examples in this book (see Fig. 0.6).

Source File	Contents
QCLSRC	CL source programs
QCMDSRC	CMD source
QDDSSRC	DDS for physical, logical, and printer files
QLBLSRC	COBOL/400 source programs
QMNUSRC	Source for menus

Figure 0.6 Source files used in this book.

To create the files listed in Fig. 0.3, enter the following commands on a command line:

```
CRTSRCPF FILE(QCLSRC)  TEXT('CL source programs')
CRTSRCPF FILE(QCMDSRC) TEXT('CMD source')
CRTSRCPF FILE(QDDSSRC) TEXT('DDS for physical, logical, format
files')
CRTSRCPF FILE(QLBLSRC) TEXT('COBOL/400 source programs')
CRTSRCPF FILE(QMNUSRC) TEXT('Source for menus')
```

0.10 Bon Voyage!

Your environment is now set up and you are ready to go. You are encouraged to try all of the examples in this book. Entering them will give you the opportunity to alter them and see how the programs really work. As an added bonus, your typing skills are likely to improve.

1

"Hello AS/400"

This section introduces the following topics:

- The COBOL/400 language and its evolution
- Basic AS/400 objects and their characteristics
- Library and library list concepts
- System/36 to AS/400 relationships
- A brief description of the IBM tools available for developing applications on the AS/400

This introduction is intended to familiarize you with the basic concepts related to IBM's OS/400 Operating System. Because this book focuses exclusively on the development of applications for the AS/400 computer, it is important that you have a basic understanding of the vocabulary used throughout this book. If you are already experienced with AS/400 development, you may choose to skip this chapter.

1.1 COBOL/400—The Language

COBOL/400 is IBM's version of the COBOL language for use on the AS/400. The name COBOL stands for COmmon Business Oriented Language. As its name implies, COBOL is particularly powerful for processing business-type problems.

Since its introduction in 1959, COBOL has undergone a number of modifications. It was updated in 1968, 1974, and most recently in 1985. The latest revision is ANSI X3.23-1985.

COBOL is often criticized for its verbosity. Variable names tend to be long (such as PAST-DUE-BALANCE). Its English-like structure for performing math (SUBTRACT TRANSACTION-AMOUNT FROM CURRENT-BALANCE GIVING NEW-BALANCE) has never won the hearts of anyone but the best typists. COBOL's roots are in the English language, and therefore a program's procedure division is constructed of paragraphs, sentences, verbs, and clauses. Use of punctuation is strict—a missing period can inadvertently alter the flow of a paragraph and cause hours of searching for a logic error that does not exist.

Some of the so-called drawbacks to COBOL also contribute to its strengths. Long variable names tend to make programs easier to understand. It is easier to determine the contents of a variable named PAST-DUE-BALANCE than it is for one named PDBALN. The action performed by SET INVALID-CUSTOMER-NUMBER TO TRUE is much easier to understand than SETON 55 or ERRFLAG = "Y". It is also no secret that many programmers forget (or choose not) to document their programs. COBOL's wordiness lends to a self-documenting language and therefore can usually be understood without excessive commenting.

Based on the 1985 standard of COBOL, COBOL/400 has outgrown many of the initial problems found in earlier implementations. For example, verbose math can now be expressed in standard algebraic format (COMPUTE AMT-DUE = CURR-BAL + TRAN-AMT). Input/output verbs have been enhanced to include scope terminators that allow easy coding of exception processing (AT END, NOT AT END). The in-line PERFORM statement makes it easier to write more structured code. The EVALUATE statement has virtually eliminated the need for complex nested IF statements. The LIKE clause makes COBOL more relational, allowing program data elements to inherit characteristics of other data elements. In general, COBOL has become a mature, powerful, and structured programming language while maintaining compatibility with its earlier versions.

1.2   The AS/400

The AS/400 was introduced as the successor of IBM's System/36 and System/38. Despite the fact that System/36 and System/38 use completely different operating systems, the AS/400 was able to merge both operating environments into a single one. AS/400 models range in size from desktop units supporting one or two users to desk size units that can support more than a thousand users. OS/400 is the AS/400's operating system. It is a multiuser multitasking operating system. OS/400 closely resembles the operating system from System/38; however, it has been greatly enhanced and made much friendlier.

OS/400 maintains compatibility with the System/36 by providing a System/36 environment that is capable of executing System/36 OCL

(Operation Control Language). Although OS/400 does not provide object code compatibility with System/36, it does provide compatible language compilers, making porting between the two platforms relatively easy.

1.3 OS/400 Objects

OS/400 is an object-based operating system. Everything on the AS/400, from devices to programs, are considered to be objects. In the most elementary definition, an object is simply a named item such as a program or a file that is stored in the system. An object can be a data file, library, command, program, source file, etc. Object names are ten characters long and must begin with an alphabetic character. You should not begin object names with the letter Q, as such names beginning with Q are assumed to be OS/400 objects that are provided by IBM or created by OS/400.

Objects are usually manipulated through OS/400 commands. A command's function is obvious once you understand OS/400 command naming conventions. The naming convention is based on the *action + object* metaphor. For instance, to create a source physical file, the CRTSRCPF command is used. Likewise, to create a data area, the CRTDTAARA command is used.

Occasionally, you may find that you know either the action you want to perform or the object you want to perform an action against, but you do not know the appropriate OS/400 command. In this case, you can take advantage of OS/400's extensive menu system. Entering the GO CMDxxx command where xxx is either an object or an action will result in OS/400 displaying a menu of commands that may be appropriate for your requirement. For example, if you want to see a list of all the commands that display something, you can enter the GO CMDDSP command. Likewise, if you want to see all the commands that work with library lists, you can enter GO CMDLIBL.

Every OS/400 object is identified by its name and its object type. Two objects in the same library cannot share the same name and object type. They may, however, share the same name but have different object types. Each object also has an attribute. This attribute provides additional information about the object. As an example, a compiled program object's attribute will contain the language in which the original program was written (such as RPG, COBOL, etc.).

The following list contains some of the basic objects you will encounter throughout this book.

*LIB   An OS/400 library. Although a library is an object itself, it contains a collection of other objects such as files and programs. An OS/400 library can be thought of as an MS-DOS directory; however, libraries cannot be stored within libraries (subdirectories). A library object's attribute indicates whether the library is a test library or a production library.

*PGM   A compiled program object. The object attribute indicates the language used to write the program (COBOL, RPG, etc.).

*MENU   A menu object.

*FILE   An OS/400 file. The object attribute indicates the type of file (physical file, logical file, printer file, display file, etc.)

*CMD   A command. Commands are used as entry points to programs. They serve as front-end processors that can set up parameter lists, validate input from the user, and finally call a program with a valid parameter list.

*DTAARA   A data area. A data area is similar to a data file that contains only one record. They are often used for program defaults, counters, and run dates. For instance, if a program creates general ledger entries and must put a serial number on each record, the last serial number used could be kept in a data area and retrieved at the beginning of program execution.

*DTAQ   A data queue. This is a special high-speed file that you can send data to and receive data from. It can be accessed either first-in–first-out, last-in–first-out, or keyed.

*PNLGRP   A panel group. Panel groups are most often used for providing an application with help text. With the introduction of OS/400 V2R2, IBM provided a set of APIs (Application Programming Interface) to access more advanced features of panel groups, called the User Interface Manager (UIM).

*JRN   An OS/400 journal. Journals are used for tracking changes to, rebuilding, and recovering database files when the system abnormally ends. Journals are also used with commitment control, which is a function that allows transactions to be "undone" if a program determines it is necessary. Journal objects interact directly with journal receivers.

*JRNRCV   An OS/400 journal receiver. The journal receiver works in conjunction with the journal to provide a method to track changes to a file. When changes are made to a journaled database file, the changes are recorded in the journal receiver.

1.4   Libraries and Library Lists

OS/400 library lists are similar to the MS-DOS path. When OS/400 searches for a particular object (a program, a file, etc.), it will search the library list from top to bottom.

The library list is actually made up of several smaller lists, some of which are set up by the system. These lists are as follows:

System list   Libraries in the system part of the library list are searched before libraries in other parts of the list. The libraries in this portion contain objects necessary to run system functions. The system part of the library list consists of the system library (QSYS, QSYS2), the system file for user data (QUSRSYS), and the system help information (QHLPSYS). *Note:* this layout may change in future releases. Furthermore, installations in which secondary languages are used may have a different system library list.

Product list   The product library part is changed by the system as users run commands or menus to include the library in which the program is stored. The product library will vary while a job is running, based on the function being performed.

Current library The current library is the default library used for the creation of objects. A developer would most likely have his or her personal development library set as the current library. This is synonymous with DOS's "Current Directory."

User list   The user part contains the libraries used by application programs to perform their functions. When the system is installed, this part contains the general-purpose library (QGPL) and the job's temporary library (QTEMP).

A typical library list would look as follows:

QSYS QSYS2 QHLPSYS	System Portion
QLBL	Product Library (COBOL)
YOURLIB	Current Library
APPDTA APPOBJ QGPL QTEMP	User Portion

1.4.1 Qualified object names

Object names are always qualified, meaning that the name is paired with the library where the object resides. Qualified names have the form of *libname/objectname*. Examples of qualified names are as follows.

*LIBL/CUSTMAST	Causes OS/400 to search the library list for the first occurrence of an object named CUSTMAST.
MYLIB/PROG1	Causes OS/400 to look only in library MYLIB for a program named PROG1.
*CURLIB/HISTFILE	Causes OS/400 to search in the user's current library for an object named HISTFILE.

If the library name is omitted when specifying an object's name, OS/400 usually assumes either *LIBL (for the user's library list) or *CURLIB (for the user's current library) depending on whether the requested function is searching for the object or creating the object. If the requested function must locate a preexisting object and the library name was not specified, OS/400 will usually search through the library list. If the requested function must create an object and no library name was specified, OS/400 usually creates the object in the user's current library (*CURLIB). Examples of commands that require object names are as follows:

`CRTSRCPF FILE(MYLIB/QLBLSRC)`	Causes OS/400 to create a source physical file in library MYLIB.
`CRTSRCPF FILE(QLBLSRC)`	Similar to the previous CRTSRCPF command, except that no library name is specified. This results in OS/400 creating a source physical file named QLBLSRC in the user's current library (for more information on the current library, see Chap. 0, Sec. 0.3).
`DSPPFM FILE(HISTFILE)`	Causes OS/400 to search the current library list for a file named HISTFILE and then display its contents. Since no library name is specified, OS/400 defaults to searching *LIBL (the current library list).

Some of the commands used to manipulate libraries are the following:

`CHGCURLIB`	Changes the current library to a different library
`CRTLIB`	Creates a new library
`DLTLIB`	Deletes a library from the system
`DSPLIB`	Displays the objects within a library

You can view additional commands for managing libraries by typing

`GO CMDLIB`

1.5   Source Physical Files

It is within source physical files that you keep all program source code. A one-source physical file may contain multiple source members. Each member is itself a source program that can be compiled by one of the AS/400 language compilers. The member type identifies the type of program that is stored within the member. COBOL members have a member type of CBL.

1.5.1   Naming conventions

IBM has defined the following names for source physical files. You are free to use them when you create your own applications, or you can choose to use a different name.

QLBLSRC	COBOL/400 Source files. QCBLSRC is used for System/38 COBOL source programs.
QDDSSRC	DDS source files
QCMDSRC	Command (CMD) source files
QCLSRC	CL source files
QMNUSRC	Menu source files
QPNLSRC	Panel group source files

Although you are not restricted to using these names, it is recommended that you do. One benefit of using IBM's naming convention becomes apparent when including (or copying) other COBOL source files (such as copy books, data structures, etc.) into a program at compile time. The COBOL COPY directive will automatically search QLBLSRC without having to specify a source file name.

Use the CRTSRCPF command to create a source physical file. To create the COBOL source physical file (QLBLSRC), you would use the following command:

```
CRTSRCPF FILE(QLBLSRC) TEXT('COBOL Source Files')
```

This command will create a source physical file in the current library. The library name can be specified in the create command as follows:

```
CRTSRCPF FILE(YOURLIB/QLBLSRC) TEXT('COBOL Source Files')
```

1.6   System/36 Environment Considerations

The next few sections describe several aspects that relate to the System/36 environment on the AS/400. If you are going to be migrating applications from a System/36, you may want to read through this section.

1.6.1   System/36 libraries

The System/36's operating system organizes its file system differently than the AS/400. On the System/36, there is one master directory (or Volume Table of Contents—VTOC) that contains the addresses of areas of disk reserved for three types of information: libraries, files, and folders. Libraries are typically used to hold OCL procedures and program source members, files are used to hold data or indexes to other files, and folders are used to hold documents (see Fig. 1.1). This differs considerably from that of the native OS/400 environment in which libraries are used to logically organize any type of OS/400 ob-

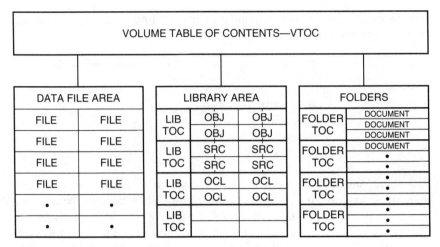

Figure 1.1 System/36 disk organization.

jects (see Fig. 1.2). On the AS/400, libraries cannot be nested within other libraries.

To compensate for these differences, OS/400 simulates the System/36 environment. When a user is logged into the System/36 environment (accomplished with the STRS36 command or by setting the user's pro-

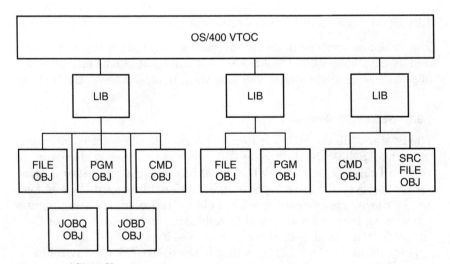

Figure 1.2 AS/400 file system.

file to automatically log them into the System/36 environment), they will find several additional libraries in their library list:

#LIBRARY   This library is used as the System/36's root library (it relates directly to the System/36's #LIBRARY).

QSSP   This library contains System/36 operating system programs (SSP) and utilities.

QS36F   This library is where System/36 programs will search for data files and indexes. You may designate any library to be the "current file library" by using the FLIB command, or alternatively you can reconfigure the System/36 environment to default to a different file library by using the CHGS36 command.

1.6.2   System/36 OCL and source members

When you create a System/36 compatible library on the AS/400 (using the System/36 BLDLIBR command), a regular OS/400 library is created for you, as well as two special source files within that library. These source files are as follows:

QS36PRC   A source physical file that is used to hold System/36 OCL procedures.

QS36SRC   A source physical file that is used to hold all System/36 program source members.

When a System/36 OCL procedure is invoked (either from the command line or by another job), only the QS36PRC source file will be searched to locate the procedure. If a source file named QS36PRC appears in more than one library in your library list, each QS36PRC will be searched for the procedure (starting with the user's current library) until the procedure is found.

Source programs for System/36 compatible compilers are usually kept in the source physical file named QS36SRC. The System/36 compatible COBOL compiler expects COBOL source members to have a type of CBL36.

When an OCL procedure attempts to load a program (using //LOAD), OS/400 will start looking for the program object in the current library, then proceed to traverse through the user's library list.

1.6.3   System/36 to AS/400 object mapping

Table 1.1 shows the mapping of some of the System/36 types of information to objects on the AS/400.

1.7   Tools for Development

IBM provides the following tools for editing source programs, creating screens and menus, creating reports, and maintaining data in database files.

TABLE 1.1   System/36 to AS/400 Object Mappings

System/36 object	AS/400 object
Alternative index	Logical file
Compiled display formats	Display file
Compiled message member	Message file
Compiled program	Program
Data dictionary folder	Data dictionary and set of files
Date-differentiated files	Multiple member physical file
Direct file	Physical file
Document	Document library object (DLO)
Document folder	Folder DLO
Folder	Folder DLO
Indexed file	Physical file
Library	Library
Library #LIBRARY	Library #LIBRARY
Load member	Program
	Display file
	Message File
Network resource directory (NRD)	DDM files
Procedure member	Member of source physical file QS36PRC
Sequential file	Physical file
Source member	Member of source physical file QS36SRC
Subroutine member	Program

1.7.1 PDM—Program development manager

PDM is an integrated and customizable environment for performing development tasks such as editing files, compiling programs, and copying objects. PDM is invoked with the STRPDM command. Chapter 2 will provide a brief introduction to using PDM. For more information on PDM, see *Programming Development Manager User's Guide*.

1.7.2 SEU—Source entry utility

SEU is OS/400's full-screen editor. It has all the capabilities found on mainframe editors. It provides instant syntax checking for most AS/400 languages, as well as assisted prompting for column-sensitive languages such as RPG/400. Chapter 2 will provide a brief introduction to using SEU. For more information on SEU, see *Source Entry Utility User's Guide*.

1.7.3 SDA—Screen design aid

SDA is a full-function screen design program. It is used to design, create, and maintain screens, menus, and online help. For more information on SDA, see *Screen Design Aid User's Guide*.

1.7.4 RLU—Report layout utility

RLU is similar to SDA in that it assists the developer in designing, creating, and maintaining printed report layouts. For more information on RLU, see *Report Layout Utility User's Guide*.

1.7.5 DFU—Data file utility

DFU provides the developer with a convenient way of quickly populating or editing records within a database file (both physical and logical). It allows for entry, update, and deletion of database records. A brief introduction to the use of DFU can be found in Chap. 7. For more information on DFU, see *Data File Utility User's Guide*.

1.8 Summary

AS/400 objects are named items (such as programs or files) that are stored in the system. Object names can be up to 10 characters long and must begin with an alphabetic character. Names should not begin with the letter Q.

OS/400 commands always use the *action + object* metaphor. Actions and objects are almost always abbreviated to three characters. Examples of actions are CRT (create), RMV (remove), and DSP (display). Objects are also abbreviated to three characters. Occasionally, frequently used object names are abbreviated to a single character, such as the letter L for list and D for description. Examples of objects are LIB (library), LIBL (library list), DEV (device), and DEVD (device description). A typical combination would be DSPLIBL for display library list.

Object names are always qualified. A qualified name consists of the object's name as well as the library name where the object is located. A qualified name is in the form xxxxxxxxxx/yyyyyyyyyy, where xxxxxxxxxx is the library name and yyyyyyyyyy is the object name. In most cases, the library name may be left blank or substituted with *LIBL. Two objects cannot reside in the same library if they have the same name and object type. They can reside in the same library if their object types are different.

Library lists are comprised of several smaller lists: the system list, product list, current library, and user list. When an object is requested and the library name is not specified, each library in the library list is searched for the object. The list is searched in top to bottom order.

OS/400 source physical files are files that contain source programs that are readable by OS/400 language compilers. SEU is used to edit source files. The CRTSRCPF command is used to create a source physical file.

The AS/400 provides a simulated System/36 environment. When the environment is active, the user's library list will contain #LIBRARY, SSP, and QS36F. When System/36 programs request a file, the environment will only check the current System/36 file library (QS36F). OCL procedures must be kept in source physical files named QS36PRC.

Tools used for development and maintenance on the AS/400 include PDM (Program Development Manager), SEU (Source Entry Utility), SDA (Screen Design Aid), RLU (Report Layout Utility), and DFU (Data File Utility).

2

"Hello World"

In order to keep with tradition, this chapter introduces the first complete example of a COBOL/400 program—the "Hello world" program. This particular version of the "Hello world" program may be the first ever written in COBOL for the AS/400; however, I cannot completely substantiate this claim. Credit is due to the original author, whomever he or she is, for such a brilliant piece of sophisticated programming artwork. In converting the program from its original C code, I have tried my best to preserve all of the original program's functionality and flair. You are sure to have hours of fun and excitement in this chapter.

This chapter will also provide you with a brief introduction to using the programming development manager (PDM), the source entry utility (SEU), and the screen design aid (SDA).

2.1 README.TXT

Make sure you have completed the preparations described in the Introduction. This chapter will assume that you have created a library and that it is your current library. Furthermore, it is assumed that you have created the necessary source physical files in which to save your source and that your user profile has the necessary authority to create and manage objects on the AS/400.

2.2 OS/400 Library, File, and Member Structure

A library is a special object that is used to hold and organize objects (see Fig. 2.1). It is easiest to visualize a library as a collection of com-

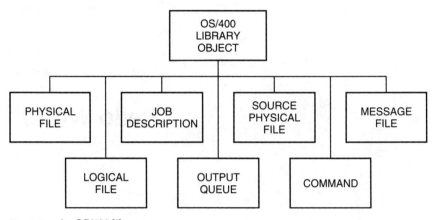

Figure 2.1 An OS/400 library.

mands, programs, files, and other miscellaneous objects such as message queues and output queues.

An OS/400 database file is composed of zero or more members. It is within the member that the data are stored. Regardless of how many members a file may have, each member has the same identical physical record description. The most common type of a file is one that has a single member (Fig. 2.2).

A file is not restricted to a single member; however, each member must be identical in its attributes and field layout. An example of a file with multiple members would be a sales transaction file that contains a member for each day of the month, with each member containing that day's transactions (see Fig. 2.3).

Source physical files are just like regular files, except they have predetermined fields and record length. Each member within the source physical file represents a different source program (see Fig. 2.4).

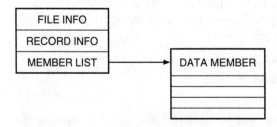

Figure 2.2 A single-member database file.

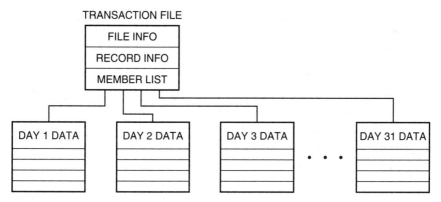

Figure 2.3 An OS/400 file.

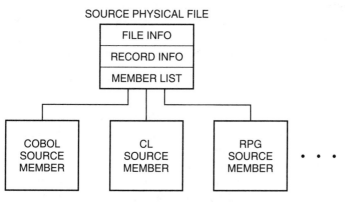

Figure 2.4 An OS/400 source physical file (SRCPF).

When you finish this chapter, your library will contain the following objects (including files and their members):

YOURLIB library (created in Chap. 0)
    HELLO1 Program object (compiled)
    HELLO2 Program object (compiled)
    HELLO3 Program object (compiled)
    HELLOWORLD Compiled display file object
    QLBLSRC Source physical file to hold COBOL source
        HELLO1 First "Hello world" COBOL source (member)
        HELLO2 Second "Hello world" COBOL source (member)
        HELLO3 Third "Hello world" COBOL source (member)
    QDDSSRC Source physical file to hold DDS source
        HELLOWORLD screen definition (source)

- HELLO1, HELLO2, HELLO3 (program objects) are executable program objects.
- HELLOWORLD is the compiled display definition.
- QLBLSRC is the source physical file for COBOL source programs.
- QDDSSRC is the source physical file for data description specifications (DDS) source programs. DDS are used to describe database files, display files, and printer files.
- The members within QLBLSRC and QDDSSRC are the actual source members that you will edit and compile.

2.3   Overview of the Examples

There are three versions of the "Hello world" program in this chapter. The first demonstrates the simplest form of output using COBOL's DISPLAY statement. The second example illustrates the use of extended ACCEPT/DISPLAY statements. The third example demonstrates the use of an external display file (coded using DDS).

2.4   "Hello World" using DISPLAY

The following program illustrates the simplest form of output in a COBOL/400 program. The DISPLAY statement is used to send the text "Hello world" to the user's terminal.

There is one quirk with simple DISPLAY output. When the program runs, you may see the words "Hello world" appear on the screen for a moment, but then disappear. This is because standard DISPLAY output is treated as program messages. The messages can be seen by displaying the job log (DSPJOBLOG).

2.4.1   Starting PDM

The programming development manager (PDM) provides an easy way of working with lists of libraries, objects, and members. PDM's environment makes it easy to perform operations such as editing, copying, renaming, compiling, and printing (to name a few), without having to know the details of OS/400 underlying command language (CL).

To start PDM, type STRPDM on a command line and then press Enter. After you press Enter, the main PDM menu will be displayed (see Fig. 2.5). Select option 2—"Work with objects"—from PDM's main menu. This will bring up the screen in Fig. 2.6.

In the library field, specify either YOURLIB or *CURLIB. Specifying *CURLIB will cause PDM to use your current library. After you press Enter, PDM will display the "Work with Objects Using PDM" display (as shown in Fig. 2.7).

```
                    AS/400 Programming Development Manager (PDM)

  Select one of the following:

      1. Work with libraries
      2. Work with objects
      3. Work with members

      9. Work with user-defined options




  Selection or command
  ===> _____
 _____
  F3=Exit       F4=Prompt      F9=Retrieve       F10=Command entry
  F12=Cancel    F18=Change defaults
                                    (C) COPYRIGHT IBM CORP. 1981, 1993.
```

Figure 2.5 PDM's main menu.

```
                        Specify Objects to Work With

  Type choices, press Enter.

      Library . . . . . . . . .   YOURLIB    *CURLIB, name

      Object:
        Name . . . . . . . . . .  _____ *ALL, name, *generic*
        Type . . . . . . . . . .  _____ *ALL, *type
        Attribute  . . . . . . .  _____ *ALL, attribute, *generic,
                                             *BLANK




  F3=Exit      F5=Refresh     F12=Cancel
```

Figure 2.6 Specifying which objects to work with.

PDM displays all of the objects in YOURLIB. If you have prepared your environment as described in Chapter 0, you should have five source physical files in your library: QCLSRC, QCMDSRC, QDDSSRC, QLBLSRC, and QMNUSRC.

The option field is where you type actions to perform against each object in the list. For instance, if you put a "3" in front of QCLSRC, you would be telling PDM that you want to create a copy of QCLSRC and all source members within it. Take a quick moment to notice what options are available to you.

You may have noticed that option 11 (Move) is followed by an ellipsis

```
                      Work with Objects Using PDM

    Library . . . . .    YOURLIB        Position to . . . . . . . .  _____
                                        Position to type . . . . .   _____

    Type options, press Enter.
       2=Change        3=Copy        4=Delete       5=Display      7=Rename
       8=Display description          9=Save        10=Restore     11=Move ...

    Opt   Object      Type        Attribute   Text
    __    QCLSRC      *FILE       PF-SRC      CL source programs
    __    QCMDSRC     *FILE       PF-SRC      CMD source
    __    QDDSSRC     *FILE       PF-SRC      DDS for physical, logical, format files
    __    QLBLSRC     *FILE       PF-SRC      COBOL/400 source programs
    __    QMNUSRC     *FILE       PF-SRC      Source for menus



                                                                        Bottom
    Parameters or command
    ===> _____
    F3=Exit          F4=Prompt            F5=Refresh         F6=Create
    F9=Retrieve      F10=Command entry    F23=More options   F24=More keys
```

Figure 2.7 Working with objects within your library.

(. . .). This indicates that there are more options to choose from. Function key F23 is used to display more options (function key F24 is used to display more function key assignments). Press F23 once to expose the next set of options.

```
                      Work with Members Using PDM

    File . . . . . .    QLBLSRC
      Library . . . .     YOURLIB            Position to . . . . .  _____

    Type options, press Enter.
       2=Edit         3=Copy       4=Delete       5=Display      6=Print
       7=Rename       8=Display description       9=Save         13=Change text ...

    Opt   Member      Type        Text

       (No members in file)




                                                                        Bottom
    Parameters or command
    ===> _____
    F3=Exit          F4=Prompt            F5=Refresh         F6=Create
    F9=Retrieve      F10=Command entry    F23=More options   F24=More keys
```

Figure 2.8 Working with members within source file QLBLSRC.

Since the first task that you will need to perform is to create a source *member* within the QLBLSRC source file, you will need to select option 12, which corresponds with PDM's "Work with" option. Move the cursor down to the option field in front of the QLBLSRC source file, type "12," and then press Enter. The "Work with Members Using PDM" screen should appear, as shown in Fig. 2.8.

2.4.2 Using the source entry utility for editing

At this time, there are no source members in QLBLSRC so you must create one. Function key F6 is used to create a new source member. Press F6 now. The "Start Source Entry Utility" screen will be displayed, as shown in Fig. 2.9.

You must now specify the name for this new source member, its source type, and optionally a text description. If *PRV is shown in the source member name field, change it to HELLO1. For the source type, specify CBL. Finally, for the text description, type: Hello world, version 1. Press Enter after completing this information. The source entry utility (SEU) editing screen will be displayed (see Fig. 2.10).

Although SEU is a full screen editor, all actions are performed against individual lines. This means that editing commands are applied a line at a time rather than on a per character basis.

The editing area of the screen is broken into two parts: the left side (which is filled with apostrophes) is where you type line editing commands such as move, delete, copy, etc. The area to the right of that is where the actual text goes.

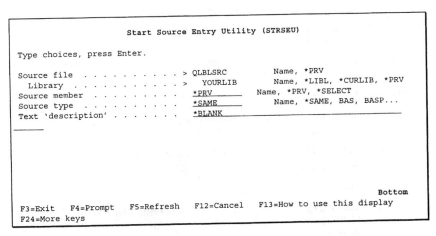

Figure 2.9 The "Start Source Entry Utility" screen.

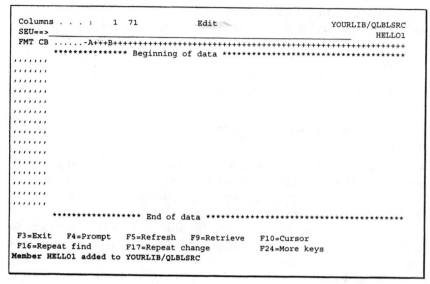

```
Columns . . . :    1  71              Edit                      YOURLIB/QLBLSRC
SEU==>_____ HELLO1
FMT CB ......-A++B++++++++++++++++++++++++++++++++++++++++++++++++++++++++++++++
        *************** Beginning of data ********************************
/ / / / / / /
/ / / / / / /
/ / / / / / /
/ / / / / / /
/ / / / / / /
/ / / / / / /
/ / / / / / /
/ / / / / / /
/ / / / / / /
/ / / / / / /
/ / / / / / /
/ / / / / / /
/ / / / / / /
/ / / / / / /
/ / / / / / /
        ***************** End of data ********************************

F3=Exit    F4=Prompt    F5=Refresh    F9=Retrieve    F10=Cursor
F16=Repeat find         F17=Repeat change            F24=More keys
Member HELLO1 added to YOURLIB/QLBLSRC
```

Figure 2.10 SEU's full screen editor.

Table 2.1 summarizes the most commonly used editing commands in SEU. The *current line* refers to the line where the cursor is positioned at the time the command is typed.

TABLE 2.1   Editing Commands Available under SEU

I	Insert a blank line after the current line.
Inn	Insert *nn* blank lines after the current line.
IB	Insert a blank line before the current line.
C and A	Copy/After. Put a "C" on the line to be copied; put an "A" on the line that it should be copied after.
C and B	Copy/Before. Same as above, except the destination of the copied line is in front of the line where the B is located.
CC and A	Copy a block of lines to be placed after the line where the A is located. Put a "CC" at the beginning of the block and a "CC" at the end of the block. Then scroll to where the block should be copied and type an "A" so that the block is copied after the line.
CC and B	Same as above except the block is copied before the line with the B.
D	Delete the current line.
Dnn	Delete *n* number of lines forward.
DD	Delete a block of lines. Put a "DD" at the beginning of the block and a "DD" at the end of the block. After pressing Enter, the block will be deleted.

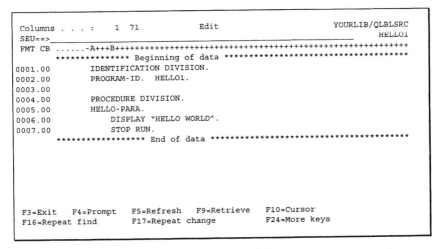

```
Columns . . . :   1  71              Edit              YOURLIB/QLBLSRC
SEU==>_                                                         HELLO1
FMT CB ......-A+++B+++++++++++++++++++++++++++++++++++++++++++++++++++++++++
         *************** Beginning of data ********************************
0001.00        IDENTIFICATION DIVISION.
0002.00        PROGRAM-ID.  HELLO1.
0003.00
0004.00        PROCEDURE DIVISION.
0005.00        HELLO-PARA.
0006.00            DISPLAY "HELLO WORLD".
0007.00            STOP RUN.
         ***************** End of data ****************************************




      F3=Exit    F4=Prompt    F5=Refresh   F9=Retrieve   F10=Cursor
      F16=Repeat find         F17=Repeat change          F24=More keys
```

Figure 2.11 Source entry of program HELLO1.

You are now ready to start typing in the source code for the first "Hello world" program. If you have problems using SEU, press the Help key on your keyboard (or if you do not have a Help key, press the F1 key).

Make sure to observe the COBOL rules of areas A and B. SEU performs syntax checking while entering source lines, so if you do not put the COBOL statements in the correct areas, SEU will flag each line as an error. Furthermore, SEU will attempt to prevent you from exiting if syntax errors exist in the source code.

Type the code shown in Fig. 2.11. If you pressed the Enter key before typing anything, the empty lines may disappear. Use the insert command (I to insert 1 line, I5 to insert 5 lines) in the left area to insert some blank lines.

After you have entered the source in Fig. 2.11, press the F3 key to exit SEU and save the source. When the "Exit SEU" screen is shown, just press Enter to continue and return to the PDM.

2.4.3 Compiling the HELLO1 program from within the PDM

When SEU terminates, you will be returned to the "Work with Members using PDM" screen, but this time you will notice that the new source member is now in the member list (see Fig. 2.12). You are now ready to compile the source program. PDM's option 14 is used for compiling source members (COBOL, RPG, DDS, all compilable source). You

```
                        Work with Members Using PDM

File  . . . . . .    QLBLSRC
    Library . . . .     YOURLIB          Position to  . . . . .  _____

Type options, press Enter.
    2=Edit          3=Copy       4=Delete        5=Display      6=Print
    7=Rename        8=Display description        9=Save         13=Change text ...

Opt  Member     Type        Text
 __    HELLO1     CBL         Hello World, version 1




                                                                      Bottom
Parameters or command
===> _____
F3=Exit          F4=Prompt           F5=Refresh        F6=Create
F9=Retrieve      F10=Command entry   F23=More options  F24=More keys
```

Figure 2.12 The HELLO1 source member.

can use the F23 key to scroll through the options until you see 14=
Compile, although you do not have to see the option to use it.

With the cursor in the option field in front of the HELLO1 source
member, put in the number 14 and then press the Enter key. Your compile request will then be submitted to the batch queue.

If your current job's message delivery mode is set to *BREAK, then
you will receive a message on your display when the compile completes
(it will indicate whether the compile was successful or not). If your job's
message delivery mode is set to *NOTIFY, then you must watch for the
"Message Waiting" (or "MW") indicator to turn on. When the indicator
turns on, type DSPMSG to display your message and find out if the
program compiled successfully. If your program did not compile successfully and you must make changes to your source member, use option 2 for editing.

2.4.4 Running your program from within PDM

When your program compiles successfully, you can execute it in one of
two ways: First, you can move the cursor to the command line (use the
Tab key) and type:

```
CALL HELLO1
```

and then press Enter. The other way to execute the program is to position the cursor next to the source member HELLO1 and put the letter

"C" in the option column. Once you press Enter, PDM will begin executing your program.

2.5 "Hello World" Program Using Extended DISPLAY/ACCEPT

This version of "Hello world" uses a special type of input/output that makes COBOL/400 compatible with other non-IBM versions of COBOL. The DISPLAY and ACCEPT statements have been extended to allow for full screen functionality, including control of display attributes and the terminal bell.

Because extended DISPLAY/ACCEPT programming is not the standard or "normal" way of programming the AS/400, the PROCESS EXTACCDSP statement must be included at the beginning of a COBOL/400 program that uses this type of input/output.

Using SEU, type the following source (Listing 2.1) into a member named HELLO2. You can start SEU as you did in the preceding section by pressing F6 from the "Work with Members using PDM" screen, or from the command line with the following command:

```
STRSEU SRCFILE(QLBLSRC) SRCMBR(HELLO2) TYPE(CBL)
```

Once SEU begins, enter the COBOL program in Listing 2.1.

Listing 2.1 "Hello world" using extended DISPLAY/ACCEPT.

```
MEMBER NAME: HELLO2        FILE: QLBLSRC
....-..A...B..-....2....-....3....-....4....-....5....-....6....
         PROCESS EXTACCDSP

         IDENTIFICATION DIVISION.
         PROGRAM-ID. HELLO2.

         DATA DIVISION.
         WORKING-STORAGE SECTION.
         77  REPLY  PIC X.

         PROCEDURE DIVISION.
         HELLO-PARA.
             DISPLAY "HELLO WORLD" UPON CRT
                 LINE 12 COLUMN 20 WITH BLANK SCREEN.
             ACCEPT REPLY FROM CRT AT LINE 24 COLUMN 1.
             STOP RUN.
```

After you have entered the source, press the F3 key to exit SEU and save the source. You can compile the program from the "Work with Members using PDM" screen by putting option 14 in front of the HELLO2 source member or from the command line as follows:

```
CRTCBLPGM PGM(HELLO2) SRCFILE(QLBLSRC)
```

Once again, you can execute the program by putting a "C" in the option column in front of the HELLO2 source member and pressing Enter or by typing the following command on a command line:

```
CALL HELLO2
```

2.6 "Hello World" Using an External Display File

This version of "Hello world" is by far the closest to a realistic COBOL/400 program. It utilizes an external display file that contains the description of how the screen should look.

There are two steps in creating this example:

1. Create a display file that displays the words "Hello world" on the screen.

2. Create the COBOL program that opens the display file and displays the record format on the display.

2.6.1 Creating the display file

There are two basic ways of creating display files on the AS/400:

1. Manually describe the screen layout using DDS and enter them using SEU.

2. Use screen design aid (SDA) to "paint" the screen. After painting the screen layout, SDA will generate the required DDS for you.

Manually describing a screen is very tedious and time consuming; therefore the preferred method is to use SDA. This section will introduce you to using SDA for a simple example; however, subsequent chapters will provide the DDS specifications for you to enter using SEU.

To start SDA, type STRSDA on a command line and then press Enter. The start "Screen Design Aid" main menu will be displayed (see Fig. 2.13). Select option 1 to begin the screen design process (see Fig. 2.14). The source file should be specified as QDDSSRC (SDA will create the DDS source for your screen; therefore the DDS source should be put in the QDDSSRC source physical file). The library should be YOURLIB (or *CURLIB), and the member should be HELLOWORLD.

When SDA starts, the screen shown in Fig. 2.15 will be displayed. A display file consists of one or more display records. Each record can be displayed independently or in combination with other records on the workstation. You will now add the first record to the display file.

```
                    AS/400 Screen Design Aid (SDA)

Select one of the following:
     1. Design screens
     2. Design menus
     3. Test display files




Selection or command
===> _____
_____
F1=Help    F3=Exit    F4=Prompt    F9=Retrieve    F12=Cancel
```

Figure 2.13 SDA's main menu.

```
                         Design Screens

Type choices, press Enter.

     Source file . . . . . . . .    QDDSSRC    Name, F4 for list

       Library . . . . . . . . .    YOURLIB    Name, *LIBL, *CURLIB

     Member  . . . . . . . . . .    HELLOWORLD Name, F4 for list






F3=Exit      F4=Prompt      F12=Cancel
```

Figure 2.14 Starting the screen design process with SDA.

With the cursor in the option column, type the number 1, then press
the Tab key to move to the record field and type the record name
HELLO. Press the Enter key when you have completed this.

The next screen displayed will ask what type of display record you
are creating. The default value should be RECORD, so just press Enter
once again.

You are now ready to start designing the "Hello world" screen. Move
the cursor to line 12, column 20, and type 'Hello world' (the single
quotes are required), and then press Enter. After pressing Enter, the
single quotes will disappear.

The screen is now complete. You can press F12 to exit from the de-

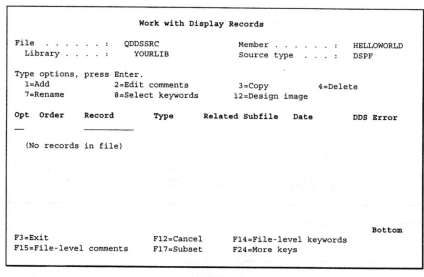

```
                    Work with Display Records
File . . . . . . :    QDDSSRC              Member . . . . . . :    HELLOWORLD
   Library . . . . :    YOURLIB              Source type  . . . :    DSPF

Type options, press Enter.
  1=Add               2=Edit comments      3=Copy            4=Delete
  7=Rename            8=Select keywords    12=Design image

Opt  Order   Record        Type      Related Subfile  Date         DDS Error
 __          _____

  (No records in file)




                                                                      Bottom
F3=Exit                     F12=Cancel      F14=File-level keywords
F15=File-level comments     F17=Subset      F24=More keys
```

Figure 2.15 SDA's "Work with Display Records" screen.

sign screen. When you return to the "Work with Display Records" screen, press the Enter key again to tell the SDA that you are finished designing records.

The "Save DDS—Create Display File" screen will be displayed. For now, just press Enter to accept the choices SDA has made for you. After pressing Enter, SDA will save the DDS specifications for the HELLOWORLD member and submit the compile of the display file to batch.

Use the F3 key as many times as necessary to return to the "Work with Members Using PDM" screen. If you press F3 too many times, you can always use the STRPDM command to start PDM again.

Using PDM, you can work with source physical file QDDSSRC to see that SDA added a source member called HELLOWORLD. PDM's option 5 will display the DDS generated by SDA.

2.6.2 Creating the COBOL program

The COBOL program opens the display file and writes record "HELLO" to the workstation. Start SEU with the following command and type in the COBOL source code in Listing 2.2:

```
STRSEU SRCFILE(QLBLSRC) SRCMBR(HELLO3) TYPE(CBL)
```

Listing 2.2 "Hello world" using an external display file.

```
MEMBER NAME: HELLO3              FILE: QLBLSRC
....-..A...B..-....2....-....3....-....4....-....5....-....6....
            IDENTIFICATION DIVISION.
            PROGRAM-ID.  HELLO3.

            ENVIRONMENT DIVISION.
            INPUT-OUTPUT SECTION.
            FILE-CONTROL.
                SELECT DISPFILE ASSIGN TO WORKSTATION-HELLOWORLD
                    ORGANIZATION IS TRANSACTION.

            DATA DIVISION.
            FILE SECTION.
            FD  DISPFILE.
            01  DISPREC PIC X(100).

            PROCEDURE DIVISION.
            HELLO-PARA.
                OPEN I-O DISPFILE.
                WRITE DISPREC FORMAT "HELLO".
                READ DISPFILE.
                CLOSE DISPFILE.
                STOP RUN.
```

Compile the program with the following command:

```
CRTCBLPGM PGM(HELLO3) SRCFILE(QLBLSRC)
```

Execute the program with the following command:

```
CALL HELLO3
```

2

COBOL/400
Enhancements

COBOL-85's introduction brought with it a variety of enhancements that bring COBOL in line with other structured programming languages.

This section introduces you to the new features found in COBOL/400. You will learn about the following:

- *Scope terminators*
- *The in-line PERFORM statement*
- *The EVALUATE statement*
- *The INITIALIZE statement*
- *Calling subprograms*

3

Scope Terminators and Conditional Phrases

This chapter discusses the mechanics of using scope terminators and conditional phrases. Explicit scope terminators are words that define the end of a procedure division statement. Examples of COBOL/400 scope terminators are the END-IF, END-EVALUATE, and END-PERFORM.

Conditional phrases specify what action to perform following the successful and/or unsuccessful completion of an operation. Prior versions of COBOL provided only unsuccessful (or exception) phrases. Examples of COBOL/400 conditional phrases are the INVALID-KEY, AT END, and NOT ON SIZE ERROR.

All of the COBOL statements that provided unsuccessful conditional phrases were enhanced to include a phrase for successful completion. This allows a program to specify what action to take if an operation is completed successfully, as well as unsuccessfully.

The addition of scope terminators and successful completion phrases rectified many shortcomings with earlier versions of COBOL, specifically those dealing with periods within nested IFs. Consistent use of scope terminators and exception phrases can lead to succinct, clean, and easy-to-read programs.

3.1 Definitions

Before diving into the depths of explicit scope terminators, it is a good idea to understand a few basic (but important) COBOL definitions.

3.1.1   Definition of an Imperative Statement

An imperative statement either specifies an unconditional action to be taken by the program or is a conditional statement terminated by its explicit scope terminator. (This will be explained in more detail in Sections 3.1.2 and 3.2.) All COBOL statements, in their simplest form, are imperative statements. Listing 3.1 illustrates an imperative statement:

Listing 3.1 Imperative statement.

```
ADD 5 TO COUNTER GIVING NEW-COUNTER.
```

3.1.2   Definition of a Conditional Statement

A conditional statement specifies that a truth value of a condition is to be evaluated and that the following action of the program is dependent on this truth value. Listing 3.2 illustrates a simple conditional statement in which the truth value that is evaluated is whether COUNTER is greater than 5. If it is, imperative-statement-1 is executed; otherwise imperative-statement-2 is executed.

Listing 3.2 Conditional statement.

```
IF COUNTER > 5
    imperative-statement-1
ELSE
    imperative-statement-2.
```

Some COBOL statements become conditional statements when a conditional phrase is included (such as the READ statement's INVALID KEY conditional phrase). Listing 3.3 shows how the ADD statement can become a conditional statement when the ON SIZE ERROR phrase is specified.

Listing 3.3 ADD as a conditional statement.

```
ADD 5 TO COUNTER GIVING NEW-COUNTER
    ON SIZE ERROR
        PERFORM ERROR-PARA.
```

Figure 3.1 is a list of COBOL statements that become conditional statements when their conditional phrases are specified.

3.2   Explicit Scope Terminators

Explicit scope terminators are amongst the most valuable enhancements to COBOL. In general, an explicit scope terminator is used to turn a conditional statement into an imperative statement. Once a con-

```
ADD...ON SIZE ERROR
ADD...NOT ON SIZE ERROR

COMPUTE...ON SIZE ERROR
COMPUTE...NOT ON SIZE ERROR

DIVIDE...ON SIZE ERROR
DIVIDE...NOT ON SIZE ERROR

MULTIPLY...ON SIZE ERROR
MULTIPLY...NOT ON SIZE ERROR

SUBTRACT...ON SIZE ERROR
SUBTRACT...NOT ON SIZE ERROR

STRING...ON OVERFLOW
STRING...NOT ON OVERFLOW

UNSTRING...ON OVERFLOW
UNSTRING...NOT ON OVERFLOW

ACCEPT...ON EXCEPTION
ACCEPT...NOT ON EXCEPTION

DELETE...INVALID KEY
DELETE...NOT INVALID KEY

READ...AT END
READ...NOT AT END
READ...INVALID KEY
READ...NOT INVALID KEY
READ...NO DATA

REWRITE...INVALID KEY
REWRITE...NOT INVALID KEY

START...INVALID KEY
START...NOT INVALID KEY

WRITE...AT END-OF-PAGE
WRITE...NOT AT END-OF-PAGE
WRITE...INVALID KEY
WRITE...NOT INVALID KEY

RETURN...AT END
RETURN...NOT AT END

CALL...ON EXCEPTION
CALL...NOT ON EXCEPTION
```

Figure 3.1 Imperative statements shown as conditional statements.

ditional statement becomes an imperative statement, it can be nested or used as any other imperative statement. This provides a clean solution to the COBOL rule that states "A conditional statement not terminated by its scope terminator cannot be contained within another statement." To illustrate this problem, consider the following logic flow shown in Listing 3.4a.

Listing 3.4a Example logic that cannot intuitively be expressed in COBOL-74.

```
if condition-1
do action # 1
if condition-2
do action # 2
end-if
do action # 3
end-if
```

The main focus in listing 3.4a is "do action #3". The required logic is that condition-1 must be true and that action #3 must occur after action 2 (whether or not action 2 ever executes). This type of problem is most often seen when performing I/O such as reading a file and having to test whether the record was found or not. In an earlier version of COBOL, this would have to be written as in listings 3.4b or 3.5a. (Remember that a period ends the scope of *all* conditional statements.)

Listing 3.4b Solution 1—expressing the logic in listing 3.4a without the END-IF scope terminator.

```
IF condition-1 THEN
    PERFORM paragraph-1
    IF condition-2 THEN
        PERFORM paragraph-2
        PERFORM paragraph-3
    ELSE
        PERFORM paragraph-3.        (repeated)
```

Listing 3.5a Solution 2—expressing the logic in listing 3.4a without the END-IF scope terminator.

```
IF condition-1 THEN
    PERFORM paragraph-1
    IF condition-2 THEN
        PERFORM paragraph-2.
IF condition-1 THEN         (repeated)
    PERFORM paragraph-3.
```

Although listings 3.4b and 3.5a provide workable solutions, they are neither elegant nor intuitive. Listing 3.5b shows how this problem would be expressed using the END-IF scope terminator. Both IF conditions are terminated by END-IFs, thus each condition is viewed as an imperative statement.

Listing 3.5b Solution 3—expressing the logic in listing 3.4 with the END-IF scope terminator.

```
IF condition-1
imperative-statement-1
    IF condition-2              ( this IF statement is now
    imperative-statement-2       treated as a single
    END-IF                       imperative statement )
imperative-statement-3
END-IF
```

Explicit scope terminators mark the end of certain procedure division statements. Figure 3.2 shows explicit scope terminators:

END-ACCEPT	END-EVALUATE	END-REWRITE
END-ADD	END-IF	END-SEARCH
END-CALL	END-MULTIPLY	END-START
END-COMPUTE	END-PERFORM	END-STRING
END-DELETE	END-READ	END-SUBTRACT
END-DIVIDE	END-RETURN	END-UNSTRING
END-WRITE		

Figure 3.2 Explicit scope terminators.

The simplest example of scope termination can be seen with the IF statement in Listing 3.6.

Listing 3.6 IF statement with scope terminator.

```
IF PREV-BAL-DUE > 1000
    PERFORM REJECT-INVOICE
ELSE
    PERFORM PROCESS-INVOICE
END-IF.
```

Earlier versions of COBOL did not have explicit scope terminators. The do-nothing NEXT SENTENCE statement (or place holder) was required simply to balance IFs and ELSEs. NEXT SENTENCE was most commonly used in cases such as that shown in Listing 3.7.

Listing 3.7 Using NEXT SENTENCE to balance nested IFs.

```
IF PREV-BAL-DUE > 1000
    PERFORM REJECT-INVOICE
    IF PREV-BAL-DUE > 2000
        PERFORM NOTIFY-CUSTOMER-REP
    ELSE
        NEXT SENTENCE       END-IF
ELSE
    PERFORM PROCESS-INVOICE
END-IF
```

Omitting the NEXT SENTENCE phrase in this listing would cause a compiler error. Omitting one of the ELSEs would cause a logic error. In COBOL/400, this same piece of code can be expressed using explicit scope terminators (see Listing 3.8).

Listing 3.8 Solution to Listing 3.7 using a scope terminator.

```
IF PREV-BAL-DUE > 1000
   PERFORM REJECT-INVOICE
   IF PREV-BAL-DUE > 2000
      PERFORM NOTIFY-CUSTOMER-REP
   END-IF
ELSE
   PERFORM PROCESS-INVOICE
END-IF.
```

Scope terminators are not intended to reduce program size. In fact, if consistently used, they may add to the length of the program. The primary benefits of using scope terminators are simplification of program logic, program clarity, and ease of maintainability.

3.3 Exception Phrases

Exception phrases define the action(s) to be taken when a statement is completed unsuccessfully. The clearest example of a COBOL exception phrase can be seen with COBOL's READ statement:

```
READ file-name INVALID KEY imperative-statement
```

The INVALID KEY phrase allows you to specify what action to take if the READ statement is completed unsuccessfully. COBOL/400 has been enhanced to include "nonexception" phrases as well. This allows programs to contain logic on what to do if an operation is completed successfully as well as unsuccessfully. This indirectly eliminates the need for setting flags and performing additional tests for success.

Listing 3.9 Traditional method of testing for successful completion.

```
01 CUST-STATUS     PIC X.
   88 VALID-CUST        VALUE "V".
   88 INVALID-CUST      VALUE "I".
        .
        .
SET VALID-CUST TO TRUE.
READ CUSTOMER-FILE
   INVALID KEY SET INVALID-CUST TO TRUE.
IF VALID-CUST
   PERFORM DISPLAY-ADDRESS
ELSE
   PERFORM ERROR-MESSAGE.
```

In Listing 3.9, a boolean variable is used to maintain the status of the file operation. Prior to executing the READ, the status is set to "success." If the READ fails, the status is changed to "fail." The status code is then checked to determine whether to display the customer's address (if successful, READ) or display an error message. This same code can be written in COBOL/400—see Listing 3.10.

Listing 3.10

```
READ CUSTOMER-FILE
   INVALID KEY
      PERFORM ERROR-MESSAGE
   NOT INVALID KEY
      PERFORM DISPLAY-ADDRESS
END-READ.
```

The use of success and failure phrases in combination with scope terminators makes this code easy to understand.

The remaining part of this chapter will introduce the various statements that have been enhanced to include explicit scope terminators as well as successful completion phrases. Details regarding the cause of the unsuccessful completion code have been included for your reference. The samples of code are not complete syntax diagrams. For the complete syntax of each of the listed statements, see Appendix C.

3.4 Arithmetic Statements

The ADD, COMPUTE, DIVIDE, MULTIPLY, and SUBTRACT statements have been enhanced to include the NOT ON SIZE ERROR phrases, as well as explicit scope terminators (see Listing 3.11).

Listing 3.11 Math statements.

```
ADD identifier-1 TO identifier-2 ROUNDED
   ON SIZE ERROR
      imperative-statement-1
   NOT ON SIZE ERROR
      imperative-statement-2
END-ADD

SUBTRACT identifier-1 FROM identifier-2
   ON SIZE ERROR
      imperative-statement-1
   NOT ON SIZE ERROR
      imperative-statement-2
END-SUBTRACT

MULTIPLY identifier-1 BY identifier-2 GIVING identifier-3
   ON SIZE ERROR
      imperative-statement-1
   NOT ON SIZE ERROR
      imperative-statement-2
END-MULTIPLY
```

```
DIVIDE identifier-1 INTO identifier-2 GIVING identifier-3
    ON SIZE ERROR
        imperative-statement-1
    NOT ON SIZE ERROR
        imperative-statement-2
END-DIVIDE

COMPUTE identifier-1 ROUNDED = arithmetic-expression
    ON SIZE ERROR
        imperative-statement-1
    NOT ON SIZE ERROR
        imperative-statement-2
END-COMPUTE
```

The SIZE ERROR phrase is the same as in prior versions of COBOL. A size error condition can occur in the following ways:

- When the absolute value of the result of an arithmetic evaluation, after decimal-point alignment, exceeds the largest value that can be contained in the result field
- When division by zero occurs
- When zero is raised to the exponent zero
- When zero is raised to a negative exponent
- When a negative number is raised to a fractional exponent

If any of these conditions are met, then a SIZE ERROR condition exists. When a size errors occurs, the subsequent action of the program depends on whether or not the ON SIZE ERROR phrase is specified.

If a size error condition exists and the ON SIZE ERROR phrase is not specified, the value of the resultant identifier is unpredictable. If the ON SIZE ERROR phrase is specified and a size error condition exists, the resultant identifier remains unmodified, and control passes to the imperative statement in the ON SIZE ERROR phrase.

During an ADD CORRESPONDING, the ON SIZE ERROR imperative statement is not executed until all individual additions or subtractions have been completed.

If the size error condition does not exist, and the NOT ON SIZE ERROR phrase has been specified, control is transferred to the NOT ON SIZE ERROR imperative statement.

3.5   Data Movement Statements

The STRING and UNSTRING statements have been enhanced to include the NOT ON OVERFLOW phrases, as well as explicit scope terminators.

Listing 3.12 STRING statement.

```
STRING identifier-1 DELIMITED BY literal-2 INTO identifier-3
   WITH POINTER identifier-4
   ON OVERFLOW
      imperative-statement-1
   NOT ON OVERFLOW
      imperative-statement-2
END-STRING
```

For the STRING statement (see Listing 3.12), an OVERFLOW condition occurs when the pointer value (explicit or implicit):

- Is less than 1
- Exceeds a value equal to the length of the receiving field

If any of these conditions are met and the ON OVERFLOW phrase has been specified, control is transferred to the ON OVERFLOW imperative statement, otherwise control is transferred to the NOT ON OVERFLOW phrase (if specified).

Listing 3.13 UNSTRING statement.

```
UNSTRING identifier-1 DELIMITED BY literal-1
   INTO identifier-4 DELIMITER IN identifier-5 COUNT identifier-6
   WITH POINTER identifier-7 TALLYING IN identifier-8
   ON OVERFLOW
      imperative-statement-1
   NOT ON OVERFLOW
      imperative-statement-2
END-UNSTRING
```

For the UNSTRING statement (see Listing 3.13), an OVERFLOW condition occurs when:

- The pointer value (explicit or implicit) is less than 1
- The pointer value (explicit or implicit) exceeds a value equal to the length of the sending field
- All data receiving fields have been acted upon, and the sending field still contains unexamined characters

If any of these conditions are met and the ON OVERFLOW phrase has been specified, control is transferred to the ON OVERFLOW imperative statement; otherwise control is transferred to the NOT ON OVERFLOW phrase (if specified).

3.6   Subprogram Linkage

The CALL statement allows specification of both ON EXCEPTION and
NOT ON EXCEPTION phrases (see Listing 3.14).

Listing 3.14 The CALL statement.

```
CALL literal-1 USING identifier-2
    ON EXCEPTION
        imperative-statement-1
    NOT ON EXCEPTION
        imperative-statement-2
END-CALL
```

For the CALL statement, an EXCEPTION condition occurs when the
called subprogram cannot be made available (locked or not found).

3.7   Ordering

The RETURN statement now includes a NOT AT END phrase (see
Listing 3.15).

Listing 3.15 RETURN statement.

```
RETURN file-name-1 RECORD INTO identifier-1
    AT END
        imperative-statement-1
    NOT AT END
        imperative-statement-2
END-RETURN
```

The imperative-statement specified on the AT END phrase is executed after all records have been returned from file-name-1.

3.8   Input/Output Statements

The various input/output statements all have scope terminators as
well as successful completion phrases (see Listing 3.16). The conditions
that will cause the unsuccessful completion status to be raised vary
with each input/output statement, as well as with the file mode being
used for the target file, therefore it is recommended to consult the
COBOL/400 reference for specific information pertaining to each
statement.

Listing 3.16 Input/output statements.

```
DELETE file-name
    INVALID KEY
        imperative-statement-1
    NOT INVALID KEY
        imperative-statement-2
END-DELETE

READ file-name
    AT END
        imperative-statement-1
    NOT AT END
        imperative-statement-2
END-READ

REWRITE record-name
    INVALID KEY
        imperative-statement-1
    NOT INVALID KEY
        imperative-statement-2
END-REWRITE

START file-name KEY IS > EXTERNALLY-DESCRIBED-KEY
    INVALID KEY
        imperative-statement-1
    NOT INVALID KEY
        imperative-statement-2
END-START

WRITE record-name FROM identifier-1 BEFORE ADVANCING 1 LINE
    AT END-OF-PAGE
        imperative-statement-1
    NOT AT END-OF-PAGE
        imperative-statement-2
END-WRITE
```

3.9 Summary

Scope terminators can be used to change a conditional statement into an imperative statement. Since there are few COBOL rules that govern the use of imperative statements, the programmer now has greater flexibility in program design. Conditional statements can now be nested (if the appropriate scope terminator is used) without regard to period (.) placement.

The inclusion of successful completion phrases provides the programmer with an even greater degree of control in program design, eliminating the need for variables to track the status of operations.

Conditional: DO "IF";

Imperative: Just DO.

4

The PERFORM Statement

The COBOL/400 PERFORM verb has been updated to include features found in more modern structured programming languages. Of course, the PERFORM statement can still be used in its earlier formats. The biggest change to the PERFORM statement is the ability to code the body of the PERFORM statement in-line, which means you can include the statements to be executed right after the PERFORM statement. This eliminates the need for coding a separate paragraph for the PERFORM body.

4.1 In-Line versus Out-of-Line Perform Statement

Previous versions of COBOL only allowed out-of-line PERFORM statements. An out-of-line PERFORM causes the program to execute the paragraph specified in the PERFORM statement. After the last statement in the paragraph has been executed, control returns to the statement following the PERFORM statement.

Listing 4.1 Out-of-line PERFORM statement flow.

```
FOO-PARA.
       .
       .
       .
    PERFORM GET-CUSTOMER-DATA.
    MOVE CUST-NAME TO SHIP-TO-NAME.
       .
       .
       .
GET-CUSTOMER-DATA.
    MOVE REQUESTED-NAME TO CUST-KEY.
    READ CUST-FILE
        INVALID KEY
            MOVE SPACES TO CUST-NAME
    END-READ.
```

In Listing 4.1, the PERFORM statement causes control to transfer to the GET-CUSTOMER-DATA paragraph. After the last statement is executed in the GET-CUSTOMER-DATA paragraph, control returns to the statement following the PERFORM; in this case, the MOVE CUST-NAME TO SHIP-TO-NAME statement is executed.

Listing 4.2 shows an example of an in-line PERFORM statement.

Listing 4.2 In-Line PERFORM statement flow.

```
01  FILE-STAT1          PIC XX.
    88 END-OF-FILE          VALUE "10".
    .
    .
CALCULATE-AVERAGE.
    MOVE ZERO TO TRAN-COUNT.
    PERFORM WITH TEST AFTER UNTIL END-OF-FILE        LOOP
        READ TRANSACTION-FILE NEXT RECORD
            AT END
                DIVIDE GROSS-TOTAL BY TRAN-COUNT GIVING AVG
                PERFORM DISPLAY-TOTALS
            NOT AT END
                ADD TRAN-TOTAL TO GROSS-TOTAL
                ADD 1 TO TRAN-COUNT
        END-READ
    END-PERFORM.
```

Here the statements between the PERFORM and the END-PERFORM will repeat until the END-OF-FILE condition becomes TRUE; then execution will continue with the first statement following the END-PERFORM. The only imperative statement between the PERFORM and END-PERFORM is the READ statement. Some points to note about this example are as follows:

- The WITH TEST AFTER phrase causes the END-OF-FILE condition to be tested AFTER the READ statement, rather than before. This forces the code to be executed at least once.

- There are no periods between the PERFORM and END-PERFORM.

- The FILE-STAT-1 variable is updated automatically by OS/400 after each input/output (I/O) operation on the file; therefore no direct manipulation of this file-status flag is necessary.

- The PERFORM statement specifies that only an imperative statement may be included between the PERFORM and the END-PERFORM. When the AT END and/or NOT AT END conditions are specified on the READ statement, the READ statement becomes a conditional statement and therefore would normally not be acceptable as an imperative statement; however, since the END-READ scope terminator is used, the READ statement was considered an imperative statement and therefore meets the requirements of the PERFORM statement.

- By using the AT END and NOT AT END conditional phrases, it was unnecessary to code any separate paragraphs for the calculations. It was also easy to avoid using any conditional statements such as the IF statement.

4.2   PERFORM Statement Formats

There are four formats to the PERFORM statement:

- Basic PERFORM *(unconditional)*
- PERFORM with the TIMES phrase specified
- PERFORM with the UNTIL phrase specified
- PERFORM with the VARYING phrase specified

The first format of the PERFORM statement is unconditional, that is, there is no condition specified as to whether or not to execute the specified paragraph (subroutine) or in-line statements. It will always execute. The last three formats contain conditional phrases, thus allowing possible execution of the specified paragraph or the in-line statements depending on the condition.

4.3   Unconditional PERFORM

The unconditional form of the PERFORM statement executes a block of code or a specified paragraph exactly once without discretion.

Listing 4.3 Unconditional PERFORM.

```
        .
        .
PERFORM CALCULATE-BALANCE.
        .
        .
PERFORM
    ADD 1 TO PAGE-NUMBER
    MOVE ZERO TO LINE-COUNTER
END-PERFORM.
        .
        .
```

The two PERFORM statements in Listing 4.3 are unconditional. They will always execute. The first will execute a paragraph named CALCULATE-BALANCE. The second PERFORM will execute the two lines of code between the PERFORM and the END-PERFORM (referred to as the in-line statements) exactly once; the PERFORM statement in this case is unnecessary but serves to show that blocks of code can be grouped together by using the PERFORM and END-PERFORM statements.

4.4 Conditional PERFORM

A conditional PERFORM allows a condition to be tested before or after execution of the specified paragraph or in-line statements. There are two types of conditional statements:

- PERFORM with the TIMES phrase
- PERFORM with the UNTIL phrase

The TIMES phrase allows the program to specify the number of times that the PERFORM should execute. The UNTIL phrase allows the program to specify a condition that is tested either before or after the PERFORM executes. If the condition evaluates to TRUE, then the PERFORM statement is executed; otherwise control transfers to the next statement following the PERFORM.

4.5 The TIMES Phrase

The TIMES phrase allows the program to specify the number of times to repeat the PERFORM statement. The actual number of times can be expressed as a constant or as an identifier. If an identifier is specified, then the value of the identifier is used to determine the repeat factor. If the identifier contains the value zero, then the PERFORM statement will not be executed.

Listing 4.4 PERFORM with TIMES phrase specified.

```
        .
        .
        .
PERFORM GET-SCREEN-DETAILS 10 TIMES.
        .
        .
MOVE 5 TO INVOICE-COUNT.
PERFORM INVOICE-COUNT TIMES
    PERFORM GET-NEXT-INVOICE
    ADD INVOICE-TOTAL TO CUST-TOTAL
END-PERFORM.
        .
        .
```

Listing 4.4 illustrates the two ways of specifying the TIMES phrase. The first PERFORM will execute GET-SCREEN-DETAILS exactly

ten times. The second PERFORM uses identifier INVOICE-COUNT
to determine how many times to repeat the PERFORM block. Since
the value 5 was moved into INVOICE-COUNT prior to execution
of the PERFORM statement, the PERFORM will execute exactly 5
times.

It should be noted that the value of the identifier is referenced only
during the first iteration; therefore any modifications to the identifier
will have no effect on the number of iterations performed.

Listing 4.5 Ineffective TIMES Counter Modification

```
        .
        .
        .
MOVE 10 TO LOOP-COUNT.
PERFORM LOOP-COUNT TIMES
    imperative-statement-1
    imperative-statement-2
    MOVE 5 TO LOOP-COUNT       ** Ineffective **
END-PERFORM.
        .
        .
        .
```

In Listing 4.5, the highlighted line is intended to modify the number
of iterations of the loop from 10 to 5; however, since the contents of the
LOOP-COUNT are only evaluated once (during the first iteration), the
modification has no effect and the loop will continue to iterate ten
times.

4.6   The UNTIL Phrase

The UNTIL phrase allows a condition to be specified that will control
the duration of time that the PERFORM is executed. When the WITH
TEST BEFORE phrase is specified, the PERFORM acts as a "DO
WHILE". When the WITH TEST AFTER phrase is specified, the PER-
FORM acts as a "DO UNTIL". The only difference between a DO
WHILE and a DO UNTIL is that the DO UNTIL will always execute at
least once.

It is important to note that the default handling of a PERFORM
UNTIL is WITH TEST BEFORE (equivalent to a DO-WHILE). Therefore, the words "PERFORM UNTIL" should not be assumed to be
equivalent to "DO-UNTIL"; exactly the opposite is true. If the program
logic requires a DO-UNTIL condition, then you must write the statement in the form of "PERFORM WITH TEST AFTER UNTIL [some
condition]."

Listing 4.6 Conditional PERFORM.

```
        .
        .
PERFORM GET-RECORDS UNTIL REC-TYPE EQUAL "T".
        .
        .
PERFORM WITH TEST AFTER UNTIL END-OF-FILE
    READ IN-FILE
        AT END
            SET END-OF-FILE TO TRUE
            PERFORM SUM-UP-TOTALS
        NOT AT END
            ADD 1 TO NUM-RECORDS-PROCESSED
            PERFORM PROCESS-RECORD
    END-READ
END-PERFORM.
        .
        .
```

In Listing 4.6, the first PERFORM illustrates an out-of-line DO-WHILE condition, while the second PERFORM illustrates an in-line DO-UNTIL condition. In the first PERFORM, the condition REC-TYPE EQUAL "T" will be tested before the GET-RECORDS paragraph is executed. If the REC-TYPE is already equal to "T" prior to the PERFORM statement, then the GET-RECORDS paragraph will never be executed. In the second PERFORM example, the WITH TEST AFTER phrase will force the READ statement to be executed at least once.

4.7   The VARYING Phrase

Although the basic format of the PERFORM ... VARYING statement has not changed, it has been extended to allow in-line statements. The VARYING phrase is most often used for iterative processes, and now that in-line coding is supported, it is no longer necessary to create separate paragraphs for the iterative code.

Listing 4.7 PERFORM with VARYING phrase and 1 iterator.

```
        .
        .
PERFORM VARYING INDX-A FROM 1 BY 1 UNTIL INDX-A > 99
    ADD ARRAY-VALUE(INDX-A) TO GRAND-TOTAL
END-PERFORM.
        .
        .
```

Listing 4.7 illustrates a simple iterative loop with one identifier. This PERFORM statement results in the following actions:

1. INDX-A is initialized to 1.
2. Check the condition—is INDX-A greater than 99? If so, go to step 6.

3. Perform the body of the PERFORM statement.

4. Increment INDX-A by 1 (the value specified in the BY phrase).

5. Go back to step 2.

6. Continue execution with the statement following the END-PERFORM.

The PERFORM statement can specify more than one iterator, which has the same effect as nesting PERFORM statements. For instance, the two pieces of code in Listing 4.8 perform the identical task. All elements of a three-dimensional array are summed up into GRAND-TOTAL.

Listing 4.8 Nested PERFORM vs. multi-identifier PERFORM.

```
PERFORM VARYING INDX-1 FROM 1 BY 1 UNTIL INDX-1 > 10
   PERFORM VARYING INDX-2 FROM 1 BY 1 UNTIL INDX-2 > 2
      PERFORM VARYING INDX-3 FROM 1 BY 1 UNTIL INDX-3 > 3
         ADD TABLE-VALUE(INDX-1, INDX-2, INDX-3,) TO GRAND-TOTAL
      END-PERFORM
   END-PERFORM
END-PERFORM.

PERFORM VARYING INDX-1 FROM 1 BY 1 UNTIL INDX-1 > 10
   AFTER INDX-2 FROM 1 BY 1 UNTIL INDX-2 > 2
      AFTER INDX-3 FROM 1 BY 1 UNTIL INDX-3 > 3
         ADD TABLE-VALUE(INDX-1, INDX-2, INDX-3,) TO GRAND-TOTAL
END-PERFORM.
```

In some cases, it will not be possible to use the multi-identifier format of the PERFORM...VARYING statement. The code in Listing 4.9 cannot be expressed in a single PERFORM statement because imperative-statement-2 is outside the innermost code block. The multi-identifier format of the PERFORM statement can iterate up to seven identifiers; however, only one block of code can be executed for all of them.

Listing 4.9 Nested PERFORM with nested imperative statements.

```
PERFORM VARYING INDX-1 FROM 1 BY 1 UNTIL INDX-1 > 10
   PERFORM VARYING INDX-2 FROM 1 BY 1 UNTIL INDX-2 > 2
      imperative-statement-1
   END-PERFORM
   imperative-statement-2
END-PERFORM.
```

4.8 Summary

The PERFORM statement has been enhanced to include many essential features for writing clean structured code. The most important change is the ability to include in-line statements rather than having to write separate paragraphs for each iterative loop. The addition of the WITH TEST AFTER phrase adds the ability to write DO-UNTIL phrases that were previously not possible with the PERFORM statement alone.

New programs should always utilize the in-line PERFORM statement for all looping. Out-of-line PERFORM statements should be utilized for subroutines that are executed from several different places within the program.

The EVALUATE
Statement

The EVALUATE statement is another of COBOL/400's powerful enhancements. It can be thought of as a shorthand for a series of nested IF statements. The EVALUATE statement has its roots in structured programming methodology. It can best be compared to PL/I's SELECT statement and C/C++'s switch/case statement.

5.1 Understanding EVALUATE by Example

In order to avoid a large amount of rhetoric to describe the EVALUATE statement, examples will be presented to illustrate its functionality. It may however, be necessary to clarify some definitions.

The basic format of the EVALUATE statement is given in Listing 5.1.

Listing 5.1 Basic syntax of EVALUATE statement.

```
EVALUATE identifier-1
   WHEN phrase-1
      imperative-statement-1
   WHEN phrase-2
      imperative-statement-2
   WHEN OTHER
      imperative-statement-3
END-EVALUATE
```

Operands *before* the first WHEN phrase are interpreted in one of two ways, depending on how they are specified:

- Individually, they are called selection *subjects*.

- Collectively, they are called a *set* of selection subjects.

Operands *in* the WHEN phrase are interpreted in one of two ways, depending on how they are specified;

- Individually, they are called selection *objects*.
- Collectively, they are called a *set* of selection objects.

In Listing 5.1, identifier-1 is considered the selection subject. Phrase-1 is a selection object.

5.2   Basic EVALUATE Functionality

To illustrate the basic functionality of the EVALUATE statement, consider an interactive application that responds to requests from a user. After the user presses Enter, the program will receive an account number and an action code from the display. The user may have specified any of the following action codes:

- DEL = Delete the account
- DEA = Deactive the account
- CHG = Request a change screen to update the account data
- DSP = Display the account data

Based on the code specified by the user, the program should call an appropriate program to execute the action against the specified account code.

The EVALUATE statement in Listing 5.2 satisfies the above-noted requirements.

Listing 5.2   Evaluate with one selection subject.

```
EVALUATE ACTION-CODE
    WHEN "DEL"
        CALL "DELACT" USING ACCT-NUMBER
    WHEN "DEA"
        CALL "DEAACT" USING ACCT-NUMBER
    WHEN "CHG"
        CALL "CHGACT" USING ACCT-NUMBER
    WHEN "DSP"
        CALL "DSPACT" USING ACCT-NUMBER
    WHEN OTHER
        PERFORM ERROR-MESSAGE
END-EVALUATE.
```

Identifier ACTION-CODE contains the requested action code, and ACCT-NUMBER contains the desired account number. In this case, the selection subject is ACTION-CODE, and each of the selection objects are "DEL", "DEA", "CHG", and "DSP". Each WHEN statement compares a constant value (each action code) with the selection subject (ACTION-CODE). If the result is a TRUE comparison, then the associated statements following the WHEN are executed until the next WHEN, at which point control is transferred to the next statement following the END-EVALUATE. The WHEN OTHER clause is the default handler when none of the previous WHEN statements successfully evaluates to TRUE. If WHEN OTHER is not specified, then control would continue with the next statement following the END-EVALUATE.

The equivalent IF-ELSE statement is not quite as elegant, as shown in Listing 5.3.

Listing 5.3 Equivalent code using IF statement.

```
IF ACTION-CODE = "DEL"
   CALL "DELACT" USING ACCT-NUMBER
ELSE
   IF ACTION-CODE = "DEA"
      CALL "DEAACT" USING ACCT-NUMBER
   ELSE
      IF ACTION-CODE = "CHG"
         CALL "CHGACT" USING ACCT-NUMBER
      ELSE
         IF ACTION-CODE = "DSP"
            CALL "DSPACT" USING ACCT-NUMBER
         ELSE
            PERFORM ERROR-MESSAGE
         END-IF
      END-IF
   END-IF
END-IF.
```

5.3 EVALUATE Using Two Subjects

The EVALUATE statement is not limited to a single selection subject. The word ALSO is used to separate selection subjects within a set of selection subjects. It also separates selection objects within a set of selection objects.

Say a company has three types of customers, "risky," "regular," and "special," and are represented as "RSK", "REG", and "SPC". The policy of the company relating to exceeding the defined credit limit depends on what type of customer is requesting the charge. If a charge request is rejected due to exceeding the credit limit, a letter should be sent to the customer explaining the reason for denial.

- If the customer is classified as risky, then the credit limit may not be exceeded.

- If the customer is classified as regular, then the credit limit may be exceeded; however, the customer should receive a warning letter.

■ If the customer is classified as special, then no charge is denied; thus the charge request should be processed.

The requirement can be written using the EVALUATE statement as presented in Listing 5.4.

Listing 5.4 EVALUATE with two selection subjects.

```
EVALUATE CUST-TYPE ALSO BAL-DUE > CREDIT-LIMIT
    WHEN "RSK" ALSO TRUE
        PERFORM REJECT-CHARGE-REQUEST
        PERFORM SEND-EXCEED-LIMIT-LETTER
    WHEN "REG" ALSO TRUE
        PERFORM ALLOW-CHARGE-REQUEST
        PERFORM SEND-WARNING-LETTER
    WHEN "SPC" ALSO ANY
        PERFORM ALLOW-CHARGE-REQUEST
END-EVALUATE.
```

There are several points worth noting in this listing. First, there are two selection subjects: CUST-TYPE and BAL-DUE > CREDIT-LIMIT. The second selection subject is an expression which evaluates to either TRUE or FALSE. The two selection subjects are separated by the word ALSO. Each of the WHEN phrases must specify two selection objects to be compared against the two selection subjects. The first WHEN specifies two objects, "RSK" and the word TRUE. RSK will be compared with CUST-TYPE, and TRUE will be compared against the evaluated result of BAL-DUE > CREDIT-LIMIT. If both result to TRUE, the WHEN phrase evaluates successfully and the statements following it will be executed. When the next WHEN statement is encountered, control will transfer to the next statement after the END-EVALUATE.

Notice also on the third WHEN statement, the use of the word ANY. ANY will automatically evaluate to a TRUE comparison against its related selection subject. In this case, the comparison of the balance and credit limit is ignored.

5.4 Using TRUE and FALSE in the Selection Set

If you find that you have several different types of expressions to evaluate, you can take advantage of using TRUE and/or FALSE in the selection set.

Listing 5.5 Using TRUE as a selection subject.

```
EVALUATE TRUE
    WHEN CODE = "DLT"
        PERFORM DELETE-ACTION
    WHEN BAL-DUE > CREDIT-LIMIT
        PERFORM REJECT-REQUEST
```

```
    WHEN END-OF-FILE
        PERFORM RESET-FILE
    WHEN BAL-DUE + CHARGE-AMT > CREDIT-LIMIT
        PERFORM REJECT-REQUEST
END-EVALUATE.
```

As shown in Listing 5.5, any logical expression can be compared against TRUE. The first WHEN compares two character fields; the second WHEN compares two values; the third tests a BOOLEAN identifier (88 level); the fourth evaluates an expression (BAL-DUE + CHARGE-AMT) and compares the result with CREDIT-LIMIT resulting in a TRUE or FALSE condition.

5.5   Using THROUGH (or THRU)

Ranges of values can be tested by using THROUGH. THROUGH may be used only in a selection object, that is, it can only be used after the first WHEN statement. THROUGH and THRU are functionally equivalent (see Listing 5.6).

Listing 5.6 EVALUATE using THRU.

```
EVALUATE RENT
    WHEN ZERO
        PERFORM UNOCCUPIED
    WHEN .01 THROUGH 499.99
        PERFORM LOW-RENT
    WHEN 500 THROUGH 999.99
        PERFORM MID-RENT
    WHEN 1000 THRU 2699.99
        PERFORM HI-RENT
    WHEN OTHER
        PERFORM VERY-HI-RENT
END-EVALUATE.
```

The THROUGH clause may be specified anywhere that a selection object may appear, as long as the associated selection subject is of the same type (i.e., 1 THRU 10 must be associated with a numeric subject; "A" THRU "Z" must be associated with a character subject).

5.6   Summary

The EVALUATE statement is extremely powerful and should be used whenever multiple conditions exist. It is clearly easier to follow the logic of an evaluate statement as opposed to nested IF statements. Whenever coding a conditional IF statement, if nesting starts to exceed more than two or three levels, the EVALUATE statement should be considered. Nested IF statements are particularly difficult to read and especially difficult to modify when new conditions are introduced.

6

Other Noteworthy Points

This chapter is a collection of miscellaneous enhancements and noteworthy points that will be helpful when writing COBOL/400 programs.

6.1 The INITIALIZE Statement

The INITIALIZE statement is a fast and easy way to initialize data items to predetermined values. It accomplishes the same task as one or more MOVE statements.

The INITIALIZE statement may be used against all data types except under the following conditions:

- The identifier being initialized, as well as all subordinate items to it, may not contain the DEPENDING ON phrase of the OCCURS clause.

- The identifier being initialized may not contain a RENAMES clause.

- The identifier being initialized cannot be an index data item.

The results of a simple INITIALIZE statement depend upon the category (or data type) of the destination identifier.

- If the data item is alphabetic, alphanumeric, or alphanumeric-edited, it is initialized to spaces.

- If the data item is numeric or numeric-edited, it is initialized to zero.

The following examples illustrate the use of the INITIALIZE statement, as well as its equivalent MOVE statements.

Listing 6.1 Example of INITIALIZE statement.

```
....-..A...B..-....2....-....3....-....4....-....5....-....6
    01  ELEM-1                PIC X(10).
    01  ELEM-2                PIC 9(3).
    01  ELEM-3                PIC Z(3)9.
    01  GROUP-1.                            .
        03  ELEM-4            PIC X(5).
        03  ELEM-5            PIC 9(3).
        03  GROUP-2 OCCURS 10 TIMES.
            05  ELEM-6        PIC 9(2).
            05  ELEM-7.       PIC X(2).
    .
    .
    PROCEDURE DIVISION.
    INIT-PARA.
        INITIALIZE ELEM-1.
        INITIALIZE ELEM-2 ELEM-3.
        INITIALIZE GROUP-1.
```

In Listing 6.1, the first INITIALIZE statement will set ELEM-1 to spaces. The second INITIALIZE will set ELEM-2 equal to 000 (all zeros), as well as setting ELEM-3 to 0. The final INITIALIZE statement will initialize all of the data items in GROUP-1 depending on their data category (alphabetic, numeric, etc.). Furthermore, each of the elements within the GROUP-2 table will be initialized appropriately. The code in Listing 6.2 achieves the same results without using the INITIALIZE statement.

Listing 6.2 Same results as from program in Listing 6.1.

```
....-..A...B..-....2....-....3....-....4....-....5....-....6
    INIT-PARA.
        MOVE SPACES TO ELEM-1.
        MOVE ZERO TO ELEM-2, ELEM-3.
        MOVE SPACES TO ELEM-4.
        MOVE ZERO TO ELEM-5.
        PERFORM VARYING INDX FROM 1 BY 1 UNTIL INDX > 10
            MOVE ZERO TO ELEM-6(INDX)
            MOVE SPACES TO ELEM-7(INDX)
        END-PERFORM.
```

6.1.1 The REPLACING phrase

By specifying the REPLACING phrase, you can specify exactly what value the data item should be initialized to. This has a similar result as using MOVE ALL. In Listing 6.3, SEPARATOR-LINE will be initialized to 132 equal signs.

Listing 6.3 INITIALIZE with REPLACING phrase.

```
....-..A...B..-....2....-....3....-....4....-....5....-....6
    01  SEPARATOR-LINE PIC X(132).
        INITIALIZE SEPARATOR-LINE REPLACING
            ALPHANUMERIC DATA BY "=".
```

The replacing phrase allows you to specify initialization values for the following data categories:

- Alphabetic
- Alphanumeric
- Numeric
- Alphanumeric-edited
- Numeric-edited

6.2   The LIKE Clause

The LIKE clause gives COBOL the ability to base one data item's characteristics (PICTURE, USAGE, and SIGN) on the characteristics of another data item or database field within the same program. Some of the characteristics may be changed as well, such as length or usage.

If a program requires temporary holding variables for data that come from external files (database, printer, display, etc.), the characteristics of the temporary variable no longer need to be explicitly defined; rather they can be copied (or inherited) from the file's field definition (see Listings 6.4 and 6.5).

Listing 6.4   Definition of a simple database file.

```
.....A..........T.Name++++++RLen++TDpB......Functions++++++++++++
A          R PHONEREC
A            NAME          30          TEXT('CUSTOMER NAME')
A            PHNUMBER      15          TEXT('PHONE NUMBER')
A
A
```

Listing 6.5   Inheriting fields from a file definition based on Listing 6.4.

```
....-..A...B..-....2....-....3....-....4....-....5....-....6....
          .
          .
          .
      DATA DIVISION.
      INPUT-OUTPUT SECTION.
      FD  PHONE-FILE.
      01  PONE-REC.
[1]       COPY DDS-ALL-FORMATS OF PHONEFILE.
[2]         03 PHONEREC                          PHONEFILE
               05 NAME         PIC X(30).        PHONEFILE
               05 PHNUMBER     PIC X(15).        PHONEFILE
          .
          .
      WORKING-STORAGE SECTION.
[3]       01  TEMP-NAME LIKE NAME.
[4]       01  TEMP-PHONENUM LIKE PHNUMBER(+5).
```

1. The COPY DDS statement will cause the COBOL compiler to search the library list for a file named PHONEFILE. Note that the compiler does *not* go to the DDS source in Listing 6.4, rather it goes to the actual database file.

2. These lines are inserted by the COBOL compiler. The two fields (NAME and PHNUMBER) are copied from the file definition.

3. TEMP-NAME's characteristics are based on NAME (which was copied from the file in part [2] in Listing 6.5).

4. TEMP-PHONENUM's characteristics are based on PHNUMBER; however, the length is being increased by five characters.

By using the LIKE clause in conjunction with a field reference file or a COBOL copybook (see Listing 6.6), a generic data type file can be used to standardize data types in a system. For example, there are a variety of formats for storing dates (i.e., MMDDYY, YYMMDD, CYYMMDD, CCYYMMDD). If a data type copybook is used, all dates can be based on a single generic date field.

Listing 6.6 Sample COBOL data types copybook.

```
COBOL copybook DATATYPES
....-..A...B..-....2....-....3....-....4....-....5....-....6....
        01  GEN-DATE        PIC 9(8).
        01  GEN-INT         PIC 9(7).
        01  GEN-INDX        PIC 9(4) USAGE COMP-3.
        01  GEN-MONEY       PIC S9(9)V99.
        01  GEN-FLOAT       PIC S9(9)V9(7).
        01  GEN-ADDRESS     PIC X(30).
        01  GEN-ZIP         PIC X(15).
        .
        .
```

Listing 6.7 Using a copybook for data type references.

```
....-..A...B..-....2....-....3....-....4....-....5....-....6....
        .
        .
    WORKING-STORAGE SECTION.
    COPY DATATYPES.
        .
        .
    01  INVOICE-DATE    LIKE GEN-DATE.
    01  CALC-DATE       LIKE GEN-DATE.
    01  LOOP-INDX       LIKE GEN-INDX.
    01  TEMP-BALANCE    LIKE GEN-MONEY.
        .
        .
```

Listing 6.7 illustrates the use of a data type file using a COBOL copybook. The source file DATATYPES (Listing 6.6) is included in the program source file; all data items are defined by referencing generic identifiers from the copybook.

6.2.1 Using DDS as a reference file

DDS can also be used to create a generic data type file (see Listing 6.8). The same method that is used to create a data file is used; however, the file will be used for reference purposes only—it will never be populated with data.

Listing 6.8 Sample of a generic field reference file.

```
DDS SOURCE FOR DATATYPES
.....A..........T.Name+++++++RLen++TDpB......Functions+++++++++++++++
     A           R DATATYPES
     A             GENDATE      8S 0
     A             GENINT       7S 0
     A             GENINDX      4  0
     A             GENMONEY     9S 2
     A             GENFLOAT    16S 7
     .
     .
```

Listing 6.9 Program that uses an externally described physical file (defined in 6.8) for generic data types.

```
....-..A...B..-....2....-....3....-....4....-....5....-....6....
     .
     .
     WORKING-STORAGE SECTION.
     01  GENERIC-DATATYPES.
         COPY DDS-ALL-FORMATS OF DATATYPES.
         05 GENDATE           PIC S9(8)                DATATYPES
         05 GENINT            PIC S9(7)                DATATYPES
         05 GENINDX           PIC S9(4) COMP-3         DATATYPES
         05 GENMONEY          PIC S9(7)V99             DATATYPES
         05 GENFLOAT          PIC S9(9)V9(7)           DATATYPES
     .
     .
     01  INVOICE-DATE  LIKE GENDATE.
     01  CALC-DATE          LIKE GENDATE.
     01  LOOP-INDX          LIKE GENINDX.
     01  TEMP-BALANCE       LIKE GENMONEY.
     .
     .
```

Listing 6.9 shows how to use an externally described file as a generic data type file. First, a file is created containing the generic data type fields; then the definition of the file is copied into the WORKING-STORAGE section as a group data item. Finally, the LIKE clause is used to define identifiers based on the fields from the data type file.

6.3   The LENGTH OF Special Register

Occasionally it is necessary to know the defined length of an identifier within a program. The LENGTH OF special register provides a program with a way of accessing an identifier's defined length (see Listing 6.10).

Listing 6.10   Using the LENGTH OF special register.

```
....-..A...B..-....2....-....3....-....4....-....5....-....6....
    01  PHNUMBER        PIC X(15).
      .
      .
    CALL "FMTNBR" USING PHNUMBER, LENGTH OF PHNUMBER.
```

The LENGTH OF special register has the implicit definition of PIC 9(9) USAGE IS BINARY.

The LENGTH OF register is useful when calling other programs that require the calling program to indicate the lengths of character-based parameters. This command calls a program named FMTNBR and passes two parameters: the first is PHNUMBER and the second is the length of identifier PHNUMBER. The receiving program must be expecting two parameters: the first is a string and the second is a binary number defined as PIC 9(9) USAGE BINARY.

6.4   The CONTINUE Statement

The CONTINUE statement does absolutely nothing but hold a place where an imperative or conditional statement may be (see Listing 6.11). It has no effect on the execution of the program.

Listing 6.11   Examples of using CONTINUE.

```
....-..A...B..-....2....-....3....-....4....-....5....-....6....
      .
      .
    READ INPUT-FILE
       INVALID KEY CONTINUE
    END-READ.
      .
      .
    IF UNIT-IS-OCCUPIED
       CONTINUE
    ELSE
       ...
    END-IF.
```

6.5   Calling Subprograms

It is often necessary for a COBOL program to call other programs. OS/400 supports the ability for COBOL programs to call one another, as well as programs written in other languages such as RPG/400 and CL (command language).

When a COBOL/400 program starts, it becomes part of a COBOL run unit. The run unit starts with the first COBOL program called in the program stack and includes all programs (of any language) that are below it. A program stack is a list of programs linked together as a result of programs calling other programs.

6.5.1 Returning from a called program

The first COBOL program in the run unit is defined as the main program. A subprogram is any program that has been called after the main program has started. For example, if program A calls program B, and program B calls program C, then program A is the main program, and program B and C are both subprograms. It is important to know whether a program is a main program or a subprogram when determining how control is returned from a called program when an error occurs or a program ends.

There are three statements that end programs: STOP RUN, EXIT PROGRAM, and GOBACK. The resultant actions of these statements depend on whether the ending program is a main program or a subprogram.

6.5.1.1 Exiting from a main program.
To terminate a main program, use either STOP RUN or GOBACK. These statements will end the entire run unit, and control is returned to the caller of the main program. The EXIT PROGRAM statement will have *no* effect in a main program, and execution will continue with the statement immediately following the EXIT PROGRAM statement.

6.5.1.2 Exiting from a subprogram.
The actions taken upon exiting a subprogram depend completely upon which statement is used to terminate the subprogram. In a subprogram, there are four ways to exit.

If execution ends with a STOP RUN statement, all COBOL programs in the run unit are terminated and control returns to the *caller of the main program.*

If execution ends with EXIT PROGRAM, GOBACK, or by an implicit EXIT PROGRAM, control returns to the subprogram's immediate caller without ending the entire run unit. An implicit EXIT PROGRAM statement is generated if there is no next executable statement in a called program.

When a subprogram ends by EXIT PROGRAM or GOBACK, all of its data items are preserved and remain intact until the next time it is called. Value initialization will *not* take place again. That is, any values associated with VALUE clauses are only initialized the *first* time a program is called. Files are also left open (unless explicitly closed) and the file position remains unchanged (unless) the open data path for the file is shared by other programs.

The following code in Listing 6.12 shows one way to manage initialization each time that a subprogram is executed.

Listing 6.12 Subprogram initialization logic.

```
....-..A...B..-....2....-....3....-....4....-....5....-....6....
        WORKING-STORAGE SECTION.
        01  INITIALIZATION-STATUS        PIC X VALUE "N".
[1]         88  NOT-INITIALIZED                 VALUE "N".
            88  INITIALIZED                     VALUE "I".
            .
            .
        PROCEDURE DIVISION.
        MAIN-PARA.
[2]         PERFORM INITIALIZATION.
            .
            .
[3]         PERFORM SHUT-DOWN.
            GOBACK.
        INITIALIZATION.
            IF NOT-INITIALIZED
                set one-time initialization values
[4]             OPEN any files necessary
                SET INITIALIZED TO TRUE
            ELSE
[5]             code not to be executed first time thru goes here
            END-IF.
[6]         Every-time initialization code goes here.
            .
            .
            .
        SHUT-DOWN.
[7]         CLOSE only files that are opened in the every-time
                initialization code.
```

1. A data item is set up to hold the status of whether the program has been initialized or not. The VALUE clause will force the value to be NOT-INITIALIZED the first time the subprogram is executed. Each subsequent time the program is called, the VALUE clause will have no effect.

2. Every time the subprogram starts, it performs a paragraph called INITIALIZATION.

3. Before the program exits, it performs a paragraph called SHUT-DOWN.

4. This block of code is only performed ONCE; therefore any one-time initialization code (including opening files) should be placed in this block.

5. This block will be executed each subsequent time the subprogram is called.

6. Everything from this point to the end of the paragraph will be executed every time the subprogram is called, regardless of whether it is the first time or not.

7. This block of code will be executed each time the subprogram exits. Only files that are opened in part [6] should be closed.

Arguments: Data items (calling)

6.5.2 Passing data using BY REFERENCE
Parameters: Data items (callers)

Arguments refer to the data items being passed by a calling program. Parameters refer to the data items being received by a called program.

When a CALL statement contains a USING phrase, the way that the arguments are passed to the called program is determined by whether the BY REFERENCE or the BY CONTENT phrase is specified. If neither phrase is specified, BY REFERENCE is implied.

BY REFERENCE means that the subprogram is referring to and processing the data items in the calling program's storage rather than a copy of the data. Any changes that the called program makes to the parameter will affect the argument in the calling program.

Listing 6.13 Using BY REFERENCE.

```
Program A (PGMA)     CALLING   IS  WORKING
....-..A...B..-....2....-....3....-....4....-....5....-....6....
      WORKING-STORAGE SECTION.
      01  VAR-A    PIC X(3).        ''
      ...
      PROCEDURE DIVISION.
      ...
         MOVE "ABC" TO VAR-A.
         CALL "PGMB" USING BY REFERENCE VAR-A.
         DISPLAY VAR-A.
Program B (PGMB)      Caller  IS  LINKED
....-..A...B..-....2....-....3....-....4....-....5....-....6....
      LINKAGE SECTION.
      01  PARM-1   PIC X(3).
      PROCEDURE DIVISION USING PARM-1.
      ...
         MOVE "XXX" TO PARM-1.
         GOBACK.
```

In Listing 6.13, program A (PGMA) declares VAR-A as three characters and moves the value ABC into it. Then program B (PGMB) is called with one parameter VAR-A BY REFERENCE. PGMB then modifies parameter PARM-1 by moving "XXX" into it. When the DISPLAY statement executes in PGMA, the value "XXX" will be displayed.

6.5.3   Passing data using BY CONTENT

BY CONTENT means that the calling program is passing only the contents of the parameter. The contents of the argument are copied to a temporary storage area before the CALL executes; then the CALL passes a reference to the copied data, rather than the original data. With a CALL...BY CONTENT, the called program can change the value of the parameter; however, it will have no effect on the argument in the calling program.

Listing 6.14 Using BY CONTENT.

```
Program A (PGMA)
....-..A...B..-....2....-....3....-....4....-....5....-....6....
        WORKING-STORAGE SECTION.
        01  VAR-A    PIC X(3).
        ...
        PROCEDURE DIVISION.
        ...
        MOVE "ABC" TO VAR-A.
        CALL "PGMB" USING BY CONTENT VAR-A.
        DISPLAY VAR-A.

Program B (PGMB)
....-..A...B..-....2....-....3....-....4....-....5....-....6....
        LINKAGE SECTION.
        01  PARM-1   PIC X(3).
        PROCEDURE DIVISION USING PARM-1.
        ...
        MOVE "XXX" TO PARM-1.
        GOBACK.
```

In Listing 6.14, PGMA initializes the variable VAR-A to "ABC", then calls PGMB using VAR-A. This time, however, VAR-A is being passed by content, rather than by reference. PGMB then modifies PARM-1. Upon returning to PGMA, the value of VAR-A remains "ABC".

Literal values can also be passed with the BY CONTENT phrase (see Listing 6.15).

Listing 6.15 Passing literal values BY CONTENT.

```
CALL...BY CONTENT "some literal value".
```

Within a single CALL statement, both the BY REFERENCE and BY CONTENT phrases can be used (see Listing 6.16).

Listing 6.16 Mixing BY REFERENCE and BY CONTENT.

```
CALL "PGMA" USING BY CONTENT LENGTH OF identifier-1
              USING BY REFERENCE identifier-1.
```

6.5.4 Defining Arguments and Parameters

In the calling program, arguments may be defined anywhere in any of the sections of the data division. They may be fields from a file or identifiers from the WORKING-STORAGE or LINKAGE sections.

In the called program, parameters must be described in the linkage section. The USING clause after the PROCEDURE DIVISION header causes the program to receive the parameters.

The linkage section in the called program must be set up to match the arguments being passed from the calling program. Argument and parameter relationships are not checked at compile time; therefore if they do not match, or if the data categories do not match, run-time errors are likely to occur. There is a one-to-one positional correspondence of arguments to parameters; the first argument in the calling program is matched with the first parameter in the called program.

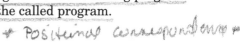

6.5.5 Argument-grouping techniques

As long as the called program knows what parameters to expect, there is no right or wrong way of constructing an argument list; however, some grouping schemes are easier to maintain and use. Since calling BY CONTENT does not utilize the original arguments in the calling program, a copy must be made in temporary storage. This will cause some performance overhead; however, it may be trivial.

Grouping data items together into a single level-01 item makes the argument list easy to pass. Furthermore, putting the entire level-01 record in a copybook eliminates the possibility of mismatched arguments to parameters.

Listing 6.17 Copybook containing PARMLIST parameter list.

```
....-..A...B..-....2....-....3....-....4....-....5....-....6....
       01  REGISTER-ACCT-PARMS.
           05 PARM-ACCT-NUM          PIC X(5).
           05 PARM-ACCT-TYPE         PIC X(2).
           05 PARM-ACCT-NAME         PIC X(20).
```

Listing 6.18 PGMA—calling program.

```
....-..A...B..-....2....-....3....-....4....-....5....-....6....
       ...
       WORKING-STORAGE SECTION.
       COPY PARMLIST.
       ...
       PROCEDURE DIVISION.
       ...
           CALL "REGACT" USING REGISTER-ACCT-PARMS.
       ...
```

Listing 6.19 PGMB—called program.

```
....-..A...B..-....2....-....3....-....4....-....5....-....6....
    ...
    LINKAGE SECTION.
    COPY PARMLIST.
    PROCEDURE DIVISION USING REGISTER-ACCT-PARMS.
    ...
```

As an example, see Listings 6.17 to 6.19. Listing 6.17 defines the parameters used in PGMB (Listing 6.19). The program that calls REGACT (PGMA in Listing 6.18) copies the parameter list (PARM-LIST) into the working storage section. PGMB copies the parameters into the linkage section. Since both programs copy the exact same member (PARMLIST), they are guaranteed to match at run time.

6.6 Executing a CL Command using QCMDEXC

It is sometimes necessary to be able to execute an OS/400 command from within a COBOL/400 program. For example, the program may provide its user with the option of displaying the user's current spooled files. The normal command for viewing the current user's spool file is WRKSPLF. Commands are different from CL programs in that they cannot be called directly with COBOL's CALL statement. A special IBM supplied program named QCMDEXC is used for this purpose.

Listing 6.20 Calling QCMDEXC.

```
....-..A...B..-....2....-....3....-....4....-....5....-....6....
    ...
    WORKING-STORAGE SECTION.
    01  CMD-STRING      PIC X(100) VALUE "WRKSPLF".
    01  CMD-LENGTH      PIC 9(10)V9(5) COMP-3 VALUE 7.
    ...
    PROCEDURE DIVISION.
    ...
        CALL "QCMDEXC" USING CMD-STRING, CMD-LENGTH.
    ...
```

Listing 6.20 shows how to call QCMDEXC to execute an OS/400 command. CMD-STRING contains the command to execute. CMD-LENGTH specifies the command's length. The specified length should be the actual number of characters that the command executor should look at. In this example, the length is specified as 7, even though the length of CMD-STRING is 100. You may specify 100, but you must also make sure that there are no stray characters in the remaining positions of CMD-STRING.

6.7   Accessing the Local Data Area (LDA)

Each job running under OS/400 has a special data area for storing temporary application-related information. The data are maintained as long as the job is active. The job is active as long as the user is signed on or as long as there are additional job steps in a batch job. Once the user signs off or the batch job is completed, the local data area for that job are deleted and unrecoverable.

The local data area (LDA) is used primarily for communication between programs. Most, if not all languages under OS/400, support the local data area, whether directly or through the use of application program interfaces (APIs).

The LDA is accessed exactly the same as any other data area under OS/400. The main difference is that regular data areas are named objects and remain after the job ends; the LDA is a special system data area and is referenced as *LDA.

The commands in CL to read and modify the LDA are given in Listing 6.21.

Listing 6.21 CL commands that use the local data area (LDA).

```
CHGDTAARA DTAARA(*LDA (startPos length)) VALUE(aValue)
RTVDTAARA DTAARA(*LDA (startPos length)) RTNVAR(aCLvarName)
DSPDTAARA DTAARA(*LDA)
```

COBOL/400 programs access the local data area with the DISPLAY and ACCEPT statements. The local data area must be defined in the SPECIAL-NAMES paragraph.

Listing 6.22 Using the LDA in a COBOL program.

```
....-..A...B..-....2....-....3....-....4....-....5....-....6....
     IDENTIFICATION DIVISION.
     PROGRAM-ID.  ADDPHNE.
     ENVIRONMENT DIVISION.
     CONFIGURATION SECTION.
     SPECIAL-NAMES.   LOCAL-DATA IS LDA.
         .
         .
     WORKING-STORAGE SECTION.
     01  LDA-DATA-AREA.
         05  LDA-ACCT    PIC X(5).
         05  LDA-FIRM    PIC X.
         .
         .
     PROCEDURE DIVISION.
         ...
         ACCEPT LDA-DATA-AREA FROM LDA.
         ...
         DISPLAY LDA-DATA-AREA UPON LDA.
         ...
```

Listing 6.22 shows how to read and write to the LDA. The environment name LOCAL-DATA is assigned to the program mnemonic name LDA. Once assigned, the program can use LDA with the DISPLAY and ACCEPT statements to transfer data to and from the local data area.

6.8 Reference Modification

In COBOL/400, it is possible to reference substrings of a data item. This is accomplished by specifying a starting position within a string and the length of the substring. The length of the substring is optional; if omitted, it automatically extends to the end of the data item.

Both the starting position and the length can be expressed as an integer value, a literal value, another data item, or an arithmetic expression. The starting position and length must be at least 1 and cannot be greater than the length of the source data item.

As an example, consider an application that reads a field from the display but must ensure that the field is left justified before writing the value to a database.

Listing 6.23 Left justify using reference modification.

```
....-..A...B..-....2....-....3....-....4....-....5....-....6....
      PROCESS EXTACCDSP
      IDENTIFICATION DIVISION.
      PROGRAM-ID.  LJUST.
      ENVIRONMENT DIVISION.
      SPECIAL-NAMES.  CONSOLE IS CRT, CRT STATUS IS CRT-STATUS.
      DATA DIVISION.
      WORKING-STORAGE SECTION.
      01  CRT-STATUS.
          03 STATUS-1                   PIC 9(2).
             88 CRT-OK                        VALUE 0.
             88 CRT-FKEY                       VALUE 1.
          03 STATUS-2                   PIC 9(2).
             88 FKEY-3                         VALUE 3.
          03 STATUS-3                   PIC 9(2).
      01  UNJUST-TEXT                    PIC X(30).
      01  JUSTIFIED-TEXT                 PIC X(30).
      01  INDX                          PIC 9(9) USAGE BINARY.
      PROCEDURE DIVISION.
      DEMONSTRATE-LEFTJUST.
          PERFORM WITH TEST AFTER UNTIL CRT-FKEY AND FKEY-3
             PERFORM JUSTIFY-FIELD
             DISPLAY "TEXT TO JUSTIFY:" AT 0510 WITH BLANK SCREEN
                "F3 = EXIT" AT 2402
                "JUSTIFIED TEXT:" AT 0610
                JUSTIFIED-TEXT AT 0635 WITH UNDERLINE
             ACCEPT UNJUST-TEXT LINE 5 COL 35 WITH UNDERLINE
          END-PERFORM.
          STOP RUN.
      JUSTIFY-FIELD.
          INITIALIZE INDX
          INSPECT UNJUST-TEXT TALLYING INDX FOR LEADING SPACES.
```

```
IF INDX < LENGTH OF JUSTIFIED-TEXT
    MOVE UNJUST-TEXT (INDX + 1 : LENGTH OF UNJUST-TEXT - INDX)
        TO JUSTIFIED-TEXT
ELSE
    MOVE UNJUST-TEXT TO JUSTIFIED-TEXT
END-IF.
```

The main point in Listing 6.23 is the MOVE statement found in the JUSTIFY-FIELD paragraph. After the INSPECT statement, the value of INDX will specify how many leading spaces were found in UNJUST-TEXT. Adding 1 to INDX computes the offset of the first nonblank character in UNJUST-TEXT. To determine the length of the substring, subtract the number of leading blanks from the actual length of UNJUST-TEXT. The length of UNJUST-TEXT is determined by using the special LENGTH of register (see Fig. 6.1).

```
Initially:
   UNJUST-TEXT = "ƀƀƀƀSOME TEXTƀƀƀƀƀƀƀƀƀƀƀƀƀƀƀƀƀƀ"
   INDX = 0
   LENGTH OF UNJUST-TEXT = 30

After the INSPECT statement:
   INDX = 4    -- there are 4 leading spaces
   INDX + 1 = 5    -- The beginning of the substring is the 5th char
   LENGTH OF UNJUST-TEXT - INDX =  26
   (length equals 30 and index equals 4, therefore 30-4=26)

The resultant MOVE statement is:
   MOVE UNJUST-TEXT (5 : 26) TO JUSTIFIED-TEXT

Which means:
   Move 26 characters from UNJUST-TEXT starting with the 5th
   character.
```

Figure 6.1 Results of example program in Listing 6.23.

6.9 MOVE with De-editing

COBOL/400 also supports move with deediting. This means that a numeric-edited data item can be moved into a numeric or numeric-edited data field. Internally, this is accomplished by first determining the value of the numeric-edited item, then moving that value to the receiver. Move with deediting should not be confused with parsing of a string field for its numeric value. The following example does *not* demonstrate MOVE with deediting and will result in a run-time error (see Listing 6.24).

Listing 6.24 Erroneous MOVE.

```
.....-..A...B..-....2....-....3....-....4....-....5....-....6....
    01  CHAR-FIELD  PIC X(15) VALUE " $100.00".
    01  NUM-FIELD   PIC S9(5)V99.
        ...
        MOVE CHAR-FIELD TO NUM-FIELD.   *** Decimal data error
```

Deediting takes place only when a numeric-edited data field is the sender. The receiver may be either numeric-edited or numeric (see Listing 6.25).

Listing 6.25 Proper MOVE with de-editing.

```
.....-..A...B..-....2....-....3....-....4....-....5....-....6....
    01  NUM-EDIT-FLD  PIC $$$,$$9.99CR.
    01  DEST-NUMBER   PIC S9(5)V99.
        ...
        MOVE 100.00 TO NUM-EDIT-FLD.
        MOVE NUM-EDIT-FLD TO DEST-NUMBER.
```

The program in Listing 6.26 demonstrates move from numeric-edited values to regular values and vice versa.

Listing 6.26 Example to show MOVE with de-editing.

```
.....-..A...B..-....2....-....3....-....4....-....5....-....6....
    PROCESS EXTACCDSP
    IDENTIFICATION DIVISION.
    PROGRAM-ID.  DEEDIT.
    DATA DIVISION.
    WORKING-STORAGE SECTION.
    01  NUM-VAL       PIC S9(9)V9(5).
    01  PIC-1         PIC S9(5)V9(5) USAGE IS DISPLAY.
    01  PIC-2         PIC S9(5)V9(5) USAGE IS BINARY.
    01  PIC-3         PIC S9(5)V9(5) USAGE IS PACKED-DECIMAL.
    01  PIC-4         PIC $$$$,$$$.$$CR.
    01  PIC-5         PIC ----,---.99.
    01  PIC-6         PIC $++++9999.
    01  PIC-7         PIC 9(5).99-.
    PROCEDURE DIVISION.
    DEMONSTRATE-DE-EDITING.
        INITIALIZE PIC-1 PIC-2 PIC-3 PIC-4 PIC-5 PIC-6 PIC-7.
        DISPLAY "F3 = EXIT" AT 2202 WITH BLANK SCREEN
                "S9(5)V9(5) USAGE DISPLAY:" AT 0705
                "S9(5)V9(5) USAGE IS BINARY:" AT 0805
                "S9(5)V9(5) USAGE IS PACKED-DECIMAL:" AT 0905
                "$$$$,$$$.$$CR:" AT 1005
                "----,---.99:"  AT 1105
                "$++++9999:"    AT 1205
                "9(5).99-:"     AT 1305.
        ACCEPT PIC-1 AT 0745.
        MOVE PIC-1 TO NUM-VAL.
        PERFORM SET-VALS.
        ACCEPT PIC-2 AT 0845.
        MOVE PIC-2 TO NUM-VAL.
        PERFORM SET-VALS.
        ACCEPT PIC-3 AT 0945.
```

```
       MOVE PIC-3 TO NUM-VAL.
       PERFORM SET-VALS.
       ACCEPT PIC-4 AT 1045.
       MOVE PIC-4 TO NUM-VAL.
       PERFORM SET-VALS.
       ACCEPT PIC-5 AT 1145.
       MOVE PIC-5 TO NUM-VAL.
       PERFORM SET-VALS.
       ACCEPT PIC-6 AT 1245.
       MOVE PIC-6 TO NUM-VAL.
       PERFORM SET-VALS.
       ACCEPT PIC-7 AT 1345.
       MOVE PIC-7 TO NUM-VAL.
       PERFORM SET-VALS.
       DISPLAY "PRESS ENTER TO END" AT 2202 WITH REVERSE-VIDEO.
       ACCEPT END-PGM AT 2260.
       STOP RUN.
   SET-VALS.
       MOVE NUM-VAL TO PIC-1 PIC-2 PIC-3 PIC-4 PIC-5 PIC-6 PIC-7.
       DISPLAY PIC-1 AT 0745 WITH BLANK LINE
           PIC-2 AT 0845 WITH BLANK LINE
           PIC-3 AT 0945 WITH BLANK LINE
           PIC-4 AT 1045 WITH BLANK LINE
           PIC-5 AT 1145 WITH BLANK LINE
           PIC-6 AT 1245 WITH BLANK LINE
           PIC-7 AT 1345 WITH BLANK LINE.
```

6.10   Performance Considerations

This section outlines points that should be considered when designing programs in COBOL/400.

6.10.1   PICTURE clauses for numeric items

Since the AS/400 represents numbers internally with a sign, you can improve performance by including an S in a picture clause whenever possible.

If you are declaring a data item for usage of COMP-3 (packed decimal), you can improve performance by specifying an odd number of numeric character positions in the picture clause. Internally, the rightmost byte of a packed decimal item contains a digit and a sign; all remaining bytes contain two digits. If you specify an odd number of digits, the compiler will not have to supply the missing digit.

6.10.2   Eight-byte binary items

Avoid using 8-byte binary items. The compiler must make conversions in order to use them.

6.10.3   Segmentation

Use of segmentation increases the compile and run times of COBOL/400 programs. Segmentation is provided only for compatibility with other systems. It is not necessary to be concerned with storage management when writing COBOL/400 programs.

6.10.4 Debugging

By default, the COBOL/400 compiler includes information in the object program for use when debugging the program. Compile time, as well as run time, is longer when debugging information is present in the object program. You can obtain increased performance by turning off debugging information when it is not required. To compile without debugging information, specify the *NOSRCDBG in the source listing options field.

6.10.5 *NORANGE compile-time option

The *NORANGE generation option instructs the COBOL/400 compiler to omit run-time range checking for subscripts and reference modifications. For example, range checking ensures that you do not attempt to access the 21st element of a 20-element array. Specifying *NORANGE can improve performance when:

- The program makes frequent references to tables

- The program often uses reference modification

Specifying *NORANGE prevents the COBOL/400 compiler from generating code to check subscripts or reference modification ranges. Unpredictable results may occur if a program attempts to reference array elements outside the array's defined size.

6.10.6 *DUPKEYCHK compile-time option

The *DUPKEYCHK compile-time option instructs the COBOL/400 compiler to check for duplicate keys when using an INDEXED file. Using this option while reading INDEXED files can adversely affect performance.

6.10.7 Commitment control

The use of commitment control will increase the run time of a COBOL/400 program. Additionally, commitment control causes locks on records that may cause delays for other jobs using the same file.

6.10.8 Initializing variables

By default, when a COBOL/400 program begins, any variables that do not specify a VALUE clause are initialized to zero or blanks. Specifying the *NOSTDINZ generation option instructs the COBOL/400 compiler not to initialize all variables. The compiler will initialize only those variables that have value clauses declared.

If you specify the *NOSTDINZ, you must ensure that a variable contains valid data before attempting to manipulate it.

6.10.9   Blocking records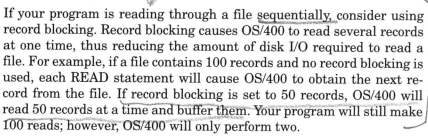

If your program is reading through a file sequentially, consider using record blocking. Record blocking causes OS/400 to read several records at one time, thus reducing the amount of disk I/O required to read a file. For example, if a file contains 100 records and no record blocking is used, each READ statement will cause OS/400 to obtain the next record from the file. If record blocking is set to 50 records, OS/400 will read 50 records at a time and buffer them. Your program will still make 100 reads; however, OS/400 will only perform two.

3

AS/400 File Concepts

COBOL programs interact with a variety of file types such as physical files, logical files, query files, printer files, and display files. This part explains in detail the various file types that you will use when developing COBOL/400 applications.

Chapter 7 discusses physical and logical files. Physical and logical files act as the heart of all database applications.

Chapter 8 discusses display files. Display files are used to communicate with the user. For the most part, all workstation I/O operations are performed through the use of display files.

Chapter 9 discusses printer files. Printer files are used to contain report layouts in much the same way as display files contain display layouts.

7

Physical and Logical Files

At the heart of the OS/400 operating system is a flexible and powerful database engine capable of handling virtually all database-related requirements.

This chapter discusses some of the basic ideas and techniques underlying OS/400 databases. For more detailed information regarding any of the topics, you should obtain the *AS/400 Database Guide* or the *AS/400 DDS Reference*.

7.1 Physical and Logical Files Defined

There are two classifications for database files on the AS/400: physical files and logical files. Physical files can be thought of as actual data files. Logical files can be thought of as the access path (or index) to a separately defined physical file. A logical file must be associated with a physical file.

Physical files on the AS/400 relate directly to regular data files on the System/36. AS/400 logical files relate to System/36 alternate indexes.

7.1.1 Physical files

In contrast to files on most systems, a database file on the AS/400 consists of two main components: a header section that contains detailed information about the contents of the file (such as the names of the fields, attributes of each field, record formats, etc.) and a collection of zero or more members that contain the data. Each member can be thought of as a separate file and therefore must have a unique name.

All members share the exact same record layout (which is defined in the file's header). Prior to executing a program, the override database file command (OVRDBF) can be used to direct the program to access a specific member within the file. The OVRDBF command can also instruct the program to view all members as a single member.

7.1.2   Logical files

Logical files contain no data. They are used to arrange data from one or more physical files into different formats and sequences. For example, a physical file may contain a database of customers ordered by customer number. A logical file can be created that will order the records by customer name. Logical files are often referred to as *logical views*.

Logical files can also be set up to omit certain types of records from the access path, thus preventing a program from ever reading them. For example, a database system may be set up never to delete a customer record (for historical purposes); rather it would set a status field to indicate that the account is inactive. A logical view could be created that omits any records that have an inactive status; thus if a program were to read the logical file from beginning to end, it would never encounter any inactive accounts.

Logical files can also be used to connect two or more physical files together based on common keys (this is called a JOIN file). For example, a file that contains order-header information and another that contains order details may be logically connected to form a single logical file that contains both header and detail information in each record.

7.2   Externally Described versus Program Described Database Files

Records can be described on the AS/400 either at the field level or at the record level. Files that are described at the field level contain specific information relating to each field within the file. Files that are described at the field level are referred to as *externally described* files. Files that are described at the record level only specify the length of the record; the system does not know about fields in the file. Files that are described in this fashion are referred to as *program-described* files.

Programs written on the AS/400 can use either externally described files or program-described files. However, there is much power and flexibility to be gained by using externally described files.

If a file is set up as an externally described file, a program can read and access it as a program-described file as well. This is helpful when migrating programs from a system that does not support externally described files (such as the System/36). When migrating, a file can be externally described on the AS/400 but old programs can continue to read it as a flat file (or a program-described file). Later, should the programs be updated, they can be changed to use the external descriptions.

7.2.1 Describing a file at the record level   (*Progrma Descibed*)

To describe a file at the record level, you would use the create physical file (CRTPF) command and specify the record length (RCDLEN) parameter. This instructs OS/400 to create a physical file with the specified record length.

```
CRTPF FILE(library-name/file-name)  RCDLEN(rec-length)
```

Figure 7.1 The create physical file command for a flat file.

Figure 7.1 shows how to enter the create physical file command from the command line. The library-name/file-name represents the qualified name of the file that you are creating. If you omit the library part of the qualified name, the file will be created in the current library (*CURLIB). The rec-length parameter specifies the record length of the file. If you specify a record length when creating a file, the file will be created as a flat file for use as a program-described file.

7.2.2 Describing a file at the field level   (*Externally described*)

There are several methods for describing a database file at the field level. Among these methods are interactive data definition utility (IDDU), SQL/400 commands (structured query language), and data description specifications (DDS). Since DDS is the most widely used method for describing database files on the AS/400, this book will focus on discussing files using DDS.

7.3 Using DDS to Describe Files

When describing a database file using DDS, you can describe attributes at the file, record format, join, field, key, and select/omit levels:

- File-level attributes supply information relevant to the entire file. For example, you can specify whether the file allows for duplicate keys or not.

- Record-format level attributes specify information about a specific record format within the file. For example, when describing a logical file, you would specify what physical file it is based on at the record-format level.

- Join-level information specifies the relationship between physical files to be included in the join.

- Field-level information defines various aspects of an individual field such as its data type, length, precision, and validation rules.

- Key-level fields define the order in which the records are returned (also known as the access path for the file).

- Select/omit field information specifies which records are to be returned to a program when processing the file.

DDS is entered and edited using source entry utility (SEU). DDS source members should be kept within a source physical file named QDDSSRC. The CRTPF command is used to create physical files; the CRTLF command is used to create logical files. If the compile is completed successfully, a file will be created in the specified (or current) library.

7.3.1 Physical file DDS

DDS for a physical file must be in the following order:

1. File-level entries (optional)

2. Record-format-level entries

3. Field-level entries

4. Key-field-level entries (optional)

The member type for a physical file is PF. To create and edit a physical file description, you can use the command in Fig. 7.2.

```
STRSEU SRCFILE(library-name/file-name) SRCMBR(member-name) TYPE(PF)
```

Figure 7.2 Starting source entry utility (SEU).

Replace (library-name) with the name of the source physical file (such as QDDSSRC) where the DDS source member resides (or should reside if you are creating it). Replace (member-name) with the name of the physical file you want to describe. The source physical file must already exist; if the member does not exist, it will be created for you. The PF in the TYPE parameter specifies to SEU that the member will define a physical file. SEU uses this TYPE to help you when entering source statements. SEU will automatically syntax check source statements based on this type. SEU also offers intelligent prompting for a source statement by positioning the cursor on a source line and pressing F4. A full-screen prompt will guide you through all the fields of a DDS record.

Listing 7.1 DDS source file.

```
FILE NAME:    CLAIMHDR
.....A..........T.NAME++++++RLEN++TDPB......FUNCTIONS+++++++++++++
     A* PATIENT CLAIM HEADER RECORD
1    A                                      UNIQUE      — NO DUPLICATES
2    A          R CLAIMHDR
3    A            CLAIMKEY     4A            TEXT('CLAIM ID')
4    A            PATACCT      4             TEXT('PAT CHART #')
5    A            CLAIMDATE    8S 0          TEXT('CLAIM DATE')
6    A            CARRIER      30            TEXT('INS CARR NAME')
7    A            CLAIMSTAT    1             TEXT('CLAIM STATUS')
8    A          K CLAIMKEY
```

Listing 7.1 is an example of a DDS source listing, and shows the definition of a physical file with the following attributes:

- Line 1 specifies that the file is to have unique key values—that is, no duplicate keys are allowed in the file. The UNIQUE keyword is a file-level keyword and must appear before the first record definition.

- Line 2 begins the definition of the record. The R in column 17 (under the letter T) indicates the beginning of the definition. The record format name is CLAIMHDR.

- Line 3 defines a field named CLAIMKEY which is four characters long. The TEXT keyword allows you to provide a textual description of the field that will be kept in the file's header. When a program includes this file, the text will appear as comments in the compiler source listing. The "A" which appears next to the "4" (in position 35) specifies the data type for the field. The following are valid data types:

Entry	Meaning
A	Character
P	Packed decimal
S	Zoned decimal
B	Binary
F	Floating point
H	Hexadecimal
L	Date
T	Time
Z	Time stamp

If no data type is specified (as in lines 4, 6, and 7 of Listing 7.1), the decimal position entry is used to determine the data type. If the decimal positions (positions 36–37) are blank, the data type is assumed to be character (A); if they contain a number 0 through 31, the data type is assumed to be packed decimal (P).

- Lines 4 and 6 define a character field names PATACCT and CARRIER. No data type and decimal positions are specified; therefore the compiler will automatically assume they are character fields.

- Line 5 defines a zoned decimal field of length 8 with two decimal positions. In COBOL/400, this translates to

```
PIC S9(8).
```

- Line 7 defines another character field called CLAIMSTAT, which is 1 character long.

- Line 8 begins the key definitions. In this example, there is only one field defined as the key. The "K" in column 17 specifies that a key is being defined.

7.3.2 README.TXT

Before proceeding, it is necessary to ensure that your environment is set up correctly and that any previously created example files are deleted (if you plan to create them again).

First, make sure that your current library is set properly as discussed in Chap. 0.

Next, check that any previously created examples are deleted before attempting to create them again. If you try to create a physical file that already exists, you will receive an error message stating that the file already exists. Furthermore, you cannot delete a physical file when there are logical files still attached to it.

If you prefer to check whether or not the files exist, you can use OS/400's work with objects command (WRKOBJ) to check for the existence of an object. If the object (in this case, a file object) exists, OS/400 will show you information regarding the file (i.e., what library it is located in, etc.). To use the WRKOBJ command to see any objects in your library list whose name begins with CLAIM, type the following command on the command line, then press Enter. The display will look similar to the one in Fig. 7.3.

```
WRKOBJ CLAIM*
```

To delete any files previously created from this chapter's examples, put "4" in the option column of the work with objects output display and

```
                       Work with Objects

  Type options, press Enter.
    2=Edit authority        3=Copy    4=Delete    5=Display authority
  7=Rename
    8=Display description   13=Change description

  Opt  Object     Type     Library   Attribute   Text
    __   CLAIMDTL   *FILE    YOURLIB   PF          Claim details
    __   CLAIMHDR   *FILE    YOURLIB   PF          Claim headers
    __   CLAIMPAT   *FILE    YOURLIB   PF          Claim patients
    __   CLAIMS     *FILE    YOURLIB   LF          Join all hdrs, dtls, pats
    __   CLAIMSOPEN *FILE    YOURLIB   LF          Open claims only
```

Figure 7.3 Output from WRKOBJ command.

```
  DLTF CLAIMS            (logical files must be deleted first)
  DLTF CLAIMSOPEN
  DLTF CLAIMHDR          (finally, delete all physical files)
  DLTF CLAIMDTL
  DLTF CLAIMPAT
```

Figure 7.4 Commands to delete example files.

then press Enter, or use the following commands (note—you must delete the logical files first) (see Fig. 7.4).

7.3.3 Creating a file and manually loading data using data file utility

In this section, you will create three physical files relating to insurance claim processing.

- CLAIMHDR: This file contains information regarding each claim in the system. Each claim may have several detail records associated with it.
- CLAIMDTL: This file is the "detail" file and contains one record for each transaction.
- CLAIMPAT: This file contains patient names.

Use SEU to enter the source shown in Listing 7.1. Start SEU with the following command:

```
STRSEU QDDSSRC CLAIMHDR TYPE(PF) TEXT('Claim headers')
```

After editing the file, exit SEU (F3 = Exit) and compile the DDS using the following command:

```
CRTPF FILE(CLAIMHDR)
```

You can display any compiler messages that might be sent to your workstation by using the DSPMSG command. Also, you can view any spooled output (compiler listing, etc.) using the WRKSPLF command. Repeat the above steps for the files shown in Listing 7.2.

Listing 7.2 DDS for file CLAIMDTL.

```
FILE NAME:    CLAIMDTL
......A..........T.Name+++++RLen++TDpB......Functions++++++++++++++++++
      A*  PATIENT CLAIM DETAIL RECORDS
      A                                          UNIQUE
      A          R CLAIMDTL
      A            CLAIMKEY      4                TEXT('CLAIM ID')
      A            TRANDATE      8S 0             TEXT('CLAIM DATE')
      A            TRANKEY       2S 0             TEXT('TRANS KEY')
      A            TRANDESC     30                TEXT('INS CARR NAME')
      A            TRANAMT      11   2            TEXT('TRANSACT AMT')
      A          K CLAIMKEY
      A          K TRANDATE
      A          K TRANKEY
```

Use this command to start SEU for this file:

```
STRSEU QDDSSRC CLAIMDTL TYPE(PF) TEXT('Claim detail')
```

Use this command to create the file:

```
CRTPF FILE(CLAIMDTL)
```

The file definition in Listing 7.2 is similar to the CLAIMHDR file except the file holds the details relating to each claim. In this file, there are three key fields (CLAIMKEY, TRANDATE, and TRANKEY). Together, these three fields form a single complex key. The file will be kept in CLAIMKEY, TRANDATE, and TRANKEY order.

Listing 7.3 DDS for file CLAIMPAT.

```
FILE NAME:  CLAIMPAT
......A..........T.Name+++++RLen++TDpB......Functions+++++++
      A*  PATIENT NAME RECORD
      A                                          UNIQUE
      A          R PATREC
      A            PATACCT       4                TEXT('PAT CHART #')
      A            PATNAME      30                TEXT('INS CARR NAME')
      A          K PATACCT
```

Listing 7.3 defines the patient file. Use the following command to start SEU for this file:

```
STRSEU QDDSSRC CLAIMPAT TYPE(PF) TEXT('Claim patients')
```

Use this command to create the file:

```
CRTPF FILE(CLAIMPAT)
```

7.3.3.1 Using the data file utility to manually load data. An easy way to load data into a file (physical or logical) is to use data file utility (DFU). You can request DFU to create a temporary program for data entry. Because all details relating to all fields and record formats are saved in the actual physical file, DFU can look at the file to determine what fields exist and how to build an entry screen. To request a temporary program for data entry, use the following command:

```
UPDDTA CLAIMHDR
```

When DFU presents you with an entry display, enter the data shown in Fig. 7.5. When finished, press F3 = Exit to end the DFU session.

CLAIMKEY	PATACCT	CLAIMDATE	CARRIER	CLAIMSTAT
C001	P001	19950301	Aetna Casualty	O
C002	P002	19940328	Blue Cross/Blue Shield	C

Figure 7.5 Data to populate the CLAIMHDR file.

7.3.3.2 Displaying data in a physical file. There are two simple ways to display the data in the file. You can use the display physical file member (DSPPFM) command or the run query (RUNQRY) command. The DSPPFM command will display the file in a flat record format; the RUNQRY command will show the values of each field in table format.

The following command displays the contents of the CLAIMHDR file using the DSPPFM command:

```
DSPPFM CLAIMHDR    (display physical file member)
```

Results from DSPPFM command are shown in Fig. 7.6.

```
*...+....1....+....2....+....3....+....4....+..
C001P00119950301Aetna Casualty          O
C002P00219940328Blue Cross/Blue Shield  C
                ****** END OF DATA ******
```

Figure 7.6 Output from DPPFM on CLAIMHDR.

The following command displays the contents of the CLAIMHDR file using the RUNQRY command:

```
RUNQRY *NONE CLAIMHDR    (builds a temporary query and runs it)
```

Results from RUNQRY command are shown in Fig. 7.7.

```
....+....1....+....2....+....3....+....4....+....5....+....6....+....7...
CLAIMKEY  PATACCT   CLAIMDATE   CARRIER                          CLAIMSTAT
  C001      P001    19,950,301  Aetna Casualty                       O
  C002      P002    19,940,328  Blue Cross/Blue Shield               C
********  End of report  ********
```

Figure 7.7 Output from RUNQRY on CLAIMHDR.

If you have been following the command sequence, you can now populate the remaining two files. Use the commands below and data tables shown in Figs. 7.8 and 7.9 to populate the CLAIMDTL and CLAIMPAT files:

```
UPDDTA CLAIMDTL
```

CLAIMKEY	TRANDATE	TRANKEY	TRANDESC	TRANAMT
C001	19941201	01	Physical examination	200.00
C001	19941205	02	Injection	25.00
C002	19941210	01	Vertebral manipulation	50.00
C002	19941210	02	Lumbar X-Rays	75.00

Figure 7.8 Data to populate the CLAIMDTL file.

```
UPDDTA CLAIMPAT
```

PATACCT	PATNAME
P001	Gerry Kaplan
P002	Donald Myers
P003	Shayna Pearl
P004	Mercedes Hennessy

Figure 7.9 Data to populate CLAIMPAT.

The next section will show how to build a logical file over these physical files.

7.3.4 Logical file DDS

DDS for a logical file must be in the following order:

1. File-level entries (optional)
2. Record-format-level entries
3. Field-level entries (optional)
4. Key-field-level entries (optional)
5. Select/omit field-level entries (optional)

Since logical files may contain multiple record formats, items 2 through 5 may be repeated for each defined record format.

The member type for a logical file is LF. Use the command shown in Fig. 7.10 to start SEU and edit a logical file description.

```
STRSEU SRCFILE(library-name/file-name) SRCMBR(member-name) TYPE(LF)
```

Figure 7.10 Command to enter logical file DDS.

Listing 7.4 DDS source file.

```
FILE NAME: CLAIMSOPEN
......A..........T.Name++++++RLen++TDpB......Functions+++++++
      A* CLAIMSOPEN - CLAIMS WITH OPEN STATUS
1     A                                       UNIQUE
2     A          R CLAIMREC                   PFILE(CLAIMHDR)
3     A          K CLAIMKEY
4     A          S CLAIMSTAT                  CMP(EQ 'O')
```

Listing 7.4 is an example of a DDS source listing for a logical file. This logical file is also sorted by CLAIMKEY; however, only records that have a claim status of "O" will be included in the file.

- Line 1 indicates that the logical file should have no duplicate keys allowed.

- Line 2 begins the definition of record CLAIMHDR. The function PFILE specifies the name of the physical file that this record format is based on.

- Line 3 specifies CLAIMKEY as the key for this logical file.

- Line 4 is a select line. The "S" is required in column 17 for selection criteria lines. The value in field CLAIMSTAT will be compared to the value "O", and if it matches, it will be included in the logical file. In this example, status "O" represents open records.

If a program opens this logical file and reads from beginning to end, it will only receive records that have an open status.

7.3.5 Creating the logical file

Use SEU to enter the source shown in Listing 7.4. Start SEU with the following command:

```
STRSEU QDDSSRC CLAIMSOPEN TYPE(LF) TEXT('OPEN CLAIMS ONLY')
```

After editing the file, exit SEU (F3 = Exit) and compile the DDS using the following command:

```
CRTLF FILE(CLAIMSOPEN)
```

7.3.5.1 Displaying a logical file. A logical file does not actually contain data—it is just an access path (or an index) to a physical file; therefore you cannot display it using the display physical file member command as you can for physical files. Instead, you can use the RUNQRY command:

```
RUNQRY *NONE CLAIMSOPEN
```

The output will resemble that shown in Fig. 7.11. Notice that only one record is shown. This is because the logical file defines a select/omit clause that specifies selection of only records with a claim status of "O". The other record has a claim status of "C" and therefore is not included in the logical file.

```
....+....1....+....2....+....3....+....4....+....5....+....6....+...
CLAIMKEY  PATACCT   CLAIMDATE   CARRIER                 CLAIMSTAT
  C001      P001    19,950,301  Aetna Casualty              O
********  End of report ********
```

Figure 7.11 Output from RUNQRY on CLAIMSOPEN.

7.3.6 Join logical files

A join file is a special logical file that represents one or more files that are logically related. Relationships between files are described using DDS. Once created, the file can be read as any other normal database file, without the COBOL program having any knowledge of what files are actually being accessed.

To present a realistic example, consider the files that you created in Sec. 7.3.3—a header file, a transaction file, and a patient name file. There is a clear relationship between all three of these files. Each record in the header file is logically connected to one or more records in the detail file. Furthermore, each header record is bound to exactly one patient record. Without join logical files, a COBOL program would have to process all three files to obtain one complete set of details. Joining all three files together as a single file allows a COBOL program to open a single file and obtain all necessary details for each transaction in one read. As an added bonus, the join logical file can also have a select/omit section specified that will present the COBOL program with only transactions for open claims.

The source in Listing 7.5 shows how to code a join logical file over three separate files.

Listing 7.5 DDS for a JOIN logical file.

```
FILE NAME: CLAIMS
.....A..........T.Name++++++RLen++TDpB......Functions++++++++++++++++++++
     A* CLAIMS - HEADERS & DETAILS WITH PATIENT
[1]  A          R JOINREC               JFILE(CLAIMHDR CLAIMDTL +
     A                                  CLAIMPAT)
[2]  A          J                       JOIN(CLAIMHDR CLAIMDTL)
[3]  A                                  JFLD(CLAIMKEY CLAIMKEY)
[4]  A                                  JDUPSEQ(TRANDATE)
[5]  A          J                       JOIN(CLAIMHDR CLAIMPAT)
[6]  A                                  JFLD(PATACCT PATACCT)
[7]  A            CLAIMKEY              JREF(1)
[8]  A            PATACCT              JREF(1)
     A            PATNAME
     A            CLAIMDATE
     A            CARRIER
     A            CLAIMSTAT
     A            TRANDATE
     A            TRANDESC
     A            TRANAMT
     A          K PATACCT
     A          K CLAIMDATE
[9]  A          S CLAIMSTAT            CMP(EQ'O')
```

- The keyword JFILE on line 1 indicates that the record being defined is a joined record. All files connected by the join must be listed. If there is not enough room to list all file names, they can be continued on subsequent lines by using the + sign at the end of the line to indicate continuation.

- Line 2 has a J coded in column 17 that indicates the beginning of a join relationship definition. Line 2 specifies that file CLAIMHDR and CLAIMDTL are to be logically connected. The actual relationship will be defined on following lines.

- Line 3 defines the relationship between the two files specified on line 2. The first field represents the field to be matched from the first file on line 2 (CLAIMHDR); the second field is the name of the field to connect to in the second file listed on line 2 (CLAIMDTL). In this case, both files use the same name for the field; thus the same name appears twice.

- Line 4 specifies how to order records from this join when the resultant keys from the two files are identical. In this case, identical keys should then be sorted by transaction date.

- Line 5 begins another join relationship between CLAIMHDR and CLAIMPAT. This relationship will connect a claim record to a patient record by matching PATACCT as specified in line 6.

- Line 7 begins the list of fields to include in the record definition. Lines 7 and 8 contain the JREF( ) function. This is used because more than one file contains CLAIMKEY and PATACCT; therefore it must be qualified explicitly. JREF(1) indicates to take the field from the first file in the list of JFILE files (in this case, from CLAIMHDR). The same is true for line 8.

- Line 9 is a select line. The "S" is required in column 17 for selection criteria lines. The value in field CLAIMSTAT will be compared to the value "O", and if it matches, it will be included in the logical file. In this example, status "O" represents open records.

Enter the DDS from Listing 7.5 into source member CLAIMS. Use the following command to start SEU:

```
STRSEU QDDSSRC CLAIMS TYPE(LF) TEXT('JOIN ALL HDRS, DTLS, PATS')
```

After entering the file, compile it with the following command:

```
CRTLF FILE(CLAIMS)
```

Use the RUNQRY command to view the CLAIMS logical file:

```
RUNQRY *NONE CLAIMS
```

Because the output is wider than the standard display, you will probably have to scroll horizontally. Check the function keys at the bottom of the display for left or right scrolling. The output should resemble that shown in Fig. 7.12 (wrapped over several lines).

Notice that there are only two records displayed (even though the file contained four transactions). This is because the header file

```
....+....1....+....2....+....3....+....4....+....5....+....6....
CLAIMKEY  PATACCT  PATNAME                           CLAIMDATE
  C001     P001    Gerry Kaplan                      19,950,301
  C001     P001    Gerry Kaplan                      19,950,301

+....7....+....8....+....9....+...10....+...11....+...12
CARRIER                       CLAIMSTAT    TRANDATE
Aetna casualty                    O       19,941,201
Aetna casualty                    O       19,941,205

....+...13....+...14....+...15....+...16....+..
TRANDESC                      TRANAMT
Physical examination           200.00
Injection                       25.00

********  End of report  ********
```

Figure 7.12 Output from RUNQRY on CLAIMS.

(CLAIMHDR) only has one record with an "O" status; therefore only records in other files relating to the one open claim were returned. Furthermore, you can see that each record contains data from all three files.

7.3.7 Logical file considerations

As powerful as logical files are, they should be used cautiously and wisely. Each logical file that is added to a physical file will affect performance when updating related files. Remember that each time a record is added to a file, all indexes in other files must be updated to reflect the change. Consider the patient claim example. Each time a record is added to the claim header file, updates are also made to both logical files connected to it (CLAIMSOPEN and CLAIMS). If a program requires a special logical file, but the program is only run once a month, using the open query file command (OPNQRYF) may be a better solution. The OPNQRYF command is discussed later in Sec. 7.7.

Another way of managing how logical files affect performance is by the way in which their access paths are maintained. Access path maintenance refers to how and when a logical file's index is updated. Access path maintenance can be done three different ways:

- *Immediate update:* As soon as a record is added, changed, or deleted from its related physical file(s), the logical file will be immediately updated.

    Benefit: Programs reading the logical file will run faster.
    Drawback: Programs adding records to the physical file may become slower as more logical views are added.

    This method should be considered for logical files that are frequently accessed or when there are not many logical files attached to a dependent physical file.

- *Rebuild:* When a program opens the logical view, the entire access path (index) is rebuilt. When other programs add records to files related to the logical file, no changes occur to the logical file's access path.

    Benefit: No effect on performance exists since file updates will not be recorded in the logical file's access path.
    Drawback: When a program finally does open the logical file, it will have to wait until the access path is entirely rebuilt.

    This method works well for history files that are usually maintained or accessed during night batch runs. It is probably not wise to use this type of access path maintenance for logical files accessed by interactive programs.

- *Delayed:* Changes that affect the logical file are collected, and when the logical file is opened, those changes are applied.

    Benefit: Other programs will not be adversely affected during up-dates to the related files since no access path maintenance takes place during updates.

    Drawback: There may be a delay when opening the logical file if many changes are waiting to be applied to its access path.

This type of access path maintenance is good for infrequently used logical views, both interactive and batch.

Access path maintenance options are specified when the database file is created. A file's access path maintenance setting can also be changed with the CHGPF (for physical files) and CHGLF (for logical files) commands. For more information pertaining to these options, see the *AS/400 Database Guide.*

Note: if the file being defined specifies UNIQUE KEYS, rebuild and delay cannot be specified.

7.4   Field Reference Files

A field reference file acts as a data dictionary—you can define all fields used in a system in a single location (the field reference file) and have all files look to the field reference file for field definitions. The source in Listing 7.6 shows a file that defines the fields used in the previous example.

Listing 7.6   Example of a field reference file.

```
FILE NAME: FIELDREF
.....A..........T.Name++++++RLen++TDpB......Functions+++++++++++++
     A* FIELD REFERENCE FILE
     A                                       UNIQUE
     A           R FIELDREF
     A*
     A* CLAIM HDR FIELDS
     A             CLAIMKEY      4           TEXT('CLAIMKEY')
     A             CLAIMDATE     8S  0       TEXT('CLAIM DATE')
     A             CARRIER      30           TEXT('INS CARR NAME')
     A             CLAIMSTAT     1           TEXT('CLAIM STATUS')
     A*
     A* CLAIM DTL FIELDS
     A             TRANDATE      8S  0       TEXT('CLAIM DATE')
     A             TRANKEY       2S  0       TEXT('TRAN KEY')
     A             TRANDESC     30           TEXT('INS CARR NAME')
     A             TRANAMT      11   2       TEXT('TRANSACT AMT')
     A*
     A* PATIENT ACCOUNT FIELDS
     A             PATACCT       4           TEXT('PAT CHART #')
     A             PATNAME      30           TEXT('INS CARR NAME')
```

All of the fields used so far in this chapter are contained within this single file. Once this file has been compiled, all other files can reference this file for field attributes (including display files and printer files). The physical files from Sec. 7.3.3 can be rewritten as in Listing 7.7.

Listing 7.7 File DDS using a field reference file.

```
FILE NAME: CLAIMHDR
.....A..........T.Name+++++RLen++TDpB......Functions+++++++
    A* PATIENT CLAIM HEADER RECORD
    A                                          REF(FIELDREF)
    A                                          UNIQUE
    A          R CLAIMHDR
    A            CLAIMKEY    R
    A            PATACCT     R
    A            CLAIMDATE   R
    A            CARRIER     R
    A            CLAIMSTAT   R
    A          K CLAIMKEY
FILE NAME: CLAIMDTL
.....A..........T.Name+++++RLen++TDpB......Functions+++++++
    A* PATIENT CLAIM DETAIL RECORDS
    A                                          UNIQUE
    A                                          REF(FIELDREF)
    A          R CLAIMDTL
    A            CLAIMKEY    R
    A            TRANDATE    R
    A            TRANKEY     R
    A            TRANDESC    R
    A            TRANAMT     R
    A          K CLAIMKEY
    A          K TRANDATE
    A          K TRANKEY
FILE NAME: CLAIMPAT
.....A..........T.Name+++++RLen++TDpB......Functions+++++++
    A* PATIENT NAME RECORD
    A                                          REF(FIELDREF)
    A                                          UNIQUE
    A          R PATREC
    A            PATACCT     R
    A            PATNAME     R
    A          K PATACCT
```

The REF keyword specifies the name of a file that contains field references. When a field is defined with an "R" in the reference column, the DDS compiler will look to the reference file for the field's attributes.

Notice now that PATACCT's attributes are no longer defined twice—previously they were defined in both the CLAIMPAT file as well as the CLAIMHDR file. Furthermore, CLAIMKEY's attributes were also defined twice—in the CLAIMHDR and CLAIMDTL file. A field reference file can help to prevent fields from being defined with different attributes in different files. Additionally, if a field's attributes must be changed (i.e., length must become longer), the length can be changed in the field reference file; all other files must simply be recompiled.

7.5   Using COPY to Obtain Externally Described File Layouts into a COBOL Program

The INPUT–OUTPUT section of the data division is where COBOL programs define the files declared in the environment division. If the program is accessing externally described files, it is not necessary to define each field within the file—the COBOL/400 compiler can extract the fields directly from the file. This section focuses on the various options for copying file descriptions into a COBOL program.

Listing 7.8   COBOL program using the COPY statement.

```
.....-..A...B..-....2.....-....3....-....4....-....5....-....6....-....-
         ENVIRONMENT DIVISION.
         INPUT-OUTPUT SECTION.
         FILE-CONTROL.
             SELECT CLAIMHDR-FILE ASSIGN TO DATABASE-CLAIMHDR
                 ORGANIZATION IS INDEXED
                 ACCESS MODE IS RANDOM
                 RECORD KEY IS EXTERNALLY-DESCRIBED-KEY.
         DATA DIVISION.
         FILE SECTION.
         FD  CLAIMHDR-FILE.
         01  HEADER-REC.
             COPY DDS-ALL-FORMATS OF CLAIMHDR.
             .
             .
             .
         WORKING-STORAGE SECTION.
```

The COPY statement directs the COBOL/400 compiler to obtain field descriptions from a file and generate group-level data definitions, as shown in Listing 7.8. The claim header file (CLAIMHDR) that is being copied is the same from Sec. 7.4. It is defined in Listing 7.9.

Listing 7.9   DDS source for a CLAIMHDR file.

```
FILE NAME: CLAIMHDR
.....A...........T.Name++++++RLen++TDpB......Functions+++++++
     A* PATIENT CLAIM HEADER RECORD
     A                                     UNIQUE
     A           R CLAIMHDR
     A             CLAIMKEY    4A          TEXT('CLAIM ID')
     A             PATACCT     4           TEXT('PAT CHART #')
     A             CLAIMDATE   8S 0        TEXT('CLAIM DATE')
     A             CARRIER     30          TEXT('INS CARR NAME')
     A             CLAIMSTAT   1           TEXT('CLAIM STATUS')
     A           K CLAIMKEY
```

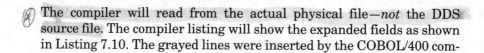
The compiler will read from the actual physical file—*not* the DDS source file. The compiler listing will show the expanded fields as shown in Listing 7.10. The grayed lines were inserted by the COBOL/400 com-

piler. The lines beginning with asterisks (*) are comments (also inserted by the compiler). When copying an external file, you must provide the first level group identifier (in this example, "01 HEADER-REC." since the compiler will always start numbering at a higher level; here the compiler started numbering at level 05).

Listing 7.10 Compiler results of using a COPY statement.

```
ENVIRONMENT DIVISION.
INPUT-OUTPUT SECTION.
FILE-CONTROL.
    SELECT CLAIMHDR-FILE ASSIGN TO DATABASE-CLAIMHDR
        ORGANIZATION IS INDEXED
        ACCESS MODE IS RANDOM
        RECORD KEY IS EXTERNALLY-DESCRIBED-KEY.
DATA DIVISION.
FILE SECTION.
FD  CLAIMHDR-FILE.
01  HEADER-REC.
    COPY DDS-ALL-FORMATS OF CLAIMHDR.
        05  CLAIMHDR-RECORD PIC X(47).                          <-ALL-FMTS
*       I-O FORMAT:CLAIMHDR  FROM FILE CLAIMHDR  OF LIBRARY BOOK  <-ALL-FMTS
*                                                               <-ALL-FMTS
*THE KEY DEFINITIONS FOR RECORD FORMAT  CLAMIHDR                <-ALL-FMTS
*   NUMBER      NAME                 RETRIEVAL    TYPE ALTSEQ   <-ALL-FMTS
*   0001    CLAIMKEY                 ASCENDING     AN   NO      <-ALL-FMTS
        05  CLAIMHDR        REDEFINES CLAIMHDR-RECORD.          <-ALL-FMTS
            06 CLAIMKEY               PIC X(4).                 <-ALL-FMTS
            06 PATACCT                PIC X(4).                 <-ALL-FMTS
            06 CLAIMDATE              PIC S9(8).                <-ALL-FMTS
            06 CARRIER                PIC X(30).                <-ALL-FMTS
            06 CLAIMSTAT              PIC X(1).                 <-ALL-FMTS
        .
        .
        .
WORKING-STORAGE SECTION.
```

7.5.1   COPY statement formats DD, DDR, DDS, and DDSR

There are four different formats of the COPY statement when copying external file descriptions:

- COPY DD-*formatName* or COPY DD-ALL-FORMATS
- COPY DDR-*formatName* or COPY DDR-ALL-FORMATS
- COPY DDS-*formatName* or COPY DDS-ALL-FORMATS
- COPY DDSR-*formatName* or COPY DDSR-ALL-FORMATS

The *formatName* refers to the record format name defined in the DDS with the "R" in column 17 in Listing 7.9. Since it is possible for logical, display, and printer files to have more than one record format, you can optionally specify which format to include. Since physical files can only have one record format, it is easier to specify ALL-FORMATS for physical files.

The DD option is used to reference ALIAS (alternative) names specified by using the ALIAS keyword in the file's DDS (the ALIAS keyword will be covered later in this section). When the DD option is used, any ALIAS names present replace the corresponding DDS field names. All underscores in the ALIAS names are translated into hyphens.

The DDR option performs the same function as the DD option, except that it replaces any invalid COBOL characters (@, #, $, and _) with valid COBOL characters A, N, D, and - accordingly. This is useful when files are being used that were defined for RPG programs in which these characters are valid.

The DDS option copies the internal DDS format field names. This is the format used in all examples in this book. The DDSR option is the same as the DDS option, except that it replaces invalid characters as does the DDR option.

7.5.2   Using the ALIAS keyword

The ALIAS keyword is used to provide an alternative name for a particular field. All DDS field names can be no longer than 10 characters. The ALIAS keyword allows an alternate name to be specified which can be up to 30 characters long.

Listing 7.11   Example of using the ALIAS keyword.

```
.....A..........T.Name+++++RLen++TDpB......Functions++++++++++++++++++
    A          R CLAIMHDR
    A            CLAIMKEY     4A        ALIAS(CLAIM_KEY)
    A            PATACCT      4         ALIAS(PATIENT_ACCOUNT)
    A            CLAIMDATE    8S 0      ALIAS(DATE_CLAIM_CREATED)
```

If the file shown in Listing 7.11 is copied into a COBOL program using the COPY statement with the DD or DDR options, the compiler will use CLAIM-KEY, PATIENT-ACCOUNT, and DATE-CLAIM-CREATED instead of CLAIMKEY, PATACCT, and CLAIMDATE.

7.6   Overriding Files

Before a program begins executing, it is possible to redirect input or output to a different file (including display and printer files). This process is referred to as *file overriding*.

File overriding occurs before a COBOL program is executed. The override with database file (OVRDBF) CL command accomplishes the override function.

Consider a system that has a current month's transaction file and a history file that contains all transactions for the year. Each month, the transaction file is dumped into the history file and then cleared for the next month. The transaction and history file's layouts are identical. There is no difference between the two files except for the data that they hold. One requirement of the system is to have a program that can print a detailed description of every trade in the file. Using overrides, only one program would need to be written. At run time, an override can be initiated to specify which of the two files to read. The following command overrides the file so that the program reads from the history file instead of the monthly transaction file:

```
OVRDBF FILE(MONTHLY) TOFILE(HISTORY)
```

This is a simple but useful example of how overrides are used. The override command, however, has many additional options not covered in this book. Also, it is important to understand the relationship between the override and the job's program stack. For more information on file overrides, see the *AS/400 Database Guide*.

7.7   Using OPNQRYF

The open query file (OPNQRYF) command is a CL command that allows you to perform many data-processing functions on database files—before the high-level language program (COBOL, RPG, etc.) opens the file. Basically, the OPNQRYF command acts as a filter between the processing program and the database records. The database file can be a physical or a logical file.

If you are familiar with SQL, you may see many similarities between the OPNQRYF command and SQL. For example, the OPNQRYF FILE parameter is similar to the SQL FROM statement, the QRYSLT parameter is similar to the SQL WHERE statement, the GRPFLD parameter is similar to the SQL GROUP BY statement, and the GRPSLT parameter is similar to the SQL HAVING statement.

The OPNQRYF command can dynamically perform the following operations on a file before the file is used by a program:

- Dynamic record selection
- Dynamic keying of the file (ordering)
- Dynamic keyed sequence access path over a join
- Dynamic join
- Handling missing records in secondary join files
- Unique-key processing
- Mapped field definitions

- Group processing
- Final total-only processing

The most common use of the OPNQRYF command is to select, arrange, and format data so it can be read sequentially by a high-level language program. You can see a complete description of all the capabilities of the OPNQRYF command in the CL reference.

Because the OPNQRYF command is a CL command, details of its usage will be covered in the chapter on CL programming.

7.8   Using QTEMP for Temporary Work Files

QTEMP is a special library that can be used to contain any temporary work files for the current job. Each time a job is initiated on the AS/400, a QTEMP library is allocated and assigned to it. Once the job terminates, QTEMP also disappears, along with everything that was in it.

7.9   DDS for Physical and Logical Files

See Table 7.1 for a list of DDS for physical and logical file functions.

7.10   Summary

Physical files are OS/400 objects that contain data organized in records. Physical files contain two parts: a header part that contains detailed descriptions of each field and record format in the file, and a collection of members where the data are actually stored. Members can be accessed individually or collectively. Physical files can contain key fields for keyed access.

Logical files are OS/400 objects that act as an alternative view of physical files. Logical files do not contain data—they only contain access path information. When defining the DDS for a logical view, field tests can be declared to determine whether records should be included or excluded from the logical view.

Join logical files provide a view over two or more related physical or logical files. The relationships between fields in the various files are declared when defining the DDS. Programs that read join logical files are unaware of how many files are actually processed during each READ.

File redirection is accomplished using overrides. The OVRDBF command is a CL command that allows dynamic changing of file attributes before a high-level language program accesses the file.

To display a physical file, use either the DSPPFM command or the RUNQRY command. The RUNQRY command is used to display logical files.

TABLE 7.1   DDS for Physical and Logical File Functions

DDS keyword	Level	Description
ABSVAL	Key	Causes sign to be ignored when ordering a file
ALIAS	Field	Specifies an alternative name for a field
ALL	Select/omit	Specifies action to be taken after other select/omit specifications have been processed
ALTSEQ	File	Use an alternative collating sequence
ALWNULL	Field	Allows a field to have null values
CHECK	Field	Used for validity checking when referred to in a display file
CHKMSGID	Field	Specifies error message for validity checking keywords
CMP	Field	See COMP
COLHDG	Field	Specifies column headings
COMP	Field	Used for validity checking when referred to in a display file
CONCAT	Logical field	Combines two or more fields into one
DATFMT	Field	Specifies the format of a date field
DATSEP	Field	Specifies the date separator
DESCEND	Key	Orders values in descending order
DFT	Field	Defines default value for the field
DIGIT	Key	Causes only the digit portion of each byte to be used when creating a key value (zone portion is zero-filled)
DYNSLT	Logical file	Selection/omission is done at processing time rather than access path select/omit
EDTCDE	Field	Used for editing when referenced by a display file
FCFO	File	Used for duplicate key processing--the record with the key value that was changed first is the first record retrieved
FIFO	File	Duplicate keys are processed in first-in[nd]first-out basis
FLTPCN	Field	Specifies floating-point precision
FORMAT	Format	Shares field specifications for a previously defined record format
JDFTVAL	Logical file	Specifies system-provided default value for fields when a join does not produce any records
JDUPSEQ	Join	Specifies order in which records with duplicate join fields are returned when reading a join logical file

TABLE 7.1 (*Continued*)

DDS keyword	Level	Description
JFILE	Record	Specifies physical files for a join
JFLD	Join	Identifies from and to fields for a join
JOIN	Join	Identifies file pairs for joining
JREF	Join field	Identifies a field when the same name appears in more than one file within a join
LIFO	File	Duplicate key records are returned in last-in-first-out order
NOALTSEQ	Field	Specifies that the ALTSEQ keyword specified at the file level does not apply to this field
PFILE	Logical record	Identifies physical file associated with this logical record
RANGE	Field or select/omit	Used for validity checking when referred to by a display file or for selecting/omitting when referenced in the select/omit section section
REF	File	Specifies the file from which field descriptions are retrieved
REFACCPTH	File	Used to reference another file's access path
REFFLD	Field	Used to reference another field
REFSHIFT	Field	Specifies keyboard shift when referenced by a display file
RENAME	Logical field	Renames a field in a logical file
SIGNED	Field	Honors the sign when ordering a numeric field in the key
SST	Logical field	Specifies a subset of an existing field
TEXT	Record or field	Supplies a text description
TIMFMT	Field	Specifies format of a time field
TIMSEP	Field	Specifies separator character for a time field
UNIQUE	File	Specifies no duplicate keys for file
UNSIGNED	Key field	Numeric fields are sequenced as a string of unsigned binary data
VALUES	Field/select/omit	Used for validation when referenced by a display file; also used when selecting/omitting records
VARLEN	Field	Defines field as variable length
ZONE	Key field	Causes only the zone portion of each byte of the key field to be used when constructing a key value (digits are filled with zeros)

Chapter

8

Display Files

Display files are used by OS/400 languages as a means for communicating with users through display stations. Display files are defined using data description specifications (DDS). This chapter will describe the ways in which COBOL uses display files.

A display file defines the format of the information to be presented on a workstation and how that information is processed by the system on its way to and from the workstation. COBOL/400 programs can describe and use display screens in any of three ways:

- Using extended DISPLAY/ACCEPT statements (an example of this type of I/O can be seen in Chap. 2, "Hello World")
- Using external display files described using DDS (as explained in this chapter)
- Using the OS/400 user interface manager (UIM) in combination with calls to the OS/400 UIM System APIs

Since DDS is the most widely used of the above-listed methods, this book will focus primarily on using DDS to describe display files.

Display files described with DDS can be entered directly using the source entry utility (SEU) or can be automatically generated by painting the screen image using the screen definition aid (SDA). SDA is by far the easiest way of creating and designing display files. A brief introduction to SDA is provided in Chap. 2. In lieu of lengthy descriptions of using SDA to define the example screens in this book, the DDS source code for the display files will be provided for you to enter with SDA. The *Screen Design Aid User's Guide and Reference* provides good descriptions and examples of using SDA.

8.1   Externally Described Display Files

A COBOL program communicates with a workstation through the use of a display file in a very similar way as it communicates with regular database files. Data are written to a display file with the WRITE statement and read from the display with the READ statement.

The file description (written in DDS) for a display file describes data at three different levels:

- *File level:* a display file is an organized set of records. Entries at the file level define attributes applicable to all formats within the file. For example, specifying the PRINT keyword at the file level enables the print key within all record formats.

- *Record level:* A record is an ordered set of one or more fields. The record-level description specifies how a record format looks when it is displayed. In addition, it also describes what function keys are available when the record is displayed.

- *Field level:* Information for each field specifies the following:

  Where on the screen the field is to appear
  What type of data is valid for the field
  Whether the field should be highlighted in some way
  Whether the field is an input-capable or output-capable field
  Validity checking for the field

Listing 8.1   Example of a display file DDS source listing.

```
FILE NAME: EX0801FM
.....AAN01N02N03T.Name++++++RLen++TDpBLinPosFunctions++++++++++++++++++
[1]   A                                       INDARA
[2]   A          R ENTERDATA
[3]   A                                       CA03(03 'Exit')
[4]   A                                       CA05(05 'Refresh')
[5]   A                                       PRINT
[6]   A                                     1 31'Enter Arbitrary Data'
[7]   A                                       DSPATR(HI)
[8]   A                                     3  2'Type choices, press Enter.'
[9]   A                                       DSPATR(HI)
[10]  A                                       COLOR(BLU)
[11]  A                                     6  2'Name . . . . . . . . .'
[12]  A                                     7  4'Addresss1 . . . . . . . .'
[13]  A                                     8  4'Address2 . . . . . . . .'
[14]  A                                     9  4'City, State, Zip . . . .'
[15]  A                                    23  2'F3=Exit'
[16]  A                                       DSPATR(HI)
[17]  A                                       COLOR(BLU)
[18]  A                                    23 13'F5=Refresh'
[19]  A                                       DSPATR(HI)
[20]  A                                       COLOR(BLU)
[21]  A            NAME          35    B  6 32
[22]  A 90                                    DSPATR(RI PC)
[23]  A            ADDRESS1      40    B  7 32
[24]  A            ADDRESS2      40    B  8 32
```

```
[25]  A           CITY        15  B  9 32
[26]  A           STATE        2  B  9 49VALUES ('AL' 'AK' 'AZ' +
[27]  A                                     'AR' 'CA' 'CO' 'CT' +
[28]  A                                     'DE' 'DC' 'FL' 'GA' +
[29]  A                                     'HI' 'ID' 'IL' 'IN' +
[30]  A                                     'IA' 'KS' 'KY' 'LA' +
[31]  A                                     'ME' 'MD' 'MA' 'MI' +
[32]  A                                     'MN' 'MS' 'MO' 'MT' +
[33]  A                                     'NE' 'NV' 'NH' 'NJ' +
[34]  A                                     'NM' 'NY' 'NC' 'ND' +
[35]  A                                     'OH' 'OK' 'OR' 'PA' +
[36]  A                                     'RI' 'SC' 'SD' 'TN' +
[37]  A                                     'TX' 'UT' 'VT' 'VA' +
[38]  A                                     'WA' 'WV' 'WI' 'WY' ' ')
[39]  A           ZIP          5  0B  9 53EDTCDE (X)
```

Listing 8.1 shows an example of an externally described display file. The source in this listing shows a complete DDS source file with a small variety of functions:

- On line 1, the INDARA file-level keyword specifies that indicators are to be maintained separately from other fields in the display file. This will be discussed in more detail in Sec. 8.3.

- Line 2 defines a record format named ENTERDATA. All fields following this record format definition will be part of format ENTERDATA until the next record format is defined or the end of the source file.

- Lines 3 and 4 define two function keys that are available when the screen is displayed. CA03 maps to command key 3, and CA05 maps to command key 5. Within the parentheses, the number 03 is specified, indicating that if the user presses the F3 key, indicator 03 should be turned on.

- Line 5 enables the PRINT key for the record format. When the record is displayed, the user will have the ability to press PRINT to obtain a screen copy.

- Lines 6, 8, 11, 12, 13, 14, 15, and 18 define constants that will appear at the designated row and column numbers. Lines followed by the word DSPATR(HI) will be displayed in high intensity; lines followed by the word COLOR(BLU) will be shown in blue (if displayed on a color display).

- Lines 21, 23, 24, 25, and 26 define field that are both input/output capable (indicated by the letter "B"). A COBOL program will initialize the fields prior to displaying them; once displayed, they can be changed by the user.

- The name field on line 21 is followed by a conditional display attribute keyword. If indicator 90 is on (or TRUE) when the record format is displayed, the name field will be shown in reverse image (RI) and the cursor will be positioned at the beginning of the field (PC = position cursor).

- Line 26 defines the STATE field, which has an associated VALUES function specified. Any entries typed into the STATE field will be validated against the list of possible values. If a match does not exist, the field will be in error and the user will receive an error message. Notice that the last value specified is blank, which permits the user to leave the field blank.

- The ZIP field on line 39 has an edit code of "X" specified. Edit code "X" specifies that zero suppression should not take place and that all positions to the left of the number should be padded with zeros.

You can enter the source in Listing 8.1 with SEU by using the following command:

```
STRSEU QDDSSRC EX0801FM TYPE(DSPF)
```

To create the display file, use the following command:

```
CRTDSPF EX0801FM QDDSSRC
```

You can test the display file using SDA. Use the following command to start SDA's testing function (see Fig. 8.1):

```
STRSDA OPTION(3) TSTFILE(EX0801FM)
```

```
                          Test Display File

  Type choices, press Enter.

      Display file . . . . . . . . . . . . .    EX0801FM_    Name, F4 for list
        Library  . . . . . . . . . . . . .      COBOLBOOK_   Name, *LIBL ...

      Record to be tested  . . . . . . . .      ENTERDATA__  Name, F4 for list

      Additional records to display  . . . .    _____   Name, F4 for list
                                                _____
                                                _____




  F3=Exit    F4=Prompt    F12=Cancel
                                          (C) COPYRIGHT IBM CORP. 1981, 1993.
```

Figure 8.1 SDA's test display file function.

Specify the record to be tested: ENTERDATA, then press Enter. You can ignore the next two screens for now, so press Enter two more times. Finally you will see the screen in Fig. 8.2.

```
                          Enter Arbitrary Data

Type choices, press Enter.

Name . . . . . . . . . . .  BBBBBBBBBBBBBBBBBBBBBBBBBBBBBBBBBBB
    Address1 . . . . . . . .  BBBBBBBBBBBBBBBBBBBBBBBBBBBBBBBBBBBBBBBBB
    Address2 . . . . . . . .  BBBBBBBBBBBBBBBBBBBBBBBBBBBBBBBBBBBBBBBBB
    City, State, Zip . . . . .  BBBBBBBBBBBBBBB  BB  99999













F3=Exit     F5=Refresh
```

Figure 8.2 Output from EX0801 (Listing 8.1).

Listing 8.2 shows a complete COBOL program that uses the display file in Listing 8.1.

Listing 8.2 COBOL declaring external display file.

```
MEMBER NAME: EX0801 FILE: QLBLSRC
....-..A...B..-....2....-....3....-....4....-....5....-....6....-....-
        IDENTIFICATION DIVISION.
        PROGRAM-ID. EX0801.

        ENVIRONMENT DIVISION.
        INPUT-OUTPUT SECTION.
        FILE-CONTROL.
[1]        SELECT DISPFILE ASSIGN TO WORKSTATION-EX0801FM-SI
               ORGANIZATION IS TRANSACTION.
        DATA DIVISION.
        FILE SECTION.
[2]     FD   DISPFILE.
        01   DISP-REC PIC X (500).

        WORKING-STORAGE SECTION.
[3]        01   ENTERDATA-IN.
               COPY DDS-ENTERDATA-I OF EX0801FM.
[4]        01   ENTERDATA-OUT.
               COPY DDS-ENTERDATA-O OF EX0801FM.
```

```
      01  INDIC-AREA.
[5]       03  EACH-IND OCCURS 99 TIMES PIC 1 INDICATOR 1.
              88 IND-OFF VALUE B"0".
              88 IND-ON  VALUE B"1".

      01  INDICATOR-USAGE.
[6]       03  F03-EXIT      PIC 99 VALUE 03.
          03  F05-REFRESH   PIC 99 VALUE 05.
          03  NAME-ERROR    PIC 99 VALUE 90.

      PROCEDURE DIVISION.
      MAIN-PARA.
[7]       OPEN I-O DISPFILE.
          INITIALIZE ENTERDATA-O.
[8]       PERFORM WITH TEST AFTER UNTIL IND-ON(F03-EXIT)

          WRITE DISP-REC FROM ENTERDATA-OUT
              FORMAT "ENTERDATA" INDICATORS ARE INDIC-AREA
[9]       READ DISPFILE INTO ENTERDATA-IN FORMAT "ENTERDATA"
              INDICATORS ARE INDIC-AREA

[10]      SET IND-OFF(NAME-ERROR) TO TRUE

          IF IND-OFF (F05-REFRESH)
[11]          MOVE CORRESPONDING ENTERDATA-I TO ENTERDATA-O
          END-IF

          IF NAME OF ENTERDATA-I EQUAL SPACES
[12]          SET IND-ON(NAME-ERROR) TO TRUE
          END-IF
      END-PERFORM.

      CLOSE DISPFILE.
      STOP RUN.
```

1. The SELECT statement associates DISPFILE with a WORKSTATION device and declares EX0801FM as the display file to use when performing input/output operation. The SI (Separate Indicator) instructs COBOL to maintain a separate indicator area for this display file. This will be discussed later in Sec. 8.3.

2. The FD entry for DISPFILE declares a single record of 500 characters. This is a chosen arbitrary number that is big enough to hold the biggest record format in the display file.

3. ENTERDATA-IN is declared as a level-01 group, and is followed by a COPY command that extracts any fields that are input-capable from file description EX0801FM. The results of this COPY will be shown in the compiler listing that follows.

4. ENTERDATA-OUT is declared as a level-01 group as is ENTERDATA-IN; however, ENTERDATA-OUT contains only output-capable fields.

5. INDIC-AREA defines an area in storage that holds 99 separate indicators (or BOOLEAN values). Indicators are used to communicate special conditions to the display file.

6. INDICATOR-USAGE contains a variety of constants used to define the meanings of various indicators used in the display file.

7. The program opens a display file as "I-O" (both input and output).

8. The main PERFORM loop is processed until the user presses the F3 key.

9. Within the loop, record format "ENTERDATA" is written to the workstation—all data sent to the workstation are taken from ENTERDATA-OUT. The same format is then read from the workstation; however, the data are retrieved and placed in a separate buffer named ENTERDATA-IN. In both the WRITE and the READ, the INDICATORS clause specifies that the indicators to use can be found in the level-01 group named INDIC-AREA.

10. After reading the display, the NAME-ERROR indicator is turned off.

11. If the user did not press F5 (refresh), the values that were just read from the display are moved to their corresponding output fields to be redisplayed again. If the user did press F5, then no move will take place, resulting in the original values from the last WRITE remaining in the output buffer. This will cause the display to be "refreshed" with the prior cycle's output values.

12. Finally, if the NAME field was left blank, the appropriate indicator is turned on to position the cursor to the NAME field and reverse video the field.

You can enter the COBOL source program using SEU with the following command:

```
STRSEU QLBLSRC EX0801 TYPE(CBL)
```

Compile the program with the following command:

```
CRTCBLPGM EX0801
```

To run the program, use the following command:

```
CALL EX0801
```

Listing 8.3 shows the expansion of the COPY DDS statements.

Listing 8.3 Expansion of the COPY statement for a display file.

```
      .
      .
      .
WORKING-STORAGE SECTION.
```

```
01 ENTERDATA-IN.
   COPY DDS-ENTERDATA-I OF EX0801FM.
*INPUT FORMAT:ENTERDATA    FROM FILE EX0801FM    OF LIBRARY COBOLBOOK
*                                                               ENTERDATA
   05 ENTERDATA-I.                                              ENTERDATA
      06 PHONENUM             PIC X(20).                        ENTERDATA
      06 NAME                 PIC X(35).                        ENTERDATA
      06 ADDRESS1             PIC X(40).                        ENTERDATA
      06 ADDRESS2             PIC X(40).                        ENTERDATA
      06 CITY                 PIC X(15).                        ENTERDATA
      06 STATE                PIC X(2).                         ENTERDATA
      06 ZIP                  PIC X(10).                        ENTERDATA
01 ENTERDATA-OUT.
   COPY DDS-ENTERDATA-O OF EX0801FM.
*OUTPUT FORMAT:ENTERDATA    FROM FILE EX0801FM    OF LIBRARY COBOLBOOK
*                                                               ENTERDATA
   05 ENTERDATA-O.                                              ENTERDATA
      06 PHONENUM             PIC X(20).                        ENTERDATA
      06 NAME                 PIC X(35).                        ENTERDATA
      06 ADDRESS1             PIC X(40).                        ENTERDATA
      06 ADDRESS2             PIC X(40).                        ENTERDATA
      06 CITY                 PIC X(15).                        ENTERDATA
      06 STATE                PIC X(2).                         ENTERDATA
      06 ZIP                  PIC X(10).                        ENTERDATA
```

8.2   Defining a Panel

As stated earlier, a screen can be made up of several different types of
record formats. The screen displayed in Fig. 8.2 demonstrated a simple
display file with a single record format. The COBOL program that uses
that record format does a single WRITE to display the panel on the
workstation followed by a single READ to retrieve the data. Not all
panels are as simple.

The screen in Fig. 8.3 contains four visible record formats. The first
format is a regular record format; the second is a subfile record format;
the third is a subfile control record format; the last one is a message
subfile record format. All fields are output-only except for the "Position
to . . . " field and the column headed by "Opt."

8.2.1   Field types

There are several different types of fields that you can utilize when defining a display file.

- Input fields are fields that are passed from the display to the program when the program reads a record from the display. They can be
  initialized with a default value (specified in the record format). If the
  user does not change the field and the field is selected for input, the
  default value is passed to the program. Uninitialized fields are displayed as blanks into which the user can enter data. By default, input fields are underlined on the display.

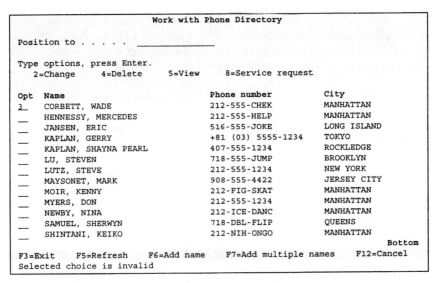

```
                         Work with Phone Directory

Position to . . . . .    _____

Type options, press Enter.
  2=Change     4=Delete      5=View     8=Service request

Opt  Name                      Phone number        City
3_   CORBETT, WADE             212-555-CHEK         MANHATTAN
__   HENNESSY, MERCEDES        212-555-HELP         MANHATTAN
__   JANSEN, ERIC              516-555-JOKE         LONG ISLAND
__   KAPLAN, GERRY             +81 (03) 5555-1234   TOKYO
__   KAPLAN, SHAYNA PEARL      407-555-1234         ROCKLEDGE
__   LU, STEVEN                718-555-JUMP         BROOKLYN
__   LUTZ, STEVE               212-555-1234         NEW YORK
__   MAYSONET, MARK            908-555-4422         JERSEY CITY
__   MOIR, KENNY               212-FIG-SKAT         MANHATTAN
__   MYERS, DON                212-555-1234         MANHATTAN
__   NEWBY, NINA               212-ICE-DANC         MANHATTAN
__   SAMUEL, SHERWYN           718-DBL-FLIP         QUEENS
__   SHINTANI, KEIKO           212-NIH-ONGO         MANHATTAN
                                                             Bottom
F3=Exit    F5=Refresh    F6=Add name    F7=Add multiple names    F12=Cancel
Selected choice is invalid
```

Figure 8.3 Panel containing multiple record formats.

- Output fields are fields that are passed from the program to the display station when the program writes a record to a display. Output fields contain data provided by the program, not by the user. In the case of subfiles, which are special records used to display lists of information, output fields are returned to the program as if they were output/input fields.

- Output/input fields are fields that are passed from the program when the program writes a record to a display and are passed to the program when the program reads a record from the display. Output/input fields are usually used when the program displays data that can be changed by a user.

- Hidden fields are fields that are passed from and to the program but are not shown on the display. Hidden fields are useful in applications that use subfiles and cannot be seen by the user when the subfile is displayed.

- Constant fields are fields that are passed to the display but are unknown to the program.

- Message lines are output fields that are treated as messages.

- Program-to-system fields are output-only fields that are used to communicate between an application program and the system. Program-to-system fields do not appear on the display. That is, your program can place data in these fields and the system will use those data to control its processing on an output operation, but the user cannot see the contents of these fields.

8.2.2 Modified data tag

Input-capable fields have a special attribute called a modified data tag (MDT). The MDT is set on by the display station when any data are typed into the field. It can also be set on and cleared by the application program.

Modified data tags are most commonly used with subfiles (lists). A special COBOL/400 format of the READ statement includes a NEXT MODIFIED clause that instructs the display station to return the next record that has been modified in the list.

The MDT tag can also be manually set on by a COBOL program. This is useful when the user keys erroneous data into a subfile record. To illustrate, consider an application that allows the user to key several account numbers into a subfile list. When the user presses the Enter key, each account number must be validated. To do this, the COBOL program enters into a loop and executes a READ NEXT MODIFIED clause until there are no more modified subfile records. If an invalid account number is encountered, the account number should be REWRITTEN back to the subfile with an indicator on, which causes the account to be shown in reverse image. When the subfile is then re-displayed, the account in error will be highlighted and the user can change it. However, suppose that the user just presses the Enter key again without correcting the erroneous account number. When the program enters the loop and executes the READ NEXT MODIFIED clause, the erroneous record will not be returned since the user did not type anything into it; thus it will not be rechecked and the user may be able to proceed without correcting the error.

To solve this problem, when the program rewrites the record with the reverse image specified, it can also specify MDT on, so that whether the user types anything into the field or not, it will be returned to the program for validation during the next cycle.

8.3 Indicators

AS/400 COBOL programs communicate special conditions to display (and print) files through the use of indicators. An indicator represents either an *on* or *off* condition.

8.3.1 Option and response indicators

There are two types of indicators for display files:

- Option indicators pass information from an application program to the system. These typically are used to control display attributes such as reverse image or blink.

- Response indicators pass information from the system to an application program when an input request is completed. Response indicators usually indicate which function was pressed or whether the MDT tag is on or off.

8.3.1.1 Option indicators. An example of an option indicator used for formatting can be seen in Listing 8.4. Indicator 90 is used to condition whether or not the field is displayed in reverse image. If indicator 90 is on, the field will be reversed. If it is off, the field will be displayed as normal.

Listing 8.4 Option indicator used for display attributes.

```
.....AAN01N02N03T.Name++++++RLen++TDpBLinPosFunctions++++++++++++++++
      .
      .
   A           NAME       35    B  6 32
   A    90                                  DSPATR(RI)
```

Testing the off condition of an indicator is also possible. Listing 8.5 shows how to condition an indicator on a negative condition (or a NOT condition). Multiple indicators can also be tested—up to three per line. All indicator conditions must be TRUE in order for the DDS function to take effect. In other words, a positive AND condition must exist between all indicators listed on the line to cause a TRUE condition.

Listing 8.5 Option indicator based on the off condition.

```
...AAN01N02N03T.Name++++++RLen++TDpBLinPosFunctions++++++++++++++++++++
      .
      .
   A           NAME       35    B  6 32
   A  N90                                  DSPATR(RI)
      .
      .
```

The example in Listing 8.6 tests indicators 90, 30, and 31. If 90 and 30 are both on and indicator 31 is off, the field will be displayed in reverse image.

Listing 8.6 Testing multiple indicator conditions.

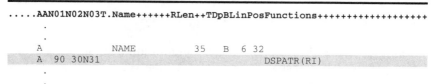

If the application requires more than three indicators, they can be continued as shown in Listing 8.7. This example requires that indicators 25, 90, and 30 be on, and indicator 31 be off. You can also use an OR condition in the indicator test area, as shown in Listing 8.8, which shows an example that requires either indicator 30 or 25 be on in order to display the NAME field in reverse image.

Listing 8.7 Testing more than three indicators.

```
.....AAN01N02N03T.Name++++++RLen++TDpBLinPosFunctions+++++++++++++++++++
       .
       .
    A                    NAME          35   B   6 32
    A   90 30N31
   AA 25                                          DSPATR(RI)
       .
       .
```

Listing 8.8 Testing an OR condition.

```
.....AAN01N02N03T.Name++++++RLen++TDpBLinPosFunctions+++++++++++++++++++
       .
       .
    A                    NAME          35   B   6 32
    A   30
   AO 25                                          DSPATR(RI)
       .
       .
```

8.3.1.2 Response indicators. An example of a response indicator that is used for determining what key was pressed by the user can be seen in Listing 8.9.

Listing 8.9 Using response indicators.

```
.....AAN01N02N03T.Name++++++RLen++TDpBLinPosFunctions+++++++++++++++++++
    A                                             INDARA
    A            R ENTERDATA
    A                                             CA03(03 'Exit')
    A                                             CA05(05 'Refresh')
    A                                             PRINT
```

If the user presses the F3 key, indicator 03 will be turned on; if the user presses the F5 key, indicator 05 will be turned on.

8.3.2   Using a separate indicator area

A display file can use the indicator area (INDARA) keyword to separate the option and response indicators from the input and output records used by the program. If you use the INDARA keyword, the indicators are placed in a separate 99-character area rather than being integrated into the input and output record formats.

Listing 8.10   DDS source that does not use the INDARA keyword.

```
.....AAN01N02N03T.Name++++++RLen++TDpBLinPosFunctions++++++++++++++++++
     A           R DSPREC1
     A                                   CA03(03 'Exit')
     A                         6   2'Name . . . . . . . . . . .'
     A                         7   2'Age . . . . . . . . . ., .'
     A             NAME       35  B  6 32
     A 90                                DSPATR(RI)
     A             AGE         3  0B  7 32
     A                        23   2'F3=Exit'
```

Listing 8.10 shows how indicators are integrated into the input and output buffers when the INDARA keyword is not used. This example shows a simple screen with two fields that are both input and output. The user can press F3 to exit the screen. This display format does *not* include the separate indicator area keyword (INDARA); thus variables will be created for both indicator 03 (used for the F3 key) and indicator 90 (used for turning on the reverse image in the NAME field). The results of the COBOL COPY statement are shown in Listing 8.11.

Listing 8.11   Integrated indicators and data fields.

```
     .
     .
     WORKING-STORAGE SECTION.
     01  DSPREC1-IN.
         COPY DDS-DSPREC1-I OF EXINDAFM.
     * INPUT FORMAT:DSPREC1 FROM FILE EXINDAFM OF LIBRARY COBOLBOOK   DSPREC1
     *                                                                DSPREC1
         05  DSPREC1-I.                                               DSPREC1
             06  DSPREC1-I-INDIC.                                     DSPREC1
                 07  IN03            PIC 1  INDIC 03.                  DSPREC1
             06  NAME                PIC X(35).                       DSPREC1
             06  AGE                 PIC S9(3).                       DSPREC1
     01  DSPREC1-OUT.
         COPY DDS-DSPREC1-O OF EXINDAFM.
     * OUTPUT FORMAT:DSPREC1 FROM FILE EXINDAFM OF LIBRARY COBOLBOOK  DSPREC1
     *                                                                DSPREC1
         05  DSPREC1-O.                                               DSPREC1
             06  DSPREC1-O-INDIC.                                     DSPREC1
                 07  IN90            PIC 1  INDIC 90.                  DSPREC1
             06  NAME                PIC X(35).                       DSPREC1
             06  AGE                 PIC S9(3).                       DSPREC1
     .
     .
```

Notice in both the input and output buffers that a level-06 identifier named DSPREC1-?-INDIC that contains the indicators used for either input or output has been added. If the INDARA keyword had been included in the DDS, the indicators would not be included in the record layout; however, the program would be responsible for declaring and maintaining the separate indicator area.

Although there are benefits to using both ways, experience has shown that using a separate indicator area proves to be more flexible and easier to maintain. To use a separate indicator area, note the following:

- The DDS keyword INDARA must be included at the file level in the display file source (as seen in Listing 8.1).

- The COBOL program must append the -SI flag to the display file name specified in the SELECT clause (as seen in COBOL Listing 8.2).

- A separate indicator area must be declared as follows:

```
01   INDIC-AREA.
    03   EACH-IND OCCURS 99 TIMES PIC 1 INDICATOR 1.
        88 IND-OFF VALUE B"0".
        88 IND-ON  VALUE B"1".
```

- Optionally, a set of constants should be defined to indicate the meanings of the various indicators:

```
01   INDICATOR-USAGE.
    03   F03-EXIT       PIC 99 VALUE 03.
    03   F05-REFRESH    PIC 99 VALUE 05.
    03   NAME-ERROR     PIC 99 VALUE 90.
```

If the constants are defined as above, then you can set indicators on by name:

```
SET IND-ON(NAME-ERROR) TO TRUE
```

instead of by number

```
SET IND-ON(90) TO TRUE
```

Indicators can be tested in the following manner:

```
IF IND-ON(F03-EXIT)...
```

8.3.3   Using integrated indicators

If you choose to use indicators that are integrated with each record format, it is likely that each indicator will have to be qualified when being used. This is not necessary in the prior example because there was only one record format; however, in a display file that contains multiple record formats, it is likely that more than one record will use the same indicator assignments (for example, it is probable that many record formats will contain the F3=Exit assignment of indicator 03). In this case, each record format will contain a boolean variable named IN03. You can test the value of IND03 as follows:

```
IF IN03 OF INPUT-REC1 ...
IF IN03 OF INPUT-REC2 ...
```

To set the indicator on or off:

```
SET IN90 OF OUTPUT-REC1 TO TRUE
SET IN90 OF OUTPUT-REC2 TO FALSE
```

8.4   Command Keys

There are two distinct types of command keys that can be defined in display files: command attention (CA) and command function (CF) keys. The difference between the two is whether or not data are returned to the input buffer when the function key is pressed. CA01 ... CA24 do *not* return data from the workstation to the COBOL program. CF01 ... CF24 do return data to the COBOL program. Response indicators are set in both cases to indicate which key was pressed.

Care must be taken when using command attention keys. When a user presses a key that is defined as a command attention key, data in COBOL's input buffers are *not* updated; therefore it will contain data from the previous input operation.

8.5   Overlaying Records

As seen in Fig. 8.3, a panel may contain several record formats. The DDS OVERLAY keyword specifies that a record is not to erase the display before it is shown. The OVERLAY keyword causes only those records that are completely or partially overlapping to be erased; all other records remain on the display. The OVERLAY keyword does not prevent the screen from being erased if it is in effect for the first WRITE operation after a file is opened unless the DDS keyword ASSUME is specified for any record format in the display file.

You can use the OVERLAY keyword to display information from an application that needs to be presented together but naturally falls into two or more pieces. For example, one record format can be used for patient account information at the top of the display, and information pertaining to their insurance carrier can be shown in another area.

If an application is presenting the same record format repeatedly, the

OVERLAY keyword can prevent a flickering effect caused by repetitive clearing of the display. If the DDS OVERLAY keyword is not specified in a record format, the screen will be cleared when the record is displayed.

8.6 Subfiles

A subfile is a special type of record format that is used for presenting lists of information. All records within the subfile have the exact same record layout. The entire group of records is written to the display in a single WRITE operation. In Fig. 8.4, the subfile record is shaded.

```
                        Work with Phone Directory

  Position to . . . . .    _____

  Type options, press Enter.
    2=Change      4=Delete      5=View      8=Service request

  Opt  Name                        Phone number        City
  __   CORBETT, WADE               212-555-CHEK        MANHATTAN
  __   HENNESSY, MERCEDES          212-555-HELP        MANHATTAN
  __   JANSEN, ERIC                516-555-JOKE        LONG ISLAND
  __   KAPLAN, GERRY               +81 (03) 5555-1234  TOKYO
  __   KAPLAN, SHAYNA PEARL        407-555-1234        ROCKLEDGE
  __   LU, STEVEN                  718-555-JUMP        BROOKLYN
  __   LUTZ, STEVE                 212-555-1234        NEW YORK
  __   MAYSONET, MARK              908-555-4422        JERSEY CITY
  __   MOIR, KENNY                 212-FIG-SKAT        MANHATTAN
  __   MYERS, DON                  212-555-1234        MANHATTAN
  __   NEWBY, NINA                 212-ICE-DANC        MANHATTAN
  __   SAMUEL, SHERWYN             718-DBL-FLIP        QUEENS
  __   SHINTANI, KEIKO             212-NIH-ONGO        MANHATTAN
                                                             More...
  F3=Exit     F5=Refresh     F6=Add name    F7=Add multiple names    F12=Cancel
  Selected choice is invalid
```

Figure 8.4 Panel containing a subfile.

The subfile in Fig. 8.4 contains one input/output field (under the "Opt" column), and three output-only fields (name, phone number, and city). The word "More . . . " at the end of the subfile indicates that there are more records in the subfile, and that the user can use the Page down key to view the next subfile page. If the last page of the subfile is displayed, the word "Bottom" is displayed.

A subfile does not have to have any input fields—it may be output only. Figure 8.5 is an output-only subfile.

```
                    Display Account Transactions

Account . . :   01303
  Name   . . :   The Kaplan Software Group

Date       Chk#    Description                        Amount
95/01/01   103222  Goldman & Abene Family Planning    3,302.25
95/01/01   103223  Kosaka Kanji Entertainment         3,441.20
95/01/01   103224  Binder & Binder, CPA               4,271.00
95/01/01   103225  Stanley S. Kaplan, D.C.              925.00
95/01/01   103226  Karen Condon Interiors             1,023.55
95/01/01   103227  Jeff Salzman Leather Works           857.00



                                                        Bottom
Press Enter to continue.

F3=Exit    F12=Cancel
```

Figure 8.5 Example of output-only subfile.

```
Office/Dr. . : Cocoa Chiropractic Center
Chart   . . . : 92-001
  Patient  . : Kaplan, Lisa H.

ICD/Description
723.1  Pain in neck
729.5  Pain in someone else's neck
123.4  Always has a pain somewhere

CPT/TrnCd  Date     Description
72148      1/28/95  MRI - LUMBAR               A 4 3 I  1  960.00
72149-22   1/28/95  Add'l sequences with Gad.  A 4 3 I  1  200.00
39070      1/25/95  Injection - gadolinium - DTPA A 4 3 I 1 250.00
                                               _ _ _ _  _  _____
                                               _ _ _ _  _  _____

D=Related ICD Code or A for All       Total charges . . :  1,410.00
T=Type of Service      P=Place of Service   Total payments . :       .00
R=Responsible (I=Insurance, P=Patient)  New balance . . . :  1,410.00

F3=Exit    F8=Save
```

Figure 8.6 Example of a panel with input capable fields.

Similarly, a subfile can consist of primarily input capable fields (see Fig. 8.6). This panel contains two subfiles:

- The first is under "ICD/Description" and is an output-only subfile—three lines are displayed.

- The second is under "CPT/TrnCd". All fields are output/input fields so that the user can supply just the CPT code and the system will return with the default data for the remaining fields.

Two records are required when defining a subfile: a subfile record format and a subfile control record format.

8.6.1   The subfile record

The subfile record format defines the fields in one row of the subfile. The COBOL program uses the subfile record format to add records to the subfile, as well as update and delete subfile records. When any of these actions occur against a subfile record, there is no change on the workstation. The subfile record *must* be defined before the subfile control record in the DDS source file.

8.6.1.1   Subfile record addressibility.   A subfile is organized similar to a relative file in that each record is identified by a unique record number—the first record is record number 1. This number is referred to as the subfile record number. The subfile record number is defined within the COBOL program, not in the DDS source. It must be declared in the RELATIVE KEY clause of the SELECT statement and should be defined in the WORKING-STORAGE section as PIC 9(7).

8.6.2   The subfile control record

The subfile control record performs several functions:

- It defines the associated subfile's attributes such as size, page size, and appearance.

- It performs actions against its associated subfile such as clearing, initializing, and displaying.

- It optionally defines header or footer information that can be displayed at the same time the subfile is displayed.

A COBOL program will use the subfile control record to display the subfile records on the workstation or read the subfile records from the workstation.

Writing the subfile control record does not always result in output being displayed on the workstation. If the SFLDSPCTL and SFLDSP keywords are disabled (by turning off their associated indicators) and the SFLCLR keyword is enabled, writing the subfile control record will result in the subfile being cleared—nothing will happen on the display.

8.6.3   Subfile control record required keywords

The following DDS keywords are required on a subfile control record format:

- *SFLCTL:* Subfile control keyword, which associates the control record being defined with the subfile record that immediately precedes it in the source file

- *SFLSIZ:* Subfile size keyword, which specifies the size (in records) of the subfile

- *SFLPAG:* Subfile page keyword, which specifies the size of a single subfile page (how many records to display at one time).

- *SFLDSP:* Subfile display keyword, which specifies whether or not to display the subfile on the workstation when the subfile control record is written

8.6.4   Subfile size

When defining a subfile, you must specify the size of the subfile and the number of subfile records to be displayed at one time with the SFLSIZ and SFLPAG keywords. There are basically three different ways of using subfiles:

- The subfile size equals the subfile page size. In this case, the application loads a single page at a time. When the user presses Page up or Page down, the COBOL application is responsible for clearing and reloading the subfile with the next or previous page.

- The subfile size is greater than the subfile page size and all records are initially loaded. Once displayed, OS/400 manages scrolling within the subfile.

- The subfile size is greater than the subfile page size and only the first page of the subfile is loaded. Each time the user presses Page down, the system requests the next page from the application program. If the user presses Page up, OS/400 handles this request and scrolls backward through the subfile.

8.6.4.1   Subfile size is equal to the page size.   The use of subfile size equal to page size is recommended when the number of subfile records to be displayed will fit on one page or when the number of records to be placed in the subfile is unknown and large. If the number of records to be placed in the subfile is extremely large, the subfile may exceed the maximum size (9999 records). Furthermore, the user may have to wait an excessive amount of time while the subfile is loaded.

When subfile size is equal to the page size, the system does not automatically support the use of the Page up and Page down keys. If the user is to have the ability to scroll through the subfile using these keys, you must specify the PAGEUP and PAGEDOWN keywords in the subfile control record. The application program is then responsible for clearing and loading the appropriate page into the subfile.

Listing 8.12 illustrates the use where subfile size is equal to page size. The display contains a simple subfile that contains one output-only field. An array is used to simulate a database file. When the program begins, the simulated file is filled with account numbers. The first page of the subfile is then loaded and displayed. The user can press the Page up or Page down key to scroll through the account numbers in the simulated file.

Listing 8.12 Example DDS of a subfile size equal to the subfile page size.

```
FILE NAME: EX0802FM
.....AAN01N02N03T.Name++++++RLen++TDpBLinPosFunctions++++++++++++++++
      A                                       INDARA
[1]   A            R ACCTLIST                 SFL
[2]   A              ACCTNUM      5S 0O  7  7
[3]   A            R ACCTLSTCTL               SFLCTL(ACCTLIST)
[4]   A                                       PAGEDOWN(40)
[4]   A                                       PAGEUP(41)
[5]   A                                       CF03(03)
[6]   A   30                                  SFLDSP
      A                                       SFLDSPCTL
[7]   A   31                                  SFLCLR
[8]   A   32                                  SFLEND(*MORE)
[9]   A                                       SFLSIZ(0010)
[9]   A                                       SFLPAG(0010)
      A                                    6  7'Acct#'
      A                                       DSPATR(HI)
      A                                    3  3'Use PageUp and PageDown -
      A                                       to scroll through the -
      A                                       list.'
      A                                       DSPATR(HI)
      A                                    4  3'Press F3 to Exit.'
      A                                       DSPATR(HI)
```

1. ACCTLIST defines the subfile record (by using the SFL keyword).

2. ACCTNUM is defined as numeric with five positions and is output only.

3. ACCTLSTCTL defines the subfile control record and is associated with subfile record ACCTLIST.

4. If the Page down key is pressed, indicator 40 is turned on. If the Page up key is pressed, indicator 41 is turned on.

5. If the user presses F3, indicator 03 is turned on.

6. If indicator 30 is on when the control record is written, the subfile should be displayed on the workstation (SFLDSP).

7. If indicator 31 is on, the subfile will be cleared (SFLCLR).

8. If indicator 32 is on, the subfile will be displayed with the word "Bottom", indicating that there are no more records in the underlying file. If it is off, the words "More . . . " will be shown, indicating that the user can scroll to see more records.

9. The subfile size and page size are defined to be the same size (SFLSIZ and SFLPAG). The user will be able to see 10 records on the display.

The program that processes this display file is shown in Listing 8.13.

Listing 8.13 Example COBOL program where subfile size is equal to a subfile page size.

```
MEMBER NAME:   EX0802        FILE:   QLBLSRC
....-..A...B..-....2....-....3....-....4....-....5....-....6....-....-
[1]      PROCESS FS9MTO0M.
         IDENTIFICATION DIVISION.
         PROGRAM-ID. EX0802.

         ENVIRONMENT DIVISION.
         CONFIGURATION SECTION.
         INPUT-OUTPUT SECTION.
         FILE-CONTROL.
             SELECT DISPFILE ASSIGN TO WORKSTATION-EX0802FM-SI
                 ORGANIZATION IS TRANSACTION
                 ACCESS MODE IS DYNAMIC
                 RELATIVE KEY IS SFL-RECNUM.

         DATA DIVISION.
         FILE SECTION.
         FD  DISPFILE.
         01  DISP-REC              PIC X(100).

         WORKING-STORAGE SECTION.
         77  SFL-PAGESIZE          PIC 99 VALUE 10.
         77  SFL-RECNUM            PIC 9(7).
         77  FIL-RECNUM            PIC 9(7).
         77  FILE-SIZE             PIC 99 VALUE 33.
         77  NUM-EXTRA             PIC 99.
         77  NUM-PAGES             PIC 999.
         77  LAST-DSP-REC          PIC 999.

         01  SIMULATED-FILE.
             03  ONE-RECORD OCCURS 1 TO 40 TIMES DEPENDING ON FILE-SIZE.
                 05  ACCT-NBR          PIC 9(5).

         01  SUBFILE-REC-OUT.
             COPY DDS-ACCTLIST-O OF EX0802FM.

         01  INDIC-AREA.
             03  EACH-IND OCCURS 99 TIMES PIC 1 INDICATOR 1.
                 88 IND-OFF VALUE B"0".
                 88 IND-ON  VALUE B"1".
```

```
      01  INDICATOR-USAGE-CONSTANTS.
          03  I-SFLDSP              PIC 99 VALUE 30.
          03  I-SFLCLR             PIC 99 VALUE 31.
          03  I-SFLEND             PIC 99 VALUE 32.
          03  FK-EXIT              PIC 99 VALUE 03.
          03  FK-PAGEDOWN          PIC 99 VALUE 40.
          03  FK-PAGEUP            PIC 99 VALUE 41.

      PROCEDURE DIVISION.
      MAIN-PARA.
          OPEN I-O DISPFILE.
[2]       PERFORM LOAD-SIMULATED-FILE.
[3]       MOVE 1 TO FIL-RECNUM.
[4]       PERFORM LOAD-SFL-PAGE.

[5]       PERFORM UNTIL IND-ON (FK-EXIT)

[6]           WRITE DISP-REC FORMAT "ACCTLSTCTL" INDIC INDIC-AREA
              READ DISPFILE FORMAT "ACCTLSTCTL" INDIC INDIC-AREA

              EVALUATE TRUE
[7]               WHEN IND-ON (FK-PAGEDOWN) PERFORM LOAD-NEXT-PAGE
                  WHEN IND-ON (FK-PAGEUP)   PERFORM LOAD-PREV-PAGE
              END-EVALUATE
          END-PERFORM.

          CLOSE DISPFILE.
          STOP RUN.

      LOAD-NEXT-PAGE.
          IF FIL-RECNUM NOT GREATER THAN FILE-SIZE
[8]           PERFORM LOAD-SFL-PAGE
          END-IF.

      LOAD-PREV-PAGE.
[9]       COMPUTE LAST-DSP-REC = FIL-RECNUM - 1.
[10]      IF LAST-DSP-REC > SFL-PAGESIZE

[11]          DIVIDE LAST-DSP-REC BY SFL-PAGESIZE GIVING NUM-PAGES
                  REMAINDER NUM-EXTRA
              IF NUM-EXTRA = ZERO
                  COMPUTE FIL-RECNUM = FIL-RECNUM - (SFL-PAGESIZE * 2)
              ELSE
                  SUBTRACT NUM-EXTRA SFL-PAGESIZE FROM FIL-RECNUM
              END-IF
              PERFORM LOAD-SFL-PAGE
          END-IF.

      LOAD-SFL-PAGE.
[12]      PERFORM CLEAR-SUBFILE.

[13]      PERFORM WITH TEST BEFORE UNTIL (SFL-RECNUM = SFL-PAGESIZE)
          OR (FIL-RECNUM > FILE-SIZE)

[14]          MOVE ACCT-NBR (FILE-RECNUM) TO ACCTNUM

              ADD 1 TO SFL-RECNUM
[15]          WRITE SUBFILE DISP-REC FROM SUBFILE-REC-OUT
                  FORMAT "ACCTLIST" INDIC INDIC-AREA
              ADD 1 TO FIL-RECNUM
          END-PERFORM.
```

```
          IF SFL-RECNUM EQUAL ZERO
              SET IND-OFF(I-SFLDSP) TO TRUE
[16]      ELSE
              SET IND-ON(I-SFLDSP) TO TRUE
  .       END-IF.

          IF FIL-RECNUM NOT LESS THAN FILE-SIZE
              SET IND-ON(I-SFLEND) TO TRUE
[17]      ELSE
              SET IND-OFF(I-SFLEND) TO TRUE
          END-IF.

      CLEAR-SUBFILE.
[18]      SET IND-ON(I-SFLCLR) IND-OFF(I-SFLDSP) TO TRUE.
          WRITE DISP-REC FORMAT "ACCTLSTCTL" INDIC INDIC-AREA.
[19]      SET IND-OFF(I-SFLCLR) IND-ON(I-SFLDSP) TO TRUE.
          MOVE ZERO TO SFL-RECNUM.

      LOAD-SIMULATED-FILE.
          PERFORM VARYING FILE-RECNUM FROM 1 BY 1
              UNTIL FIL-RECNUM > FILE-SIZE
              ADD 90000 TO FIL-RECNUM GIVING ACCT-NBR(FIL-RECNUM)
          END-PERFORM.
```

1. The PROCESS FS9MTO0M instructs the COBOL run time system to translate file status 9M to 0M. File status 9M occurs when the last record is written to a subfile. The subfile is defined as 10 records. When the program attempts to write the 10th record, file status 9M is raised and a message would normally interrupt the program. The PROCESS FS9MTO0M statement prevents this message by having COBOL translate the file status to 0M, which is not considered critical enough to send a message to the workstation.

2. The simulated file is loaded.

3. FIL-RECNUM is used as a relative record number into the simulated file.

4. The first subfile page is then loaded.

5. The main PERFORM loop continues until the user presses F3=Exit.

6. Each iteration of the loop displays the subfile control record (as well as the subfile records) and then reads the subfile control record.

7. If either the Page up or Page down key was pressed, the appropriate paragraph is performed.

8. LOAD-NEXT-PAGE first checks whether we are at the end of the file for the simulated file. If not, it attempts to load the next subfile page by performing LOAD-SFL-PAGE.

9. The LOAD-PREV-PAGE paragraph must first determine how many simulated records there are to "back-up." This is because it is possible that the last display contained fewer records than one subfile page. For example, if the file contains 33 records, the last page would only have three records displayed (since each subfile page holds 10 re-

cords). To determine the last displayed record (LAST-DSP-REC), 1 is subtracted from the current file record number since the record number always points to the next record.

10. "IF LAST-DSP-REC > SFL-PAGESIZE" makes sure that the currently displayed subfile page is not the first page. If it is the first page, the user cannot scroll back any further and the paragraph exits.

11. If the current subfile page is not the first page, then the number of records to back-up is calculated and FIL-RECNUM is adjusted to point to the new "next" record to be read. The LOAD-SFL-PAGE paragraph is then executed.

12. The LOAD-SFL-PAGE paragraph first clears the subfile (which also initializes the subfile record number to zero).

13. It then enters into a loop and continues until either the subfile has been filled (SFL-RECNUM = SFL-PAGESIZE) or the end of the simulated file is reached (FIL-RECNUM > FILE-SIZE).

14. Each iteration moves the data from the simulated file's account number to the subfile record buffer's account number field (ACCTNUM).

15. The subfile record number is incremented and the subfile record is written. Notice that the WRITE statement has the special SUBFILE word to distinguish it from a regular WRITE.

16. After the subfile page has been loaded, the subfile record number is compared to zero. If it is zero, then no records were added to the subfile (indicating that the database file may be empty); thus the indicator associated with displaying the subfile is turned off. The program may also decide to display an "Empty" message if this indicator is off.

17. Finally, the last IF checks whether the program has reached the end of the file, and if so, turns on the I-SFLEND indicator to show the word "Bottom". If I-SFLEND is off, the word "More . . . " will show at the bottom of the subfile.

18. Indicator I-SFLCLR is turned on, which tells the subfile control record to clear the subfile. I-SFLDSP is turned off to prevent the control record from attempting to display the subfile on the workstation at the same time it is clearing the subfile.

19. After the subfile has been cleared (by writing the subfile control record), the I-SFLCLR indicator is turned off and the subfile display indicator is turned on. Aftwards, the subfile record number (SFL-REC-NUM) is reset to zero.

When the program is run, it will appear as illustrated in Fig. 8.7.

8.6.4.2 Subfile size is greater than the page size. Subfile size not equal to page size should be used when a finite number of records can be placed in the subfile and that number is relatively small (less than 50).

```
Use PageUp and PageDown to scroll through the list.
Press F3 to Exit.

   Acct#
   90001
   90002
   90003
   90004
   90005
   90006
   90007
   90008
   90009
   90010
                                                              More...
```

Figure 8.7 Output from the program in Listing 8.13.

When the display file is opened, the system allocates space to contain the subfile records based on the value specified for SFLSIZ. If the application program places a record in the subfile at a record number greater than the subfile size, the system will extend the subfile to contain it (up to a maximum of 9999 records).

When the subfile size is not equal to the page size, the use of the Page up and Page down keys is automatically supported by the system; thus the application program does not have to handle paging as the example given in Sec. 8.6.4.1.

8.6.4.3 Subfile size is greater than the page size and application program handles page down. In some applications, loading the subfile may take more time than is acceptable. This is often the case when each record in the subfile contains data that are obtained from several database files. Filling the subfile then takes an unacceptable amount of time. A technique that is used to improve performance is to write only one page of subfile records at a time but to use OS/400 system's support for scrolling through the subfile. To do this, you need to define the PAGEDOWN and SFLRCDNBR keywords. The application program would then fill the first subfile page and display that page. When the user wants to see the next page, they would press the Page down key. The program then writes another page of records to the subfile, places the relative record number of a record from the second page into the SFLRCDNBR field, and displays the subfile again. At this point, the second page of the subfile is displayed. If the user presses the Page up key, OS/400 handles it by automatically scrolling to the previous page. If the user presses the Page down key while the first subfile page is displayed, OS/400 will handle it by displaying the second subfile page. If the user then presses the Page down key once again, OS/400 will notify the application program to provide records for the third subfile page.

The example in Listing 8.14 shows how to create and use a subfile in which the subfile size is greater than the page size and the application program will handle the Page down key.

Listing 8.14 DDS Example of subfile size > subfile page size.

```
FILE NAME: EX0803FM
     .....AAN01N02N03T.Name++++++RLen++TDpBLinPosFunctions++++++++++++++++
        A                                       INDARA
[1]     A             R ACCTLIST                SFL
        A               ACCTNUM      5S 00  7  7
[2]     A             R ACCTLSTCTL              SFLCTL(ACCTLIST)
[3]     A                                       PAGEDOWN(40)
[4]     A                                       CF03(03)
[5]     A  30                                   SFLDSP
        A                                       SFLDSPCTL
[6]     A  31                                   SFLCLR
[7]     A  32                                   SFLEND(*MORE)
[8]     A                                       SFLSIZ(0050)
[8]     A                                       SFLPAG(0010)
        A                                    6  7'Acct#'
        A                                       DSPATR(HI)
        A                                    3  3'Use PageUp and PageDown-
        A                                       to scroll through the-
        A                                       list.'
        A                                       DSPATR(HI)
        A                                    4  3'Press F3 to Exit.'
        A                                       DSPATR(HI)
[9]     A               CRSR         4S 0H      SFLRCDNBR(CRSR)
```

1. ACCTLIST defines the subfile record (by using the SFL keyword).

2. ACCTLSTCTL defines the subfile control record. This control record is associated with subfile record ACCTLIST.

3. If the Page down key is pressed, then indicator 40 is turned on. In this example, OS/400 handles the Page up key.

4. If the user presses F3, then indicator 03 is turned on.

5. If indicator 30 is on when the control record is written, then the subfile will be displayed on the workstation (SFLDSP).

6. If indicator 31 is on, then the subfile will be cleared (SFLCLR).

7. If indicator 32 is on, then the subfile will be displayed with the word "Bottom," indicating that there are no more records in the underlying file. If indicator 32 is off, the words "More . . . " will be shown, indicating that the user can scroll to see more records.

8. The subfile size is defined to be greater than the subfile page size.

9. The SFLRCDNBR (CRSR) statement defines a variable named CRSR that contains the subfile record number whose page should be

shown when the subfile is displayed. For example, if the subfile page size is 10 and the CRSR's value is 17, the second subfile page would be displayed because subfile record number 17 is on the second subfile page.

The program that processes this display file is shown in Listing 8.15.

Listing 8.15 COBOL programs example where subfile size > subfile page size.

```
MEMBER NAME:  EX0803         FILE:  QLBLSRC
....-..A...B..-....2....-....3....-....4....-....5....-....6....-....-
     PROCESS FS9MTO0M.
     IDENTIFICATION DIVISION.
     PROGRAM-ID. EX0803.

     ENVIRONMENT DIVISION.
     CONFIGURATION SECTION.
     INPUT-OUTPUT SECTION.
     FILE-CONTROL.
         SELECT DISPFILE ASSIGN TO WORKSTATION-EX0709FM-SI
             ORGANIZATION IS TRANSACTION
             ACCESS MODE IS DYNAMIC
             RELATIVE KEY IS SFL-RECNUM.

     DATA DIVISION.
     FILE SECTION.
     FD  DISPFILE.
     01  DISP-REC                PIC X(100).

     WORKING-STORAGE SECTION.
     77  SFL-PAGESIZE            PIC 99 VALUE 10.
     77  SFL-RECNUM              PIC 9(7).
     77  FIL-RECNUM              PIC 9(7).
     77  FILE-SIZE               PIC 99 VALUE 33.
     77  ADD-COUNT               PIC 99.

     01  SIMULATED-FILE.
         03  ONE-RECORD OCCURS 1 TO 40 TIMES DEPENDING ON FILE-SIZE.
             05  ACCT-NBR        PIC 9(5).
     01  SUBFILE-REC-OUT.
         COPY DDS-ACCTLIST-O OF EX0803FM.
     01  SFL-CTL-REC.
         COPY DDS-ACCTLSTCTL-O OF EX0803FM.

     01  INDIC-AREA.
         03  EACH-IND OCCURS 99 TIMES PIC 1 INDICATOR 1.
             88  IND-OFF VALUE B"0".
             88  IND-ON  VALUE B"1".
     01  INDICATOR USAGE CONSTANTS.
         03  I-SFLDSP            PIC 99 VALUE 30.
         03  I-SFLCLR            PIC 99 VALUE 31.
         03  I-SFLEND            PIC 99 VALUE 32.
         03  FK-EXIT             PIC 99 VALUE 03.
         03  FK-PAGEDOWN         PIC 99 VALUE 40.

     PROCEDURE DIVISION.
     MAIN-PARA.
         OPEN I-O DISPFILE.
         PERFORM LOAD-SIMULATED-FILE.
```

```
                MOVE 1 TO FIL-RECNUM.
                MOVE 0 TO SFL-RECNUM.
                PERFORM LOAD-SFL-PAGE.

[1]             PERFORM UNTIL IND-ON(FK-EXIT)
                    WRITE DISP-REC FROM SFL-CTL-REC
                        FORMAT "ACCTLSTCTL" INDIC INDIC-AREA
                    READ DISPFILE INTO SFL-CTL-REC
                        FORMAT "ACCTLSTCTL" INDIC INDIC-AREA
                    EVALUATE TRUE
[2]                     WHEN IND-ON(FK-PAGEDOWN) PERFORM LOAD-NEXT-PAGE
                    END-EVALUATE
                END-PERFORM.

                CLOSE DISPFILE.
                STOP RUN.

[3]         LOAD-NEXT-PAGE.
                IF FIL-RECNUM NOT GREATER THAN FILE-SIZE
                    PERFORM LOAD-SFL-PAGE
                END-IF.

            LOAD-SFL-PAGE.
[4]             ADD 1 TO SFL-RECNUM GIVING CRSR.
                PERFORM VARYING ADD-COUNT FROM 1 BY 1 UNTIL
                (ADD-COUNT > SFL-PAGESIZE) OR (FIL-RECNUM > FILE-SIZE)
                    MOVE ACCT-NBR(FIL-RECNUM) TO ACCTNUM
                    ADD 1 TO SFL-RECNUM
                    WRITE SUBFILE DISP-REC FROM SUBFILE-REC-OUT
                        FORMAT "ACCTLIST" INDIC INDIC-AREA
                    ADD 1 TO FIL-RECNUM
                END-PERFORM.

[5]             IF SFL-RECNUM EQUAL ZERO
[6]                 SET IND-OFF(I-SFLDSP) TO TRUE
                ELSE
                    SET IND-ON(I-SFLDSP) TO TRUE
                END-IF.

                IF FIL-RECNUM > FILE-SIZE
                    SET IND-ON(I-SFLEND) TO TRUE
                END-IF.
            LOAD-SIMULATED-FILE.
                PERFORM VARYING FIL-RECNUM FROM 1 BY 1
                    UNTIL FIL-RECNUM > FILE-SIZE
                    ADD 90000 TO FIL-RECNUM GIVING ACCT-NBR(FIL-RECNUM)
                END-PERFORM.
```

This program is almost identical to that in Listing 8.15 except for a few minor differences:

1. The main perform loop continues until the user presses F3=Exit.

2. If the user presses the Page down key, then the LOAD-NEXT-PAGE paragraph is executed.

3. The LOAD-NEXT-PAGE paragraph checks to see if the user is already at the end of the file, and if not, performs the LOAD-SFL-PAGE paragraph.

4. When the LOAD-SFL-PAGE paragraph starts, the SFL-RECNUM variable points to the last subfile record filled by the program. By adding one to this number, the first record of the next page is calculated and saved in the CRSR field from the subfile control record. This specifies that the next time the subfile is displayed, the page containing subfile record number CRSR will be shown.

5. The subfile record number is checked for zero to determine if the subfile is empty (indicating an empty database file).

6. If it is zero, the subfile display indicator is turned off. The next test checks whether the user is now at end of file.

8.6.5   Output-only and output-input subfiles

A subfile that displays a list of items but contains no input fields is considered an output-only subfile. The examples in the preceding section showed output-only subfiles. A subfile that displays a list of items and allows the user to make changes is considered an output/input subfile. Both output only and output/input subfiles are initialized the same way; however, using an output/input subfile contains additional logic for record retrieval.

8.6.6   Output/input subfiles

An output/input subfile is initialized in the same way as an output-only subfile. The difference is that data can now be read from the subfile to determine if the user made any changes.

The READ SUBFILE and READ SUBFILE NEXT MODIFIED statements are used to retrieve records from a subfile. The NEXT MODIFIED clause causes the read statement to return a record only if the user has typed into any of its fields or if the field's MDT tag is turned on.

The following examples, beginning with Listing 8.16, show a program that displays a list of names and allows the user to select a color for each name. When the user presses Enter, the COBOL program will check for each choice made by the user and update the subfile record to be displayed in the chosen color.

Listing 8.16 Panel with an output/input subfile.

```
FILE NAME: EX0804FM
.....AAN01N02N03T.Name++++++RLen++TDpBLinPosFunctions+++++++++++++++++
      A                                        INDARA
      A          R NAMELIST                    SFL
      A            CUSTNAME      30A  O  7  7
      A  40                                     COLOR(BLU)
      A  41                                     COLOR(GRN)
```

```
        A  42                              COLOR(PNK)
[1]     A  43                              COLOR(RED)
        A  44                              COLOR(TRQ)
        A  45                              COLOR(WHT)
        A  46                              COLOR(YLW)
        A*
[2]     A           OPT         1A  I  7   3VALUES (' ' '1' '2' '3' -
        A                                  '4' '5' '6' '7')
        A*
        A       R NAMELSTCTL               SFLCTL(NAMELIST)
[3]     A                                  SFLSIZ(0020)
        A                                  SFLPAG (0005)
        A                                  CA03(03 'Exit')
        A                                  SFLDSPCTL
[4]     A  30                              SFLDSP
[5]     A  31                              SFLCLR
[6]     A  32                              SFLEND
        A                           6  7'Name'
        A                                  DSPATR(HI)
        A                           6  2'Clr#'
        A                                  DSPATR(HI)
        A                           4  2'Choose color: 1=Blue, -
        A                                    2=Green, 3=Pink, 4=Red, -
        A                                    5=Turquoise, 6=White, -
        A                                    7=Yellow'
        A                           2  2'Press F3 to Exit'
        A                                  DSPATR(HI)
[7]     A           CRSR        4S  0H     SFLRCDNBR(CRSR)
```

Notes about Listing 8.16 are as follows:

1. The CUSTNAME field has seven color keywords conditioned by indicators 40 through 46. If one of these indicators are on when the subfile record is either written or rewritten to the subfile, the customer name will appear in the indicator's associated color.

2. The OPT field is an input-only field that has the VALUES validation keyword specified. Eight values are listed, which correspond to a blank entry and seven possible color choices.

3. In the NAMELSTCTL record format, the subfile is defined to be 20 records long with a page size of five records. This means that only five records will be shown at once and that the user will be able to use the Page up and Page down keys to scroll through the list.

4. If indicator 30 is on when the subfile control record is written, the associated subfile records will be displayed on the workstation.

5. If indicator 31 is on, all records in the subfile will be cleared.

6. Turning indicator 32 on identifies the subfile as complete. The optional keyword *MORE is specified, which puts the word "More . . ." or "Bottom" at the end of the subfile instead of a "+", which is the default indicator to show that there are more records.

7. For more information on the SFLRCDNBR keyword, see the notes for Listing 8.15.

The COBOL program to use the display file in Listing 8.16 is given in Listing 8.17:

Listing 8.17 COBOL program to use the output/input subfile.

```
MEMBER NAME:  EX0804          FILE:  QLBLSRC
....-..A...B..-....2....-....3....-....4....-....5....-....6....-.....-
      IDENTIFICATION DIVISION.
      PROGRAM-ID.  EX0804.

      ENVIRONMENT DIVISION.
      CONFIGURATION SECTION.
      INPUT-OUTPUT SECTION.
      FILE-CONTROL.
          SELECT DISPFILE ASSIGN TO WORKSTATION-EX0704FM-SI
          ORGANIZATION IS TRANSACTION
          ACCESS MODE IS DYNAMIC
          RELATIVE KEY IS SFL-RECNUM.

      DATA DIVISION.
      FILE SECTION.
      FD  DISPFILE.
      01  DISP-REC                    PIC X(100).

      WORKING-STORAGE SECTION.
      77  SFL-RECNUM                  PIC 9(7).

      01  SFL-STATUS                  PIC X.
          88 MORE-CHANGED-RECORDS            VALUE SPACE.
          88 NO-MORE-CHANGED-RECORDS         VALUE "X".
      01  SUBFILE-REC-IN.
          COPY DDS-NAMELIST-I OF EX0804FM.
      01  SUBFILE-REC-OUT.
          COPY DDS-NAMELIST-O OF EX0804FM.
      01  SUBFILE-CTL-REC.
          COPY DDS-NAMELSTCTL-O OF EX0804FM.

      01  NAME-TABLE.
          03 TABLE-DATA.
             05 PIC X(20) VALUE "Samuel, Sherwyn".
             05 PIC X(20) VALUE "Newby, Nina".
             05 PIC X(20) VALUE "Corbet, Wade".
             05 PIC X(20) VALUE "Moir, Ken".
             05 PIC X(20) VALUE "Kaplan, Marcia".
             05 PIC X(20) VALUE "Leone, Michelle".
[1]          05 PIC X(20) VALUE "Kaplan, Stanley".
             05 PIC X(20) VALUE "Lutz, Steve".
             05 PIC X(20) VALUE "Hennessy, Mercedes".
             05 PIC X(20) VALUE "Maysonet, Mark".
             05 PIC X(20) VALUE "Kaplan, Lisa".
             05 PIC X(20) VALUE "Santagada, Alex".
             05 PIC X(20) VALUE "Onuma, Jun".
             05 PIC X(20) VALUE "Goldman, Bessie".
             05 PIC X(20) VALUE "Kepke, Dorothy".
          03 EACH-NAME REDEFINES TABLE-DATA
             OCCURS 15 TIMES INDEXED BY TBL-INDX PIC X(20).
```

```
       01  INDIC-AREA.
           03  EACH-IND OCCURS 99 TIMES PIC 1 INDICATOR 1.
               88  IND-OFF VALUE B"0".
               88  IND-ON  VALUE B"1".
       01  INDICATOR-USAGE-CONSTANTS.
           03  FK-EXIT             PIC 99 VALUE 03.
           03  I-SFLDSP            PIC 99 VALUE 30.
           03  I-SFLCLR            PIC 99 VALUE 31.
           03  I-SFLEND            PIC 99 VALUE 32.
           03  CLR-BLUE            PIC 99 VALUE 40.
[2]        03  CLR-GREEN           PIC 99 VALUE 41.
           03  CLR-PINK            PIC 99 VALUE 42.
           03  CLR-RED             PIC 99 VALUE 43.
           03  CLR-TURQUOISE       PIC 99 VALUE 44.
           03  CLR-WHITE           PIC 99 VALUE 45.
           03  CLR-YELLOW          PIC 99 VALUE 46.

       PROCEDURE DIVISION.
       MAIN-PARA.
           OPEN I-O DISPFILE.
[3]        PERFORM CLEAR-SUBFILE.
           PERFORM VARYING TBL-INDX FROM 1 BY 1 UNTIL TBL INDX > 15
               ADD 1 TO SFL-RECNUM
               MOVE EACH-NAME (TBL-INDX) TO CUSTNAME OF SUBFILE-REC-OUT
               WRITE SUBFILE DISP-REC FROM SUBFILE-REC-OUT
                   FORMAT "NAMELIST" INDIC INDIC-AREA
                   INVALID KEY CONTINUE
               END-WRITE
           END-PERFORM.
[4]        SET IND-ON(I-SFLEND) TO TRUE.

           IF SFL-RECNUM NOT EQUAL ZERO
[5]            SET IND-ON(I-SFLDSP) TO TRUE
           END-IF.

           PERFORM WITH TEST BEFORE UNTIL IND-ON(FK-EXIT)
               WRITE DISP-REC FROM SUBFILE-CTL-REC
[6]                FORMAT "NAMELSTCTL" INDIC INDIC-AREA
               READ DISPFILE INTO SUBFILE-CTL-REC
                   FORMAT "NAMELSTCTL" INDIC INDIC-AREA

               IF NOT IND-ON(FK-EXIT)
[7]                PERFORM CHECK-FOR-COLOR-CHOICES
               END-IF
           END-PERFORM.

           CLOSE DISPFILE.
           STOP RUN.

       CHECK-FOR-COLOR-CHOICES.
[8]        SET MORE-CHANGED-RECORDS TO TRUE.
[9]        PERFORM UNTIL NO-MORE-CHANGED-RECORDS
[10]           READ SUBFILE DISPFILE NEXT MODIFIED INTO SUBFILE-REC-IN
                   FORMAT "NAMELIST"
                   AT END
                       SET NO-MORE-CHANGED-RECORDS TO TRUE
                   NOT AT END
                       SET IND-OFF(CLR-BLUE)   IND-OFF(CLR-GREEN)
                           IND-OFF(CLR-RED)    IND-OFF(CLR-PINK)
                           IND-OFF(CLR-WHITE)  IND-OFF(CLR-TURQUOISE)
                           IND-OFF(CLR-YELLOW) TO TRUE
                       EVALUATE OPT
```

```
                    WHEN "1" SET IND-ON(CLR-BLUE) TO TRUE
                    WHEN "2" SET IND-ON(CLR-GREEN) TO TRUE
                    WHEN "3" SET IND-ON(CLR-PINK) TO TRUE
                    WHEN "4" SET IND-ON(CLR-RED) TO TRUE
                    WHEN "5" SET IND-ON(CLR-TURQUOISE) TO TRUE
                    WHEN "6" SET IND-ON(CLR-WHITE) TO TRUE
                    WHEN "7" SET IND-ON(CLR-YELLOW) TO TRUE
                    END-EVALUATE
[11]                MOVE CUSTNAME OF SUBFILE-REC-IN TO SUBFILE-REC-OUT
                    REWRITE SUBFILE DISP-REC FROM SUBFILE-REC-OUT
                    FORMAT "NAMELIST" INDICATORS ARE INDIC-AREA
                    INVALID KEY CONTINUE
                    END-REWRITE
                    MOVE SFL-RECNUM TO CRSR
              END-READ
        END-PERFORM.

    CLEAR-SUBFILE.
        SET IND-ON(I-SFLCLR) TO TRUE.
        WRITE DISP-REC FORMAT "NAMELSTCTL" INDICATORS INDIC-AREA.
        SET IND-OFF(I-SFLCLR) TO TRUE.
        MOVE ZERO TO SFL-RECNUM.
        MOVE 1 TO CRSR.
```

1. NAME-TABLE is used to simulate the file input to simplify this example.

2. INDICATOR-USAGE-CONSTANTS associates descriptive names with indicator numbers used in the display file. This is optional but helps make the actions in the procedure division more clear.

3. MAIN-PARA first clears the subfile—this is not really necessary since the subfile is empty to begin with, but the CLEAR-SUBFILE paragraph also initializes some variables. Following this, the subfile is loaded from the entries in NAME-TABLE.

4. After loading the table, the SFLEND indicator is turned on to declare the subfile as being complete.

5. The next step is included for illustrative purposes—the subfile record number is checked to see if any records were added to the file, and if there were, the associated indicator for displaying the subfile is turned on. This example always loads records so the test is unnecessary; however, in real applications, this would not be the case, and the test would be necessary.

6. The program then enters into a loop that continues until the user presses the F3=Exit key. The loop writes the subfile control record with the SFLDSP keyword in effect. This causes the subfile to be displayed as well as any fields in the subfile control record. The following READ commands suspends operation of the program and waits for the user to do something.

7. When control returns to the program (after the user did something), the Exit function key is tested to determine whether or not

to check for any selections. If the user pressed the Exit function key, the loop terminates and the program ends. If the user pressed the Enter key, the CHECK-FOR-COLOR-CHOICES paragraph is executed.

8. The CHECK-FOR-COLOR-CHOICES paragraph begins by setting the subfile status flag to MORE-CHANGED-RECORDS. This resets any previous status and ensures that the following loop will execute at least once.

9. The PERFORM UNTIL NO-MORE-CHANGED-RECORDS will loop through all changed records in the subfile one at a time.

10. Each READ SUBFILE NEXT MODIFIED will only return a record that has been changed by the user (i.e., the user put a color number in the option column). The READ SUBFILE NEXT MODIFIED statement fetches the next modified record. If it encounters the end of the file, then the NO-MORE-CHANGED-RECORDS flag is set to TRUE and the loop terminates; otherwise all color indicators are reset and the EVALUATE statement proceeds to set on the appropriate indicator based on the color selection made by the user.

11. Afterwards, CUSTNAME is copied from the subfile's input buffer (which was filled by the READ SUBFILE) to the subfile's output buffer, which will then be rewritten to the subfile.

When this program is executed, it will show the display shown in Fig. 8.8.

```
Press F3 to Exit

Choose color:  1=Blue, 2=Green, 3=Pink, 4=Red, 5=Turquoise, 6=White, 7=Yellow

Opt  Name
 _    Samuel, Sherwyn
 _    Newby, Nina
 _    Corbet, Wade
 _    Moir, Ken
 _    Kaplan, Marcia
                                                                  More...
```

Figure 8.8 Panel with an output/input subfile.

8.6.7 Input-only subfiles

A subfile that is used for input-only must initialize all the records prior to displaying the subfile; otherwise the subfile will contain uninitialized records and cannot be displayed. The SFLINZ keyword initializes all records in the subfile, causing the subfile to appear to have records, even though they are all empty. When the subfile is then displayed, each line in the subfile will be displayed (as blanks). Reading through the subfile is exactly identical to that of output/input subfiles as described in Sec. 8.6.6.

Figure 8.9 illustrates an input-only subfile.

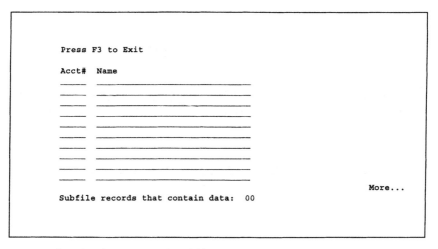

Figure 8.9 Panel with an input-only subfile.

The DDS source for this display file is shown in Listing 8.18. This example contains three records: a subfile record, a subfile control record, and a regular record called DATAREC. Both records (DATAREC and NAMELSTCTL), which can be displayed, are defined with the OVERLAY keyword to allow both to be displayed at the same time.

Listing 8.18 Example of DDS for an input-only subfile.

```
FILE NAME: EX0805FM
.....AAN01N02N03T.Name++++++RLen++TDpBLinPosFunctions+++++++++++++++++++
     A                                        INDARA
     A          R NAMELIST                    SFL
     A            ACCTNUM       5   I  7   9
     A            ACCTNAME     30   I  7  16
     A          R NAMELSTCTL                   SFLCTL(NAMELIST)
     A                                         CF03(03 'Exit')
```

```
A                                             OVERLAY
A                                             SFLCSRRRN(&SFLRRN)
A  30                                         SFLDSP
A                                             SFLDSPCTL
A  31                                         SFLINZ
A  32                                         SFLCLR
A  33                                         SLFEND(*MORE)
A                                             SFLSIZ(0030)
A                                             SFLPAG(0010)
A                                    6  9'Acct#'
A                                             DSPATR(HI)
A                                    6 16'Name'
A                                             DSPATR(HI)
A                                    4  9'Press F3 to Exit'
A                                             DSPATR(HI)
A          CRSR          4S  0H              SFLRCDNBR (CRSR)
A          SFLRRN        5S  0H
A        R DATAREC
A                                             OVERLAY
A                                   19  9'Subfile records that -
A                                             contain data:'
A                                             DSPATR(HI)
A          TTLRECS       2  00 19 46
```

The SFLCSRRRN keyword identifies a variable that will contain the
subfile record number where the cursor was when the enter key was
pressed (see Listing 8.19).

Listing 8.19 COBOL program for example EX0805.

```
MEMBER  NAME  EX0805       FILE:  QLBLSRC
....-..A...B..-....2....-....3....-....4....-....5....-....6....-.....-
     IDENTIFICATION DIVISION.
     PROGRAM-ID. EX0805.

     ENVIRONMENT DIVISION.
     CONFIGURATION SECTION.
     INPUT-OUTPUT SECTION.
     FILE-CONTROL.
         SELECT DISPFILE ASSIGN TO WORKSTATION-EX0706FM-SI
             ORGANIZATION IS TRANSACTION
             ACCESS MODE IS DYNAMIC
             RELATIVE KEY IS SFL-RECNUM.

     DATA DIVISION.
     FILE SECTION.
     FD  DISPFILE.
     01  DISP-REC                 PIC X(100).

     WORKING-STORAGE SECTION.
     77  SFL-RECNUM               PIC 9(7).
     77  SFL-SIZE                 PIC 99 VALUE 30.

     01  SUBFILE-REC-IN.
         COPY DDS-NAMELIST-I OF EX0805FM.
     01  SUBFILE-CTL-OUT.
         COPY DDS-NAMELSTCTL-O OF EX0805FM.
     01  SUBFILE-CTL-IN.
         COPY DDS-NAMELSTCTL-I OF EX0805FM.
     01  DATAREC-OUT.
```

```
        COPY DDS-DATAREC-O OF EX0805FM.

    01  INDIC-AREA.
        03  EACH-IND OCCURS 99 TIMES PIC 1 INDICATOR 1.
            88 IND-OFF VALUE B"0".
            88 IND-ON  VALUE B"1".
    01  INDICATOR-USAGE-CONSTANTS.
        03  FK-EXIT            PIC 99 VALUE 03.
        03  I-SFLDSP          PIC 99 VALUE 30.
        03  I-SFLINZ          PIC 99 VALUE 31.
        03  I-SFLCLR          PIC 99 VALUE 32.
        03  I-SFLEND          PIC 99 VALUE 33.


    PROCEDURE DIVISION.
    MAIN-PARA.
        OPEN I-O DISPFILE.
```
[1]   ```   PERFORM INIT-SUBFILE.```

```
        MOVE 1 TO CRSR OF SUBFILE-CTL-OUT.
        SET IND-ON(I-SFLDSP) TO TRUE.
```
[2]   ```   PERFORM WITH TEST BEFORE UNTIL IND-ON(FK-EXIT)```

[3]   ```
            WRITE DISP-REC FROM SUBFILE-CTL-OUT
                FORMAT "NAMELSTCTL" INDIC INDIC-AREA
            READ DISPFILE INTO SUBFILE-CTL-IN
                FORMAT "NAMELSTCTL" INDIC INDIC-AREA
```

[4]     ```        MOVE SFLRRN OF SUBFILE-CTL-IN TO CRSR OF SUBFILE-CTL-OUT```

```
            IF IND-OFF(FK-EXIT)
```
[5]     ```            PERFORM CHECK-FOR-CHOICES```
```
                WRITE DISP-REC FROM DATAREC-OUT FORMAT "DATAREC"
            END-IF
        END-PERFORM.

        CLOSE DISPFILE.
        STOP RUN.
```

[6]     ```CHECK-FOR-CHOICES.```
```
        MOVE ZERO TO TTLRECS.
        PERFORM VARYING SFL-RECNUM FROM 1 BY 1
            UNTIL SFL-RECNUM > SFL-SIZE
            READ SUBFILE DISPFILE INTO SUBFILE-REC-IN
                FORMAT "NAMELIST"
            IF ACCTNUM NOT EQUAL SPACES OR ACCTNAME NOT EQUAL SPACES
                ADD 1 TO TTLRECS
            END-IF
        END-PERFORM.

    INIT-SUBFILE.
```
[1]     ```
        SET IND-ON(I-SFLINZ) TO TRUE.
        WRITE DISP-REC FORMAT "NAMELSTCTL" INDICATORS INDIC-AREA.
        SET IND-OFF (I-SFLINZ) TO TRUE.
```
```
        MOVE ZERO TO SFL-RECNUM.
        SET IND-ON(I-SFLEND) TO TRUE.
```

1. The program starts by initializing the subfile. This is accomplished
   by turning on the I-SFLINZ indicator and writing to the subfile control record (NAMELSTCTL). After this, the subfile will contain 30
   initialized records (SFLSIZ = 30).

2. The main PERFORM loop is then entered and continues until the user presses F3=Exit.

3. In each iteration, the subfile control record is written and then read.

4. The SFLRRN variable is moved to CRSR. This is done to ensure that when the subfile is redisplayed, the displayed subfile page will not change. SFLRRN will contain the subfile record number the cursor was on when the enter key was pressed. This number is then put in the CRSR variable to instruct OS/400 to display the same page again when the subfile is redisplayed.

5. If F3=Exit was not pressed, the CHECK-FOR-CHOICES paragraph executes, and then the DATAREC display record is shown.

6. The CHECK-FOR-CHOICES paragraph reads through the entire subfile. If a record is read that has been filled in by the user, the TTLRECS variable is incremented. This example does not use the NEXT MODIFIED clause, and thus shows an example of how to read ALL records within the subfile.

8.7 Displaying Messages

Messages are used to communicate program conditions to the user. You can specify that a message is to be displayed on the message line with the ERRMSG or ERRMSGID keyword.

- The ERRMSG keyword is used when the message text is defined as a constant within the DDS or when the message is passed in a field from the COBOL program. Message help is not supported for these kinds of messages.

- The ERRMSGID keyword directs OS/400 to locate the message in a message file. Message help is supported when this keyword is used.

An application program would usually associate a particular indicator with an error condition. If the error indicator is on when the record format is displayed, then the message will appear on the message line (usually the last line of the display), the field in error will be displayed in reverse image, and the keyboard will be locked.

Listing 8.20 illustrates how to use both of these keywords.

Listing 8.20 ERRMSGID and ERRMSG keywords.

```
.....AAN01N02N03T.Name++++++RLen++TDpBLinPosFunctions++++++++++++++++++
      A           R NAMEREC
      A             NAME          35   B  6 32
[1]   A  10                                    ERRMSGID(MSG0001 MSGF1 10)
[2]   A  11                                    ERRMSG('This is an error -
      A                                          msg.' 11)
      A             ADDRESS1      40   B  7 32
```

1. If indicator 10 is on when the record format is displayed, the NAME field will appear in reverse image and message MSG0001 from message file MSGF1 will be displayed on the message line.

2. If indicator 11 is on, the field will be displayed in reverse image and the text "This is an error msg." will appear on the message line. In both cases, the cursor will be positioned to the field and the keyboard will be locked.

8.7.1 Using a subfile for error messages

The ERRSFL (error subfile) keyword can be used to indicate that the error messages associated with ERRMSG and ERRMSGID be displayed on the message line using a system-supplied error subfile. Using an error subfile allows the user to roll through a subfile of error messages. One error message is displayed at a time. The COBOL program would handle the validity checking of the fields, setting on the option indicators for the appropriate ERRMSG or ERRMSGID for the fields in error. The system handles putting the message in the error subfile and displaying them. When the error subfile is displayed, the keyboard is not locked; thus it is not necessary to press the Reset key prior to correcting the fields in error.

To use an error subfile, include the ERRSFL keyword at the beginning of the display file (see Listing 8.21).

Listing 8.21 ERRSFL keyword.

```
.....AAN01N02N03T.Name++++++RLen++TDpBLinPosFunctions++++++++++++++++++
A                                          ERRSFL
A             R NAMEREC
A               NAME        35    B  6 32
A   10                                     ERRMSGID(MSG0001 MSGF1 10)
A   11                                     ERRMSG('This is an error -
A                                          msg.' 11)
A               ADDRESS1    40    B  7 32
```

8.8 Level Checks

When the DDS source for a display file is compiled, a special level identifier is generated and included in the file header. When a COBOL program is complied, this level number is noted and saved in the generated object program. During run time, the level number is compared with that of the file. If the level number does not match, a level check error is sent to the workstation. Basically, a level check is an indication that the file no longer matches the layout that the COBOL program is expecting.

Not all changes to a display file will result in the level number changing. For instance, if you change the color of a display field or add additional constants to a record format, the level number will not change. If, however, you add an additional field to a record format or you change the length of a field, the file's level number will change, thus causing a level check in any program that references the file. A level check error can easily be rectified by recompiling the COBOL program so that it includes the description and level identifier of the newer file.

8.9 Summary

COBOL/400 programs communicate with display stations by using display files. Display files are described with DDS and then complied. A display file's description contains descriptions of record formats and fields.

Record formats describe a single logical part of the screen. A COBOL program can display several record formats at the same time to construct a screen. Record formats contain detailed descriptions of each field within the record.

Field descriptions contain information such as where the field should be displayed on the screen, what type of data the field contains (alphabetic, numeric, etc.), display attributes (color, underline, bold, etc.), as well as validity checks.

Subfiles are used for displaying and managing lists of related information. Subfiles are constructed from two parts: a subfile record and a subfile control record. The control record is used for functions that affect the entire list such as clearing, initializing, inserting, etc. The control record also determines how the list is presented to the user. This includes how many subfile records are displayed at once and whether "More . . . " or "Bottom" appears. Headers or footers can also be defined in the control record.

The subfile record defines what fields appear in each line of the subfile. When a COBOL program is filling a subfile, it will write subfile records one at a time.

There are three ways of controlling scrolling with subfiles. If the subfile size is equal to the subfile page size (a screen page equals the size of the entire subfile), the COBOL program will be responsible for handling all scrolling. When the user presses Page up or Page down, the COBOL program will have to clear the subfile and load the next or previous page. This is the preferred method when the list tends to be large or of unknown size.

If the subfile size is greater than the page size, then the COBOL program can load the entire subfile before displaying it and OS/400 workstation management will handle all scrolling requests from the user. This is the preferred method when the list is small.

If the subfile size is greater than the page size but the PAGEDOWN keyword has been specified in the DDS, then the COBOL program will be responsible for loading only one page at a time. When the user presses the Page down key, the COBOL program will be notified that the next page is needed. If the user scrolls backwards, OS/400 will redisplay previously filled records. This is the preferred method when the list is not too long and/or creating each subfile record takes an unusually long amount of time.

9

Printing

When a program generates output destined for the printer, a number of intermediate steps occur prior to the actual printing. In most cases, the application program writes data to a printer file that performs any necessary formatting. The formatted printer data are then accumulated in a spool file and held in a print queue until the application program indicates that the output is complete. If the output queue is associated with a print writer, the spool file then begins to print.

Although this scenario defines the most common path that data may take on its way to a printer, it is not the only way. Printed output may be held in an output queue that is not associated with a printer (thus it will not be printed until it is moved into a queue that is associated with a printer). A printer file may also define that the printed output is not to be spooled at all and should go directly to the printer.

It is clear that printing can be customized exactly for the need of the application. Before explaining how this is done, it is important to understand the various components that make up the entire printing process.

9.1   Printers and Writers

Each printer connected to the AS/400 has an associated device description (DEVD). It should never be necessary to work directly with a device except for varying it on-line and off-line.

Each printer device on the AS/400 is associated with a print *writer.* The writer relates directly to the physical printer device (see Fig. 9.1). A writer can be started, stopped, held, and released. Each writer is associated with exactly one output queue. The associated output queue is usually named the same as the writer. Any printed output that is

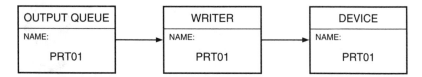

Figure 9.1 Queue–writer–printer relationship.

placed in this output queue will automatically be printed (unless the spooled file, print queue, or print writer has a "held" status). You can see the various writers on your system by entering the WRKWTR command.

9.2 Output Queues

When a spooled file is produced as a result of printing, it is placed on an output queue. Each output queue contains an ordered list of spooled files. The current job usually indicates which output queue to use. You can see which output queue your job uses by displaying the current job with the DSPJOB command and then displaying the job definition attributes. The default output queue may be set up in the user's profile, the job description, or the workstation description, in addition to a variety of other places within the system. Setting up user profiles, group profiles, and job descriptions is outside the scope of this book; however, you can find more details in the *AS/400 Work Management Guide*.

When programs generate output, the output is placed in a spool file. There are two ways to see what spooled files are ready to print:

- The WRKOUTQ command lets you specify exactly which output queue you want to see.

- The WRKSPLF command lets you see all generated spool files for your job, regardless of what output queue they are in.

9.3 Printer Files

Printer files are used to define the formatting characteristics of printed output from a program. They define attributes such as lines per inch (LPI), characters per inch (CPI), number of copies to print, and destination printer queue to name just a few. They also define exactly where each data should appear on the printed page. This chapter describes how to use printer files, and how COBOL/400 interacts with the different types of printer files.

Traditional systems left the housekeeping of printer activity to the application program or job control language. It was the application program that defined the exact column layout of each printed line, the number of characters per line, and the length limits of a page. With OS/400, most of these characteristics are found in the printer file definition; the application program is responsible only for providing the data fields and specifying which record formats within the printer file to write to the printer.

There are two different types of printer files:

- *Program-described printer files:* This type of printer file relies heavily on the high-level language (COBOL) program to define printer layouts as well as line spacing. Traditional programs use this type of printing.

- *Externally described printer files:* This type of printer file uses data description specifications (DDS) rather than the high-level language to define records and fields to be printed. This is the standard way for producing printed reports on the AS/400.

All program output must go to a printer file. If no printer file is specified in the COBOL SELECT statement, the default printer file QPRINT will be used.

9.4 Program-Described Printer Files

IBM provides several predefined printer files that you can use for program described printer output:

- *QSYSPRT:* Standard program-described printer file

- *QPRINT:* Default spooled output printer file

- *QPRINTS:* Printer file for use with special forms

- *QPRINT2:* Printer file that produces two copies of output

- *QPSPLPRT:* Spooled output printer file for the spooling subsystem

You can easily create a new printer file tailored specifically to a job's requirements. The CRTPRTF command is used to create a new printer file. You can also change the attributes of a preexisting printer file using the CHGPRTF command. The command in Fig. 9.2 will create a printer file named THREEPART in the current library. When a spooled file that was based on this printer file is printed, OS/400 will print three copies.

```
CRTPRTF FILE(THREEPART) COPIES(3)
```

Figure 9.2 Command to create a printer file that produces three copies.

To see the wide variety of options available for printer files, type the CRTPRTF command and then press the F4=Prompt key. The F10 key can be used to display all available options.

It is not always necessary to create a new printer file for each job. Previously defined printer files can be used and attributes can be "overridden." For example, it it not necessary to create a new print file if a job requires five copies. Instead, the QPRINT printer file can be overridden with the COPIES parameter set to 5.

9.4.1   Using program-described printer files

To use a program-described printer file, the COBOL program must specify a device of PRINTER in the SELECT statement.

```
SELECT REPORT-FILE ASSIGN TO PRINTER.
```

This SELECT statement will send all output to a spool file based on the IBM-supplied printer file QPRINT.

```
SELECT REPORT-FILE ASSIGN TO PRINTER-THREEPART.
```

This SELECT statement will send all output to a spool file based on the printer file created in Fig. 9.2. Any output printed to this file will be printed in triplicate.

9.4.2   Using special names CSP and C01

A program can use the special CSP and C01 environment names in the ADVANCING phrase. CSP relates directly to ADVANCING 0 LINES and C01 relates directly to ADVANCING PAGE. These special keywords must first be declared in the SPECIAL-NAMES paragraph in Listing 9.1.

Listing 9.1   Using CSP and C01.

```
....-..A...B..-....2....-....3....-....4....-....5....-....6....-....-
        SPECIAL-NAMES. CSP IS NO-LINE-FEED,
        C01 IS FORM-FEED.
        .
        .
        WRITE REPORT-FILE AFTER NO-LINE-FEED.
        WRITE REPORT-FILE AFTER FORM-FEED.
        .
        .
```

The CSP and C01 special names cannot be used for externally described printer files.

9.4.2.1 CSP and C01 example. The following example illustrates the use of C01 and CSP (see Listing 9.2). The first WRITE statement will write the word HELLO. The next WRITE statement writes five underscore characters using the NO-LINE-FEED special name that was associated with CSP in the SPECIAL-NAMES statement. The result is the underlined word HELLO. The next WRITE uses FORM-FEED, which is associated with C01. This causes a page eject prior to writing the print line.

Listing 9.2 COBOL program using C01 and CSP.

```
MEMBER NAME: EX0901          FILE: QLBLSRC
....-..A...B..-....2....-....3....-....4....-....5....-....6....-.....-
          IDENTIFICATION DIVISION.
          PROGRAM-ID. EX0901.

          ENVIRONMENT DIVISION.
          SPECIAL-NAMES.  C01 IS FORM-FEED, CSP is NO-LINE-FEED.
          CONFIGURATION SECTION.
          INPUT-OUTPUT SECTION.
          FILE-CONTROL.
              SELECT OUTFILE ASSIGN TO PRINTER.

          DATA DIVISION.
          FILE SECTION.
          FD  OUTFILE.
          01  PRINT-LINE PIC X(132).

          PROCEDURE DIVISION.
          MAIN-PARA.
              OPEN OUTPUT OUTFILE.
              MOVE "HELLO" TO PRINT-LINE.
              WRITE PRINT-REC.
              MOVE "_____" TO PRINT-LINE.
              WRITE PRINT-REC AFTER ADVANCING NO-LINE-FEED.
              MOVE "NEW-PAGE" TO PRINT-LINE.
              WRITE PRINT-REC AFTER ADVANCING FORM-FEED.
              CLOSE OUTFILE.
              STOP RUN.
```

9.4.3 The Linage clause

When the LINAGE clause is specified for a file associated with the PRINTER device (through the SELECT statement), all spacing and paging for WRITE statements are controlled internally. For a file that has a LINAGE clause and is assigned to PRINTER, paging consists of spacing to the end of the logical page and then spacing past the bottom and top margins—the physical size of the page (known to the spooler) is ignored.

Use of the LINAGE clause degrades performance. If the physical paging performed by OS/400 is acceptable, the LINAGE clause is not necessary. The LINAGE clause should not be used for files assigned to FORMATFILE (externally described printer files).

9.4.4 Using first-character form control

Program-described printer files can control printer actions through the use of first-character form control. This is done by including an ANS-defined control code in the first position of each printed line.

Programs being migrated from mainframe computers may require the use of first-character form control.

First-character form control is supported only for program-described printer files. It cannot be used if the file is defined using DDS.

If first-character form-control data is used, any print control information generated by the COBOL program (such as AFTER ADVANCING) is ignored—only the character in position 1 of each print line is used for printer control.

To create a program-described printer file that uses first-character form-control data, specify the CTLCHAR(*FCFC) parameter on the CRTPRTF command.

Table 9.1 lists the ANS Control Codes that can be put in column 1 of the print-line. Any other character found in the first column will be interpreted as a blank (space one line).

TABLE 9.1 First-Character Form-Control Codes

Control Code	Action before printing a line
' '	Space one line
0	Space two lines
-	Space three lines
+	Supress space
1	Skip to channel 1
2	Skip to channel 2
3	Skip to channel 3
4	Skip to channel 4
5	Skip to channel 5
6	Skip to channel 6
7	Skip to channel 7
8	Skip to channel 8
9	Skip to channel 9
A	Skip to channel 10
B	Skip to channel 11
C	Skip to channel 12

9.4.4.1 First-character form-control example. The example in Listing 9.3 shows how to use first-character form control in a COBOL/400 program.

Listing 9.3 COBOL program using first-character form control.

```
MEMBER NAME: EX0902          FILE: QLBLSRC
....-..A...B..-....2....-....3....-....4....-....5....-....6....-.....-
         IDENTIFICATION DIVISION.
         PROGRAM-ID. EX0902.

         ENVIRONMENT DIVISION.
         CONFIGURATION SECTION.
         INPUT-OUTPUT SECTION.
         FILE-CONTROL.
             SELECT OUTFILE ASSIGN TO PRINTER-FCFCPRTF.

         DATA DIVISION.
         FILE SECTION.
         FD OUTFILE.
         01  PRINT-REC.
             03 FCFC        PIC X.
             03 PRINT-LINE  PIC X(131).

         PROCEDURE DIVISION.
         MAIN-PARA.
             OPEN OUTPUT OUTFILE.
             MOVE "USING 1 - MOVES TO FIRST LINE" TO PRINT-LINE.
 [1]         MOVE "1" TO FCFC.
             WRITE PRINT-REC.
             MOVE "SKIP 3 LINES" TO PRINT-LINE.
 [2]         MOVE "-" TO FCF.
             WRITE PRINT-REC.
             MOVE "NEXT PAGE- FIRST LINE" TO PRINT-LINE.
 [3]         MOVE "1" TO FCFC.
             WRITE PRINT-REC.
             CLOSE OUTFILE.
             STOP RUN.
```

Before this program can run, a printer file named FCFCPRTF must be created with the CTLCHAR(*FCFC) option specified. This can be done with the following command:

```
CRTPRTF FILE(FCFCPRTF) CTLCHAR(*FCFC)
```

1. The first WRITE statement uses the character "1" in the FCFC position. This causes a "Skip to Channel 1" to occur that forces the printer to move to line 1.

2. The next WRITE statement uses the hyphen "-" character, which is defined as "Skip 3 lines", thus the text "Skip 3 lines" will be printed after the carriage advances three lines.

3. The next WRITE statement uses the "1" character in the FCFC position, which will cause the text "NEXT PAGE-FIRST LINE" to be printed at the top of the next page.

9.5   Externally Described Printer Files

When an externally described printer file is used, the COBOL program does not define how each line will look. These details are kept in the printer file. The COBOL program will COPY the field layout from the external file exactly as it would for a display file or an externally described physical file.

Using externally described printer files is the standard way for producing printed output on the AS/400. To use an externally described printer file, you must specify a device type of FORMATFILE instead of PRINTER in the SELECT statement (see Fig. 9.3).

```
SELECT PRINT-FILE ASSIGN TO FORMATFILE-CUSTLIST-SI.
```

Figure 9.3   SELECT statement for an externally described printer file.

This associates the internal file name PRINT-FILE with an externally described printer file named CUSTLIST. The -SI tells COBOL that a separate indicator area will be maintained. For more information on indicators and separate indicator areas, see Sec. 8.3 on indicators.

There are advantages to using externally described printer files rather than program-described printer files:

- Multiple lines can be printed by one WRITE statement.

- Fields can be conditioned with indicators. If the field's indicator is not on, the field will not be printed.

- Field editing is done by OS/400 instead of within the COBOL program.

- Field attributes can easily be defined (such as color, underline, fonts, bold, etc.).

- The report layout is easily maintained using the report layout utility (RLU) or source entry utility (SEU) (additional report formatting tools are available from other vendors).

- The same printer file can be used by more than one program (printer files are language independent).

Externally described printer files must contain a DDS source file to describe how the printer output should look. You can use SEU to create printer file DDS, or you can use RLU. If you are entering and trying the examples in this book, you may find it easier to use SEU rather than RLU.

9.5.1   External printer file example

This example demonstrates how to create and use an externally defined printer file. Listing 9.4 defines a printer file with two record formats and four output fields.

Listing 9.4 DDS for an externally described printer file.

```
FILE NAME: EX0903PR
.....AAN01N02N03T.Name++++++RLen++TDpBLinPosFunctions++++++++++++++++
[1]    A              R HEADER
[2]    A                                      SKIPB(002)
[3]    A                              2
[4]    A                                      'SERVICE REQUEST LOG'
[5]    A                            +48
[6]    A                                      'Page:'
[7]    A                             +2
[8]    A                                      PAGNBR
[9]    A                              2
[10]   A                                      'Date'
[11]   A                                      SPACEB(002)
[12]   A                             +6
[13]   A                                      'Time'
[14]   A                             +6
[15]   A                                      'Phone number'
[16]   A                            +15
[17]   A                                      'Request details'
[18]   A                              2
[19]   A                                      '_____'
[20]   A                                      SPACEB(001)
[21]   A                             +2
[22]   A                                      '_____'
[23]   A                             +2
[24]   A                                      '_____'
[25]   A                             +2
[26]   A                                      '_____'
[27]   A              R DETAIL
[28]   A                                      SPACEB(001)
[29]   A                REQDAT       6S   O    2
[30]   A                                      EDTCDE(Y)
[31]   A                REQTIM       6S  OO   12
[32]   A                                      EDTWRD ('  :  :  ')
[33]   A                REQNBR      25A   O   22
[34]   A                REQDTL      30A   O   +2
```

- Line 1 begins the definition of the HEADER record.

- Line 2 instructs the printer to skip to printer line 2 before printing the next item in the record format.

- The words "SERVICE REQUEST LOG" will begin printing in column 2.

- The plus sign preceding some column numbers specifies a "relative position" rather than an absolute position. When no plus sign is specified, the number represents an absolute column (as in line 3). When a plus is present (as in line 5), printing begins *n* positions relative to the end of the previously printed item. In line 5, the words "Page:" will be printed 48 spaces after the words "SERVICE REQUEST LOG", which were printed on line 4.

- Two spaces following "Page:" will be the current page number. The PAGNBR keyword causes the system page number to be printed. This page number is maintained by OS/400.

- After all headings have been printed, line 19 defines the first set of underlines to be printed; since line 20 specifies SPACEB(001), a line feed will occur before the underlines are printed. All keywords following the definition of a new field (i.e., a new column number) are all applied to the field until the next field definition begins. Therefore, lines 18 through 20 are viewed as one field.

- Line 27 begins the definition of the DETAIL record. Before each detail record is printed, the printer will advance forward one line as a result of the SPACEB(001) keyword on line 28.

- Lines 29 through 34 define the four fields that will print each time the DETAIL record format is printed. These fields will have a direct relationship to the output buffer in the COBOL program.

Enter the source in Listing 9.4 using SEU. For the member name, use EX0903PR. Create the printer file with the following command:

```
CRTPRTF FILE(EX0903PR) SRCFILE (QDDSSRC)
```

9.5.3 Creating the COBOL program

The COBOL program in Listing 9.5 uses the printer file defined in Listing 9.4.

Listing 9.5 COBOL program that uses an external printer file.

```
MEMBER NAME  EX0903           FILE: QLBLSRC
....-..A...B..-....2....-....3....-....4....-....5...-....6....-....-
        IDENTIFICATION DIVISION.
        PROGRAM-ID. EX0903.

        ENVIRONMENT DIVISION.
        INPUT-OUTPUT SECTION.
        FILE-CONTROL.
[1]        SELECT RPTFILE ASSIGN TO FORMATFILE-EX0903PR.
        DATA DIVISION.
        FILE SECTION.
        FD  RPTFILE.
        01  RPTFILE-REC.
[2]        COPY DDS-ALL-FORMATS-O OF EX0903PR.

        WORKING-STORAGE SECTION.
        01  DETAIL-TABLE.
            03  RAW-DATA.
```

```
              07 PIC X(40) VALUE "950301100520555-1212NO DIAL TONE".
              07 PIC X(40) VALUE "950328130233555-1213BROKEN PHONE".
              07 PIC X(40) VALUE "950507231000555-1214NO RINGER TONE".
              07 PIC X(40) VALUE "950615080000555-1215BAD STATIC".
[3]           07 PIC X(40) VALUE "950726173321555-1216NO DIAL TONE".
           03 DETAIL-DATA REDEFINES RAW-DATA OCCURS 5 TIMES
              INDEXED BY INDX.
              07 REQDAT        PIC S9(6).
              07 REQTIM        PIC S9(6).
              07 REQNBR        PIC X(8).
              07 REQDTL        PIC X(20).
        PROCEDURE DIVISION.
        MAIN-PARA.
[4]        OPEN OUTPUT RPTFILE.
           PERFORM PRINT-HEADER.
           PERFORM VARYING INDX FROM 1 BY 1 UNTIL INDX > 5
              MOVE CORRESPONDING DETAIL-DATA(INDX) TO DETAIL-O
[5]           WRITE RPTFILE-REC FORMAT "DETAIL"
              AT EOP PERFORM PRINT-HEADER
              END-WRITE
           END-PERFORM.
           CLOSE RPTFILE.
           STOP RUN.
        PRINT-HEADER.
[6]        WRITE RPTFILE-REC FORMAT "HEADER".
```

1. The externally described printer file EX0903PR is associated with the internal file RPTFILE.

2. This will cause the COBOL compiler to create data structures for all records found in printer file EX0903PR. It will copy two formats: HEADER and DETAIL. The HEADER record format will contain no fields and the DETAIL format will have four fields.

3. An internal table will contain test data to avoid having to include a physical file in this example.

4. The printer file is opened for output processing.

5. The DETAIL record will be written to the spool file here. If an end-of-page condition occurs, the PRINT-HEADER paragraph will be performed.

6. The HEADER record will be written here. Since this record is defined (in the DDS) with the SKIPB(002) keyword, the printer will advance to the next page and move to line 2.

It should also be noted that the sizes of the data items in the COBOL program do not exactly match the sizes defined the printer file. Specifically, the size of REQNBR in the DDS is defined as 25 characters as opposed to being defined as 8 characters in the COBOL program. Also, REQDTL is defined as 30 characters in the DDS and only 20 in the COBOL program. In fact, there is no direct relationship between the fields in the COBOL program and those in the DDS. The names were made the same simply for convenience so that the MOVE CORRE-SPONDING statement could be used. The COPY DDS-ALL-FORMATS in line [2] of Listing 9.5 will include a data structure that matches exactly that of the DDS. The fields from DETAIL-DATA will be moved to the fields with the same names in RPTFILE-REC. The output from this program looks like that shown in Fig. 9.4.

```
SERVICE REQUEST LOG                                     Page:  0001

Date      Time      Phone number              Request details
--------  --------  ------------------------  ------------------------------
95/03/01  10:05:20  555-1212                  NO DIAL TONE
95/03/28  13:02:33  555-1213                  BROKEN PHONESET
95/05/07  23:10:00  555-1214                  NO RINGER
95/06/15   8:00:00  555-1215                  BAD STATIC
95/07/26  17:33:21  555-1216                  NO DIAL TONE
```

Figure 9.4 Output from an externally described printer file example.

9.6 Overriding Printer Files

Overrides are used to temporarily specify a different printer file or temporarily change some of the attributes of a printer file. Override commands may be entered interactively from a display station or as part of a command language (CL) program. Regardless of how they are issued, overrides remain in effect only for the job, program, or sign-on session in which they are issued. Overrides have no effect on other jobs that may be running at the same time.

Examples of when overrides may be used are as follows:

- Specifying a different printer file for output (i.e., a foreign language version of the report)

- Changing printer characteristics such as lines per inch and number of copies

- Changing the output queue or printer device

Printer files are associated with a COBOL program by the file names specified in the SELECT statement. You can override the file name when you compile or run a program.

Overrides may be used to change most, but not all, of the attributes that are specified when the printer file is created. Overriding a file is different from changing a file in that an override does not permanently change the attributes of a file. For example, if you override the number of copies specified in a printer file by requesting six copies instead of two, the file description for the printer file still specifies two copies, but six copies are printed.

9.6.1 Overriding printer file attributes

The simplest use of a printer file override is to temporarily change some attributes of a preexisting printer file. For example, suppose that you created a program that uses the IBM-supplied QPRINT printer file for standard output. The program gives the user the choice of either regular paper (66 lines × 132 characters at 6 lines per inch) or long paper (88 lines × 132 characters at 8 lines per inch). Furthermore, you want to make sure that the system will request the proper paper to be loaded into the printer. Depending on the choice made by the user, one of the two overrides shown in Fig. 9.5 may be used.

```
Regular paper:
    OVRPRTF FILE(QPRINT) PAGESIZE(66 132) LPI(6) FORMTYPE(*STD)
Long paper:
    OVRPRTF FILE(QPRINT) PAGESIZE(88 132) LPI(8) FORMTYPE(LONG)
```

Figure 9.5 Examples of the OVRPRTF command.

The COBOL program does not have to account for the page overflow line number since OS/400 will raise the end-of-page condition at the appropriate time (based on the page size). The COBOL program will continue to write records and handle the end-of-page condition when it occurs.

9.6.2 Overriding printer file names

It is sometimes necessary to redirect output to a completely different print file. Consider an application that contains reports that are available in a variety of foreign languages. The data fields in the print files must be defined similarly; however, the constants and page formatting may be different. The OVRPRTF command can be used to redirect the output to a different printer file (see Fig. 9.6). This override would cause a program to write to the SALESSPN (Spanish version) of the sales report instead of the original SALESRPT printer file.

```
OVRPRTF FILE(SALESRPT) TOFILE(SALESSPN)
```

Figure 9.6 Overriding to a different printer file.

9.6.3 Using a generic override

The OVRPRTF command allows you to have one override for all the printer files in your job with the same set of values. Without the generic override, you would have to do a separate override for every printer file. By specifying *PRTF as the file name on the OVRPRTF command, you can apply one override to all printer files.

9.6.4 Overrides and the current call level

An override will remain in effect until the override is deleted, the job terminates, or the user signs off. Additionally, an override will automatically be deleted when its call level is no longer active. It is good programming practice to always delete any overrides created.

Figure 9.7 illustrates how the call stack affects an override's effectiveness. When CL Program 1 begins, it overrides printer file SALESRPT to print two copies, then it calls CL Program 2. When CL Program 2 starts, the override from CL Program 1 is in effect. It adds two additional overrides (page size and LPI), then calls a COBOL program. When the COBOL program prints, it will utilize all overrides (copies, LPI, page size). When CL Program 2 terminates, control returns to CL Program 1. The overrides specified in CL Program 2 are NOT in effect—the call level at which they were defined no longer exists; thus they were automatically deleted. When CL Program 1 then calls CL Program 3, only the COPIES(2) override is in effect.

```
CL Program 1
   OVRPRTF FILE(SALESRPT) COPIES(2)
   CALL CL Program 2
   CALL CL Program 3
End

CL Program 2
   OVRPRTF FILE(SALESRPT) PAGESIZE(88 132) LPI(8)
   CALL COBOL program
   Return
End

CL Program 3
   CALL COBOL program
End
```

Figure 9.7 Overrides based on the call level.

9.6.5 Displaying overrides

You can display the overrides that are currently in effect for a specific printer file or for all printer files. Figure 9.8 displays the overrides for printer file SALESRPT.

```
DSPOVR FILE(SALESRPT)
```

Figure 9.8 Displaying current overrides for a printer file.

You can also request to see all overrides in effect (see Fig. 9.9) for all files (not just printer files).

```
DSPOVR FILE(*ALL)
```

Figure 9.9 Displaying current overrides for a printer file.

9.6.6 Deleting overrides

Overrides can be manually deleted with the DLTOVR command.

9.7 DDS for Printer Files

Table 9.2 lists the various DDS keywords specific to printer files. For a complete description of each keyword, see the *AS/400 DDS Reference*.

9.8 Summary

COBOL/400 programs can produce printed output by using either program-described printer files or externally described printer files. A COBOL program that uses a program-described printer file is responsible for maintaining all constants, spacing, formatting, etc. A program that uses an external printer file is concerned only with providing the data fields to the printer file. Formatting instructions are maintained within the printer file.

TABLE 9.2 DDS Keywords for Printer Files

DDS keyword	Level	Description
ALIAS	Field	Alternative name to use when copying DDS at compile time
BARCODE	Field	Prints field as user-specified bar code; valid for IPDS printers

TABLE 9.2 (*Continued*)

DDS keyword	Level	Description
BLKFOLD	Field	For multiline fields; causes line folding to occur at a blank instead of at the end of the physical line
BOX	Record	Draws a box on the page
CDEFNT	Field and record	Specifies the coded font for printing named or constant fields
CHRID	Field	Specifies alternative graphic character set to use instead of the device's default
CHRSIZ	Field and record	Expands the width and height of a record or field
COLOR	Field	Specifies the color for a field if supported by the printer device
CPI	Field and record	Specifies characters per inch
CVTDTA	Field	Converts character data to hexadecimal data when the field is passed to the printer
DATE	Field	Displays the current job date
DFNCHR	File and record	For 5224/5225 printers—allows custom characters to be defined
DFT	Field	Specifies a constant value for a constant field.
DLTEDT	Field	Directs OS/400 to ignore any edit code or edit word associated with a field that was referenced from another file
DRAWER	Record	Specifies drawer from which noncontinuous forms will be selected
EDTCDE	Field	Specifies an edit code for a field
EDTWRD	Field	Specifies an edit word for a field
ENDPAGE	Record	Causes a form feed (page eject)
FLTFIXDEC	Field	Prints floating-point number in fixed decimal notation
FLTPCN	Field	Specifies floating-point number precision
FNTCHRSET	Field and record	Specifies font character set for printing fields within a record
FONT	Field and record	Specifies the font identification for printing
GDF	Record	Used for inclusion of graphic data files
HIGHLIGHT	Field and record	Causes bold printing
IGCCDEFNT	Field and record	Used to print DBCS data contained in the AFPDS
INDARA	File	Removes option indicators from the I/O buffer and puts them in a 99-byte separate indicator area

TABLE 9.2 (*Continued*)

DDS keyword	Level	Description
INDTXT	File, field, and record	Used to associate descriptive text with an indicator
LINE	Record	Causes a line to be drawn on the page
LPI	File	Specifies lines per inch
MSGCON	Field	Specifies that the text for a constant field is to be taken from a message file
OVERLAY	Record	Specifies the inclusion of an overlay to be printed at a specific location
PAGNBR	Field	Specifies a four-digit zoned decimal field to contain the page number
PAGRTT	Record	Specifies the degree of rotation of the text with respect to the way the page is loaded into the printer; valid on only some printers
PAGSEG	Record	Includes a page segment at a specific location on the page
POSITION	Field	Specifies the position of a field using the unites specified on the unit of measure (UOM) parameter on the CRTPRTF command
PRTQLTY	Field and record	Specifies the print quality
REF	File	Names a file where field descriptions are contained
REFFLD	Field	Retrieves field attributes for current field from another file
SKIPA	File, field, and record	Causes the printer to skip to a specific line number after printing
SKIPB	File, field, and record	Causes the printer to skip to a specific line number before printing
SPACEA	Field and record	Causes the printer to space some number of lines after it prints the current item
SPACEB	Field and record	Causes the printer to space some number of lines before it prints the current item
TEXT	Field and record	Used for supplying a comment relating to a record or field definition
TIME	Field	Prints the current time
TRNSPY	Field	Prevents code points you have redefined (using DFNCHR keyword) from being interpreted as SCS printer control commands when the program sends an output operation that prints the field being defined
TXTRTT	Field	Specifies text rotation for the current field
UNDERLINE	Field	Causes the current field to be underlined

Part

4

Command Language

Command language (CL) is the main job control language for OS/400. Unlike many job control languages, CL can be complied to form an executable program.

Chapter 10 will introduce you to writing programs in CL. It discusses the structure of a CL program. It also covers a wide variety of CL-related topics such as how to obtain system information, accessing data areas and data queues, and using files and the open query file (OPNQRYF) command. Chapter 10 concludes with several useful sample programs that illustrates most of the topics covered.

Chapter 11 discusses OS/400's file journaling capabilities and how to use them. File journaling is OS/400's way of recovering after an abnormal job termination (or system shutdown). It also facilitates commitment control, a function that allows programs to "undue" changes made to a database.

Chapter 12 introduces messages and message files. Programs, users, and the system can all communicate among each other using OS/400 messages. Messages either can be immediate (when the user types the message text or it is hard coded in a program) or can be taken from message files. Message files are used to hold predefined messages.

Command Language Programming Basics

On the AS/400 computer, the set of commands that control the actions of the OS/400 system are called *control language* (CL). CL is the primary mode of communication between users, programs, and the operating system. CL commands act as the front-end processors to programs written in any of the AS/400 high-level languages.

This chapter provides a compact introduction to the various aspects of writing CL programs and CL commands. Additional information can be found in the *AS/400 CL Programmer's Guide* and the *AS/400 CL Reference*.

10.1 Overview

A single control language statement is called a command. Commands can be entered by a user (at a workstation), as part of a batch job, or as source statements that form a CL program.

All CL commands use a consistent syntax and are given names that conform to the naming standard set forth by OS/400. For example, the WRKCTLD command works with controller descriptions and the WRKOBJ command works with objects. All commands use the VERB + NOUN metaphor (with some minor exceptions). Even after a limited exposure to using the AS/400, you will quickly become familiar with the intuitive command naming conventions.

Prompting is supported for all CL commands. Prompting allows the user to use the F4=Prompt key to obtain a fill-in-the-blank form containing all of the command's parameters. Default values for most command parameters are supplied. The command processor checks the validity of all entries to make sure that the command is correct before it is executed.

10.1.1 Relationship between CL programs and CL commands

A CL program is not the same as a CL command:

- A CL command is a single executable command, optionally having a set of parameters. A CL command acts as a front-end processor to an OS/400 program.

- A CL program is a collection of one or more CL commands. A CL program may contain conditional logic, looping, branching, etc. CL programs must be compiled before they can be used (unless submitted as a job stream to batch). Once compiled, it can be executed with the CALL command.

If you have been following along with the examples in this book, you have already been exposed to a variety of CL commands (CRTPF, CRTPRTF, CHGCURLIB, CRTLIB, and STRSEU to name a few).

In most instances, a CL program will perform any preexecution tasks necessary before another high-level language program is executed. For example, it may be necessary to create a temporary file, establish a file override, and set up the local data area (LDA) before executing a COBOL or RPG program. The chain of events may appear as follows:

1. A user selects an option from a menu.
2. The menu option is related to a single CL command that executes a CL program.
3. The CL program creates a temporary file in library QTEMP, overrides the printer file to make two copies of the output, and then calls a COBOL program.
4. When the COBOL program completes, control returns to the CL program, which then ends.

Starting with Sec. 10.2, the basics of writing CL programs will be explained. Section 10.9 will explain the details of creating commands.

10.1.2 Messages, message files, and message queues

OS/400 supports a variety of different types of messages:

- *Program to user:* A program can direct a message to the user of the program, other users, or the system operator.

- *Program to program:* A program can send a message to another program. Messages are not limited to just error or status alerts—they can relate any information necessary.

- *User to user:* A user can send a message to another user on the system (including the system operator).

Sending messages between programs can play an important role in the design of object-oriented systems on the AS/400; therefore the use of messages should be considered during the design phase of an application.

When a message is sent, it is sent to a message queue. Messages sent to message queues will remain in the queue until the message is received by a program or user, or until the message queue is explicitly cleared. Status messages can also be sent to the current workstation user to inform them of the progress of a job.

Messages can be defined in message files that are kept separately from the programs that use them. Using message files is efficient since their use is not restricted to a single program. Messages can be defined in the message file and used by all programs within the application. When messages are changed within the message file, the programs that use them will not require any maintenance. Message files also make translating an application into a foreign language easier.

Messages, message queues, and message files will be covered in more detail in Chap. 12.

10.1.3 Debugging

OS/400 provides the developer with a set of tools for debugging. The standard debugger allows for the following:

- Setting a breakpoint and stopping a running program at any named point in the program's source file. For CL programs, the source line number is the named point; for COBOL, it is the line number generated by the COBOL compiler.

- Displaying and/or modifying the contents of a program variable.

- Tracing the use of a variable by recording the steps in the program that modify the variable, as well as recording the changes.

A complete list of commands related to debugging can be seen by typing the GO CMDDBG command on a command line. This book will not explain the use of the debugging commands.

GO, CMD (ANY)

10.1.4   Parameter prompting while editing
with SEU using the source entry utility

Since CL commands often have many parameters, it is difficult to remember all the parameter names and possible values when writing a
CL program. To help in writing CL programs, the source entry utility
(SEU) allows you to use the F4=Prompt key when editing your programs.

To start SEU for the entry of a CL program, use the following command:

```
STRSEU SRCFILE(library-name/source-file-name) SRCMBR(member-name) TYPE(CLP)
```

The IBM-recommended name for a CL source physical file is QCLSRC.
Once in SEU, type a CL command and then press F4. SEU will invoke
the CL command prompter for the command. When you press Enter,
the command will be inserted into your source program.

10.2   CL Program Structure

Generally, a CL program is a group of CL commands that can:

- Automate a set of repetitively performed actions

- Prepare the environment for a user (such as set up library lists and
  create objects)

- Organize an application by specifying where to get input, how to
  process it, and where to place the results

Most CL commands can be processed interactively by typing the
command on the command line. Commands that are grouped together
and kept in a source file comprise a CL program.

A CL program has the following form:

```
PGM (optional)        Defines any parameters to be received by the program
DCL                   Variable declarations
DCLF                  File declarations
MONMSG                Global message handler
Program body
RETURN (optional)
ENDPGM
```

A CL program is entered using SEU with a source type of CLP (CL
program). To compile a CL program into an executable object, use the
CRTCLPGM command shown in Fig. 10.1. The following sections define in more detail the various parts of a CL program.

```
CRTCLPGM PGM(library-name/program-name) SRCFILE(QCLSRC)
```

Figure 10.1 Create a CL program command.

10.2.1 PGM command

The PGM command defines the beginning of a CL program. It is optional unless the program receives parameters. The format of the PGM command is

```
PGM    PARM(&PARM1 &PARM2 ...)
```

10.2.2 DCL and DCLF commands

The DCL and DCLF commands declare to the CL program any variables and files that are referenced. Parameters specified in the PARM keyword of the PGM command must also be declared. Figure 10.2 shows an example of using the DCL command to declare a character variable. CL variable names always begin with an ampersand (&) and are up to 10 characters long. Declaring variables will be discussed in Sec. 10.3, and using files will be discussed in Sec. 10.8.

```
PGM        PARM(&ACCTNAME)
DCL        VAR(&ACCTNAME) TYPE(*CHAR) LEN(30)
```

Figure 10.2 Example of declaring a character variable.

10.2.3 Message monitoring (local and global)

The monitor message (MONMSG) command is used to detect when a specific message has been sent back from a step within the CL program. For example, if the command

```
CHKOBJ OBJ(YOURFILE) OBJTYPE(*FILE)
```

is executed and YOURFILE is not found, the CHKOBJ command will send message CPF9801 back to the CL program that issued the command. By using the MONMSG command, the CL program can be made aware of the condition and take necessary action.

Any monitor message commands (MONMSG) that appear *before* the first executable CL statement is monitored throughout the entire CL program. For example, if the MONMSG CPF9801 command is issued at the beginning of the program, an implied MONMSG for message

CPF9801 will be issued after every command in the program. This is very useful for trapping unexpected errors or when the same operation is repeatedly executed throughout the program.

Details on message monitoring will be discussed later in this chapter in Sec. 10.2.6.

10.2.4   Program body

The program body contains the actions necessary to perform the function of the CL program. The body of the CL program can contain the following:

- Conditional control commands such as IF, THEN, ELSE, DO, ENDDO, and GOTO
- Built-in functions such as %SUBSTRING (or %SST), %BINARY, and %SWITCH
- Program control commands such as CALL, RETURN, and TFRCTL

10.2.5   ENDPGM command

The optional ENDPGM command marks the end of the CL program.

10.2.6   Monitoring for errors using MONMSG

When a CL command encounters a problem and terminates unsuccessfully, it sends an escape message to the calling program. CL programs can monitor for these escape messages and can take the appropriate action if necessary. For example, if a CL program issues the CHKOBJ command and the object is not found, an "object not found" escape message is sent to the program by the CHKOBJ command.

The monitor message (MONMSG) command directs the CL program to take a predetermined action (or no action) if a specific error occurs during the processing of the *immediately preceding* command. For a detailed description of the MONMSG command and its associated parameters, type the word MONMSG on a command line and press the F4=Prompt key.

Figure 10.3 illustrates the use of the MONMSG command for the scenario discussed earlier. The MSGID parameter specifies the message that is to be monitored after the CHKOBJ command is executed. GOTO NOTFOUND is the command that is to be executed should this condition occur.

The MONMSG command does not always have to specify the EXEC parameter. In some cases, the error condition may be acceptable. For

```
            .
            .
CHKOBJ OBJ(YOURFILE) TYPE(*FILE)
MONMSG MSGID(CPF9801) EXEC(GOTO NOTFOUND)
            .
            .
```

Figure 10.3 Checking the existence of a file with CHKOBJ and MONMSG.

example, if a file is to be deleted but it does not exist when the DLTF command is executed, an error will occur and the user will be notified. In this case, it is acceptable for the command to fail, since its failure would indicate that the file may have already been deleted. Omitting the EXEC simply accepts the escape message and allows processing to continue without interrupting the user. Figure 10.4 shows a case when no action is taken when a message is received.

```
DLTF FILE(YOURFILE)
MONMSG CPF2105
```

Figure 10.4 Taking no action when an error occurs.

Specifying the message identifier. A message identifier must take the form of "pppmmnn":

- ppp identifies the licensed program that owns the message
- mmnn indicates the message number

CPF9801 is an example of an OS/400 message identifier.

10.2.6.2 Monitoring for generic messages. Generic messages for a particular program product can be monitored by specifying the message identifier in the format pppmm00. Monitoring for message CPF5100 would result in all messages CPF5101 through CPF5199 being monitored.

You can also specify the message identifier in the form ppp0000. This will monitor for any messages starting with ppp. Monitoring for message CPF0000 would monitor for all messages beginning with CPF. Optionally, you can monitor for message CPF9999, which will match against any message sent from any program.

10.2.7   Operators in expressions

Operators are used in expressions to indicate an action to be performed on the operands in the expression or the relationship between the operands. There are four kinds of operators:

- Arithmetic operators (+, −, *, /)
- Character operators (| |, |>, |<)
- Logical operators (&, |, ¬)
- Relational operators (=, >, <, >=, <=, ¬=, ¬>, ¬<)

Table 10.1 shows the various operators that you can use in a CL program.

TABLE 10.1   CL Operators

Predefined value	Predefined symbol	Meaning	Type
	+	Addition	Arithmetic operator
	−	Subtraction	Arithmetic operator
	*	Multiplication	Arithmetic operator
	/	Division	Arithmetic operator
*CAT	| |	Concatenation	Character string operator
*BCAT	|>	Blank insertion with concatenation	Character string operator
*TCAT	|<	Blank truncation with concatenation	Character string operator
*AND	&	AND	Logical operator
*OR	|	OR	Logical operator
*NOT	¬	NOT	Logical operator
*EQ	=	Equal	Relational operator
*GT	>	Greater than	Relational operator
*LT	<	Less than	Relational operator
*GE	>=	Greater than or equal	Relational operator
*LE	<=	Less than or equal	Relational operator
*NE	¬=	Not equal	Relational operator
*NG	¬>	Not greater than	Relational operator
*NL	¬<	Not less than	Relational operator

10.2.8   Example CL program

The program in Listing 10.1 accepts two parameters: a library name and a program name. It first verifies that the program exists in the specified library. If the program exists, it is called. If it does not exist, a different program is called.

Listing 10.1 Example CL program.

```
           PGM        PARM(&LIBNAME &PGMNAME)
           DCL        VAR(&LIBNAME) TYPE(*CHAR) LEN(10)
           DCL        VAR(&PGMNAME) TYPE(*CHAR) LEN(10)
           MONMSG     CPF9999
           CHKOBJ     &LIBNAME/&PGMNAME *PGM
           MONMSG     MSGID(CPF9801) EXEC(GOTO NOTFOUND)
           CALL       &LIBNAME/&PGMNAME
           RETURN
NOTFOUND:  CALL       ERRPGM
           ENDPGM
```

- This program must be called with two parameters: a library name and a program name.

- Two string variables are declared, &LIBNAME and &PGMNAME; both are 10 characters long.

- A global MONMSG is issued for CPF9999, which will trap any message sent to the program. No EXEC parameter is specified, so processing will continue uninterrupted.

- The CHKOBJ command verifies whether the program exists or not. If the CHKOBJ command cannot find the object, message CPF9801 will be sent to this program. The MONMSG command immediately following will trap this error message and transfer control to label NOTFOUND. Otherwise, processing continues with the next statement and the specified program is called.

10.3   CL Variables

CL provides a limited, yet useful set of commands for declaring and manipulating variables. CL supports the following types of variables:

- *Character:* Strings may be up to 9999 characters long.

- *Packed decimal:* Decimal values can be up to 15 digits with as many as 9 decimal positions.

- *Logical:* Value can be either "0" (OFF or FALSE) or "1" (ON or TRUE).

If a variable is not initialized when it is declared, it is automatically initialized to zero for decimal numbers, blank for strings, and zero (or FALSE) for logical variables.

CL variable names must begin with an ampersand (&) followed by as many as 10 characters. The first character following the ampersand must be alphabetic; the remaining characters may be alphanumeric.

10.3.1 Declaring variables

Variables are declared in a CL program using the DCL command. The program in Listing 10.1 shows the following two variable declarations:

```
DCL VAR(&LIBNAME) TYPE(*CHAR) LEN(10)
DCL VAR(&PGMNAME) TYPE(*CHAR) LEN(10)
```

The first declares a string variable named &LIBNAME to have a length of 10 characters. The second DCL command declares another string named &PGMNAME, which is also 10 characters long.

The following examples show a variety of different variable declarations:

Example 1	DCL VAR(&DECVAR) TYPE(*DEC) LEN(7 2)
Example 2	DCL VAR(&COUNTER) TYPE(*DEC) LEN(3) VALUE(25)
Example 3	DCL VAR(&NAME) TYPE(*CHAR) LEN(20) VALUE('Hello')
Example 4	DCL &NAME *CHAR 15

- Example 1 shows a decimal variable named &DECVAR being declared as length 7 with 2 decimal places.

- Example 2 shows a decimal variable named &COUNTER being declared with length 3. It is also being initialized to the value 25. If the decimal position is zero, it may be omitted [if it were not omitted in this example, the variable would be declared with LEN(30) instead of LEN(3)].

- Example 3 shows a string variable named &NAME that is being initialized to the value 'Hello'. If the value was in only upper case and contained no spaces, the single quote marks could be omitted.

- Example 4 shows a shorthand method of declaring a variable. The keywords VAR, TYPE, LEN, and VALUE may be omitted if the values are presented in the correct order (name, type, length, and value). Note: If the variable is a decimal variable and the length contains one or more decimal places, the LEN keyword must be used as in the following example:

```
DCL &DECVAR *DEC LEN(7 2)
```

- Furthermore, once a keyword is specified, positional values can no longer be used.

```
DCL &DECVAR *DEC LEN(7 2) 3.5   ** Incorrect
```

- This is invalid because the initial value of 3.5 is specified without the keyword VALUE:

```
DCL &DECVAR *DEC LEN(7 2) VALUE(3.5)   ** Correct
```

10.3.2 Changing the value of a variable

You can change the value of a CL program variable using the change variable (CHGVAR) command. The following examples show how to use the CHGVAR command:

```
CHGVAR VAR(&A) VALUE(25)
```

or

```
CHGVAR &A 25
```

In this example, variable &A is changed to the value of 25. Both commands are identical—the first uses keywords for each parameter; the second uses positional parameters.

In the next example, variable &A is changed to the current value of variable &B:

```
CHGVAR VAR(&A) VALUE(&B)
```

or

```
CHGVAR &A &B
```

The next example shows variable &A being incremented by 1:

```
CHGVAR VAR (&A) VALUE(&A + 1)
```

or

```
CHGVAR &A (&A + 1)
```

10.3.3 The %SUBSTRING function

The substring function (%SUBSTRING or %SST) produces a character string that is a subset of an existing string. The substring function can be used in both the VAR and VALUE parameters of the CHGVAR command.

The format of the substring function is

```
%SUBSTRING(charVariableName startingPosition length)
```

or

```
%SST(charVariableName startingPosition length)
```

If charVariableName is specified as *LDA, the substring function is performed on the contents of the local data area.

The substring function produces a substring from the contents of the specified CL variable (or the local data area). The substring begins at the specified starting position (which can be a variable name) and continues for the length specified (which can also be a variable name).

Listing 10.2 shows examples of the substring function.

Listing 10.2 CL program with several CHGVAR commands.

```
      PGM
[1]   DCL VAR(&A) TYPE(*CHAR) LEN(15)
[2]   DCL VAR(&B) TYPE(*CHAR) LEN(15) VALUE('ABCDEFGHIJKLMNO')
[3]   CHGVAR VAR(&A) VALUE(%SST(&B 10 1)
[4]   CHGVAR VAR(%SST(&A 4 5) VALUE('HELLO')
[5]   IF (%SST(&A 1 1) *EQ 'J') THEN(...
[6]   CHGVAR %SST(*LDA 1 10) VALUE(&B)
      ENDPGM
```

1. Line 1 declares variable &A as a string of length = 15 characters.

2. Line 2 declares variable &B as a string of length = 15 characters and initializes it to the string 'ABCDEFGHIJKLMNO'.

3. Line 3 changes &A to the value of the 10th character in variable &B. After this command, &A has the value 'Jbbbbbbbbbbbbbb'.

4. Line 4 changes a substring of variable &A starting at position 4 for a length of five characters, and assigns it the value 'HELLO'. After this command executes, &A's value is 'JbbHELLObbbbbbb'.

5. Line 5 tests the first character of variable &A for the value 'J'.

6. Line 6 changes the first ten characters of the local data area (*LDA) to the first ten characters of variable &B.

10.3.4   The %SWITCH function

Each job on the AS/400 has a set of eight program switches that are available for use by CL programs. Each switch maintains one of two states: ON is represented by "1", and OFF is represented by "0". The initial values of all eight switches are determined by the job description. The default value for the switches is '00000000'.

The syntax of the %SWITCH function is

```
%SWITCH(8-character-mask)
```

The eight-character mask is used to indicate the job switches to be tested and the value each switch is to be tested for. Each position in the mask corresponds to one of the eight job switches. Each position in the mask can be specified as one of three values:

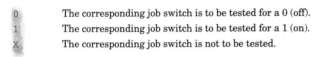

0	The corresponding job switch is to be tested for a 0 (off).
1	The corresponding job switch is to be tested for a 1 (on).
X	The corresponding job switch is not to be tested.

If %SWITCH(XX1001X1) is specified, job switches 3, 6, and 8 are tested for 1s; switches 4 and 5 are tested for 0s; and switches 1, 2, and 7 are ignored.

A CL program can change the value of one or more switches with the CHGJOB command by specifying the SWS parameter.

The program in Listing 10.3 illustrates several examples of the %SWITCH function.

Listing 10.3 Example of using the %SWITCH function.

```
      PGM
[1]   CHGJOB SWS(10110001)
[2]   IF %SWITCH(0XXXXXXX) THEN(...
[3]   IF %SWITCH(XX1X0XXX) THEN(...
[4]   IF %SWITCH(00110001) THEN(...
[5]   IF %SWITCH(10110001) THEN(...
      ENDPGM
```

1. Line 1 changes the current switch settings to 10110001.

2. Line 2 tests only the first switch for 0 (off). The results of the %SWITCH function will be FALSE.

3. Line 3 tests switch 3 for a 1 (on) and switch 5 for 0 (off). The results of the %SWITCH function will be TRUE.

4. Line 4 tests for an exact match of all eight switches against the mask 00110001. The value of %SWITCH will be FALSE, since they do not match the current job switches exactly.

5. Line 5 tests for an exact match of all eight switches against the mask 10110001. The value of %SWITCH will be TRUE, since they all match the job switches exactly.

10.3.5   The %BINARY function

It is often necessary to provide certain functions with a binary value rather than a packed decimal number. This is often the case when using OS/400 system APIs. The %BINARY (or %BIN) function interprets the contents of a specified CL character variable as a signed binary integer.

The syntax of the binary function is

```
%BINARY(variable-name starting-position length)
```

or

```
%BIN(variable-name starting-position length)
```

The starting-position and length are both optional; they will default to a starting position of 1 and a length of the character variable specified. The character variable must be declared with a length of either two or four characters.

A 2-byte character variable can hold a signed binary integer with values from −32768 through 32767. A 4-byte character variable can hold a signed binary integer with values from −2,147,483,648 through 2,147,483,647.

Listing 10.4 shows how to convert from a binary number to a decimal number. The CHGVAR command assigns the results of the %BINARY function to the numeric variable &NUM. The %BINARY function will treat &B2 as a 2-byte signed binary integer and convert to its decimal equivalent of 28. The variable &NUM will contain the value 28.

Listing 10.4 Converting from a binary to a decimal number.

```
DCL     VAR(&B2) TYPE(*CHAR) LEN(2) VALUE(X'001C')
DCL     VAR(&NUM) TYPE(*DEC) LEN(3 0)
CHGVAR &NUM %BINARY(&B2)
```

The example in Listing 10.5 shows how to convert a decimal number to a signed binary number. The value of the decimal variable &N is converted to a 2-byte signed binary number and then placed in character variable &B2. Variable &B2 will have the value of X'001C'.

Listing 10.5 Converting from a decimal to 2-byte binary number.

```
DCL     VAR(&B2) TYPE(*CHAR) LEN(2)
DCL     VAR(&NUM) TYPE(*DEC) LEN(3 0) VALUE(28).
CHGVAR %BIN(&B2) &NUM
```

10.4 Program Control

Commands in a CL program are processed consecutively, starting with the first command, until either a command alters the flow of the program or the end of the program is reached. This section deals with the various commands that can conditionally or unconditionally alter the flow of a CL program.

10.4.1 Using the GOTO command

The GOTO command unconditionally alters the flow of the program. Processing is directed to another part of the program (identified by a label). The GOTO command can cause the program to branch either forward or backward.

The GOTO command has one parameter that contains the label of the destination statement:

```
GOTO CMDLBL(label)
```

or

```
GOTO label
```

Figure 10.5 shows how to use the GOTO statement. The label in this figure is START. A label can contain up to 10 characters and must be immediately followed by a colon.

```
            PGM
            .
            .
START:      IF .....
            .
            .
            .
            GOTO START
            ENDPGM
```

Figure 10.5 Example of using the GOTO command.

10.4.2 Using the IF and ELSE commands

The IF command is used to test a condition and execute a CL command based on whether the condition is TRUE or FALSE. The syntax of the IF command is

```
IF COND(logical-expression) THEN(CL-command)
```

The logical-expression in the COND parameter is first evaluated. If the expression evaluates to TRUE, the program processes the CL command on the THEN parameter. This may be a single command, or a group of commands (see Sec. 10.4.2.3 for more details on the DO command). Listing 10.6 shows an example of using the IF command:

Listing 10.6 Examples of using the IF command.

```
        PGM      PARM(&PARM1 &PARM2)
        DCL      VAR(&PARM1) TYPE(*CHAR) LEN(1)
        DCL      VAR(&PARM2) TYPE(*CHAR) LEN(10)
[1]     IF       COND(&PARM1='1') THEN(CALL PGM1)
[2]     IF       (&PARM1 *EQ '2') CALL PGM2
[3]     IF       (&PARM1 *NE '3') CHGVAR &PARM2 'HELLO'
        ENDPGM
```

1. In line 1, the variable &PARM1 is compared for equality to the string '1', and if it is equal, program PGM1 will be called.

2. Line 2 compares &PARM2 for equality with the string '2'. If they are equal, PGM2 will be called.

3. Line 3 checks for &PARM1's inequality with the constant '3'. If it is not equal, &PARM2's value is changed to the constant 'HELLO'.

The **ELSE** command specifies the processing to perform should the condition in an **IF** statement evaluate to FALSE. The format of the **ELSE** command is

```
ELSE CMD(cl-command)
```

The cl-command can be any CL command, as well as a DO group, as discussed later in Sec. 10.4.2.3.

Figure 10.6 shows how to code an **IF-THEN-ELSE** structure. If the contents of variables &A and &B are equivalent, then program PGMX will be called, otherwise PGMY will be called.

```
IF (&A = &B) THEN(CALL PGMX)
ELSE CMD(CALL PGMY)
```

Figure 10.6 Using an IF-THEN-ELSE construct.

10.4.2.1 Nested IF statements. Up to 10 levels of IF commands may be nested. The following example shows how to code a nested IF command:

```
IF COND(&OPT = 1) THEN(CALL PGM(ADDPHNE))
    ELSE CMD(IF COND(&OPT = 2) THEN(CALL PGM(CHGPHNE)))
        ELSE CMD(IF COND(&OPT = 3) THEN(CALL PGM(DLTPHNE)))
            ELSE CMD(CALL PGM(PRTPHNE))
```

10.4.2.2 Using *AND, *OR, and *NOT. It is often necessary to test more than one condition within a single IF command. You can use the *AND, *OR, and *NOT logical operators to connect multiple conditions:

```
IF ((&A = &B) *AND (&C = &B)) CALL PGMA
```

In order for this expression to evaluate to TRUE, both logical expressions must evaluate to TRUE. &A must equal &B, and &C must equal &B.

```
IF ((&A = &B) *OR (&C = &B)) CALL PGMA
```

In this expression, either one of the two logical expressions may be true in order to make the entire IF condition true. Either &A must equal &B or &C must equal &B. If either one or both of these tests are TRUE, the entire IF evaluates to TRUE and PGMA will be called:

```
DCL VAR(&A) TYPE(*LGL)
DCL VAR(&B) TYPE(*LGL)
  .
  .
IF (&A *AND &B) CALL PGMA
```

Both variable &A and &B are declared as type logical. If &A's value is TRUE and &B's value is TRUE, then PGMA will be called.

10.4.2.3 Grouping commands with DO and ENDDO. The DO command allows you to put a group of CL commands in place of a single command. DO groups are most commonly used with the IF, ELSE, and MONMSG commands.

The following example shows a typical example of using a DO group within an IF command:

```
IF (&A *EQ &B) THEN(DO)
    DLTF QTEMP/FILE1
    DLTF QTEMP/FILE2
    DLTF QTEMP/FILE3
ENDDO
ELSE CMD(DO)
    DLTF QTEMP/FILE4
    DLTF QTEMP/FILE5
ENDDO
```

Normally, only a single command could be put in the THEN parameter. In this case, the DO group consists of three DLTF commands. The end of the group is marked by the ENDDO command.

Figure 10.7 shows how a DO group may be used with the MONMSG command. In this example, the check object command checks to see if FILE1 exists in library QTEMP. If the object does not exist, message

```
CHKOBJ QTEMP/FILE1 *FILE
MONMSG MSGID(CPF9801) EXEC(DO)
   CRTPF FILE(QTEMP/FILE1) RCDLEN(80)
   CHGDTAARA DTAARA(*LDA (1 5)) VALUE('FILE1')
ENDDO
```

Figure 10.7 Using the DO command with the MONMSG command.

CPF9801 will be sent from the CHKOBJ command to the CL program. If the MONMSG command traps message CPF9801, it will execute the CL command in the EXEC parameter (a DO group). Therefore, if the CHKOBJ command fails (does not find the file), the create physical file command will create a new file in QTEMP and the local data area will be updated with the name FILE1.

10.4.3   Calling other programs using CALL

The CALL command calls the program named on the command. When the called program finishes running, control returns to the next command in the calling program. The CALL command has the following format:

```
CALL PGM(library-name/program-name) PARM(parameter-values)
```

The program name and/or library name may be specified as variables; however, you must use separate variables for the name and library—they cannot be combined in one variable. If the called program is in a library that is not in the library list, you must specify the qualified name of the program.

Figure 10.8 shows several examples of the CALL command.

```
[1]     CALL PGM(MYPROG)
[2]     CALL PGM(MYLIB/MYPROG) PARM(25 'Y')
[3]     CALL &PGMVAR
[4]     CALL MYPROG 25
```

Figure 10.8 Examples of using the CALL command.

Line 1	A CALL command with no parameters. Since no library name was specified, the library list (*LIBL) will be searched for MYPROG. When MYPROG finishes executing, control will return to line 2.
Line 2	A CALL command that specifies a qualified program name and two parameters.
Line 3	A CALL command that has the destination program name stored in variable &PGMVAR.

Line 4   A CALL command that uses positional parameters instead of key-
                           words.

10.4.3.1 Passing parameters with the CALL command.

The CALL command has the ability to send constants and variables as parameters to a called program. A maximum of 40 parameters can be passed to the called program. The values of the parameters are passed in the order in which they appear in the CALL command, and the order must match the order in which they appear in the parameter list (or linkage section) of the called program. The names of the variables passed do not have to be the same as the names in the receiving parameter list.

All parameters are passed by reference, which means that no storage is allocated for the parameters in the called program. Instead, the variable is stored in the calling program.

When the called program makes any modifications to variables in the parameter list, the changes are reflected in the calling program as well; thus no special action is necessary to return values back to the calling program.

10.4.4 Transferring control using TFRCTL

The TFRCTL command is similar to the CALL command except that when the destination program finishes executing, control is *not* returned to the caller. The TFRCTL command has the following format:

```
TFRCTL PGM(library-name/program-name) PARM(CL-variable)
```

Both the library name and/or program name may be specified as variables.

10.4.4.1 Passing parameters with TFRCTL.

An important difference between TFRCTL and CALL is how parameters are handled. The TFRCTL command can only pass variables as parameters. Furthermore, the TFRCTL command cannot pass a variable that was not passed to the program issuing the TFRCTL command.

Listing 10.7 shows a valid and invalid TFRCTL statement. Although the logic in this program is impossible, it illustrates the restrictions on parameter passing with the TFRCTL command.

Listing 10.7 Examples of the TFRCTL command.

```
PGM PARM(&VAR1)
DCL &VAR1 *CHAR LEN(10)
DCL &VAR2 *CHAR LEN(10)
TFRCTL PROG1 PARM(&VAR1)        /* Valid */
TFRCTL PROG2 PARM(&VAR2)        /* NOT valid */
TFRCTL PROG3 PARM('abc')        /* NOT valid */
ENDPGM
```

- The first TFRCTL is valid—&VAR1 is passed from another program to this program; therefore it can be used as a parameter on the TFRCTL command.

- The second TFRCTL is not valid because &VAR2 is declared in this program.

- The third TFRCTL is not valid because you cannot pass a constant as a parameter.

10.5   Obtaining System Information

It is often necessary to obtain system information such as the current user's identification or the system date and time from within a CL program. This section will introduce you to CL commands that retrieve information relating to the system as a whole, the current job, or a specific object in the system. The commands discussed in this section cannot be executed interactively—they must be executed within a CL program.

10.5.1   Retrieving system values

A system value contains information that is used by OS/400 to control the operation of the system. For example, there is a system value that specifies the name of the controlling subsystem at startup, as well as the name of a program that should be executed during the initial program load (IPL) of OS/400.

In general, applications should never need to change any of the system values. These are usually maintained by the security or system administrator.

You can retrieve system values into your program and manipulate them as variables using the retrieve system value (RTVSYSVAL) command:

```
RTVSYSVAL SYSVAL(systemvaluename) RTNVAR(clvariablename)
```

The systemvaluename specifies the name of the system value that you want to retrieve. For a complete list of systemvaluenames, enter the command: WRKSYSVAL

The clvariablename is the name of the variable in which the retrieved information should be placed. It must be the appropriate size for the value being retrieved.

For example, to retrieve the current date format, you can retrieve the system value that contains the current date format. The name of the system value is QDATFMT. Figure 10.9 shows an example of this. The RTNVAR parameter specifies variable &DFMT as the location for the

```
PGM
DCL VAR(&DFMT) TYPE(*CHAR) LEN(3)
RTVSYSVAL SYSVAL(QDATFMT) RTNVAR(&DFMT)
  .
  .
```

Figure 10.9 Retrieving the current date format.

returned date format. To determine the size and type of the return variable, first prompt the RTVSYSVAL command (using F4=Prompt); then move the cursor to the CL variable name field and press Help (if your keyboard does not have a Help key, you can also press the F1 key). You will be presented with a list of system values and the size of their associated return values.

10.5.2 Retrieving job attributes

The retrieve job attributes (RTVJOBA) command is used to obtain information about a job. As with system values, you can retrieve information about the current job and place it in CL variables. Some of the attributes are the identification of the current user, the job identification in the system, the job date, and the current output queue.

Figure 10.10 shows an example of how to retrieve the identification (ID) of the current user. By prompting the RTVJOBA command, you can see the list of attributes that can be retrieved. The destination CL variable must be defined appropriately to hold the retrieved data. The prompt display indicates the size of the variable required for each attribute that can be retrieved.

```
PGM
DCL  VAR(&USERID) TYPE(*CHAR) LEN(10)
  .
  .
RTVJOBA USER(&USERID)
  .
  .
```

Figure 10.10 Retrieving the current user's ID.

10.5.3 Retrieving an object's attributes

The retrieve object description command (RTVOBJD) works similar to that of RTVJOBA, except that it retrieves information relating to a particular object in the system. An object can be any AS/400-supported object such as a file, program, library, job, or subsystem. The RTVOBJD command can retrieve such information as the library where the object resides, the owner of the object, or the creation date, as well as many other object-related attributes.

It is often necessary to determine exactly the library in which an object is located. The retrieve object description can obtain this information. Figure 10.11 shows how to determine the library in which a file resides. After the RTVOBJ command is executed, the name of the library in which the file was found will be placed in variable &FOUNDLIB.

```
PGM
DCL &FOUNDLIB TYPE(*CHAR) LEN(10)
RTVOBJD OBJ(YOURFILE) OBJTYPE(*FILE) RTNLIB(&FOUNDLIB)
 .
 .
```

Figure 10.11   Determining the library in which an object resides.

10.6   Using Data Areas and Data Queues

A data area is an object that is used to hold data for access by any job running on the system. A data area is like a file with only one record.

A data queue is an object to which one program can send data and from which another program can receive data. The receiving program either can be waiting for the data or can randomly check to see whether data are available.

OS/400 supports manipulation of both data areas and data queues through a set of CL commands. This section describes how to create, use, and delete data areas and data queues.

10.6.1   Using data areas

A data area is similar to a file that contains a single record. Some high-level languages have commands that can manipulate data areas directly (CL and RPG both support data areas, but COBOL does not; however, COBOL does support the special data area *LDA).

10.6.1.1   Creating a data area.   The create data area (CRTDTAARA) command is used to create a new data area. You can specify the length of the data area, the type of data that goes in the data area, and an initial value for it. The following is the syntax for the create data area command:

```
CRTDTAARA DTAARA(lib/name) TYPE(data-type) LEN(length) VALUE(init-val)
```

The data type may be either decimal, character, or logical. The length is specified the same as a CL variable. You can optionally assign an initial value to the data area in the VALUE parameter. Once created, a data area will remain on the system until it is explicitly deleted.

10.6.1.2 Changing the value of a data area. The value of a data area can be changed by using the change data area (CHGDTAARA) command. The following is the syntax of the CHGDTAARA command:

```
CHGDTAARA DTAARA(lib-name/data-area-name (start length)) VALUE(value)
```

Start specifies the beginning position within the data area, and length specifies how many positions to change. Value contains the contents to be placed into the data area. Optionally, the keyword *ALL can be used in place of start and length.

10.6.1.3 Retrieving data from a data area. The retrieve data area (RTVDTAARA) command is used to obtain the contents of a data area and place the value in a CL variable. The format of the RTVDTAARA command is

```
RTVDTAARA DTAARA(lib-name/data-area-name (start length)) RTNVAR(CL-var-name)
```

The start position specifies the location within the data area from which to start retrieving. The length specifies the number of characters to retrieve. RTNVAR specifies the CL variable in which the data is to be stored. The contents of the data area remain unchanged by this command.

10.6.1.4 Displaying a data area. The display data area (DSPDTAARA) command is used to view the contents of a data area. The format of the DSPDTAARA command is

```
DSPDTAARA DTAARA(lib-name/data-area-name) OUTPUT(dest) OUTFMT(format)
```

Only the data area name is required. Specifying *PRINT for the destination will cause the contents of the data area to be printed. Specifying the OUTFMT as *HEX will show the contents of the data area in hexadecimal format.

10.6.1.5 Deleting a data area. A data area can be deleted by using the DLTDTAARA command. The following is the syntax for the DLTDTAARA command:

```
DLTDTAARA DTAARA(lib-name/data-area-name)
```

10.6.1.6   Accessing a data area from COBOL/400. As of version 2.3 of
COBOL/400, access to data areas other than the local data area is not
supported. This does not mean that you cannot obtain the contents of a
data area from within a COBOL program, however.

One way to update a data area is by having COBOL directly execute
the CL command CHGDTAARA. The command string can be built
within the COBOL program and the QCMDEXC program can be called
to execute it. Retrieving data from a data area cannot be done this way,
since the command that retrieves the data (RTVDTAARA) returns
data and QCMDEXC cannot pass the returned data back to a COBOL
program. To retrieve data, the QWCRDTAA API is used.

The following example shows a COBOL program that reads the contents of a data area, displays them on the workstation allowing the
user to modify the data, and then writes the data back to the data area.
It is assumed that the data area already exists. To create the data area
used by this program, use the following command:

```
CRTDTAARA DTAARA(TRYDTAARA) TYPE(*CHAR) LEN(40)
```

To start SEU, use the following command:

```
STRSEU SRCFILE(QLBLSRC) SRCMBR(EX1001) TYPE(CBL)
```

Use SEU to enter the COBOL program in Listing 10.8.

Listing 10.8   Program that reads and updates a data area.

```
MEMBER NAME: EX1001          FILE: QLBLSRC
....-..A...B..-....2....-....3....-....4....-....5....-....6....
        PROCESS EXTACCDSP
        IDENTIFICATION DIVISION.
        PROGRAM-ID.  EX1001.

        DATA DIVISION.
        WORKING-STORAGE SECTION.
        01  BIN4                    PIC S9(9) BINARY.

        01  API-ERROR.
            03 ERR-BYTPRO           LIKE BIN4 VALUE 116.
            03 ERR-BYTAVA           LIKE BIN4 VALUE 0.
[1]         03 ERR-EXCID            PIC X(7) VALUE SPACES.
            03 ERR-RSRVD            PIC X VALUE SPACE.
            03 ERR-EXCDTA           PIC X(100) VALUE SPACES.

        01  QWCRDTAA-PARMS.
            03 QWCRDTAA-RECEIVER.
               05 QWCRDTAA-BYTES-AVAIL    LIKE BIN4 VALUE 20.
               05 QWCRDTAA-BYTES-RETURNED LIKE BIN4.
               05 QWCRDTAA-VALUE-TYPE      PIC X(10).
               05 QWCRDTAA-RET-LIBRARY     PIC X(10).
[2]            05 QWCRDTAA-RET-LENGTH      LIKE BIN4.
               05 QWCRDTAA-RET-DECPOS      LIKE BIN4.
```

```
          05 QWCRDTAA-DATA            PIC X(20).
       03 QWCRDTAA-RCV-SIZE          LIKE BIN4.
       03 QWCRDTAA-QUAL-NAME.
          05 QWCRDTAA-AREANAME        PIC X(10) VALUE 'TRYDTAARA'.
          05 QWCRDTAA-LIBNAME         PIC X(10) VALUE '*LIBL'.
       03 QWCRDTAA-START-POS         LIKE BIN4 VALUE 1.
       03 QWCRDTAA-LENGTH            LIKE BIN4 VALUE 20.


    01  CHGDTAARA-COMMAND           PIC X(100).
    01  CHGDTAARA-CMD-LENGTH PIC 9(10)V9(5) COMP-3 VALUE 100.


    PROCEDURE DIVISION.
    MAIN-PARA.
[3]      MOVE LENGTH OF QWCRDTAA-RECEIVER TO QWCRDTAA-RCV-SIZE.


         CALL "QWCRDTAA" USING QWCRDTAA-RECEIVER
                               QWCRDTAA-RCV-SIZE
[4]                            QWCRDTAA-QUAL-NAME
                               QWCRDTAA-START-POS
                               QWCRDTAA-LENGTH
                               API-ERROR.


    DISPLAY "DATA VALUE:" LINE 12 COLUMN 2 WITH BLANK SCREEN.
    ACCEPT DATA-HOLDER FROM CRT AT LINE 12 COLUMN 20.


         STRING
            "CHGDTAARA DTAARA(TRYDTAARA) VALUE('" DELIMITED BY SIZE
[5]         QWCRDTAA-DATA DELIMITED BY SIZE
            "')" DELIMITED BY SIZE
            INTO CHGDTAARA-COMMAND.


[6]      CALL "QCMDEXC" USING CHGDTAARA-COMMAND
                             CHGDTAARA-CMD-LENGTH.


    STOP RUN.
```

Notes about the program in Listing 10.8:

1. This data item defines the return code from the OS/400 QWCRDTAA API. Status on whether there was successful or unsuccessful completion will be found in this structure.

2. This data item defines the parameters for the QWCRDTAA API.

    BYTES-AVAIL indicates the size of the data buffer to put the contents of the data area.

    BYTES-RETURNED will contain the number of bytes returned from the API.

    VALUE-TYPE will contain either *CHAR, *EC, or *LGL depending on how the data area is defined.

    RET-LIBRARY will indicate where the data area was found.

    RET-LENGTH will indicate the number of bytes returned.

    RET-DECPOS will indicate the decimal precision of the returned value.

    DATA is the actual data taken from the data area.

    RCV-SIZE is the size of the receiver data structure RECEIVER.

QUAL-NAME contains the qualified name of the data area. START-POS and LENGTH indicate the starting position within the data area, and the number of characters to return.

3. It is easiest to use the special LENGTH OF register to determine the size of the receiver variable.

4. In this step, the QWCRDTAA API is being called. The data will be retrieved from the data area and placed in the RECEIVER variable.

5. This example will change the data area using the CHGDTAARA CL command. This is accomplished by calling QCMDEXC from the COBOL program. The QCMDEXC program takes two parameters: the command string and the length of the command. These two variables will be passed to the QCMDEXC program.

6. QCMDEXC will execute the command defined in step [5].

You can find additional information regarding the QWCRDTAA API in the *AS/400 System Programmer's Interface Reference.*

10.6.1.7 The local data area. The local data area (*LDA) is a data area that exists for each job running on the system. When a job terminates, the local data area (as well as any data that are in it) is no longer available.

In a CL program, the local data area is manipulated through the same commands that manipulate regular data areas. Instead of specifying a data area name, specify *LDA.

10.6.1.8 Sample CL program using a data area. The CL program in Listing 10.9 creates a data area in library QTEMP, writes some data to it, reads data from it, and then deletes it.

Listing 10.9 Program that performs several updates to a data area.

```
....-....1....-....2....-....3....-....4....-....5....-....6....
        PGM
        DCL  &VAR1 TYPE(*CHAR) LEN(20)
[1]     CRTDTAARA DTAARA(QTEMP/TMPDTAARA) TYPE(*CHAR) LEN(20)
[2]     CHGDTAARA DTAARA(QTEMP/TMPDTAARA) VALUE('Hello')
[3]     CHGDTAARA DTAARA(QTEMP/TMPDTAARA (7 3)) VALUE('Bye')
[4]     RTVDTAARA DTAARA(QTEMP/TMPDTAARA (1 20)) RTNVAR(&VAR1)
[5]     DLTDTAARA DTAARA(QTEMP/TMPDTAARA)
        ENDPGM
```

1. A data area is created in library QTEMP named TMPDTAARA to hold character data. It has a length of 20 characters.

2. The value of the data area is changed to the string 'Hello'. Since the starting position and length were not specified, *ALL is implied and

therefore the data area is cleared before the word 'Hello' is placed in it.

3. The value 'Bye' is placed in the data area starting at position 7 for a length of 3 characters. The value 'Hello' still remains in positions 1 through 5.

4. The value of the data area is retrieved, starting at position 1 and for a length of 20 characters. The value is placed in the variable named &VAR1. The data remain unchanged in the data area.

5. The data area is deleted from QTEMP. You can omit this line if you would like to use the DSPDTAARA command to view the contents after the program runs.

10.6.2 Using data queues

Data queues are special OS/400 objects that can act as a high-speed mode of communication between programs. There are three types of data queues:

- *First-in–first-out (FIFO):* Data put in the queue are removed from the queue in the same order as they arrived.

- *Last-in–first-out (LIFO):* The last data put into the queue will be the first data retrieved from the queue.

- *Keyed:* A key can be specified to identify the next data item to retrieve from the queue.

There are many uses for data queues. A client–server environment can be set up within an application where several "transaction" programs generate orders that are "queued" while a background (batch) job retrieves each request from the queue.

A single queue can be used by more than one job. This is advantageous if the number of transactions to process is greater than one job can handle. For example, if several printers are available to print orders, several interactive jobs could send requests to a single data queue. A separate job for each printer could receive from the data queue and print the orders.

Jobs that retrieve data from a data queue have several options when attempting to access the next data queue record:

- If an entry exists in the data queue, the data are immediately returned to the requester.

- If no data are available, the requester has the option of waiting until an entry is placed in the queue. The requester basically "sleeps" until the entry arrives.

- If no data are available, the requester can set a time limit to wait. If no entry has been put in the queue within the specified time limit, the requester is notified and can continue processing other tasks.

- If no data are available, the requester may choose not to wait at all.

Data queues can also be used when a program needs to wait for input from display files, ICF (intersystem communications functions) files, and data queues at the same time.

10.6.2.1 Creating a data queue. The create data queue (CRTDTAQ) command creates a data queue:

```
CRTDTAQ DTAQ(ORDERDTAQ) MAXLEN(128) TEXT('Order DataQ')
```

The MAXLEN parameter indicates the maximum length of a single entry within the data queue. The data queue created with this command will be a FIFO data queue.

10.6.2.2 Sending data to a data queue. To send data to a data queue, call the QSNDDTAQ program. Since this is not a CL command (it is a program), you must use the CALL command when calling it from CL and COBOL.

```
CALL QSNDDTAQ PARM(&QNAME &LIB &FLDLEN &FIELD &KEYLEN &KEY)
```

Table 10.2 defines the various parameters (optional parameters are shown in gray).

TABLE 10.2 Parameters for the QSNDDTAQ Program

Parameter name	Description
&QNAME	Ten-character field that names the data queue.
&LIB	Ten-character field that names the library containing the data queue. *LIBL or *CURLIB can be used.
&FLDLEN	Five-digit packed decimal with no decimal positions. Defines the number of characters sent to the data queue.
&FIELD	The data to be put in the data queue.
&KEYLEN	Three-digit packed decimal value with no decimal places that contains the length of the key sent to the data queue. If this field is used, the &KEY field must also be supplied.
&KEY	A character field of length &KEYLEN.

10.6.2.3 Receiving data from a data queue. To receive data from a data queue, you must call the QRCVDTAQ program. The following example shows how to call the QRCVDTAQ from a CL program:

```
CALL PGM(QRCVDTAQ) PARM(&QNAME &LIB &FLDLEN &FIELD &WAIT +
         &ORDER &KEYLEN &KEY &SNDRLEN &SNDR)
```

Table 10.3 defines the parameters for the QRCVDTAQ program (optional parameters are shown in gray).

TABLE 10.3   Parameters for the QRCVDTAQ Program

Parameter name	Description
&QNAME	Ten-character field that names the data queue.
&LIB	Ten-character field that names the library containing the data queue. *LIBL or *CURLIB can be used.
&FLDLEN	Five-digit packed decimal with no decimal positions. Defines the number of characters sent to the data queue.
&FIELD	The data to be put in the data queue.
&WAIT	Five-digit packed decimal field with no decimal positions. When no entries are on the data queue, the WAIT parameter specifies the following: A negative value indicates an unlimited wait request. Zero indicates no wait—return immediately if no entry exists in the data queue. A positive value specifies the number of seconds to wait for an entry to become available. The maximum value, 99999, allows a wait time of approximately 28 hours.
&ORDER	Two-character field that retrieves a message using the specified character key. The following character values are used: GT: Greater than LT: Less than NE: Not equal EQ: Equal GE: Greater than or equal LE: Less than or equal
&KEYLEN	Three-digit packed decimal value with no decimal places that contains the length of the key sent to the data queue. If this field is used, the &KEY field must also be supplied.
&KEY	A character field of length &KEYLEN.
&SNDRLEN	Three-digit packed decimal field with no decimal positions—specifies the length of the sender identification parameter. The sender ID length value must be 0, or have a value equal to or greater than 8.
&SNDR	A character field that identifies the variable to contain the sender ID information associated with the received message. The data returned is 4 bytes—packed 7,0 contains the number of bytes returned (i.e., the length of data actually returned). 4 bytes—packed 7,0 contains the number of bytes available. 26 bytes—character field containing the job name, user, and job number. 10 bytes—character field containing the name of the sender's current user profile.

10.6.2.4 Clearing a data queue. To clear the contents of a data queue, you must call the QCLRDTAQ program. The format of the call is

```
CALL PGM(QCLRDTAQ) PARM(&QNAME &LIB)
```

where the QNAME specifies the name of the data queue to be cleared, and &LIB specifies the library name where the data queue resides.

10.7 Libraries

Libraries are special objects on the AS/400 that are used to group other objects. They are similar to directories on personal computers. A library may contain a group of related files or programs. OS/400 locates objects in the system by using libraries.

10.7.1 Qualified name

When both the library name and object name are specified, the name is considered to be qualified. The name in Fig. 10.12 is a fully qualified name.

```
YOURLIB/WRKPHNDIR
```

Figure 10.12 A qualified object name.

Commands that require qualified names will always present two input fields: the first for the object name and the second for the library name (see Fig. 10.13). This type of command requires both an object name and a library name. Most commands that require a library name allow you to specify *CURLIB (the current library for the job) or *LIBL (the current library list for the job).

```
Object . . . . . . .  _____    Name, generic*, *ALL
   Library  . . . . .  _____    Name, *LIBL, *CURLIB,...
```

Figure 10.13 Prompt that requires a qualified name.

If the library name is not specified, one of the following scenarios happens:

- For a create command, the object created will be placed in the user's current library (*CURLIB) or in the system library, depending on the object type.

- For all other commands, the system will search the library list to find the object.

10.7.2 Library lists

The library list is a list of libraries that is searched when looking for an object. They are similar in concept to the "path" used in other operating systems such as PC-DOS, UNIX, and OS/2.

A library list consists of four parts, as shown in Fig. 10.14.

System Part	The system part of the library list (QSYSLIBL). This part contains objects needed by the system.
Product Libraries	The system uses product libraries to support languages and utilities that are dependent on libraries other than QSYS to process their commands.
Current Library	The current library can be, but does not have to be, a duplicate of any library in the library list. The value *CURLIB (current library) may be used on most commands as a library name to represent whatever library has been specified as the current library for the job. If no current library exists in the library list and *CURLIB is specified, QGPL is used. The CHGCURLIB and CHGLIBL commands can be used to change the current library.
User part	This part contains the libraries necessary to run the applications for the user. There is a limit of 25 libraries in the user part.

Figure 10.14 Library list make-up.

A typical library list may look like the list shown in Fig. 10.15. Each job on the system has a library list. The job's initial library list is usually determined by the job's job description.

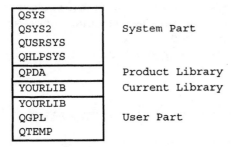

QSYS QSYS2 QUSRSYS QHLPSYS	System Part
QPDA	Product Library
YOURLIB	Current Library
YOURLIB QGPL QTEMP	User Part

Figure 10.15 Typical library list.

When the library list is used to locate an object, the library list is searched from top to bottom, starting with QSYS. If two or more objects of the same type and name exist in the list, you get the object from the library that appears first in the library list. This is particularly useful when designing new components of an existing system. The new components can be placed in a library that appears first in the user's portion of the library list. If a new version of a program appears in the "new release" library, it will be found first when the program is requested. This causes an "override" effect for new versions of old programs.

Generally, it is most advantageous not to qualify an object's name. However, there are occasions when it is advantageous (or necessary) to qualify an object's library:

- When the required object is *not* in the current library list for the job.
- When there is more than one object of the same name in the library list and you want one in a specific library.
- When a specific library must be used for security reasons.

The library list can be manipulated with the commands listed in Table 10.4.

10.7.3 Design issues

The layout of the user portion of the library list should be considered an important step during the design of an application. When applications use well-designed library lists, they are easy to understand and

TABLE 10.4   Library List Commands

Command	Description
ADDLIBLE	Adds a library to the current library list. The new library's position within the library list can be specified.
CHGLIBL	Changes the user's portion of the library list.
CHGSYSLIBL	Changes the system part of the library list.
DSPLIBL	Displays the current job's library list.
EDTLIBL	Provides a quick and easy way to edit the current library list with a full-screen editor.
RMVLIBLE	Remove a library entry from the library list.

maintain. They can also coexist with other applications within the same system easily. An organization that does a lot of in-house development may introduce standards for library naming to ease in identifying the applications contained within the libraries. Furthermore, "global" libraries may be set up to contain functions, subprograms, and source code that are common to many applications.

Each project should have its own set of libraries. It makes sense to keep programs and data files for an accounting system separate from those for a mortgage calculation system.

Figure 10.16 illustrates one way of organizing libraries for an application. All library names begin with PBS for patient billing system.

PBSLITENG	English Literals (screens, reports, commands, message files)
PBSDTA	Data files (physical files, logical files, data areas)
PBSOBJ	Executable objects (compiled programs)

Figure 10.16   Example of a user portion of an application's production library list.

A test environment should be established as well. If the above represents a production environment, the test environment could be set up as shown in Figure 10.17.

The production libraries for literal and program objects are included in the test library list; however, the production data are not. Data from

PBTLITENG	Test English literals
PBTDTA	Test data files
PBTOBJ	Test object files
PBSLITENG	Production English literals
PBSOBJ	Production object files

Figure 10.17 Example of a user portion of an application's test library list.

the production environment may be copied into the test data environment for testing purposes.

There are some hidden advantages to organizing an application's library list in this fashion. First, it becomes language independent. A German language version of the literal library (perhaps PBSLITGER) could be put at the beginning of the list; therefore German language versions of screens and commands would be displayed instead of their English counterparts found in PBSLITENG. Leaving the original PBSLITENG in the library list *below* the new German one would allow you to fall back to the original screens if they have not been implemented in that language. Remember that when an object is requested (such as a screen), the library list will be searched from top to bottom to find it. Therefore, if the screen is not found in the German literal library, the English library would be searched next. The other libraries in the library list would remain the same for both languages, as they contain no literals that are language dependent.

The developer's personal library should be the *current library*. The current library (*CURLIB) is always searched before any of the remaining libraries in the user portion of the library list. This scheme provides the developer with an easy method of using test data in a personal development library instead of data in the application's test data library (other developers may be using the data in PBTDTA).

QGPL and QTEMP should appear last in the library list. QTEMP is used for temporary files needed only while the user is signed onto the system. Developers coming from other systems often implement temporary work files by creating files with names relating to the current workstation or the user profile. This is not necessary on the AS/400. If a file is created in library QTEMP, it is available *only* to the current user. Each user has his or her own copy of QTEMP. When the user signs off the system, QTEMP disappears, along with anything in it.

10.8 Using Files in a CL Program

A CL program has the ability to send data to and receive data from a workstation, as well as read data from a database file. This section contains a very brief introduction to performing I/O within a CL program. CL supports I/O operations on two types of files:

- *Display files:* A CL program can send a simple display format to the workstation and receive data from it.

- *Database files:* A CL program can read sequentially through a database file. A CL program cannot write to a database file.

The DCLF command is used to declare the file. When the DCLF command is encountered, the description of the file is brought into the CL program and all fields within the file are declared to the program. If a database file was not created using DDS (indicating that it is a flat file), a single variable will be declared that represents one entire record. The CL program will be responsible for using the %SUBSTRING function to separate the file into fields.

A file is implicitly opened when the first file command is executed and remains open until the program returns, ends, or transfers control to another program. When a database file is opened, the first member in the file is opened unless an OVRDBF command was previously used to specify a different member.

10.8.1 Declaring the file

Before a file can be used in a CL program, it must be declared using the DCLF command. The format of the DCLF command is

```
DCLF FILE(library-name/file-name) RCDFMT(record-format-name)
```

The referenced file *must* exist when the CL program is compiled. When the DCLF is executed, each field found within the record format is declared as a variable with the same name preceded by an ampersand (&). Option indicators are translated into variables with the name &INxx, where xx is the indicator number.

10.8.2 Display files

The commands listed in Table 10.5 can be used to manipulate a display file. Subfiles are not supported from CL.

TABLE 10.5 Supported Actions Against Display Files from CL

SNDF	Sends data to the workstation
RCVF	Receives data from the workstation
SNDRCVF	Sends data to, then receives data from the workstation

The example in Listing 10.10 shows a simple CL program that displays a screen asking for the user's name. The program continues until the user presses Enter or F3. Validation is done against the name to verify that it is not blank (this validation could be done automatically in the DDS but is being left to the CL program for illustrative purposes).

Listing 10.10 Display file for a sample CL program.

```
MEMBER NAME: EX1002FM         FILE:  QDDSSRC
.....AAN01N02N03T.NAME++++++RLen++TDpBLinPosFunctions+++++++++++++++++++
    A           R GETNAME
    A                                        CA03(03 'Exit')
    A                                      1 28'Display from a CL Program'
    A                                        DSPATR(HI)
    A                                      3  2'Current job number . . :'
    A             CURJOB       6   O       3 28
    A                                      4  2'Current User ID  . . . :'
    A             CURUSR      10   O       4 28
    A                                      5  2'Current Output Queue . :'
    A             CUROUTQ     10   O       5 28
    A                                      7  2'Type choices, press Enter.'
    A                                        DSPATR(HI)
    A                                        COLOR(BLU)
    A                                      9  2'Your name  . . . . . . '
    A             USERNAME    30   B       9 32
    A  90                                     DSPATR(RI)
    A                                     22  2'F3=Exit'
    A                                        DSPATR(HI)
    A                                        COLOR(BLU)
```

Use the following commands to enter this display file:

```
STRSEU QDDSSRC EX1002FM TYPE(DSPF)
```

Use the following command to compile the display file:

```
CRTDSPF FILE(EX1002FM) SRCFILE(QDDSSRC)
```

Listing 10.11 is the CL source program that manipulates the display file.

Listing 10.11 CL program to manipulate a display file.

```
MEMBER NAME:   EX1002      FILE:  QCLSRC
....+....1....+....2....+....3....+....4....+....5....+....6....+....7
           PGM
           DCLF FILE(EX1001FM)
           RTVJOBA USER(&CURUSR) NBR(&CURJOB) OUTQ(&CUROUTQ)
LOOP:
           SNDRCVF RCDFMT(GETNAME)
           IF (*NOT &IN03) THEN(DO)
               IF (&USERNAME *EQ ' ') THEN(DO)
                   CHGVAR VAR(&IN90) VALUE('1')
                   GOTO LOOP
               ENDDO
           ENDDO
           ENDPGM
```

Use the following commands to enter this CL source:

```
STRSEU QCLSRC EX1002 TYPE(CLP)
```

Use the following command to compile the CL program:

```
CRTCLPGM EX1002
```

Use the following command to run the program:

```
CALL EX1002
```

The display shown in Fig. 10.18 will appear.

```
                        Display from a CL Program

   Current job number . . :   023331
   Current User ID  . . . :   GERRYK
   Current Output Queue . :   GERRYK

   Type choices, press Enter.

   Your name  . . . . . .        _____




   F3=Exit
```

Figure 10.18 Output from a CL program.

10.8.3   Database files

CL programs access database files by using the receive file (RCVF) command. When the RCVF command is executed, the next record in the file's access path is retrieved. You cannot read from a file randomly—only sequentially from beginning to end.

Since CL only supports character, packed decimal, and logical variables, database fields that are defined as zoned decimal or binary numbers will be converted to packed decimal as required. Database files that contain floating-point data cannot be used in a CL program.

When a CL program attempts to read past the end of a file, the RCVF command will send message CPF0864. A CL program can effectively use a MONMSG CPF0864 to check whether the end of the file has been reached.

10.8.3.1   Command output files.   Some CL commands have the ability to send the results of their execution to the workstation, the printer, or an output file. For example, if you enter the command

```
DSPFFD YOURFILE
```

the DSPFFD command will present you with a screen that gives details for each field in YOURFILE. Sometimes it is necessary to capture the output to a database file instead of viewing it on the screen. In this way, a high-level language program can process the data.

Commands that support redirecting the output will have the OUTFILE parameter. If you enter the DSPFFD command in the following format, a database file will be created that contains all the fields found in YOURFILE:

```
DSPFFD YOURFILE OUTFILE(ALIB/AFILE)
```

This command will create (or replace) a file named AFILE in library ALIB (or the current library if none is specified) that contains one record for each field found in YOURFILE.

IBM supplies a set of ready-to-use files (in library QSYS) that contain the record layouts of files created by CL commands. Each command that has the ability to create an output file also has a related file in QSYS that can be used as reference for the field layouts. The file that is related to the DSPFFD command is QADSPFFD. For a list of commands and related files, see the IBM *Application System / 400 Programming: Reference Summary*, Chap. 7.

10.8.3.2   Reading a database file.   The example in Listing 10.12 shows how to process a database file. The program takes two parameters: the first is a file name and the second is a library name. The program will use the DSPFFD command to create an output file in library QTEMP that contains a record for each field found in the specified file. After the file is created, the CL program will step through each record and count the number of fields. Each time a record is read, it will send the name of the field to the workstation, so you can actually see it processing the file. When the program ends, it will send a message to the workstation stating the total number of fields found in the file.

Listing 10.12 CL program that reads a database file.

```
MEMBER NAME: DSPFLDCNT      FILE NAME:  QCLSRC
....+....1....+....2....+....3....+....4....+....5....+....6....+....7
[1]             PGM  PARM(&FILENAME &LIBNAME)
                DCL  &FILENAME  TYPE(*CHAR) LEN(10)
                DCL  &LIBNAME   TYPE(*CHAR) LEN(10)
                DCL  &FLDCOUNT  TYPE(*DEC)  LEN(4 0)
                DCL  &FLDTXT    TYPE(*CHAR) LEN(4)
[2]             DCLF FILE(QADSPFFD)

[3]             DSPFFD FILE(&LIBNAME/&FILENAME) OUTPUT(*OUTFILE) +
                OUTFILE(QTEMP/FIELDLIST)
[4]             OVRDBF FILE(QADSPFFD) TOFILE(QTEMP/FIELDLIST)

        LOOP:
[5]             RCVF RCDFMT(QWHDRFFD)
[6]             MONMSG CPF0864 EXEC(GOTO ENDLOOP)
[7]             SNDPGMMSG MSGID(CPF9898) MSGF(QCPFMSG) +
                MSGDTA('Field:' *BCAT &WHFLDE) +
                TOPGMQ(*EXT) MSGTYPE(*STATUS)
[8]             CHGVAR &FLDCOUNT (&FLDCOUNT + 1)
                GOTO LOOP
        ENDLOOP:
[9]             CHGVAR &FLDTXT &FLDCOUNT
                SNDPGMMSG MSG('Fields in file:' *BCAT &FLDTXT)
                ENDPGM
```

Notes about the program in Listing 10.12 are as follows:

1. Two parameters are expected: a file name and a library name.

2. The DCLF command instructs the compiler to include the fields from file QADSPFFD (which is found in QSYS). This file contains the field layout for the output file generated by the DSPFFD command.

3. The DSPFFD command includes the OUTPUT keyword to direct the output to an outfile. The OUTFILE name is specified as FIELDLIST and is to be put in library QTEMP.

4. The OVRDBF command tells the CL program to read from the file in QTEMP instead of the file that it originally referenced (which was found in QSYS). If the OVRDBF command was not executed,

the RCVF command would read the file in QSYS (which is probably empty) instead of the one just created in QTEMP.

5. The RCVF command reads the next available record in the specified file with the specified record format.

6. If there is no record available, the RCVF command will send message CPF0864. In this context, the MONMSG command acts like the AT END phrase of a COBOL READ statement. If CPF0864 is encountered, control is transferred to label ENDLOOP.

7. The SNDPGMMSG command sends a message to the workstation with the name of the field. Messages are covered in Chap. 12.

8. This line increments the field counter.

9. In order to use the concatenation operator found in the next SNDMSG command, the numeric value must first be converted into a character variable.

10.9   Defining Commands

Commands are an important part of AS/400 application development. A command can act as a wrapper to a program, making the program more generic. When used directly by a user, they provide validity checking as well as default values. When commands have been used effectively throughout a system, they can act as modular components, allowing new programs to be built by combining preexisting commands.

The user can always use the F4=Prompt key when using commands. A command can be entered directly on the command line and executed, unlike programs that must be executed by using the CALL command. If parameters are set up with default values, they do not need to be entered, unlike programs—you must include each parameter passed to a program on the CALL command.

Commands, like other high-level languages, are created first in a source file, and then compiled to create an object of type *CMD. The CRTCMD command is used to translate a source member into an executable command.

When a command is compiled, you specify the name of a command processing program for the command. A command processing program is a high-level language program that is to receive the parameters entered by the user and process them.

Figure 10.19 illustrates the relationship between commands and command processing programs. Commands are usually kept in a source physical file named QCMDSRC.

This section will introduce you to the essential and most commonly

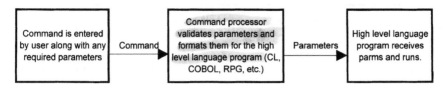

Figure 10.19 Relationship between commands and programs.

used options when creating commands. For more complete detailed information on writing commands, see the *AS/400 CL Programmer's Guide*.

10.9.1 Using the CMD statement

The CMD statement defines the beginning of a new command. The format of the CMD statement is

```
CMD PROMPT('Command Title')
```

The command title is the text that is shown to the user when the command is prompted using the F4=Prompt key.

10.9.2 Defining parameters

A command optionally contains parameters. Each parameter is associated with a keyword. For example, in the create COBOL program command, PGM is the keyword that defines the program name parameter in the command CRTCBLPGM PGM (program-name).

Parameters for the command are defined with the PARM statement. The PARM statement has many options associated with it. The easiest way to see the various options for the PARM statement is to type the word PARM on a command line and press F4=Prompt. The first page of the display is shown in Fig. 10.20. The basic function of the PARM statement is to define a parameter for the command.

Listing 10.13 Definition of a command with one parameter.

```
....+....1....+....2....+....3....+....4....+....5....+....6....+....7
        CMD         PROMPT('Delete Phone Entry')
        PARM        KWD(PHNUMBER) TYPE(*CHAR) LEN(20) +
                    PROMPT('Phone number')
```

Listing 10.13 shows the definition for a command that allows the user to specify a phone number. When this command is compiled, a command is created that has one parameter. It should be associated

```
                    Parameter Definition (PARM)

Type choices, press Enter.

Keyword  . . . . . . . . . . .    _____    Name
Type of value  . . . . . . . .    _____    Name, *DEC, *LGL, *CHAR...
Value length . . . . . . . . .    _____        Number
           + for more values
Return value . . . . . . . . .    *NO           *NO, *YES
Constant value . . . . . . . .    _____
Restricted values  . . . . . .    *NO           *NO, *YES
Default value  . . . . . . . .    _____
Valid values . . . . . . . . .    _____
           + for more values      _____
Relational expression:
  Relational operator  . . . . .  ___           *GT, *EQ, *GE, *NL, *LT...
  Value or keyword reference . .  _____
Range of values:
  Lower value or keyword ref . .  _____
  Upper value or keyword ref . .  _____
                                                          More...
F3=Exit    F4=Prompt    F5=Refresh    F12=Cancel    F13=How to use this display
F24=More keys
```

Figure 10.20 Parameters for the PARM statement.

with a high-level language program that also has one parameter. For example, Listing 10.14 would be an appropriate command processing program for the previously defined command. Notice that the CL program has exactly one parameter that matches the definition of the first PARM defined in the command in Listing 10.13.

Listing 10.14 Command processing program for command in Listing 10.13.

```
....+....1....+....2....+....3....+....4....+....5....+....6....+....7
            PGM         PARM(&PHNUM)
            DCL         VAR(&PHNUM) TYPE(*CHAR) LEN(20)
            .
            .
            .
```

The PARM statement allows you to define parameters that are decimal, logical, character, integer, names, dates, times, as well as a variety of other types. Use the F4=Prompt key on the Type of value field for a complete list of supported value types.

10.9.3 Qualified names

As defined earlier in this section, an object name that also contains a library name is considered to be qualified. The library component of a qualified name is usually shown indented when the command is prompted as in Fig. 10.21.

You can define parameters in your commands that require a quali-

```
Object . . . . . . . . _____      Name, generic*, *ALL
   Library  . . . . . _____|      Name, *LIBL, *CURLIB, ...
```

Figure 10.21 Qualified name prompt.

fied name. To do this, you create a custom "type" that contains the necessary qualified keywords. Listing 10.15 illustrates how to create a parameter that requires a qualified name. The library name will allow a default value of *LIBL. When prompted, this command will appear as shown in Fig. 10.18.

Listing 10.15 Defining a Qualified Name

```
....+....1....+....2....+....3....+....4....+....5....+....6....+....7
           CMD        PROMPT('Display File Fields')
           PARM       KWD(FILE) TYPE(QNAME) PROMPT('File name')
QNAME:     QUAL       TYPE(*NAME) LEN(10)
           QUAL       TYPE(*NAME) LEN(10) DFT(*LIBL) +
                        SPCVAL((*LIBL)) PROMPT('Library')
```

When a qualified name is passed to the command processing program, all of the QUAL fields are concatenated together to form a single parameter. Therefore, the command defined in Listing 10.15 will pass a single parameter (defined as character with length 20) to the command processing program. The CL program in Listing 10.16 shows how to receive the qualified name, as well as separate the file name from the library name.

Listing 10.16 Command processing program to receive a qualified name.

```
....+....1....+....2....+....3....+....4....+....5....+....6....+....7
           PGM        PARM(&QUALNAME)
           DCL        VAR(&QUALNAME) TYPE(*CHAR) LEN(20)
           DCL        VAR(&FILENAME) TYPE(*CHAR) LEN(10)
           DCL        VAR(&LIBNAME)  TYPE(*CHAR) LEN(10)
/* Parse the qualified name to obtain the FILENAME and LIBNAME      */
           CHGVAR     VAR(&FILENAME) VALUE(%SST(&QUALNAME 1 10))
           CHGVAR     VAR(&LIBNAME)  VALUE(%SST(&QUALNAME 11 10))
```

10.9.4 Example command

Listing 10.17 creates a command "front-end processor" for the CL program defined in Listing 10.12. The CL program takes two parameters: a file name and a library name. In this example, you will not use a qualified name, since the CL program is expecting two separate fields, each of length 10 rather than one field of length 20).

Listing 10.17   Command for display fields program in Listing 10.12.

```
MEMBER NAME: DSPFLDCNT    FILE: QCMDSRC    LIBRARY: COBOLBOOK
....+....1....+....2....+....3....+....4....+....5....+....6....+....7
          CMD         PROMPT('Display Field Count')
          PARM        KWD(FILE)TYPE(*CHAR) LEN(10) PROMPT('File name')
          PARM        KWD(LIB) TYPE(*CHAR) LEN(10) DFT(*LIBL) +
                      SPCVAL((*LIBL)) PROMPT('Library')
```

Use the following command to create the command:

```
CRTCMD CMD(DSPFLDCNT) PGM(DSPFLDCNT)
```

The program named in the PGM parameter is the program that will be called when the command is executed. This is the program from Listing 10.12.

You can now execute the DSPFLDCNT program with this command. Type DSPFLDCNT on the command line and press the F4=Prompt key to try the command.

10.10   Bringing it All Together

This section presents an example program that ties together concepts found in this chapter as well as from the chapters on display files, physical files, and the COBOL language.

The project presented in this section defines a new command used to display the fields in an OS/400 file. The file can be either a physical, logical, or device file. The syntax of the command will be

```
DSPFLDS FILE(library-name/file-name)
```

The library name should default to *LIBL if none is specified.

The project consists of the parts outlined in Table 10.6.

10.10.1   Creating the DSPFLDS command

The definition of the DSPFLDS command is shown in Listing 10.18.

Listing 10.18   Source for display file fields command.

```
MEMBER NAME: DSPFLDS         FILE: QCMDSRC
....+....1....+....2....+....3....+....4....+....5....+....6....+....7
          CMD         PROMPT('Display File Fields')
          PARM        KWD(FILE) TYPE(QNAME) PROMPT('File name')
QNAME:    QUAL        TYPE(*NAME) LEN(10)
          QUAL        TYPE(*NAME) LEN(10) DFT(*LIBL) +
                      SPCVAL((*LIBL)) PROMPT('Library')
```

The PARM field indicates that the keyword FILE is of type QNAME. QNAME is defined on line 3 as consisting of 2 individual names. The

TABLE 10.6   Components for This Project

Source file	Member name	Type	Description
QCMDSRC	DSPFLDS	CMD	The command that is used by the user
QCLSRC	DSPFLDS	CLP	A CL program that: Creates the output file in QTEMP that will contain the list of fields found in the requested file Overrides the input file for the COBOL program to the one just created in QTEMP Executes the COBOL program to display the fields from the file in QTEMP Sends a message to the user if the requested file is not found
QDDSSRC	DSPFLDS	DSPF	The display file containing the formats for the COBOL program to display.
QLBLSRC	DSPFLDS01	CBL	The COBOL program that reads the file in QTEMP and displays the list of fields

second QUAL value allows for the special value *LIBL to be entered by the user. Special values always begin with an asterisk. Also, the default value for this part of the qualified name is *LIBL (as stated in the DFT parameter).

Start SEU with the following command to enter the source in Listing 10.18:

```
STRSEU SRCFILE(QCMDSRC) SRCMBR(DSPFLDS) TYPE(CMD)
```

Compile the command with the following command:

```
CRTCMD CMD(DSPFLDS) PGM(DSPFLDS)
```

(Command and Program Linkage)

The PGM keyword specifies that when the command is actually executed, the parameters should be sent to a program named DSPFLDS (this program is the CL program that will be designed in the next step). The name DSPFLDS was used for both the CL program and the command, but this is not required.

You can test the command by typing DSPFLDS on a command line and then press the F4=Prompt key (see Fig. 10.22). If you press Enter, OS/400 will attempt to execute the command processing program (also named DSPFLDS) that has not been written yet; therefore you will receive a message indicating that program DSPFLDS was not found. You can exit the display by pressing F12 (cancel).

```
                        Display File Fields (DSPFLDS)
Type choices, press Enter.

File name  . . . . . . . . . .  _____    Name
  Library  . . . . . . . . . .  *LIBL____     Name, *LIBL




                                                              Bottom
F3=Exit   F4=Prompt   F5=Refresh   F12=Cancel   F13=How to use this display
F24=More keys
```

Figure 10.22 Results of prompting the DSPFLDS command.

10.10.2   Creating the DSPFLDS CL program

Listing 10.19 is the command processing program for the previously defined command.

Listing 10.19 Source for the DSPFLDS command processing program.

```
MEMBER NAME: DSPFLDS    FILE: QCLSRC
....+....1....+....2....+....3....+....4....+....5....+....6....+....7
            PGM         PARM(&QUALNAME)
            DCL         VAR(&QUALNAME) TYPE(*CHAR) LEN(20)
            DCL         VAR(&FILENAME) TYPE(*CHAR) LEN(10)
            DCL         VAR(&LIBNAME)  TYPE(*CHAR) LEN(10)

/* Parse the qualified name to obtain the FILENAME and LIBNAME     */

            CHGVAR      VAR(&FILENAME) VALUE(%SST(&QUALNAME 1 10))
            CHGVAR      VAR(&LIBNAME)  VALUE(%SST(&QUALNAME 11 10))

/* Use DSPFFD with *OUTFILE to create a data file in QTEMP that    */
/*   contains the field descriptions for the specified file.       */
/* DSPFFD sends CPF3012 if the file is not found.                  */
/* The MONMSG will transfer control to NOFILE if this happens.     */

            DSPFD       FILE(&LIBNAME/&FILENAME) OUTPUT(*OUTFILE +
                          OUTFILE(QTEMP/FIELDLIST)
            MONMSG      MSGID(CPF3012) EXEC(GOTO CMDLBL(NOFILE))

/* The following override makes sure that the COBOL program can    */
/*   find the newly created FIELDLIST file. This is really for     */
/*   safety in case that QTEMP is not in the library list.         */

            OVRDBF      FILE(FIELDLIST) TOFILE(QTEMP/FIELDLIST)

/* Call the COBOL program to read the file and display the fields  */

            CALL        PGM(DSPFLDS01)
            RETURN
```

```
/* If the file wasn't found, send the same message CPF3012 back    */
/* to the user's workstation. CPF3012 expects 2 data fields,        */
/* the file name and the library name (each length 10). The         */
/* original variable &QUALNAME contains both NAME and LIBNAME       */
/* already concatenated together, so &QUALNAME will be used         */

NOFILE:
            SNDPGMMSG  MSGID(CPF3012) MSGF(QCPFMSG) MSGDTA(&QUALNAME)
            ENDPGM
```

Start SEU and enter the source with the following command:

```
STRSEU SRCFILE(QCLSRC) SRCMBR(DSPFLDS) TYPE(CLP)
```

To compile this program, use the following command:

```
CRTCLPGM PGM(DSPFLDS)
```

Do not attempt to execute this program yet—there are more components to complete before it will work.

A program description for Listing 10.19 follows:

- When the command accepts the library name and file name from the user, it concatenates them together into a single field of length 20. The CL program therefore must extract the library name and the file name using the %SST function.

- The display file field descriptions (DSPFFD) command is then executed. The OUTPUT parameter is used to direct the results of the command to an output file in QTEMP instead of to the display. If the file is not found, the DSPFFD command will send message CPF3012 (which is monitored in the next line). If the message occurs, the program transfers control to the end, sends a message to the user, and then is terminated.

- If the DSPFFD command is successful, an override is established to redirect the COBOL program to read the file in QTEMP instead of the original one specified in the SELECT statement (QADSPFFD).

- The COBOL program is then called to display the fields.

- If the DSPFFD command ended in error, the same message that was sent to the program (CPF3012) is forwarded to the workstation so the user can see it. CPF3012 has two parameters: a file name and a library name. Since the original name specified in QUALNAME already has this information concatenated together, this variable is used as the message data for the message.

10.10.3 Creating the display file

Listing 10.20 is the display file used by COBOL program DSPFLDS01.

Listing 10.20 Source for the DSPFLDS display file.

```
FILE NAME: DSPFLDS          FILE: QDDSSRC
.....AAN01N02N03T.Name+++++RLen++TDpBLinPosFunctions++++++++++++++++++
    A                                           REF(*LIBL/QADSPFFD QWHDRFFD)
    A                                           PRINT
    A                                           INDARA
    A          R FIELDSFL                       SFL
    A            WHNAME    R         O  8  2
    A            WHFLDE    R         O  8 14
    A            WHFOBO    R         O  8 26EDTCDE(Z)
    A            WHIBO     R         O  8 32EDTCDE(Z)
    A            WHFLDB    R         O  8 38EDTCDE(Z)
    A            WHFLDD    R         O  8 45EDTCDE(Z)
    A            WHFLDP    R         O  8 48EDTCDE(Z)
    A            WHFLDT    R         O  8 52
    A            WHFIOB    R         O  8 55
    A            WHFTXT    R   -28   O  8 58
    A          R FIELDCTL                       SFLCTL(FIELDSFL)
    A                                           CF03 CF12 OVERLAY
    A                                           SFLDSP SFLDSPCTL
    A 30                                         SFLEND(*MORE)
    A                                           SFLSIZ(0300)
    A                                           SFLPAG(0012)
    A                                     1 32'Display Field List'
    A                                           DSPATR(HI)
    A                                     3  2'File . . . . . . :'
    A            WHFILE    R         O  3 22
    A                                     3 48'File type . . . . :'
    A            FILETYPE      10A   O  3 69
    A                                     4  4'Library  . . . :'
    A            WHLIB     R         O  4 22
    A                                     6 26'----- Buffer ----'
    A                                           DSPATR(HI)
    A                                     6 46'Dec'
    A                                           DSPATR(HI)
    A                                     7  2'Record Fmt'
    A                                           DSPATR(HI)
    A                                     7 14'Field Name'
    A                                           DSPATR(HI)
    A                                     7 27'Out'
    A                                           DSPATR(HI)
    A                                     7 33'In'
    A                                           DSPATR(HI)
    A                                     7 39'Leng'
    A                                           DSPATR(HI)
    A                                     7 45'Sz'
    A                                           DSPATR(HI)
    A                                     7 48'Pt'
    A                                           DSPATR(HI)
    A                                     7 52'T'
    A                                           DSPATR(HI)
    A                                     7 54'IOB'
    A                                           DSPATR(HI)
    A                                     7 58'Text'
    A                                           DSPATR(HI)
    A          R FOOTER
    A                                           OVERLAY
    A                                    21  2'Press Enter to continue.'
    A                                           DSPATR(HI) COLOR(BLU)
    A                                    23  2'F3=Exit'
    A                                           DSPATR(HI) COLOR(BLU)
```

Using SEU, enter the source in Listing 10.20. The following command will start SEU:

```
STRSEU SRCFILE(QDDSSRC) SRCMBR(DSPFLDS) TYPE(DSPF)
```

Compile the display file in Listing 10.20 with the following command:

```
CRTDSPF DSPFLDS QDDSSRC
```

10.10.4   Creating the COBOL program

Finally, the COBOL program that reads the file is shown in Listing 10.21.

Listing 10.21   Source for the DSPFLDS01 COBOL program.

```
MEMBER NAME: DSPFLDS01      FILE: QLBLSRC
....-..A...B..-....2....-....3....-....4....-....5....-....6....-....7
       IDENTIFICATION DIVISION.
       PROGRAM-ID.  DSPFLDS01.
       ENVIRONMENT DIVISION.
       INPUT-OUTPUT SECTION.
       FILE-CONTROL.
           SELECT DISPFILE ASSIGN TO WORKSTATION-DSPFLDS-SI
               ORGANIZATION IS TRANSACTION
               ACCESS MODE IS DYNAMIC
               RELATIVE KEY IS SFL-RECNUM.
           SELECT FIELDLIST ASSIGN TO DATABASE-FIELDLIST.
       DATA DIVISION.
       FILE SECTION.
       FD  DISPFILE.
       01  DISP-REC                  PIC X(200).
       FD  FIELDLIST.
       01  FIELD-REC.
           COPY DDS-QWHDRFFD-I OF QADSPFFD.
       WORKING-STORAGE SECTION.
       77  SFL-RECNUM               PIC 9(7).
       01  SFL-OUT.
           COPY DDS-FIELDSFL-O OF DSPFLDS.
       01  SFLCTL-OUT.
           COPY DDS-FIELDCTL-O OF DSPFLDS.
       01  INDIC-AREA.
           03 EACH-IND OCCURS 99 TIMES PIC 1 INDICATOR 1.
              88 IND-OFF VALUE B"0".
              88 IND-ON  VALUE B"1".
       01  INDIC-USAGE.
           03 I-SFLEND                 PIC 99 VALUE 30.
       PROCEDURE DIVISION.
       MAIN-PARA.
           OPEN INPUT FIELDLIST I-O DISPFILE.
           PERFORM WITH TEST AFTER UNTIL IND-ON(I-SFLEND)
              READ FIELDLIST
                 AT END
                    SET IND-ON(I-SFLEND) TO TRUE
                 NOT AT END
                    ADD 1 TO SFL-RECNUM
                    IF SFL-RECNUM = 1
```

```
                    MOVE CORR QWHDRFFD TO FIELDCTL-O
                    EVALUATE WHFTYP
                        WHEN "P" MOVE "PHYSICAL" TO FILETYPE
                        WHEN "L" MOVE "LOGICAL" TO FILETYPE
                        WHEN "D" MOVE "DEVICE" TO FILETYPE
                        WHEN OTHER MOVE "UNKNOWN" TO FILETYPE
                    END-EVALUATE
                    END-IF
                    MOVE CORR QWHDRFFD TO FIELDSFL
                    WRITE SUBFILE DISP-REC FROM FIELDSFL
                        FORMAT "FIELDSFL"
                END-READ
            END-PERFORM
            WRITE DISP-REC FORMAT "FOOTER".
            WRITE DISP-REC FROM FIELDCTL-O FORMAT "FIELDCTL"
                INDICATORS ARE INDIC-AREA.
            READ DISPFILE FORMAT "FIELDCTL".
            CLOSE FIELDLIST DISPFILE.
            STOP RUN.
```

Start SEU with the following command and enter the COBOL program in Listing 10.21:

```
STRSEU SRCFILE(QLBLSRC) SRCMBR(DSPFLDS01) TYPE(CBL)
```

To compile the COBOL program, use the following command:

```
CRTCBLPGM DSPFLDS01
```

```
                          Display File Fields

File . . . . . . : QADSPFFD          File type . . . . : PHYSICAL
    Library  . . . : QSYS

                          ----- Buffer ----   Dec
Record Fmt  Field Name   Out    In   Leng  Sz Pt  T IOB Text
QWHDRFFD    WHFILE        1     1    10            A  B  File
QWHDRFFD    WHLIB        11    11    10            A  B  Library
QWHDRFFD    WHCRTD       21    21     7            A  B  File creation date: ce
QWHDRFFD    WHFTYP       28    28     1            A  B  Type of file: P=Physic
QWHDRFFD    WHCNT        29    29     5   5        S  B  Number of record forma
QWHDRFFD    WHDTTM       34    34    13            A  B  Retrieval date: centur
QWHDRFFD    WHNAME       47    47    10            A  B  Record format
QWHDRFFD    WHSEQ        57    57    13            A  B  Format level identifie
QWHDRFFD    WHTEXT       60    70    50            A  B  Format text descriptio
QWHDRFFD    WHFLDN      120   120     5   5        S  B  Number of fields and i
QWHDRFFD    WHRLEN      125   125     5   5        S  B  Record format length
QWHDRFFD    WHFLDI      130   130    10            A  B  Internal field name
                                                                       More...
Press Enter to continue.

F3=Exit
```

Figure 10.23 Output from the DSPFLDS command.

10.10.5   Executing the command

Now that everything is complete, you can execute the DSPFLDS command. As a test, you can try and display the fields found in the IBM-supplied file QADSPFFD:

```
DSPFLDS QADSPFFD
```

You can also use the F4=Prompt function by typing the DSPFLDS command and pressing F4. The display shown in Fig. 10.23 should appear.

10.11   Using the OPNQRYF Command   (OPEN QUERY FILE)

The open query file (ONPQRYF) command is a CL command that allows you to perform many data-processing functions on database files. The OPNQRYF command acts as a filter between a high-level language program and the database records.

The OPNQRYF command consolidates much of the same functionality found in SQL (Structured Query Language) into a single CL command. For example,

- The FILE parameter is similar to the SQL "FROM" statement.

- The QRYSLT parameter is similar to the SQL "WHERE" statement.

- The GRPFLD parameter is similar to the SQL "GROUP BY" statement.

- The GRPSLT parameter is similar to the SQL "HAVING" statement.

The primary difference between OPNQRYF and SQL is that the OPNQRYF command "preprocesses" a file and makes the results available to an application program without the application having any knowledge of the OPNQRYF's existence. The results of the OPNQRYF are available until the file is closed (using the CLOF command). Once closed, the results of the OPNQRYF command are no longer available.

The following is a list of the major functions provided by OPNQRYF. For more information on these functions, please see the *AS/400 Database Guide*.

- Dynamic record selection

- Dynamic ordering of records

- Dynamic joining of several files (including ordering by selected key fields)

- Handling missing records in a secondary join file

- Unique-key processing
- Mapped field definitions
- Group processing
- Final total-only processing

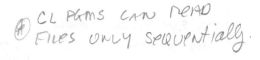

The most common use of the OPNQRYF command is to select, arrange, and format data so they can be read sequentially by a high-level language program.

10.11.1 Enhancing the DSPFLDS project

The best way to understand the power of the OPNQRYF command is to try it. In this section, we will modify the display fields command created in Sec. 10.10 to add the following enhancements:

- Provide a way to sort the fields by buffer position (as they appear in the file) or alphabetically by field name.
- Provide a way to select either all record formats or a single record format from the file.

The OPNQRYF provides an ideal solution to this requirement. No modification will be necessary to the COBOL program that processes the file. Two modifications will be required to make this enhancement:

1. The DSPFLDS command must be changed to include two additional parameters:

SORTORDER will allow the user to choose either *BUFPSN for sorting by buffer position or *NAME for sorting by field name.
FORMAT will allow the user to specify either *ALL for all formats in the file or a specific record format name.
The default selections will be *BUFPSN and *ALL.
2. The DSPFLDS CL program must be changed to include the OPNQRYF command to preprocess the input file to include only fields that meet the selection criteria based on the SORTORDER and FORMAT choices. It will also sort the results based on the user's request.

10.11.2 Modifying the DSPFLDS command

As stated above, two additional parameters must be added to the DSPFLDS command: SORTORDER and FORMAT.

The SORTORDER parameter will introduce you to replacement values. The user will be allowed to enter a meaningful special value such as *BUFPSN or *NAME (see Listing 10.22), and the command will automatically translate his or her choice to a predefined value. For example, if the user selects *BUFPSN, the command will pass the value "1" to the command processing program; if the user selects *NAME, the command will pass the value "2".

Listing 10.22 Enhanced DSPFLDS command.

```
MEMBER NAME: DSPFLDS    FILE: QCMDSRC
....+....1....+....2....+....3....+....4....+....5....+....6....+....7
              CMD      PROMPT('Display File Fields')
              PARM     KWD(FILE) TYPE(QNAME) PROMPT('File name')
              PARM     KWD(SORTORDER) TYPE(*CHAR) LEN(1) +
                         RSTD(*YES) +
                         DFT(*BUFPSN) +
                         SPCVAL((*BUFPSN '1') (*NAME + '2') +
                         PROMPT('Sort order')
              PARM     KWD(FORMAT) TYPE(*CHAR) LEN(10) +
                         DFT(*ALL) +
                         SPCVAL((*ALL)) +
                         CHOICE('*ALL or a format name')
QNAME:        QUAL     TYPE(*NAME) LEN(10)
              QUAL     TYPE(*NAME) LEN(10) DFT(*LIBL) +
                         SPCVAL((*LIBL)) PROMPT('Library')
```

Notes about Listing 10.22 follow:

- The RSTD parameter specifies that the parameter has restricted values and that the user can only choose from the values specified on the SPCVAL keyword.

- The DFT keyword is used to specify a default value for the keyword being defined. If the user does not specify a value for the SORT-ORDER keyword, the choice *BUFPSN will automatically be chosen.

- The SPCVAL keyword defines two special values, each with a replacement value. If the user chooses *BUFPSN, the command translates it to the value '1'. If the user chooses *NAME, the command translates it to the value '2'. Notice that the LEN keyword defines this field as 1 character length (not the length of the words *BUFPSN or *NAME).

- The FORMAT parameter defines the default selection to be *ALL if the user does not supply a record format name.

Make these changes to the command and recompile it the same as before.

10.11.3 Modifying the DSPFLDS CL program

The DSPFLDS CL program must be modified to accept the new parameters. The PARM keyword must have the two new parameters added (see Listing 10.23).

Listing 10.23   Enhanced DSPFLDS CL program.

```
MEMBER NAME: DSPFLDS    FILE: QCLSRC
....+....1....+....2....+....3....+....4....+....5....+....6....+....7
            PGM        PARM(&QUALNAME &SORTORD &RECNAME)
            DCL        VAR(&QUALNAME) TYPE(*CHAR) LEN(20)
            DCL        VAR(&FILENAME) TYPE(*CHAR) LEN(10)
            DCL        VAR(&LIBNAME)  TYPE(*CHAR) LEN(10)
            DCL        VAR(&SORTORD) TYPE(*CHAR) LEN(1)
            DCL        VAR(&QRYSLTSTR) TYPE(*CHAR) LEN(30)
            DCL        VAR(&RECNAME) TYPE(*CHAR) LEN(10)

/* Parse the qualified name to obtain the FILENAME and LIBNAME      */

            CHGVAR     VAR(&FILENAME) VALUE(%SST(&QUALNAME 1 10))
            CHGVAR     VAR(&LIBNAME) VALUE(%SST(&QUALNAME 11 10))

/* Use DSPFFD with *OUTFILE to create a datafile in QTEMP that      */
/*  contains the field descriptions for the specified file.         */
/* DSPFFD sends CPF3012 if the file is not found.                   */
/* The MONMSG will transfer control to NOFILE if this happens.      */

            DSPFD      FILE(&LIBNAME/&FILENAME) OUTPUT(*OUTFILE +
                       OUTFILE(QTEMP/FIELDLIST)
            MONMSG     MSGID(CPF3012) EXEC(GOTO CMDLBL(NOFILE))

/* The following override makes sure that the COBOL program can      */
/*  find the newly created FIELDLIST file. This is really for        */
/*  safety in case that QTEMP is not in the library list.            */

            OVRDBF FIELDLIST TOFILE(QTEMP/FIELDLIST) SHARE(*YES)

/* If SORTORD = 2, then an OPNQRYF must be executed. Also,           */
/*  if RECNAME isn't *ALL, an OPNQRFY must be executed.              */
/* If the user requested ALL records, change the QRYSLTSTR to be     */
/*  '*ALL', otherwise change it to be an expression that selects     */
/*  only the specified record format. The QRYSLTSTR should look      */
/*  like this: WHNAME *EQ "record-name" where the record name        */
/*  is the value specified in the &RECNAME variable. The quotes      */
/*  are required.                                                    */

            IF (&RECNAME *EQ '*ALL') THEN(DO)
            CHGVAR &QRYSLTSTR '*ALL'
            ENDDO
            ELSE DO
            CHGVAR &QRYSLTSTR ('WHNAME *EQ "' || &RECNAME || '"')
            ENDDO

            IF ((&SORTORD = '2') *OR (&RECNAME *NE '*ALL')) THEN(DO)
            IF (&SORTORD = '2') THEN(DO)
               OPNQRYF FILE((FIELDLIST)) QRYSLT(&QRYSLTSTR) +
               KEYFLD((WHFLDE *ASCEND))
               ENDDO
            ELSE DO
               OPNQRYF FILE((FIELDLIST)) QRYSLT(&QRYSLTSTR)
               ENDDO
            ENDDO

/* Call the COBOL program to read the file and display the fields  */

            CALL       PGM(DSPFLDS01)
```

```
          CLOF      OPNID(FIELDLIST)
          MONMSG    MSGID(CPF4520)

          RETURN

/* If the file wasn't found, used the same message CPF3012 back   */
/*  to the user's workstation.  CPF3012 expects 2 data fields,     */
/*  the file name and the library name (each length 10).  The      */
/*  original variable &QUALNAME contains both NAME and LIBNAME      */
/*  already concatenated together, so &QUALNAME will be used.       */

NOFILE:
          SNDPGMMSG MSGID(CPF3012) MSGF(QCPFMSG) MSGDTA(&QUALNAME)
          ENDPGM
```

Notes about Listing 10.23 follow:

- Two additional parameters were added on the PGM command to accept the SORTORDER code and the record format name. These are later declared as character variables with lengths 1 and 10, respectively.

- A new variable &QRYSLTSTR was added that will be explained later.

- The OVRDBF command must include the SHARE(*YES) parameter. This is required when a file is used in an OPNQRYF command.

- The first IF structure examines the contents of &RECNAME. If the user specified *ALL record formats, the value '*ALL' is placed in variable &QRYSLTSTR, otherwise a query selection string is built using the specified record name. Specifying *ALL as the query selection expression causes OPNQRYF to select all record formats in the file.
  If the user specified a record format name such as YOURREC, the query selection expression should be:

```
WHNAME *EQ "YOURREC"
```

- WHNAME is the field name in the physical file that contains the record name. The quotation marks are required to indicate that YOURREC is a value and not a field name. This selection will cause OPNQRYF to compare the value of the WHNAME field to the constant "YOURREC", and if it matches, the record will be included in the resulting record set.

- The first IF command in the next structure is used for speed optimization. It first compares whether or not a query must be run. If the user specified "By Buffer Position" and "All Record Formats", then it is not necessary to execute the OPNQRYF command. This combination defines the natural order of the file. If the user specified "Sort By Name" or specified a particular record format name to filter, than an OPNQRYF command must be executed.

The second IF in this structure is used to determine which OPNQRYF command to execute. The first one contains the KEYFLD parameter that is used to order the file. If the user specified *NAME, then the first version of the OPNQRYF must be used since it will order by field WHFLDE. If the user did not choose to sort the records, the second OPNQRYF is executed. Both OPNQRYF commands include the QRYSLT parameter, which specifies a selection criteria (as defined in the previous bulleted note).

- Finally, a close file (CLOF) command is executed that closes the file created by the OPNQRYF command.

- The MONMSG command is used because there is a possibility that the file was never opened by OPNQRYF. This is because the second IF statement only executes the OPNQRYF if the user specified either sorting or selection. If the user specified the default values for both parameters, the OPNQRYF was never executed, and thus the file was never opened. This MONMSG command traps the error that may occur if you try to close a file that was not previously opened. To create this program, use the following command:

```
CRTCLPGM PGM(DSPFLDS)
```

- You can now test the new enhanced command against the same file as before. Try the following commands:

`DSPFLDS QADSPFFD`	This command will produce the same results as before.
`DSPFLDS QADSPFFD SORTORDER(*NAME)`	This command will produce a list of fields in QADSPFFD but sorted by name.

11

File Journaling and Commitment Control

Journals are used to record changes that are made to one or more database files. They are used most frequently for the purpose of recovery after a system failure that has affected files. With journals, you can perform both forward and backward recovery. Forward recovery restores a file to a particular state by applying changes that are recorded in the journal to a database file. Backward recovery restores a file to an earlier state by removing changes that are recorded in the journal. Journals record all activity performed against a record such as adding, updating, and deleting. Changes to a file that are the result of changes in a logical file are also recorded. Journals also record data for the file as a whole such as file opening, closing, saving, etc.

All journaled database files are automatically synchronized with the journal when the system is started [IPL (Initial Program Load) time]. If the system ended abnormally, some database changes may be in the journal, but not yet reflected in the database itself. The system will automatically update the database files from the journal to bring them up to date.

Using journals can also make saving database files faster. If changes to a file are being recorded in a journal, it is only necessary to save the file's journal receiver each day rather than the entire database file. The complete file would be saved once per week (or any logical interval). If the file must be restored at any given time, the original file would first be restored, and then the changes for each of the following days would be applied, bringing the file to its most recent state. Saving only the journal is much faster than saving the entire file, since the journal receiver contains only the changes that have occurred to the file.

11.1 Commitment Control

Commitment control is a function that allows you to process a set of database updates as a single transaction. A transaction is defined as a group of changes that act as a single change (such as transferring billing charges from one patient's account to another). Such a transaction would include both removing the charges from one patient as well as adding the charges to the account of the other patient. With commitment control, all changes for a transaction can be undone should something go wrong during the updates, thus eliminating the possibility of only one half of the transaction being completed.

Commitment control is not limited to small transactions such as this. It is also quite convenient to use in long-running batch jobs, where it would be difficult to restart should something go wrong in the middle of the run. If all of the files are processed under commitment control, they can all be rolled back to their state at the beginning of the batch, allowing the entire batch to be rerun with little complications.

COBOL programs take advantage of commitment control with the COMMIT and ROLLBACK statements. Once a series of changes are known to be complete, they can be committed to the database file using the COMMIT statement. If it is determined that the changes are to be "undone," the ROLLBACK statement will remove all changes as far back as the most recent COMMIT (this point is also referred to as a transaction boundary).

Optionally, a notify object (such as a file, data area, or message queue) may be used to capture job information when a job ends prior to the full completion of a transaction. This information can then be used by an operator or another application program to start the failing application from the last successful transaction boundary.

11.2 Journaling Access Paths

Like regular database journals previously described, access path journals are used primarily for database recovery. During the regular journal process, images of records are recorded in a journal receiver. These changes are used to recover a file should the system end abnormally. However, after an abnormal end, the system may find that the access paths built over a file are not synchronized with the data within the file. In this case, the system will automatically rebuild the access path to match the data in the file.

Journaling access paths can reduce the amount of time necessary to rebuild files when the system is restarted. Using them causes the system to record images of the access path in the journal to provide known synchronization points between the access path and its data. If this information is available, the system can recover both the data files and the access paths, ensuring both are synchronized properly. This avoids the lengthy time required to rebuild an entire access path.

11.3 Becoming a "Journalist"

This chapter will present you with a complete working example of a program that uses commitment control. Before executing the commands, make sure you have properly established your current library.

The example in this chapter illustrates commitment control in action. When run, the program displays a panel that allows you to add, change, and delete data entries from a meaningless list. Each data entry is associated with a three-character key so that you can easily identify each item in the list. When run, the display should look like that in Fig. 11.1.

```
                        Test Commitment Control

        Type options, press Enter.
            1=Add      2=Change     4=Delete

        Opt  Key  Data

         o   ooo  ooooooooooooooooooooo
         o   ooo  ooooooooooooooooooooo
         o   ooo  ooooooooooooooooooooo
         o   ooo  ooooooooooooooooooooo
         o   ooo  ooooooooooooooooooooo
         o   ooo  ooooooooooooooooooooo
         o   ooo  ooooooooooooooooooooo
         o   ooo  ooooooooooooooooooooo
         o   ooo  ooooooooooooooooooooo
         o   ooo  ooooooooooooooooooooo
         o   ooo  ooooooooooooooooooooo
         o   ooo  ooooooooooooooooooooo

                                                       More...
        F3=Exit       F8=Commit      F10=Rollback
```

Figure 11.1 Display layout for the commitment control example.

11.3.1 Creating a file

This example will journal a single file that contains two fields: a three-character key and a 20-character data field. Start SEU with the following command, then enter the source in Listing 11.1.

Listing 11.1 Physical file used by the commitment control example.

```
MEMBER NAME:  CMTCTLPF      FILE: QDDSSRC
.....A..........T.Name+++++RLen++TDpB......Functions++++++
A                                         UNIQUE
A             R CMTREC
A               USRKEY      3
A               USRDATA    20
A             K USRKEY


STRSEU QDDSSRC CMTCTLPF TYPE(PF) TEXT('Commitment Ctl Example')
```

The following command will compile and create the file in Listing 11.1:

```
CRTPF CMTCTLPF
```

11.3.2 The display file

The DDS in Listing 11.2 defines the display pictured in Fig. 11.1. Since there is nothing special about this display, there will be no detailed discussion about it.

Listing 11.2 Display file for the commitment control example.

```
MEMBER NAME: USECMTCTL     FILE: QDDSSRC
.....AAN01N02N03T.Name+++++RLen++TDpBLinPosFunctions+++++++++++++++++++
A                                         INDARA
A                                         REF(*LIBL/CMTCTLPF)
A*********************************************************************
A             R ENTRY
A                                         OVERLAY
A                                         CF03(03 'Exit')
A                                         CF08(08 'Commit')
A                                         CF10(10 'Rollback')
A                                       1 29'Test Commitment Control'
A                                         DSPATR(HI)
A                                       3  2'Type option
A                                         COLOR(BLU)
A                                       4  4'1=Add  2=Change  4=Delete'
A                                         COLOR(BLU)
A                                       6  2'Opt'
A                                         DSPATR(HI)
A                                       6  7'Key'
A                                         DSPATR(HI)
A                                       6 13'Data'
A                                         DSPATR(HI)
A               OPT          1A  I  7  3
A               USRKEY    R      I  7  7
A               USRDATA   R      I  7 13
A*********************************************************************
A             R RECLIST                   SFL
A               USRKEY    R      O  8  7
A               USRDATA   R      O  8 13
A*********************************************************************
A             R RECLISTCTL                SFLCTL(RECLIST)
A                                         SFLSIZ(0024)
A                                         SFLPAG(0012)
```

```
A                                  OVERLAY
A    41                            SFLDSP
A                                  SFLDSPCTL
A    42                            SFLCLR
A    43                            SFLEND(*MORE)
A                           23  2'F3=Exit     F8=Commit -
A                                  F10=Rollback'
A                                  COLOR(BLU)
```

Use the following command to start SEU and enter the source in Listing 11.2:

```
STRSEU QDDSSRC USECMTCTL TYPE(DSPF) TEXT('Commitment ctl example')
```

Compile and create the display file with the following command:

```
CRTDSPF USECMTCTL QDDSSRC
```

11.3.3 The COBOL program

When run, the COBOL program in Listing 11.3 allows you to enter, update, and delete record to the file created in Sec. 11.3.1. After each action, the subfile is refreshed to show the changes.

Listing 11.3 COBOL program for the commitment control example.

```
MEMBER NAME: USECMTCTL        FILE: QLBLSRC
....-..A...B..-....2....-....3....-....4....-....5....-....6....-....7
         IDENTIFICATION DIVISION.
         PROGRAM-ID. USECMTCTL.

         ENVIRONMENT DIVISION.
         CONFIGURATION SECTION.
         INPUT-OUTPUT SECTION.
         FILE-CONTROL.
             SELECT DISPFILE ASSIGN TO WORKSTATION-USECMTCTL-SI
                 ORGANIZATION IS TRANSACTION
                 ACCESS MODE IS DYNAMIC
                 RELATIVE KEY IS SFL-RECNUM.
             SELECT COMMITMENT-FILE ASSIGN TO DATABASE-CMTCTLPF
                 ORGANIZATION IS INDEXED
                 ACCESS MODE IS DYNAMIC
                 RECORD KEY IS EXTERNALLY-DESCRIBED-KEY.

[1]      I-O-CONTROL.
             COMMITMENT CONTROL FOR COMMITMENT-FILE.

         DATA DIVISION.
         FILE SECTION.

         FD  DISPFILE.
         01  DISP-REC                       PIC X(200).
         FD  COMMITMENT-FILE.
         01  COMMITMENT-REC.
             COPY DDS-ALL-FORMATS OF CMTCTLPF.
         WORKING-STORAGE SECTION.
```

```
     77  SFL-RECNUM                          PIC 9(7).

     01  COMMITMENT-FILE-STATUS              PIC X.
         88 EOF-COMMITMENT                          VALUE "E".
         88 MID-COMMITMENT                          VALUE " ".

     01  ENTRY-IN.
         COPY DDS-ENTRY-I OF USECMTCTL.
     01  RECLIST-OUT.
         COPY DDS-RECLIST-O OF USECMTCTL.

     01  INDIC-AREA.
         03  EACH-IND OCCURS 99 TIMES PIC 1 INDICATOR 1.
             88 IND-OFF VALUE B"0".
             88 IND-ON  VALUE B"1".
     01  INDIC-USAGE.
         03  FK-EXIT                         PIC 99 VALUE 03.
         03  FK-COMMIT                       PIC 99 VALUE 08.
         03  FK-ROLLBACK                     PIC 99 VALUE 10.
         03  I-SFLDSP                        PIC 99 VALUE 41.
         03  I-SFLCLR                        PIC 99 VALUE 42.
         03  I-SFLEND                        PIC 99 VALUE 43.


     PROCEDURE DIVISION.
     MAIN-PARA.
         OPEN I-O COMMITMENT-FILE DISPFILE.
[2]      SET IND-ON(I-SFLEND) TO TRUE.

         PERFORM UNTIL IND-ON(FK-EXIT)
             PERFORM FILL-SUBFILE
             WRITE DISP-REC FORMAT "RECLISTCTL" INDIC INDIC-AREA
             WRITE DISP-REC FORMAT "ENTRY" INDIC INDIC-AREA
             READ DISPFILE INTO ENTRY-IN FORMAT "ENTRY"
                 INDICATORS ARE INDIC-AREA
             EVALUATE TRUE
                 WHEN IND-ON(FK-EXIT)          CONTINUE
[3]              WHEN IND-ON(FK-COMMIT)        COMMIT
[4]              WHEN IND-ON(FK-ROLLBACK)      ROLLBACK
                 WHEN OTHER
                     IF OPT OF ENTRY-I NOT EQUAL SPACES
                         PERFORM CHECK-FOR-ACTION
                     END-IF
             END-EVALUATE
         END-PERFORM.

         CLOSE COMMITMENT-FILE DISPFILE.
         STOP RUN.

     FILL-SUBFILE.
         SET IND-OFF(I-SFLDSP) IND-ON(I-SFLCLR) TO TRUE.
         WRITE DISP-REC FORMAT "RECLISTCTL" INDIC INDIC-AREA.
         MOVE ZERO TO SFL-RECNUM.
         SET IND-OFF(I-SFLCLR) TO TRUE.

[5]      MOVE LOW-VALUES TO USRKEY OF COMMITMENT-REC.
         START COMMITMENT-FILE
             KEY IS NOT LESS THAN EXTERNALLY-DESCRIBED-KEY
             INVALID KEY
                 CONTINUE
             NOT INVALID KEY
                 SET MID-COMMITMENT TO TRUE
                 PERFORM UNTIL EOF-COMMITMENT
                     READ COMMITMENT-FILE NEXT RECORD
```

```
                    AT END
                        SET EOF-COMMITMENT TO TRUE
                    NOT AT END
                        ADD 1 TO SFL-RECNUM
                        MOVE CORR CMTREC TO RECLIST
                        WRITE SUBFILE DISP-REC FROM RECLIST
                            FORMAT "RECLIST"
                END-READ
            END-PERFORM
            SET IND-ON(I-SFLDSP) TO TRUE
        END-START.

    CHECK-FOR-ACTION.
        MOVE USRKEY OF ENTRY-I TO USRKEY OF CMTREC.
        EVALUATE OPT OF ENTRY-IN
            WHEN "1"
                MOVE USRDATA OF ENTRY-I TO USRDATA OF CMTREC
                WRITE COMMITMENT-REC
                        INVALID KEY CONTINUE
                END-WRITE
            WHEN "2"
                READ COMMITMENT-FILE
                    INVALID KEY CONTINUE
                    NOT INVALID KEY
                        MOVE USRDATA OF ENTRY-I TO USRDATA OF CMTREC
                        REWRITE COMMITMENT-REC
                END-READ
            WHEN "4"
                DELETE COMMITMENT-FILE
                        INVALID KEY CONTINUE
                END-DELETE
        END-EVALUATE.
```

Notes about the program in Listing 11.3 follow:

1. In order to use commitment control, you must specify the I-O-CONTROL entry in the ENVIRONMENT DIVISION. Specify USE COMMITMENT CONTROL for each file name that will use commitment control.

2. The SFLEND indicator is turned on because this program always loads the entire database file into the subfile. The SFLEND indicator marks the subfile as being complete.

3. If the user presses the function key associated with committing the changes, the COMMIT statement will be executed.

4. If the user presses the function key associated with rolling back the changes, the ROLLBACK statement will be executed.

5. The LOW-VALUES constant is used in this case to reset the file to the beginning. Each time the user makes a change to the database, the subfile will be reloaded with the entire file.

Start SEU and enter the source code in Listing 11.3 with the following command:

```
STRSEU QLBLSRC USECMTCTL TYPE(CBL) TEXT('Commitment ctl example')
```

To compile and create the COBOL program, use the following command:

```
CRTCBLPGM USECMTCTL
```

Do not try and run the program yet, since it requires commitment control to be active (commitment control has not been started yet).

11.3.4 Creating a journal receiver

Before you can start journaling (or using commitment control), you must create a *journal receiver* and a *journal* to manage the journal receiver. As stated earlier, the journal receiver will contain a log of the changes made to a file which is being journaled. In this section, you will create a journal receiver called EXAMPLRCVR and a journal called EXAMPLJRN. To create a journal receiver, use the create journal receiver (CRTJRNRCV) command:

```
CRTJRNRCV JRNRCV(EXAMPLRCVR)
```

11.3.5 Creating a journal

Once the journal receiver has been created, you can create a journal to manage it. Use the create journal (CRTJRN) command to create the journal:

```
CRTJRN JRN(EXAMPLJRN) JRNRCV(EXAMPLRCVR)
```

The JRNRCV keyword specifies which journal receiver to use for logging file changes.

11.3.6 Starting the journal function

Now that all of the system-related components are in place, you are ready to start journaling the file. The following command will initiate journaling for the file CMTCTLPF.

```
STRJRNPF  FILE(CMTCTLPF) JRN(EXAMPLJRN)
```

The physical file is now being recorded journaled.

11.3.7 Starting and ending commitment control

Once the journals have been created, you must start commitment control in order to use them. The start commitment control (STRCMTCTL) command is used for this function:

```
STRCMTCTL LCKLVL(*CHG)
```

The lock level option controls how records are locked during updating. There are three options for this keyword:

- *CHG:* Every record read for update (for a file opened under commitment control) is locked. If a record is changed, added, or deleted, that record remains locked until the transaction is committed or rolled back. Records that are accessed for update operations but are released without being changed are unlocked.

- *CS:* Every record accessed for files opened under commitment control is locked. A record that is read, but not changed or deleted, is unlocked when a different record is read. Records that are changed, added, or deleted are locked until the transaction is committed or rolled back.

- *ALL:* Every record accessed for files opened under commitment control is locked until the transaction is committed or rolled back.

11.3.8 Seeing is believing

You are now ready to test the commitment-control example program. By this time, you have started journaling the physical file and started commitment control; therefore the last necessary action is to start the program:

```
CALL USECMTCTL
```

Enter several records by putting a "1" in the option column, a key value in the key field, and some data in the data column. After each entry, press Enter to see the new data moved into the subfile list.

To change some data, put a "2" in the option column and specify the key value along with the new data for the record. Option 4 will delete a record from the subfile list.

At any point, you can press the Rollback key (F10) or the Commit key (F8). Pressing the Rollback key will cause any transactions to be undone up until the last transaction boundary (the last COMMIT).

While testing, you may want to exit the program (or go to an alternate session) and view the file to see how it looks after various transactions. When you are finished trying the program, you can use the F3 key to exit.

You can end commitment control with the ENDCMTCTL command. Commitment control will automatically be ended when you sign off (journaling will not end automatically). The file will remain logically associated with the journal until you issue the end journal physical file ENDJRNPF command.

11.4   Summary

Journals and journal receivers are OS/400 objects that track changes to database files. Journals can track both changes to the data as well as to a database's access path (index). Journaling changes to a file's data provides a means of restoring (or removing) changes that have occurred to the data after an abnormal ending of the system. Journaling a file's access path provides a means of restoring a file's access path quickly without having to rebuild the entire access path completely.

Commitment control works hand in hand with journaling. When commitment control is active, changes made to a journaled file can be undone on the spot. When a set of transactions are known to be complete, the entire set can be made permanent by committing the changes to the file. The COBOL/400 COMMIT statement is used for this purpose.

If a set of transactions has not been committed and they are found to be incomplete, they can be undone by rolling back the changes as far back as the most recent COMMIT (or transaction boundary). The COBOL/400 ROLLBACK statement is used for this purpose.

Remember, commitment control is program-related—it is used for rollback and commit functions. Commitment control uses the journaling function to accomplish this.

12

Messages and Message Files

This chapter discusses the procedures for creating message files, message queues, and message descriptions. It will also discuss the various types of messages available for you to use when developing systems on the AS/400 computer.

The sample application developed in the final part of this book contains working examples of sending and receiving messages from both COBOL and CL.

12.1 System Messages

The AS/400 uses messages to communicate between programs, between jobs, between users, and between users and programs. A message can be predefined or immediate:

- A predefined message is created and exists outside the program that uses it. Predefined messages are stored in message files and have a message number.

- An immediate message is created by the sender at the time it is sent. Immediate messages are not stored in message files.

The AS/400 comes loaded with an extensive set of predefined messages for communication between programs within the system and between the system and its users. The main message file used by the operating system is QCPFMSG, which is found in library QSYS. An example of a system message found in QCPFMSG is

```
CPF9801 Object YOURFILE in library *LIBL not found.
```

Predefined messages that are kept in message files are identified by a unique seven-character code. Each message is defined by a message description that contains information such as:

- Message text
- Message help text
- Severity level
- Valid and default reply values

12.1.1 Message types

There are several different types of messages that can be used on the AS/400, as shown in Table 12.1.

TABLE 12.1 Message Types

Message Type	Description
Informational (*INFO)	A message that conveys information about the condition of a function.
Inquiry (*INQ)	A message that conveys information but also asks for a reply.
Notify (*NOTIFY)	A message that describes a condition for which a program requires corrective action or a reply from its calling program. A program can monitor for the arrival of notify messages from the programs it calls.
Reply (*RPY)	A message that is a response to a received inquiry or notify message.
Sender's copy (*COPY)	A copy of an inquiry or notify message that is kept by the sender.
Request (*RQS)	A message that requests a function from the receiving program. (i.e. a CL command can be a request message)
Completion (*COMP)	A message that conveys completion status of work.
Diagnostic (*DIAG)	A message relating to errors in the processing of a system function, in an application program, or in input data.
Status (*STATUS)	A message that describes the status of the work done by a program. A program can monitor for the arrival of status messages from the program it calls. Status messages sent to the external message queue (*EXT) are shown at the display station and can be used to inform the display station user of an operation in progress.
Escape (*ESCAPE)	A message that describes a condition for which a program must end abnormally. A program can monitor for the arrival of escape messages from the program it calls or from the system.

12.2   Message Queues

Messages are sent and received through message queues. Messages that are issued as a result of a direct request (such as a command at the workstation) are displayed on the workstation where the request was made. For all other messages, the user or program must receive the message from the queue or display it. Working with message queues will be discussed later in this chapter.

12.3   Message Files

Message files are objects that hold message descriptions. Each licensed program on the AS/400 has a message file that contains application specific messages (such as COBOL/400 compiler messages). You can create your own message files and message descriptions. By using message files and predefined messages, you can use the same message in several programs but define it only once. Using message files also aids in translating an application into another language. Changing the description in a message file has no effect on the programs that use it. Working with message files will be discussed later in this chapter.

12.4   Creating a Message Queue

Use the create message queue (CRTMSGQ) command to create a new message queue:

```
CRTMSGQ MSGQ(lib-name/queue-name) TEXT('text-description')
```

- `lib-name` defines the library where the queue should be created; if omitted, the current library (*CURLIB) will be used.
- `queue-name` defines the name of the message queue being created.
- `text-description` is optional and associates a textual description of the message queue.

Use the following command to create a message queue for the examples in this chapter:

```
CRTMSGQ MSGQ(TSTMSGQ) TEXT('Text message queue')
```

Once created, you can immediately perform operations on the message queue (see Table 12.2). To test the message queue, you can send a simple message to it, as shown in Fig. 12.1.

You can see the other options available by typing SNDMSG and then pressing the F4=Prompt key. For instance, you could specify the

TABLE 12.2   Commands for Message Queues

CHGMSGQ	Changes attributes about a message queue (such as how the messages are delivered)
CLRMSGQ	Clears a message queue
DLTMSGQ	Deletes a message queue
WRKMSGQ	Works with message queues (combines the other commands into a full-screen work-with list)

```
   SNDMSG MSG('Hello World') TOMSGQ(TSTMSGQ)
or
   SNDMSG 'Hello World' TSTMSGQ
```

Figure 12.1   Sending a message to a message queue.

TOUSR parameter instead of the TOMSGQ parameter to send the message to another user instead of a message queue.

To view the message just sent, use the DSPMSG command (see Fig. 12.2). The display shown in Fig. 12.3 should appear. You can remove an individual message by positioning the cursor over the message (using the cursor keys, not the tab or space key) and pressing the F11 key. You can also use F13 to remove all messages. When finished with this display, press Enter.

```
   DSPMSG MSGQ(TSTMSGQ)
or
   DSPMSG TSTMSGQ
```

Figure 12.2   Viewing the contents of a message queue.

```
                        Display Messages
                                          System:    S1011514
Queue . . . . . :    TSTMSGQ          Program . . . . :    *DSPMSG
   Library . . . :      YOURLIB          Library . . . :
Serverity  . . . :   00                Delivery  . . . :    *HOLD

Type reply (if required), press Enter.
   From  . . . :    GERRYK          02/16/95    15:20:50
   Hello World




                                                        Bottom
F3=Exit            F11=Remove a message             F12=Cancel
F13=Remove all     F16=Remove all except unanswered F24=More keys
```

Figure 12.3   Results of using the DSPMSG command.

12.5 Creating a Message File

In Sec. 12.4, you saw how to send an immediate message to a message queue. In this section, you will see how to create a message file and add predefined messages to it. You can then refer to the predefined messages by their message code.

To create a message file, use the create message file (CRTMSGF) command. The basic syntax for the CRTMSGF command is

```
CRTMSGF MSGF(lib-name/message-file-name) TEXT('Text description')
```

Use the following command to create a test message file for the examples in this chapter:

```
CRTMSGF MSGF(TSTMSGF) TEXT('Test message file)
```

Once created, you can use the WRKMSGD command to work with the messages held in the file (at this time, there are no messages).

```
WRKMSGD MSGF(TSTMSGF)
```

12.6 Adding Messages

You should now see a screen that allows you to add a message by pressing F6=Add. Press the F6 key and then specify the following information to create your first message:

Message identifier	TST0001
First-level message text:	'My first message'
Second-level message text:	'This is extended help'

Then press the Enter key. You will need to press the F5=Refresh key to refresh the list to include the newly created message.

You have just defined your first message. If you did it successfully, you should see it on the Work with Message Descriptions display (see Fig. 12.4).

12.6.1 Defining substitution variables

Messages that contain fill-in variables are said to have substitution variables. The message in Fig. 12.5 includes one substitution variable (expressed as &1).

When the message is displayed or retrieved, variable &1 is replaced with a phone number. This number is supplied by the sender of the message. When the message in Fig. 12.5 is sent with message data of 555-1212, it will be formatted as shown in Fig. 12.6.

Substitution variables can appear in both first- and second-level

```
                    Work with Message Descriptions
                                                    System:    S1011514
Message file:    TSTMSGF      Library:    YOURLIB

Position to . . . . . . .    _____    Message ID

Type options, press Enter.
  2=Change    4=Delete    5=Display details    6=Print

Opt  Message ID  Severity  Message Text
  _    TST0001        0     My first message




                                                             Bottom
Parameters or command
===>  _____
F3=Exit    F5=Refresh    F6=Add    F12=Cancel    F24=More keys
```

Figure 12.4 Work with Message Descriptions screen after adding a message.

```
Requested number "&1" was not found.
```

Figure 12.5 Message with one substitution variable.

```
Requested number "555-1212" was not found.
```

Figure 12.6 Message with substitution data filled in.

message text (second-level message text is also known as extended help and is shown when the user positions the cursor on an error message and presses HELP or F1). The format of a substitution variable is an ampersand (&), followed by a number from 1 through 99.

Substitution variables are defined when the message is created. For each substitution variable found within the first- and second-level messages, there must be a corresponding FMT (data format) keyword specified. The ADDMSGD command for the message in Fig. 12.5 is shown in Fig. 12.7. The FMT keyword specifies that the substitution

```
ADDMSGD MSGID(TST0002) +
        MSGF(PHONEMSGS) +
        MSG('Requested number "&1" was not found.') +
        FMT((*CHAR 20))
```

Figure 12.7 Adding a message with one substitution variable.

```
ADDMSGD MSGID(TST0003) +
        MSGF(TSTMSGF) +
        MSG('Chart &1 not found in office &2.') +
        FMT((*CHAR 5) (*CHAR 10))
```

Figure 12.8 Message definition with two variables.

variable &1 is a character variable of length 20. A message that contains two substitution variables would look like that in Fig. 12.8.

When sending a message that contains substitution variables, you must also send the data that is used in the substitution variables. The data is represented as a single character string with a length equal to the sum of the lengths of all substitution variables in the message. For example, the message defined in Fig. 12.8 would be sent as described in Fig. 12.9. When message TST0003 is formatted, it will appear as shown in Fig. 12.10.

```
SNDPGMMSG MSGID(TST0003) +
          MSGF(TSTMSGF) +
          MSGDTA(AB001SSK1ЬЬЬЬЬЬ)
```

Figure 12.9 Sending a message with two substitution variables.

```
Chart AB001 not found in office SSK1.
```

Figure 12.10 Results of the SNDPGMMSG command in Fig. 12.9.

12.7 Sending Messages to Users

There are several commands that can be used to send a message to a system user:

- **SNDMSG:** Sends an informational or inquiry message to another message queue such as the system operator's queue, a workstation's queue, or another user's queue.

- **SNDBRKMSG:** Sends an immediate message from a workstation, a program, or a job to one or more display stations to be immediately displayed upon the workstation.

- **SNDPGMMSG:** Sends a variety of message types from a CL program. This command is only available from within a CL program. It cannot be executed on a command line.

- *SNDUSRMSG:* Sends a message and optionally waits for a reply from the recipient. This command is only available from within a CL program. It cannot be executed on a command line.

The command in Fig. 12.11 shows how to send a message to the system operator. You can also replace *SYSOPR with your own user identification.

```
SNDMSG MSG('Hello') TOUSR(*SYSOPR)
```

Figure 12.11 Sending a message to the system operator.

12.8 Sending Messages from a CL Program

To send a message from a CL program, use the send program message (SNDPGMMSG) or the send user message (SNDUSRMSG) command.

12.8.1 Sending with SNDPGMMSG

The SNDPGMMSG command can send informational, inquiry, completion, diagnostic, request, escape, status, and notify messages to external message queues, message queues of programs within the current job, the system operator message queue, a workstation message queue, or another user's message queue.

Listing 12.1 Sending a message from a CL program.

```
DCL &PHONENUM TYPE(*CHAR) LEN(20) VALUE('555-1212')
    .
SNDPGMMSG MSGID(TST0002) MSGF(TSTMSGF) +
          MSGDTA(&PHONENUM) TOPGMQ(*EXT) +
          MSGTYPE(*INFO)
```

For example, to send the message defined in Fig. 12.7, you would use the commands shown in Listing 12.1 in a CL program. Using *EXT as the program queue is a convenient way of directing the message to the current user's workstation.

12.8.2 Sending messages with SNDUSRMSG

If you are developing an application that may occasionally require a response from the user, you can use the SNDUSRMSG. This command wraps the functionality of SNDPGMMSG and the receive message (RCVMSG) command into a single command.

The example in Listing 12.2 sends a message to the current workstation user and asks them to enter Y or N. A message is then sent back to the workstation indicating which choice was made.

Listing 12.2 Sending a message that requires a reply.

```
PGM
DCL VAR(&REPLY) TYPE(*CHAR) LEN(1)
SNDUSRMSG MSG('Select either Y or N') +
          VALUES(Y N) +
          TOMSGQ(*EXT) +
          MSGRPY(&REPLY)
IF (&REPLY *EQ 'Y') THEN(SNDPGMMSG 'User chose Y')
  ELSE (SNDPGMMSG 'User chose N')
ENDPGM
```

12.8.3 Receiving messages

Messages can be received from a message queue in several ways:

- By message type: You can specify to receive only a certain type of message (i.e., status, completion, etc.).
- By reference key: OS/400 assigns a unique message key to each message sent on the system.
- By location (first or last).
- By both reference key and message type.

When you receive a message from a message queue, you can specify the following:

- Which message queue to receive the message from.
- What type of message to receive.
- Whether to wait for the arrival of a message or to continue.
- Whether to remove the received message from the queue or not.
- Which group of CL variables to receive specific information such as message text, reference key, and message data.

12.9 Sending Messages from COBOL

A COBOL program cannot directly execute the SNDPGMMSG command using the QCMDEXC program, nor are there any COBOL statements that support messaging. Therefore, the only way (as of release 2.3) to send a message is via an OS/400 API.

The QMHSNDPM API is used for sending program messages from high-level languages that do not support messaging. A complete example of using QMHSNDPM can be seen in Part 6.

Part

5

Design Concepts

Good design practices and principles are essential for the successful completion of any project. This part will provide you with some useful tips to consider when designing a system for the AS/400 computer.

Chapter 13 discusses object-oriented programming and how it relates to the AS/400.

Chapter 14 touches on a number of pointers that you can use when developing an application.

Chapter 15 gives you a free (no charge) set of date routines for use in your programs. The date routines perform a variety of functions against dates.

13

Object-Oriented Design—The AS/400 Way

Traditionally, systems that were designed for use on larger systems tended to be less object oriented and more application specific than today. The AS/400 was designed as an object-oriented machine from the beginning. Its roots are in the System/38, which was also an object-oriented machine. But the words *object oriented* for the AS/400 have a slightly different meaning than object oriented in terms of object-oriented programming languages such as C++ and Smalltalk. OS/400 itself is based on objects; the languages and programming tools are not.

This limitation does not necessarily have to restrict the design of an application to traditional top-down programming design. Some object methodologies can be simulated on the AS/400. This chapter will discuss techniques that can be used to make your applications more modular and object oriented.

13.1 Before Starting

Before starting out on any large-scale AS/400 development project, you must first immerse yourself in the problem domain. That is, immerse yourself so deeply that you begin to find nuances about the task at hand that not even the user has considered. Learn as many exceptions to rules as possible. When the user makes a statement such as "this procedure will never change," consider the consequences that will occur when it does change—because it will.

Do not automate a process that is tailored to a manual environment. Systems often replicate arduous and tedious procedures—the only benefit to the user is that they use a terminal instead of paper. Ask questions if a procedure seems unreasonable. For example, if a procedure states that no more than six transactions can appear on a report, find out if that is because it is a "rule of the business" or because the first forms used by the user had room for only six transactions. In the initial design stages, questions are your most important tool.

13.2 Object-Oriented Analysis in a Nutshell

This chapter by no means intends to teach object-oriented analysis and design—it is intended to show how you can apply some of the techniques to designing applications on the AS/400. There are several activities relating to object-oriented analysis:

- Finding classes and objects
- Identifying structures
- Defining attributes
- Defining services

13.2.1 Finding classes and objects

"The most stable aspects of a system, those which are least susceptible to potential change, are the classes and objects which strictly depict the problem domain and the system's responsibilities within that domain."[1] Regardless of the budget size for a project and degree of functionality required, the classes and objects will remain the same. In the case of an air traffic control system, there will always be controllers, airplanes, airports, passengers, etc. Even if the budget is cut, these components will still be an integral part of the system. For this reason, it is important to identify the classes and objects that make up a system.

Object   An *abstraction* of something in a problem domain, reflecting the capabilities of a system to keep information about it, interact with it, or both; an *encapsulation* of attribute values and their exclusive services.

Class   A description of one or more objects with a uniform set of attributes and services, including a description of how to create new objects in the class.

Class-&-Object A term meaning "a class and the objects in that class."[2]

Classes do not always have to be tangible objects such as patients or doctors. An office visit may be considered a class, as well as a service that was rendered during an office visit.

On the AS/400, the following are classes:

- A physical file
- A device
- A program

Once a class has been determined, give it a name. Because OS/400 restricts names to 10 characters, you should try and come up with a three-character abbreviated name for the object. For example, PAT for patient, or DOC (or PHY) for doctor (or physician). These three-letter abbreviations will later be combined with the services provided for the object.

13.2.2 Identifying structures

Once the basic classes have been established, you must identify the structures associated with each class. In the case of a patient management system, there is the basic "patient" class. The structure may more realistically look like this:

Patient

Insurance patient

Medicare patient

Blue-Cross–Blue-Shield patient

Cash patient

On the AS/400, the following structure exists for files:

File

Database files

Physical files

Logical files

DDM files

Display files

Printer files

Since OS/400 does not directly support object-oriented programming, you will be unable to take advantage of inheritance. In light of this, you can avoid using descendant objects, or optionally hide the OS/400's limitation, by specifying an object type on commands. For example, when creating a new patient use

```
CRTPAT TYPE(*BLUECROSS) NAME(...)
```

or you can use different names for commands that create different patient types:

CRTPATBLC	Create Blue-Cross–Blue-Shield patient
CRTPATMED	Create Medicare patient
CRTPATCSH	Create cash patient

13.2.3 Defining attributes

Once the classes have been determined, it is necessary to decide what attributes are associated with each class. In the patient management example, the patient class may have the following attributes:

Patient class
  Name
  Address
  Phone number
  Social security number
  Height
  Weight
  Date of birth

Office class
  Office name
  Address
  Phone number
  Federal ID number

In terms of the AS/400, the attributes associated with an object will probably be kept in a database file.

13.2.4 Defining services

The services associated with an object define what actions can be performed on the object. In the patient management system, a patient may have the following services:

Patient class
  Create a new patient
  Change a patient's information
  Change a patient's billing method
  Retrieve the patient's address
  Retrieve the patient's statistics (weight, etc.)
  Remove the patient
  Post an office visit to the patient
  View the patient's account activity

In terms of the AS/400, these may all be considered separate commands (not programs—this will be discussed later in this chapter):

CRTPAT	Create a new patient
CHGPAT	Change a patient's information
CHGPATBIL	Change a patient's billing method
RTVPATDTA	Retrieve the patient's address
RTVPATDTA	Retrieve the patient's statistics (weight, etc.)
RMVPAT	Remove the patient
PSTPATVST	Post an office visit to the patient
DSPPATHST	View the patient's account activity

13.3 Using Commands and Programs

One of the main objectives of using object-oriented techniques is to provide a solution that most closely mimics the real-life situation. Encapsulation can make an object so generic that it is usable in other systems as well. For instance, in the patient billing system, the "office" object can be reused by a general ledger system. The "patient" object can be reused in a patient mailing-list system.

Commands can be an extremely powerful tool when designing a system using object-oriented techniques. Since COBOL/400 programs can execute commands directly using the QCMDEXC program, it is possible to take advantage of commands from within a COBOL program. Once a library of commands has been created, they can be used by other high-level languages such as RPG and command language (CL), as well as in batch jobs.

Using commands also helps to allow for change within the objects without affecting the programs that use them. When a command is executed, not all parameters must be specified (unless specifically designed otherwise). Some parameters can contain default values. Therefore, if additional parameters are added to the command, any programs that use the command will be unaffected.

There is a potential problem with commands, though. Commands executed from COBOL programs cannot return values. Therefore, any commands that return data will not function properly when executed using QCMDEXC since there is no way to get the data back into the COBOL program. There are three possible solutions for this limitation:

- Execute the RTV command in a CL program prior to calling the COBOL program—pass the retrieved values to the COBOL program as a parameter.
- Call a CL program from within the COBOL program—have the CL program execute the command that returns a value to CL, further returning the value to the COBOL program.

- Call the command's processing program directly (not recommended). If this is the case, the command processing program must be set up to test the number of parameters passed to it when it was called. If a program is modified to have additional parameters, it must check to see if its caller has provided all the parameters (since older programs may not be aware of the new parameters). If a COBOL program references unpassed parameters, it will receive an escape message and abort.

The most reasonable solution is the first, since most COBOL programs will be associated with a CL program anyway, and the CL program can do much of the work before the COBOL program is executed.

13.4 References

1. Peter Coad and Edward Yourdon, *Object-Oriented Analysis*, 2d ed., 1991.
2. *Ibid.*

14

Writing COBOL/400 Programs with Style

It is most likely that any program you write on an AS/400 computer will eventually be inherited by another analyst or programmer, whether to fix bugs or make enhancements. For this reason, it is important that your code be clean, efficient, and easy to understand. Furthermore, you should establish a good set of standards for file naming, field and variable naming, indicator assignments, etc. This chapter discusses some of the various points to keep in mind when designing or developing an application for the AS/400.

14.1 Standardize Source Physical File Names

If possible, use the supplied IBM source physical file names (QLBLSRC for COBOL source, QDDSSRC for DDS source, QCLSRC for CL source, QCMDSRC for CMD source, etc.). If your installation keeps separate source for each project, create a source library for the project, and within that library use the standardized source physical file names.

14.2 Standardize Variable Naming

Equally important as naming the source physical file is the naming standards you follow for files, records, and fields. Try to avoid using different names for the same data in different records. Use the entire

10 characters that DDS allows for record and field names.* A common practice is to use the first two or three characters of a field name to indicate from which file the field comes. Although this tactic easily identifies a field's owner, it prevents the use of the MOVE CORRE-SPONDING statement. Instead, try to use generic names as much as possible. In place of INVCSTNBR as the customer number in the invoice file, use just CUSTNBR. Establish the initial definition of CUSTNBR in a field-reference file, and you will never have to define it explicitly again throughout the whole software system. Establishing the field reference file takes very little setup time and can save enormous amounts of time when you must make global modifications (e.g., extend the customer number size). If multiple files within the same program have a field name CUSTNBR, you will need to use the OF qualifier:

```
MOVE CSTNBR OF CUST-RCD TO identifier.
```

By the way, if several files contain a field by the same name, each field maintains its own storage—they do *not* share the same storage location as in RPG.

Another common standard is to assign the same name to both the file name and record format name. For example, if the file name is CUST-MAST, the record format name is also CUSTMAST.

14.3 Standardize Indicator Assignments

Establish a good set of indicator standards, and place them in a copy book (perhaps labeled INDICDEF). A useful idea is to code the entire indicator array in this copy book (as seen in the example application in part 6 of this book). In this way, your program does not have to declare the indicator area or functions of the indicators. Just use COPY IN-DICDEF and the indicator area and definitions will be defined based on your predefined standards.

Once you have established the indicator assignments, give short and descriptive names to them and set up indicator constants. Avoid using keyboard legends such as F3; instead, use something more meaningful like FK-EXIT. Then you can turn indicators on and off by name instead of by number. For example, you can use

---

*If the file you are defining will be used by both COBOL and RPG programs, care should be taken when naming files, records, and fields, since standard RPG compilers restrict file names to eight characters, record names to eight characters, and field names to six characters. Furthermore, if the file name and record name are the same, the record name will need to be renamed within the RPG program.

```
SET IND-ON(I-SFLEND) TO TRUE
```

instead of

```
SET IND-ON(54) TO TRUE
```

14.4   Fill in the IDENTIFICATION DIVISION

Considered by many as pointless typing, the IDENTIFICATION DIVI-SION has hidden benefits that show up later in a program's life. Use at least the AUTHOR and DATE-WRITTEN keywords. Brief comments describing the program and its function within a job stream are also helpful.

14.5   Use Informative File Names

Try and use names that indicate the type of information contained in a data file. A file name such as CUSTOMERS clearly identifies what data is kept within the file, as opposed to a name such as JGBCMF01. Use the file's text description to give more details on the contents. When defining logical files, make sure to put a brief description of the key sequence in the file's text description. This helps prevent building multiple indexes on a file with the same key sequence.

Within the COBOL program, consider adding the suffix -FILE to file names and -REC to record names. This makes it easier to distinguish which identifiers refer to files and which refer to records.

14.6   Avoid Using ALL-FORMATS with Display Files

You should avoid using the ALL-FORMATS form of the COPY statement when including externally described display files. When the ALL-FORMATS option is specified, all the records in the file will share a single input/output buffer area. Each READ to the display device will overwrite the contents of the common buffer area, thus any other record formats that share the buffer will lose their contents. To maintain a separate buffer area for each display record, use the COPY DDS statement for each *record,* rather than once for the entire display file.

14.7   Use the LIKE Clause Whenever Possible

The LIKE keyword defines a field to have the same length and attributes as another field. For example, if you need a temporary variable to temporarily hold data from a display file, you declare the temporary variable name to be *like* the variable name found in the display file. To illustrate the power of using the LIKE keyword, assume you have a field named CUSTNBR defined in a file as six characters and a temporary holding field named SAVE-CUSTNBR defined as PIC X(6) in your program. Suppose that sometime later, you expand the CUSTNBR to eight characters. You must go through every program and find variables used for holding CUSTNBR and change them to PIC X(8). However, if you use the declaration

```
01  SAVE-CUSTNBR LIKE CUSTNBR
```

changing the definition of SAVE-CUSTNBR would not be necessary because its length is based on the CUSTNBR field (the program *would* still have to be recompiled though).

14.8 Use 88-Level Conditionals

One of COBOL's most under-used features is its ability to set and test a variable's value by using a condition name. The 88-level conditional can be used for setting a variable to a predefined value, or testing it against a predefined value. The program in Listing 14.1 shows the traditional way of setting and testing a value. In contract, Listing 14.2 shows how to do the same test but using an 88-level conditional. Using 88-level conditionals makes programs easier to understand.

Listing 14.1 Testing a condition without using 88-level conditionals.

```
01  END-OF-FILE-FLAG    PIC X.
     .
     .
READ CUST-FILE
   AT END
      MOVE "Y" TO END-OF-FILE-FLAG
   NOT AT END
      MOVE "N" TO END-OF-FILE-FLAG
END-READ.
IF END-OF-FILE-FLAG EQUAL "Y"
   PERFORM blah blah blah
END-IF.
```

Listing 14.2 Testing a condition using an 88-level conditional.

```
01  END-OF-FLAG          PIC X VALUE "N".
    88 NOT-END-OF-FILE      VALUE "N".
    88 END-OF-FILE          VALUE "Y".

READ CUST-FILE
   AT END
      SET END-OF-FILE TO TRUE
```

```
NOT AT END
    SET NOT-END-OF-FILE TO TRUE
END-READ.
IF END-OF-FILE
    PERFORM blah blah blah
END-IF.
```

14.9   Use Indents Properly

Good use of indentation in a COBOL program is a must. Use indents on all structured statements such as the in-line PERFORM statement, the EVALUATE statement, and the IF statement. Three spaces for each indent level is enough to emphasize the various levels and not too much that the code becomes too hard to read. Listing 14.3 shows several COBOL statements and how they should be indented.

Listing 14.3   Proper use of indents.

```
READ-CUSTOMER-PARA.
    IF SOMETHING-IS-GOOD
        PERFORM SOMETHING-GOOD
    ELSE
        PERFORM SOMETHING-BAD
    END-IF.
    PERFORM VARYING INDX FROM 1 BY 1 UNTIL INDX > 5
        EVALUATE TRUE
            WHEN VAR1 < VAR2
                READ AFILE
                    AT END
                        PERFORM DOUBLE-AXEL 2 TIMES
                    NOT AT END
                        PERFORM TRIPLE-LOOP 3 TIMES
                END-READ
            WHEN VAR1 > VAR2
                PERFORM SALCHOW
            WHEN OTHER
                PERFORM PASO-DOBLE
        END-EVALUATE
    END-PERFORM.
```

14.10   Paragraph Naming (Numbered versus Non-Numbered)

Controversy has always surrounded paragraph-numbering conventions. COBOL programming tradition (or religion) has always maintained paragraph numbers (e.g., 0100-MAIN-PARA) because numbering helps to locate a particular paragraph quickly, especially if the source is large.

Because developing a program is a process of constant refinements and revisions, the actual order in which program paragraphs are initially laid out is likely to change. Often procedures are found to be common with many other paragraphs and are then moved to common locations within the source. When this occurs, the paragraph numbering scheme becomes out of order and extra effort is required to renumber the paragraphs properly. For this reason my preference is not to use paragraph numbers, but to pay close attention to the logical grouping of paragraphs.

Paragraph names should be very clear. COBOL already has a reputation of being wordy, so please try and maintain this reputation. Because program documentation is usually sparse, the paragraph name should convey the true idea of what the paragraph does. You will not receive demerits for names such as "REMOVE-CANCELED-TRANS-ACTIONS" (probably nobody will check your spelling either).

14.11　Keep Paragraphs Short

As a general rule, try to keep paragraphs to no more than one page in length. If a paragraph is considerably longer than one page, you can probably break it down into smaller functional units.

14.12　Avoid the Use of GO TO

Avoid using the GO TO statement as much as possible. COBOL/400 has enough structured statements to handle almost any programming requirement.

14.13　Use Scope Terminators

Always use scope terminators on IF statements, even if the ELSE is not included (see Listing 14.4). Future code changes are much easier when the scope terminator is used. It also helps avoid logic problems with missing (or misplaced) periods.

Listing 14.4　Always use scope terminators on IF statements.

```
IF BAL-DUE GREATER THAN CREDIT-LIMIT
   PERFORM REJECT-CHARGE-REQUEST
ELSE
   PERFORM ACCEPT-CHARGE-REQUEST
END-IF.

IF ACCOUNT-IS-OK
   PERFORM PROCESS-TRANSACTION
END-IF.
```

Using scope terminators on file input/output statements allows several input/output statements to be nested within each other. Formerly, this was not possible, since the only scope terminator used to be the period

(.) and this would terminate all scopes. Listing 14.5 shows how to put a WRITE statement with an AT EOP condition within the INVALID KEY phrase of a READ statement. In previous versions of COBOL, the following PERFORM (shown in gray) would not be possible.

Listing 14.5 Nesting File Statements.

```
READ CUST-FILE
    INVALID KEY
        WRITE ERROR-RCD AFTER ADVANCING 1 LINE
        AT EOP
            PERFORM WRITE-HEADERS
        END-WRITE
        PERFORM AFTER-WRITING-TO-THE-PRINTER-PARA
    NOT INVALID KEY
        PERFORM SUCCESSFUL-READ
END-READ.
```

14.14   Use READ WITH NO LOCK for File Inquiry

Programs that read a database record for inquiry purposes should take advantage of the WITH NO LOCK phrase. When a record is read from a file that has been opened in I-O mode, the record is locked and unavailable to other programs until the program reads another record, rewrites the same record, closes the file, or ends. Using the WITH NO LOCK phrase allows a program to read from a file that has been opened in update mode (I-O) without locking the record.

14.15   Use Subprograms for Modularity

Use the CALL statement to make your programs more modular. Remove logic that can be used by other programs and create a library of subprograms that can be used throughout an entire installation. For example, if it is necessary for a program to obtain a tenant's current balance, it makes sense to put this "function" in a separate subprogram that can be used by many programs. In this way, should a change be necessary to the way a tenant's balance is calculated, it will only need to be changed in the subprogram. Subprograms should be used for such functions as date formatting, date arithmetic, account information, balance look-up, etc.

14.16   Use In-Line PERFORM Statements Whenever Possible

When you want to repeat a group of statements several times, use either an in-line or out-of-line PERFORM statement. Use an out-of-line

PERFORM only when the block of code will be used by other parts of the program. Listing 14.6 shows an out-of-line PERFORM that should be expressed using an in-line PERFORM (the preferred way is shown in Listing 14.7).

Listing 14.6 Using an out-of-line PERFORM.

```
CLEAR-ALL-INDICATORS.
    PERFORM CLEAR-ONE-INDICATOR VARYING INDX FROM 1 BY 1
        UNTIL INDX GREATER THAN 50.

CLEAR-ONE-INDICATOR.
    SET IND-ON(INDX) TO TRUE.
```

Listing 14.7 Using an in-line PERFORM.

```
CLEAR-ALL-INDICATORS.
    PERFORM VARYING INDX FROM 1 BY 1 UNTIL INDX > 50
        SET IND-ON(INDX) TO TRUE
    END-PERFORM.
```

14.17 Use the MOVE CORRESPONDING Statement

The MOVE CORRESPONDING phrase should be used when moving data fields between similarly defined data structures. If field names are standardized throughout a system, the MOVE CORRESPONDING statement prevents the need of coding multiple MOVE statements when transferring data from one record buffer to another. Listing 14.8 shows how the MOVE CORRESPONDING statement can accomplish the same results as the program in Listing 14.9. Note that only fields ACCTNBR, CUSTNAME, and CUSTADDR are moved with the MOVE CORRESPONDING statement.

Listing 14.8 Moving fields with the MOVE CORRESPONDING statement.

```
01  DISPLAY-REC.
    03  ACCTNBR      PIC X(10).
    03  DISP-STATUS  PIC X(2).
    03  CUSTNAME     PIC X(30).
    03  DISP-TIME    PIC 9(6).
    03  CUSTADDR     PIC X(30).

01  RECORD-BUFFER.
    03  ACCTNBR      PIC X(10).
    03  CUSTNAME     PIC X(30).
    03  CUSTADDR     PIC X(30).
    .
    .
MOVE CORRESPONDING DISPLAY-REC TO RECORD-BUFFER.
```

Listing 14.9 Using only the MOVE statement.

```
01  DISPLAY-REC.
    03  ACCTNBR      PIC X(10).
    03  CUSTNAME     PIC X(30).
    03  CUSTADDR1    PIC X(30).


01  RECORD-BUFFER.
    03  ACCTNBR      PIC X(10).
    03  CUSTNAME     PIC X(30).
    03  CUSTADDR1    PIC X(30).

      .
      .
      .
MOVE ACCTNBR OF DISPLAY-REC TO ACCTNBR OF RECORD-BUFFER.
MOVE CUSTNAME OF DISPLAY-REC TO CUSTNAME OF RECORD-BUFFER.
MOVE CUSTADDR OF DISPLAY-REC TO CUSTADDR OF RECORD-BUFFER.
```

14.18   Use the EVALUATE Statement
Instead of Nested IF Statements

When IF statements become nested more than two or three levels deep, you should consider using the EVALUATE statement instead. Complex nested IF statements are hard to decipher and make program maintenance difficult. Using the EVALUATE statement can make complex conditions easy to read and understand.

15

COBOL Date Routines

Convenient and accurate date routines are essential to any programmer. It is often necessary to write programs that calculate the days between days, the date 30 days from now, what the date was 180 days ago, and so on. This chapter contains a small library of routines that perform the most common of date calculation requirements.

The remaining part of this chapter is broken into three sections:

- The section titled *Copy Books* defines several COPY books that are required by most of the date routines.

- The section titled *Base Routines* defines the two main programs used by most of the date routines. These two programs convert 8-digit dates (CCYYMMDD) into a universal date and back.

- The section titled *Date Routines* gives the program listings for the data routines.

Since the date routines provided in this chapter will be useful for any programs written on the AS/400 computer, you may want to consider creating a special library specifically for these programs.

15.1 COPY Books

In order to reduce program size and make the functions more generic, a set of copy books are used. Table 15.1 defines the copy books discussed here.

TABLE 15.1   Copy Book Definitions

Copy book name	Contents
DATCONSTNT	Various constants used by all the date routines.
DATDTATYPS	Definitions of the various data types (such as generic dates, durations, days of week, etc.) used by the date routines.
DATPGMHDR	The identification division for all of the date routines.
DATRETCOD	Defines the various errors and sets up 88-level identifiers for each error.
DATWRKVARS	An assortment of commonly used variables. This is used to reduce program size.

15.1.1   DATCONSTNT—Date constants

The date constants copy book includes constants used throughout the date routines (see Listing 15.1).

Listing 15.1   Date constants.

```
MEMBER NAME:    DATCONSTNT    FILE: QLBLSRC
.....-..A...B..-....2....-....3....-....4....-....5....-....6....-....7..
    01  DATE-CONSTANTS.
        03 C-MIN-UD          LIKE GEN-UNIVDATE   VALUE 1721424.
        03 C-MAX-UD          LIKE GEN-UNIVDATE   VALUE 5373484.
        03 C-MIN-DOW         LIKE GEN-WEEKDAY    VALUE 1.
        03 C-MAX-DOW         LIKE GEN-WEEKDAY    VALUE 7.
        03 C-MIN-DOM         LIKE GEN-DAY        VALUE 1.
        03 C-MIN-MOY         LIKE GEN-MONTH      VALUE 1.
        03 C-MAX-MOY         LIKE GEN-MONTH      VALUE 12.
        03 C-MIN-YEAR        LIKE GEN-CENTYEAR   VALUE 1.
        03 C-MAX-YEAR        LIKE GEN-CENTYEAR   VALUE 9999.
        03 C-MIN-MONTH-DUR   LIKE GEN-DURATION   VALUE -119987.
        03 C-MAX-MONTH-DUR   LIKE GEN-DURATION   VALUE 119987.
        03 C-MIN-DAY-DUR     LIKE GEN-DURATION   VALUE -3652060.
        03 C-MAX-DAY-DUR     LIKE GEN-DURATION   VALUE 3652060.
        03 C-GCHGY           LIKE GEN-GREG       VALUE 1582.
        03 C-GCHGM           LIKE GEN-GREG       VALUE 10.
        03 C-OFFSET          LIKE GEN-LRGINT     VALUE 1720995.
        03 C-GREG-CUTOFF     LIKE GEN-GREG       VALUE 588829.
```

15.1.2   DATDTATYPS—Date data types

The following copy book defines the various types of data that are used in the date routines. You may notice that there are almost no PIC statements in any of the programs—instead, the LIKE statement is used to declare temporary variables to have the same attributes as the generic ones given in Listing 15.2.

Listing 15.2 Generic data types.

```
MEMBER NAME:    DATDTATYPS    FILE: QLBLSRC
....-..A...B..-....2....-....3....-....4....-....5....-....6....-....7..
   01  PRIMITIVES.
       03  GEN-CHAR10          PIC X(10).
       03  GEN-INT             PIC S9(7).
       03  GEN-LRGINT          PIC S9(15).
       03  GEN-STRING50        PIC X(50).
       03  GEN-DATEFMT         PIC X(4).
       03  GEN-DATE-STRING     PIC X(15).


   01  GENERIC-DATA-TYPES.
       03  GEN-DATE            PIC 9(8).
       03  GEN-UNIVDATE        LIKE GEN-LRGINT.
       03  GEN-WEEKDAY         LIKE GEN-INT.
       03  GEN-CENTCODE        LIKE GEN-INT.
       03  GEN-DURATION        LIKE GEN-INT.
       03  GEN-GREG            LIKE GEN-INT.
       03  GEN-RETCODE         PIC X(7).
       03  GEN-DAY             PIC 99.
       03  GEN-MONTH           PIC 99.
       03  GEN-YEAR            PIC 99.
       03  GEN-CENTURY         PIC 99.
       03  GEN-CENTYEAR        PIC 9999.
```

15.1.3 DATPGMHDR—Common program header

The common program header is used to reduce source program size (see Listing 15.3). It is used to set up the IDENTIFICATION and ENVIRONMENT divisions for all data programs.

Listing 15.3 Common program header.

```
MEMBER NAME:    DATPGMHDR    FILE: QLBLSRC
....-..A...B..-....2....-....3....-....4....-....5....-....6....-....7..
       IDENTIFICATION DIVISION.
       PROGRAM-ID.     PGMNAME.
       AUTHOR.         GERRY S KAPLAN.

       ENVIRONMENT DIVISION.
       CONFIGURATION SECTION.
       SOURCE-COMPUTER.  IBM-AS400.
       OBJECT-COMPUTER.  IBM-AS400.

       DATA DIVISION.
```

15.1.4 DATRETCOD—Return code definitions

Whether an operation is completed successfully or not can be determined by the contents of the return code. If the return code is blank, the operation was successful. For definitions, see Table 15.2 and Listing 15.4.

TABLE 15.2   Return Code Definitions

Return	Description
blanks	Successful completion
DAT0001	General error
DAT0002	Day duration error
DAT0003	Day of week error
DAT0004	Month duration error
DAT0005	Invalid date specified (regular or universal)
DAT0006	Date range error

Listing 15.4   Return code definitions.

```
MEMBER NAME:   DATRETCOD      FILE: QLBLSRC
....-..A...B..-....2....-....3....-....4....-....5....-....6....-....7..
     01  RETCODE                LIKE GEN-RETCODE.
         88 RC-NO-ERROR             VALUE SPACES.
         88 RC-ERROR-OTHER          VALUE "DAT0001".
         88 RC-ERROR-IDDER          VALUE "DAT0002".
         88 RC-ERROR-IDWER          VALUE "DAT0003".
         88 RC-ERROR-IMDER          VALUE "DAT0004".
         88 RC-ERROR-INVERR         VALUE "DAT0005".
         88 RC-ERROR-RANGE          VALUE "DAT0006".
```

15.1.5   DATWRKVARS—Common work variables

Many of the date programs perform calculations that require similar temporary variables. This copy book defines the most commonly used set of temporary variables (see Listing 15.5).

Listing 15.5   Work variables.

```
MEMBER NAME:   DATWRKVARS     FILE: QLBLSRC
....-..A...B..-....2....-....3....-....4....-....5....-....6....-....7..
     01  DATE-TEMP-VARS.
         03 TEMP-LRGINT          LIKE GEN-LRGINT.
         03 TEMP-INT             LIKE GEN-INT.
         03 TEMP-UNVDAT          LIKE GEN-UNIVDATE.
         03 TEMP-MOY             LIKE GEN-INT.
         03 TEMP-DOM             LIKE GEN-INT.
         03 TEMP-YEAR            LIKE GEN-INT.
         03 TEMP-LDM             LIKE GEN-DAY.

     01  INT-RETCODE             LIKE GEN-RETCODE.
         88 NO-ERROR                 VALUE SPACES.
```

15.1.6   DATLEAPTBL—Leap year tables

The leap year table (Listing 15.6) is used by two programs: LASTDOM (last day of the month) and DAYSINYR (days in a year).

Listing 15.6   Leap year tables.

```
MEMBER NAME:    DATLEAPTBL     FILE: QLBLSRC
....-..A...B..-....2....-....3....-....4....-....5....-....6....-....7..
     01 NOT-LEAP-TBL        PIC X(24) VALUE "312831303130313130313031".
     01 NOT-LEAP-ARRAY REDEFINES NOT-LEAP-TBL.
        03 NLP-DAYS OCCURS 12 TIMES PIC 99.

     01 LEAP-TBL            PIC X(24) VALUE "312931303130313130313031".
     01 LEAP-ARRAY REDEFINES LEAP-TBL.
        03 LP-DAYS OCCURS 12 TIMES PIC 99.
```

15.2   Base Routines

Date programs that perform math on two dates will first convert the two dates into a universal date. A universal date is an integer value that can be easily manipulated. After calculations are performed, it may be necessary to convert a universal date back to a regular date format. The two programs in this section convert between the two date formats.

15.2.1   DATETOUD—Date to universal date

The date to universal date program converts a general CCYYMMDD date into an integer based universal date (see Listing 15.7).

Listing 15.7   Date to universal date program.

```
MEMBER NAME:    DATETOUD       FILE: QLBLSRC
....-..A...B..-....2....-....3....-....4....-....5....-....6....-....7..
     COPY DATPGMHDR REPLACING PGMNAME BY DATETOUD.

     WORKING-STORAGE SECTION.

     COPY DATDTATYPS.
     COPY DATWRKVARS.
     COPY DATCONSTNT.

     01  PROGRAM-VARIABLES.
         03 YEAR              LIKE GEN-CENTYEAR.
         03 MONTH-OF-YEAR     LIKE GEN-MONTH.
         03 CENTR             LIKE GEN-LRGINT.

     LINKAGE SECTION.
     01  DATE-IN.
         03 YY1-IN            LIKE GEN-CENTYEAR.
         03 MM1-IN            LIKE GEN-MONTH.
         03 DD1-IN            LIKE GEN-DAY.
     01  UNIV-DATE-OUT        LIKE GEN-UNIVDATE.
```

```
COPY DATRETCOD.

PROCEDURE DIVISION USING DATE-IN UNIV-DATE-OUT RETCODE.
MAIN-PARA.
    SET RC-NO-ERROR TO TRUE.
    IF YY1-IN LESS THAN C-MIN-YEAR
        SET RC-ERROR-OTHER TO TRUE
    ELSE
        MOVE YY1-IN TO YEAR
        IF MM1-IN GREATER THAN 2
            ADD 1 TO MM1-IN GIVING MONTH-OF-YEAR
        ELSE
            SUBTRACT 1 FROM YEAR
            ADD 13 TO MM1-IN GIVING MONTH-OF-YEAR
        END-IF
        MULTIPLY YEAR BY 365.25 GIVING TEMP-UNVDAT
        MULTIPLY MONTH-OF-YEAR BY 30.6001 GIVING TEMP-LRGINT
        ADD TEMP-LRGINT DD1-IN C-OFFSET TO TEMP-UNVDAT
        COMPUTE TEMP-LRGINT = (YY1-IN * 12+MM1-IN) * 31 + DD1-IN
        IF TEMP-LRGINT NOT LESS THAN C-GREG-CUTOFF
            MULTIPLY YEAR BY 0.01 GIVING TEMP-LRGINT
            MOVE TEMP-LRGINT TO CENTR
            MULTIPLY CENTRY BY 0.25 GIVING TEMP-LRGINT
            ADD TEMP-LRGINT TO TEMP-UNVDAT
            SUBTRACT CENTR FROM TEMP-UNVDAT
            ADD 2 TO TEMP-UNVDAT
        END-IF
        MOVE TEMP-UNVDAT TO UNIV-DATE-OUT
    END-IF.
    GOBACK.
```

15.2.2 UDTODATE—Universal date to date

The universal date to date program (Listing 15.8) converts an integer-based universal date back into a general date (CCYYMMDD).

Listing 15.8 Universal date to regular date program.

```
MEMBER NAME:    DATPGMHDR    FILE: QLBLSRC
....-..A...B..-...2....-...3....-....4....-....5....-....6....-....7..
    COPY DATPGMHDR REPLACING PGMNAME BY UDTODATE.

    WORKING-STORAGE SECTION.

    COPY DATDTATYPS.
    COPY DATWRKVARS.
    COPY DATCONSTNT.

    01  PROGRAM-VARIABLES.
        03  FSGRUD          LIKE GEN-UNIVDATE VALUE 2299161.
        03  JA              LIKE GEN-LRGINT.
        03  JB              LIKE GEN-LRGINT.
        03  JC              LIKE GEN-LRGINT.
        03  JD              LIKE GEN-LRGINT.
        03  JE              LIKE GEN-LRGINT.
        03  JALPHA          LIKE GEN-LRGINT.
        03  TEMP-DEC        PIC S9(14)V9(4).

    LINKAGE SECTION.
```

```
01  UNIV-DATE-IN          LIKE GEN-UNIVDATE.
01  DATE-OUT.
    03  YY1-OUT           LIKE GEN-CENTYEAR.
    03  MM1-OUT           LIKE GEN-MONTH.
    03  DD1-OUT           LIKE GEN-DAY.


COPY DATRETCOD.


PROCEDURE DIVISION USING UNIV-DATE-IN DATE-OUT RETCODE.
MAIN-PARA.
    SET RC-NO-ERROR TO TRUE.
    IF UNIV-DATE-IN < C-MIN-UD OR > C-MAX-UD
        SET RC-ERROR-INVERR TO TRUE
    ELSE
        MOVE UNIV-DATE-IN TO JA
        IF JA NOT LESS THAN FSGRUD
            SUBTRACT 1867216.25 FROM JA GIVING TEMP-DEC
            DIVIDE TEMP-DEC BY 36524.25 GIVING JALPHA
            MULTIPLY JALPHA BY 0.25 GIVING TEMP-LRGINT
            SUBTRACT TEMP-LRGINT FROM JA
            ADD JALPHA 1 TO JA
        END-IF
        ADD 1524 JA GIVING JB
        SUBTRACT 2439992.1 FROM JB GIVING TEMP-DEC
        DIVIDE TEMP-DEC BY 365.25 GIVING TEMP-DEC
        ADD 6680 TO TEMP-DEC GIVING JC
        MULTIPLY JC BY 365.25 GIVING JD
        SUBTRACT JD FROM JB GIVING TEMP-LRGINT
        DIVIDE TEMP-LRGINT BY 30.6001 GIVING JE
        MULTIPLY JE BY 30.6001 GIVING TEMP-LRGINT
        SUBTRACT TEMP-LRGINT FROM JB GIVING TEMP-DOM
        SUBTRACT JD FROM TEMP-DOM
        SUBTRACT 1 FROM JE GIVING TEMP-MOY
        IF TEMP-MOY > 12
            SUBTRACT 12 FROM TEMP-MOY
        END-IF
        SUBTRACT 4715 FROM JC GIVING TEMP-YEAR
        IF TEMP-MOY > 2
            SUBTRACT 1 FROM TEMP-YEAR
        END-IF
        MOVE TEMP-YEAR TO YY1-OUT
        MOVE TEMP-MOY TO MM1-OUT
        MOVE TEMP-DOM TO DD1-OUT
    END-IF.
    GOBACK.
```

15.3   Date Routines

This section contains 15 date programs that perform a variety of different operations on dates. Table 15.3 indicates the function of the various programs.

15.3.1   ADDDURDT—Add a day's duration to date

This program adds an integer value to a date and returns a new date (see Table 15.4 and Listing 15.9). The integer value may be positive or negative.

TABLE 15.3   Summary of Date Programs in this Chapter

Program	Function
ADDDURDT	Adds an integer value (positive or negative) that represents days to a date, returning a new date
ADDDURDW	Adds a day's duration to a day of the week, returning a new day of the week
ADDMDRDT	Adds a month's (or months') duration to a date, returning a new date
CNRYCODE	Returns the century code for a date—0 = nineteenth century, 1 = twentieth century
DAYBTWDT	Returns the number of days between two dates
DATBTWDW	Returns the number of days between two days of the week
DAYSINYR	Returns the number of days in the specified year
LASTDOM	Returns the last day of the month (the number of days in the month)
LATERDAT	Returns the later of two dates
MONBTWDT	Returns the number of months between two dates
RTVDAY	Returns the day portion of a date
RTVMTH	Returns the month portion of a date
RTVYR	Returns the year portion of a date (without the century)
VLDDAT	Determines whether a date is valid or not
WEEKDAY	Returns the day of the week for a date (Sunday = 0, Monday = 1, etc.)

TABLE 15.4   Parameters for the ADDDURDT Program

Parameter	In or out	Description
Date	In	Initial date
Duration	In	Day's duration (+ or –)
Date	Out	New date
Retcode	Out	Return code

Listing 15.9   Program to add a day's duration to date.

```
MEMBER NAME:    ADDDURDT      FILE: QLBLSRC
....-..A...B..-....2....-....3....-....4....-....5....-....6....-....7..
    COPY DATPGMHDR REPLACING PGMNAME BY ADDDURDT.

    WORKING-STORAGE SECTION.

    COPY DATDTATYPS.
    COPY DATWRKVARS.
```

```
COPY DATCONSTNT.

LINKAGE SECTION.
01  DATE-IN                 LIKE GEN-DATE.
01  DURATION-IN             LIKE GEN-DURATION.
01  DATE-OUT                LIKE GEN-DATE.

COPY DATRETCOD.

PROCEDURE DIVISION USING DATE-IN DURATION-IN DATE-OUT RETCODE.
MAIN-PARA.
    SET RC-NO-ERROR TO TRUE.
    IF DURATION-IN < C-MIN-DAY-DUR OR > C-MAX-DAY-DUR
        SET RC-ERROR-IDDER TO TRUE
    ELSE
        CALL "DATETOUD" USING DATE-IN TEMP-UNVDAT INT-RETCODE
        IF NOT NO-ERROR
            SET RC-ERROR-OTHER TO TRUE
        ELSE
            ADD TEMP-UNVDAT TO DURATION-IN GIVING TEMP-LRGINT
            IF TEMP-LRGINT < C-MIN-UD OR > C-MAX-UD
                SET RC-ERROR-RANGE TO TRUE
            ELSE
                MOVE TEMP-LRGINT TO TEMP-UNVDAT
                CALL "UDTODATE" USING TEMP-UNVDAT DATE-OUT
                    INT-RETCODE
                IF NOT NO-ERROR
                    SET RC-ERROR-OTHER TO TRUE
                END-IF
            END-IF
        END-IF
    END-IF.
    GOBACK.
```

15.3.2 ADDDURDW—Add duration to day of week

This program adds an integer value to a day of the week, and returns a new day of the week (see Table 15.5 and Listing 15.10). For example, this function would be used to determine what day of the week is three days from Friday. In this case, the day of week would be specified as 6 (for Friday) and the duration would be 3. When the program returns, the new day of week would be 2 (Monday).

TABLE 15.5 Parameters for ADDDURDW

Parameter	In or out	Description
Day of week	In	Day of week (1 = Sunday)
Duration	In	Days duration (+ or −)
Day of week	Out	New day of week
Retcode	Out	Return code

Listing 15.10 Add duration to day of week.

```
MEMBER NAME:    ADDDURDW      FILE: QLBLSRC
....-..A...B..-....2....-....3....-....4....-....5....-....6....-....7..
      COPY DATPGMHDR REPLACING PGMNAME BY ADDDURDW.

      WORKING-STORAGE SECTION.

      COPY DATDTATYPS.
      COPY DATWRKVARS.
      COPY DATCONSTNT.

      LINKAGE SECTION.
      01  DOW-IN            LIKE GEN-WEEKDAY.
      01  DURATION-IN       LIKE GEN-DURATION.
      01  DOW-OUT           LIKE GEN-WEEKDAY.

      COPY DATRETCOD.

      PROCEDURE DIVISION USING DOW-IN DURATION-IN DOW-OUT RETCODE.
      MAIN-PARA.
          SET RC-NO-ERROR TO TRUE.
          IF DOW-IN < C-MIN-DOW OR > C-MAX-DOW
              SET RC-ERROR-IDWER TO TRUE
          ELSE
              IF DURATION-IN < C-MIN-DAY-DUR OR > C-MAX-DAY-DUR
                  SET RC-ERROR-IDDER TO TRUE
              ELSE
                  ADD DOW-IN TO DURATION-IN GIVING TEMP-LRGINT
                  DIVIDE TEMP-LRGINT BY C-MAX-DOW GIVING TEMP-LRGINT
                      REMAINDER DOW-OUT
                  IF DOW-OUT < 1
                      ADD C-MAX-DOW TO DOW-OUT
                  END-IF
              END-IF
          END-IF.
          GOBACK.
```

15.3.3   ADDMDRDT—Add month's duration to date

This function adds one or more months duration to a date (see Table 15.6 and Listing 15.11).

TABLE 15.6   Parameters for ADDMDRDT

Parameter	In or out	Description
Date	In	Base date
Duration	In	Duration in months
Date	Out	Resultant date
Retcode	Out	Return code

Listing 15.11   Add a month's duration to date.

```
MEMBER NAME:    ADDMDRDT      FILE: QLBLSRC
....-..A...B..-....2....-....3....-....4....-....5....-....6....-....7..
COPY DATPGMHDR REPLACING PGMNAME BY ADDMDRDT.

WORKING-STORAGE SECTION.

COPY DATDTATYPS.
COPY DATWRKVARS.
COPY DATCONSTNT.

01  DATE-STRUCT.
    03 YYEAR         LIKE GEN-CENTYEAR.
    03 MMONTH        LIKE GEN-MONTH.
    03 DDAY          LIKE GEN-DAY.

LINKAGE SECTION.
01  DATE-IN.
    03 YY1-IN        LIKE GEN-CENTYEAR.
    03 MM1-IN        LIKE GEN-MONTH.
    03 DD1-IN        LIKE GEN-DAY.
01  DURATION-IN.     LIKE GEN-DURATION.
01  DATE-OUT.
    03 YY2-OUT       LIKE GEN-CENTYEAR.
    03 MM2-OUT       LIKE GEN-MONTH.
    03 DD2-OUT       LIKE GEN-DAY.

COPY DATRETCOD.

PROCEDURE DIVISION USING DATE-IN DURATION-IN DATE-OUT RETCODE.
MAIN-PARA.
    SET RC-NO-ERROR TO TRUE.
    IF DURATION-IN < C-MIN-MONTH-DUR OR > C-MAX-MONTH-DUR
        SET RC-ERROR-IMDER TO TRUE
    ELSE
        DIVIDE DURATION-IN BY C-MAX-MOY GIVING TEMP-YEAR
            REMAINDER TEMP-MOY
        ADD MM1-IN TO TEMP-MOY
        ADD YY1-IN-TO TEMP-YEAR
        IF TEMP-MOY < C-MIN-MOY
            SUBTRACT 1 FROM TEMP-YEAR
            ADD C-MAX-MOY TO TEMP-MOY
        END-IF
        IF TEMP-YEAR < C-MIN-YEAR OR > C-MAX-YEAR
            SET RC-ERROR-RANGE TO TRUE
        END-IF
    END-IF.
    IF RC-NO-ERROR
        MOVE TEMP-YEAR TO YYEAR
        MOVE TEMP-MOY TO MMONTH
        MOVE DD1-IN TO DDAY
        CALL "LASTDOM" USING DATE-STRUCT TEMP-LDM INT-RETCODE
        IF NOT NO-ERROR
            SET RC-ERROR-OTHER TO TRUE
        ELSE
            IF DD1-IN > TEMP-LDM
                MOVE TEMP-LDM TO TEMP-DOM
            ELSE
                MOVE DD1-IN TO TEMP-DOM
            END-IF
            IF YYEAR EQUAL C-GCHGY AND TEMP-MOY EQUAL C-GCHGM AND
```

```
                    DD1-IN NOT LESS THAN 5 AND DD1-IN NOT > 14
                    MOVE 4 TO TEMP-DOM
              END-IF
           END-IF
           IF RC-NO-ERROR
              MOVE YYEAR TO YY2-OUT
              MOVE MMONTH TO MM2-OUT
              MOVE DDAY TO DD2-OUT
           END-IF
        END-IF.
        GOBACK.
```

15.3.4 CNRYCODE—Century code

This function returns a century code based on the provided date (see Table 15.7 and Listing 15.12).

TABLE 15.7 Parameters for CNRYCODE

Parameter	In or out	Description
Date	In	Base date
Century code	Out	0 = 19th Century, 1 = 20th Century
Retcode	Out	Return code

Listing 15.12 Get century code (0 or 1) from a date.

```
MEMBER NAME:   CNRYCODE      FILE: QLBLSRC
....-..A...B..-....2....-....3....-....4....-....5....-....6....-....7..
        COPY DATPGMHDR REPLACING PGMNAME BY CNRYCODE.

        WORKING-STORAGE SECTION.

        COPY DATDTATYPS.

        LINKAGE SECTION.
        01   DATE-IN.
             03 YY1-IN        LIKE GEN-CENTYEAR.
             03 MM1-IN        LIKE GEN-MONTH.
             03 DD1-IN        LIKE GEN-DAY.
        01   CENTURY-CODE     LIKE GEN-CENTCODE.

        COPY DATRETCOD.

        PROCEDURE DIVISION USING DATE1-IN CENTURY-CODE RETCODE.
        MAIN-PARA.
             SET RC-NO-ERROR TO TRUE.
             DIVIDE YY1-IN BY 100 GIVING CENTURY-CODE.
             SUBTRACT 19 FROM CENTURY-CODE.
             GOBACK.
```

15.3.5   DAYBTWDT—Days between dates

This function returns the number of days between two dates (see Table 15.8 and Listing 15.13).

TABLE 15.8   Parameters for DAYBTWDT

Parameter	In or out	Description
Date	In	First date
Date	In	Second date
Duration	Out	Days between the two dates
Retcode	Out	Return code

Listing 15.13 Calculate days between dates.

```
MEMBER NAME:    DAYBTWDT      FILE: QLBLSRC
....-..A...B..-....2....-....3....-....4....-....5....-....6....-....7..
      COPY DATPGMHDR REPLACING PGMNAME BY DAYBTWDT.

      WORKING-STORAGE SECTION.

      COPY DATDTATYPS.
      COPY DATWRKVARS.
      COPY DATCONSTNT.

      01 UNIV-DATE1              LIKE GEN-UNIVDATE.
      01 UNIV-DATE2              LIKE GEN-UNIVDATE.

      LINKAGE SECTION.
      01  DATE1-IN               LIKE GEN-DATE.
      01  DATE2-IN               LIKE GEN-DATE.
      01  DURATION-OUT           LIKE GEN-DURATION.

      COPY DATRETCOD.

      PROCEDURE DIVISION USING DATE1-IN DATE2-IN DURATION-OUT RETCODE.
      MAIN-PARA.
          SET RC-NO-ERROR TO TRUE.
          CALL "DATETOUD" USING DATE1-IN UNIV-DATE1 INT-RETCODE.
          IF NO-ERROR
              CALL "DATETOUD" USING DATE2-IN UNIV-DATE2 INT-RETCODE
              IF NO-ERROR
                  SUBTRACT UNIV-DATE1 FROM UNIV-DATE2 GIVING DURATION-OUT
              ELSE
                  SET RC-ERROR-OTHER TO TRUE
              END-IF
          ELSE
              SET RC-ERROR-OTHER TO TRUE
          END-IF.
          GOBACK.
```

15.3.6   DAYBTWDW—Days between days of the week

This function returns the number of days between two days of the week (see Table 15.9 and Listing 15.14).

TABLE 15.9   Parameters for DAYBTWDW

Parameter	In or out	Description
Day of week	In	First day (1 = Sunday)
Day of week	In	Second day
Duration	Out	Days between the two days
Retcode	Out	Return code

Listing 15.14   Calculate the days between days of the week.

```
MEMBER NAME:   DAYBTWDW      FILE: QLBLSRC
....-..A...B..-....2....-....3....-....4....-....5....-....6....-....7..
       COPY DATPGMHDR REPLACING PGMNAME BY DAYBTWDW.

       WORKING-STORAGE SECTION.

       COPY DATDTATYPS.
       COPY DATWRKVARS.
       COPY DATCONSTNT.

       LINKAGE SECTION.
       01  DOW1-IN               LIKE GEN-WEEKDAY.
       01  DOW2-IN               LIKE GEN-WEEKDAY.
       01  DURATION-OUT          LIKE GEN-DURATION.

       COPY DATRETCOD.

       PROCEDURE DIVISION USING DOW1-IN DOW2-IN DURATION-OUT RETCODE.
       MAIN-PARA.
           SET RC-NO-ERROR TO TRUE.
           IF DOW1-IN < C-MIN-DOW OR > C-MAX DOW
              SET RC-ERROR-IDWER TO TRUE
           ELSE
              IF DOW2-IN < C-MIN-DOW OR > C-MAX-DOW
                 SET RC-ERROR-IDWER TO TRUE
              ELSE
                 IF DOW1-IN > DOW2-IN
                    SUBTRACT DOW1-IN FROM DOW2-IN GIVING DURATION-OUT
                    ADD 7 TO DURATION-OUT
                 ELSE
                    SUBTRACT DOW1-IN FROM DOW2-IN GIVING DURATION-OUT
                 END-IF
              END-IF
           END-IF.
           GOBACK.
```

15.3.7 DAYSINYR—Days in the year

This function returns the number of days the year of the specified date. If you specify 19630328, the returned number of days will be for the year 1963 (see Table 15.10 and Listing 15.15).

TABLE 15.10   Parameters for DAYSINYR

Parameter	In or out	Description
Date	In	Date within desired year to check
Days in year	Out	The number of days in the year
Retcode	Out	Return code

Listing 15.15   Calculate the number of days in a specified year.

```
MEMBER NAME:    DAYSINYR     FILE: QLBLSRC
....-..A...B..-....2....-....3....-....4....-....5....-....6....-....7..
         COPY DATPGMHDR REPLACING PGMNAME BY DAYSINYR.

         WORKING-STORAGE SECTION.

         COPY DATDTATYPS.
         COPY DATWRKVARS.
         COPY DATCONSTNT.
         COPY DATELEAPTBL.

         01 REMAIN               LIKE GEN-INT.
         01 YEAR                 LIKE GEN-CENTYEAR.

         01 LEAP-YEAR-STATUS     PIC 9   VALUE 0.
            88 NOT-LEAP-YEAR             VALUE 0.
            88 IS-LEAP-YEAR              VALUE 1.

         LINKAGE SECTION.
         01  DATE-IN.
             03 YY1-IN           LIKE GEN-CENTYEAR.
             03 MM1-IN           LIKE GEN-MONTH.
             03 DD1-IN           LIKE GEN-DAY.
         01  DAYS-IN-YEAR        LIKE GEN-INT.

         COPY DATRETCOD.

         PROCEDURE DIVISION USING DATE-IN DAYS-IN-YEAR RETCODE.
         MAIN-PARA.
             SET RC-NO-ERROR TO TRUE.
             MOVE YY1-IN TO YEAR.
             PERFORM CHECK-FOR-LEAP-YEAR.
             IF RC-NO-ERROR
                 IF IS-LEAP-YEAR
                     MOVE 366 TO DAYS-IN-YEAR
                 ELSE
                     MOVE 365 TO DAYS-IN-YEAR
                 END-IF
                 IF YY1-IN EQUAL C-GCHGY
                     MOVE 355 TO DAYS-IN-YEAR
                 END-IF
```

```
            END-IF.
            GOBACK.

            CHECK-FOR-LEAP-YEAR.
                DIVIDE 4 INTO YEAR GIVING TEMP-INT REMAINDER REMAIN.
                IF YEAR < C-GCHGY
                    PERFORM JULLEP
                ELSE
                    PERFORM GRGLEP
                END-IF.

            JULLEP.
                IF REMAIN NOT EQUAL ZERO
                    SET NOT-LEAP-YEAR TO TRUE
                ELSE
                    SET IS-LEAP-YEAR TO TRUE
                END-IF.

            GRGLEP.
                IF REMAIN NOT EQUAL ZERO
                    SET NOT-LEAP-YEAR TO TRUE
                ELSE
                    DIVIDE YEAR BY 100 GIVING TEMP-INT REMAINDER REMAIN
                    IF REMAIN NOT EQUAL ZERO
                        SET IS-LEAP-YEAR TO TRUE
                    ELSE
                        DIVIDE YEAR BY 400 GIVING TEMP-INT REMAINDER REMAIN
                        IF REMAIN NOT EQUAL ZERO
                            SET NOT-LEAP-YEAR TO TRUE
                        ELSE
                            SET IS-LEAP-YEAR TO TRUE
                        END-IF
                    END-IF
                END-IF.
```

15.3.8   LASTDOM—Last day of the month

This function will return the number of days in a given month (see Table 15.11 and Listing 15.16). For instance, if you specify 19630328, the returned value will be 31 (March has 31 days). The program does account for leap years.

TABLE 15.11   Parameters for LASTDOM

Parameter	In or out	Description
Date	In	Date to inspect
Number of days	Out	The number of days in the month
Retcode	Out	Return code

Listing 15.16   Calculate the last day of the month.

```
MEMBER NAME:    LASTDOM        FILE: QLBLSRC
....-..A...B..-....2....-....3....-....4....-....5....-....6....-....7..
            COPY DATPGMHDR REPLACING PGMNAME BY LASTDOM.
            WORKING-STORAGE SECTION.
```

```
COPY DATDTATYPS.
COPY DATWRKVARS.
COPY DATCONSTNT.
COPY DATLEAPTBL.

01 DAYS-IN-YEAR            LIKE GEN-INT.

LINKAGE SECTION.
01  DATE-IN.
    03 YY1-IN             LIKE GEN-CENTYEAR.
    03 MM1-IN             LIKE GEN-MONTH.
    03 DD1-IN             LIKE GEN-DAY.
01  LAST-DAY-OF-MONTH     LIKE GEN-DAY.

COPY DATRETCOD.

PROCEDURE DIVISION USING DATE-IN LAST-DAY-OF-MONTH RETCODE.
MAIN-PARA.
    SET RC-NO-ERROR TO TRUE.
    IF MM1-IN < C-MIN-MOY OR > C-MAX-MOY
        SET RC-ERROR-OTHER TO TRUE
    ELSE
        CALL "DAYSINYR" USING DATE-IN DAYS-IN-YEAR RETCODE
        IF DAYS-IN-YEAR = 366
            MOVE LP-DAYS (MM1-IN) TO LAST-DAY-OF-MONTH
        ELSE
            MOVE NLP-DAYS (MM1-IN) TO LAST-DAY-OF-MONTH
        END-IF
    END-IF.
    GOBACK.
```

15.3.9 LATERDAT—Later date of two dates

This function compares two dates and returns the later of the two (see Table 15.12 and Listing 15.17).

TABLE 15.12 Parameters for LATERDAT

Parameter	In or out	Function
Date	In	First date to compare
Date	In	Second date to compare
Date	Out	The later of the two dates
Retcode	Out	Return code

Listing 15.17 Returns the later of two dates.

```
MEMBER NAME:    LATERDAT      FILE: QLBLSRC
....-..A...B..-....2....-....3....-....4....-....5....-....6....-....7..

    COPY DATPGMHDR REPLACING PGMNAME BY LATERDAT.

    WORKING-STORAGE SECTION.
    COPY DATDTATYPS.
    COPY DATWRKVARS.
```

```
COPY DATCONSTNT.

LINKAGE SECTION.
01  DATE1-IN.
       03 YY1-IN               LIKE GEN-CENTYEAR.
       03 MM1-IN               LIKE GEN-MONTH.
       03 DD1-IN               LIKE GEN-DAY.
01  DATE2-IN.
       03 YY2-IN               LIKE GEN-CENTYEAR.
       03 MM2-IN               LIKE GEN-MONTH.
       03 DD2-IN               LIKE GEN-DAY.
01  DATE3-OUT                  LIKE GEN-DATE.


COPY DATRETCOD.

PROCEDURE DIVISION USING DATE1-IN DATE2-IN DATE3-OUT RETCODE.
MAIN-PARA.
       SET RC-NO-ERROR TO TRUE.
       IF YY2-IN < YY1-IN OR = YY1-IN AND MM2-IN < MM1-IN
          OR YY2-IN = YY1-IN AND MM2-IN = MM1-IN
          AND DD2-IN < DD1-IN
          MOVE DATE1-IN TO DATE3-OUT
       ELSE
          MOVE DATE2-IN TO DATE3-OUT
       END-IF.
       GOBACK.
```

15.3.10   MONBTWDT—Months between dates

This function returns the number of months between two specified dates (see Table 15.13 and Listing 15.18).

TABLE 15.13   Parameters for MONBTWDT

Parameter	In or out	Description
Date	In	First date
Date	In	Second date
Duration	Out	Number of months between the dates
Retcode	Out	Return code

Listing 15.18   Returns the number of months between two dates.

```
MEMBER NAME:   MONBTWDT      FILE: QLBLSRC
....-..A...B..-....2....-....3....-....4....-....5....-....6....-....7..
       COPY DATPGMHDR REPLACING PGMNAME BY MONBTWDT.

       WORKING-STORAGE SECTION.

       COPY DATDTATYPS.
       COPY DATWRKVARS.
       COPY DATCONSTNT.

       LINKAGE SECTION.
01  DATE1-IN.
       03 YY1-IN               LIKE GEN-CENTYEAR.
       03 MM1-IN               LIKE GEN-MONTH.
```

```
      03  DD1-IN                  LIKE GEN-DAY.
  01  DATE2-IN.
      03  YY2-IN                  LIKE GEN-CENTYEAR.
      03  MM2-IN                  LIKE GEN-MONTH.
      03  DD2-IN                  LIKE GEN-DAY.
  01  DURATION-OUT                LIKE GEN-DURATION.


  COPY DATRETCOD.


  PROCEDURE DIVISION USING DATE1-IN DATE2-IN DURATION-OUT RETCODE.
  MAIN-PARA.
      SET RC-NO-ERROR TO TRUE.
      SUBTRACT YY1-IN FROM YY2-IN GIVING DURATION-OUT.
      MULTIPLY C-MAX. MOY BY DURATION-OUT GIVING DURATION-OUT.
      ADD MM2-IN TO DURATION-OUT.
      SUBTRACT MM1-IN FROM DURATION-OUT.
      GOBACK.
```

15.3.11   RTVDAY—Day portion of a date

This program returns the day portion of a date (see Table 15.14 and Listing 15.19). For example, in the date 19630328, the program will return 28.

TABLE 15.14   Parameters for RTVDAY

Parameter	In or out	Description
Date	In	Date to inspect
Day number	Out	The day number (0–31) of the date
Retcode	Out	Return code

Listing 15.19 Returns the day portion of a date.

```
MEMBER NAME:    RTVDAY          FILE: QLBLSRC
....-..A...B..-....2....-....3....-....4....-....5....-....6....-....7..
      COPY DATPGMHDR REPLACING PGMNAME BY RTVDAY.

      WORKING-STORAGE SECTION.

      COPY DATDTATYPS.

      LINKAGE SECTION.
      01  DATE1-IN.
          03  FILLER              LIKE GEN-CENTYEAR.
          03  FILLER              LIKE GEN-MONTH.
          03  DD1-IN              LIKE GEN-DAY.
          01  DAY CODE            LIKE GEN-DAY.

      COPY DATRETCOD.

      PROCEDURE DIVISION USING DATE1-IN DAY-CODE RETCODE.
      MAIN-PARA.
          SET RC-NO-ERROR TO TRUE.
          MOVE DD1-IN TO DAY-CODE.
          GOBACK.
```

15.3.12   RTVMTH—Month portion of a date

This function returns the month portion of a date (see Table 15.15 and Listing 15.20). For example, for the date 19630328, the function will return 03.

TABLE 15.15   Parameters for RTVMTH

Parameter	In or out	Description
Date	In	Date to inspect
Month number	Out	The month of the year (01–12)
Retcode	Out	Return code

Listing 15.20 Returns the month portion of a date.

```
MEMBER NAME:    RTVMTH          FILE: QLBLSRC
....-..A...B..-....2....-....3....-....4....-....5....-....6....-....7..
      COPY DATPGMHDR REPLACING PGMNAME BY RTVMTH.

      WORKING-STORAGE SECTION.

      COPY DATDTATYPS.

      LINKAGE SECTION.
      01   DATE1-IN.
           03 FILLER            LIKE GEN-CENTYEAR.
           03 MM1-IN            LIKE GEN-MONTH.
           03 FILLER            LIKE GEN-DAY.
      01   MONTH CODE           LIKE GEN-MONTH.

      COPY DATRETCOD.

      PROCEDURE DIVISION USING DATE1-IN MONTH-CODE RETCODE.
      MAIN-PARA.
           SET RC-NO-ERROR TO TRUE.
           MOVE MM1-IN TO MONTH-CODE.
           GOBACK.
```

15.3.13   RTVYR—Year portion of a date

This function returns the year portion of a date (without the century) (see Table 15.16 and Listing 15.21). For example, for the date 19630328, the function will return 63.

TABLE 15.16   Parameters for RTVYR

Parameter	In or out	Description
Date	In	Date to inspect
Year number	Out	A year number without the century
Retcode	Out	Return code

Listing 15.21 Returns the year portion of a date.

```
MEMBER NAME:    RTVYR         FILE: QLBLSRC
....-..A...B..-....2....-....3....-....4....-....5....-....6....-....7..
        COPY DATPGMHDR REPLACING PGMNAME BY RTVYR.

        WORKING-STORAGE SECTION.

        COPY DATDTATYPS.

        LINKAGE SECTION.
        01  DATE1-IN.
            03 FILLER              LIKE GEN-CENTURY.
            03 YY1-IN              LIKE GEN-YEAR.
            03 FILLER              LIKE GEN-MONTH.
            03 FILLER              LIKE GEN-DAY.
        01  YEAR CODE              LIKE GEN-YEAR.

        COPY DATRETCOD.

        PROCEDURE DIVISION USING DATE1-IN YEAR-CODE RETCODE.
        MAIN-PARA.
            SET RC-NO-ERROR TO TRUE.
            MOVE YY1-IN TO YEAR-CODE.
            GOBACK.
```

15.3.14   VLDDAT—Validate a date

This program checks whether the specified date is valid or not. For parameters and source, see Table 15.17 and Listing 15.22.

TABLE 15.17   Parameters for VLDDAT

Parameter	In or out	Description
Date	In	Date to validate
Retcode	Out	Return code (blank if valid date)

Listing 15.22 Checks whether a date is valid.

```
MEMBER NAME:    VLDDAT        FILE: QLBLSRC
....-..A...B..-....2....-....3....-....4....-....5....-....6....-....7..
        COPY DATPGMHDR REPLACING PGMNAME BY VLDDAT.

        WORKING-STORAGE SECTION.

        COPY DATDTATYPS.
        COPY DATWRKVARS.
        COPY DATCONSTNT.

        LINKAGE SECTION.
        01  DATE-IN.
            03 YY1-IN              LIKE GEN-CENTYEAR.
            03 MM1-IN              LIKE GEN-MONTH.
            03 DD1-IN              LIKE GEN-DAY.

        COPY DATRETCOD.
```

```
PROCEDURE DIVISION USING DATE-IN RETCODE.
MAIN-PARA.
    SET RC-NO-ERROR TO TRUE.
    IF DATE-IN IS NOT NUMERIC
        SET RC-ERROR-INVERR TO TRUE
        GO TO DONE
    END-IF.
    IF YY1-IN < C-MIN-YEAR OR > C-MAX-YEAR
        SET RC-ERROR-INVERR TO TRUE
        GO TO DONE
    END-IF.
    IF MM1-IN < C-MIN-MOY OR > C-MAX-MOY
        SET RC-ERROR-INVERR TO TRUE
        GO TO DONE
    END-IF.
    CALL "LASTDOM" USING DATE-IN TEMP-LDM INT-RETCODE.
    IF NOT NO-ERROR
        SET RC-ERROR-OTHER TO TRUE
        GO TO DONE
    END-IF.
    IF DD1-IN < C-MIN-DOM OR > TEMP-LDM
        SET RC-ERROR-INVERR TO TRUE
    END-IF.

DONE.
    GOBACK.
```

15.3.15   WEEKDAY—Day of the week

This function inspects a date and returns a code for the day of the week (see Table 15.18 and Listing 15.23). For example, if you specify 19630328 for the date, the function will return 5 (Thursday).

TABLE 15.18   Parameters for WEEKDAY

Parameter	In or out	Description
Date	In	Date to inspect
Day of week	Out	Day of the week for the date (0 = Sunday)
Retcode	Out	Return code

Listing 15.23 Returns the day of the week for a specified date.

```
MEMBER NAME:    WEEKDAY        FILE: QLBLSRC
....-..A...B..-....2....-...3....-....4....-....5....-....6....-....7..
    COPY DATPGMHDR REPLACING PGMNAME BY WEEKDAY.

    WORKING-STORAGE SECTION.

    COPY DATDTATYPS.
    COPY DATWRKVARS.
    COPY DATCONSTNT.

    01  TEMP-UNVDAT2           LIKE GEN-UNIVDATE.
```

```
LINKAGE SECTION.
01   DATE1-IN.
       03  YY1-IN           LIKE GEN-CENTYEAR.
       03  MM1-IN           LIKE GEN-MONTH.
       03  DD1-IN           LIKE GEN-DAY.
01   DOW-OUT                LIKE GEN-WEEKDAY.


COPY DATRETCOD.


PROCEDURE DIVISION USING DATE1-IN DOW-OUT RETCODE.
MAIN-PARA.
       CALL "DATETOUD" USING DATE1-IN TEMP-UNVDAT INT-RETCODE.
       IF NO-ERROR
           ADD 1 TO TEMP-UNVDAT GIVING TEMP-UNVDAT2
           DIVIDE TEMP-UNVDAT2 BY C-MAX-DOW GIVING DOW-OUT
               REMAINDER DOW-OUT
           ADD 1 TO DOW-OUT
           SET RC-NO-ERROR TO TRUE
       ELSE
           SET RC-ERROR-OTHER TO TRUE
       END-IF.
       GOBACK.
```

Application Development with COBOL/400

This section takes you on a guided tour that will show you the sights and sounds of developing an application from beginning to end of the IBM AS/400 computer. By the end of the tour, you will have seen and experienced a variety of AS/400 landmarks and programs covering, but not limited to, the following topics:

- *Creating physical and logical files*
- *Creating a menu*
- *Creating a pop-up window*
- *Use of function keys*
- *Creating a handful of commands*
- *Creating a handful of COBOL/400 programs, both interactive and batch*
- *Programs that both send and receive messages*
- *Creating a report program with an externally described printer file*
- *Using QCMDEXC to execute a command from within a COBOL program*
- *Using an OS/400 API to send a message from within a COBOL program*

- *Using a COBOL copy book*
- *Creating a message file and filling it with messages*
- *Creating a message queue*
- *Creating a subsystem and a JobQ*

16

Project Definition

You have been asked to design an interactive telephone directory system that has the following functionality:

- Ability to add and delete phone numbers, as well as update information pertaining to the owner of a phone number.
- Both single-entry and multiple-entry capability should exist (i.e., enter one number at a time, or multiple numbers).
- The user should have the ability to mark a phone number for service. A background program should maintain a log of all service requests.
- Keep an audit of the last person to update each phone listing record.
- Provide a single AS/400 "work with" style entry point for the user to perform all necessary tasks.

This chapter will define the requirements for each of the modules in this project. The actual steps required to create each module will be presented in the remaining chapters of this book.

16.1 Database Requirement

Based on exhaustive meetings with your client (me), you have established the list of fields given in Table 16.1 that will be necessary for the application.

16.2 Module Definitions

The modules listed in Table 16.2 have been defined for this application.

TABLE 16.1   Main Phone Directory Database Fields

Field	Description
PHONENUM	Phone number (key)
NAME	Owner's name
TITLE	Owner's professional title
COMPANY	Owner's company (employer)
ADDRESS1	Address line 1
ADDRESS2	Address line 2
CITY	City
STATE	State
ZIP	Zip code
COUNTRY	Country

TABLE 16.2   Functional Modules for this Project

Module	Function performed
WRKPHNDIR	Main task manager for all phone directory functions
ADDPHNE	Add phone entry (both single and multiple) to database
DSPPHNE	Display phone entry
CHGPHNE	Change phone entry
DLTPHNE	Delete phone entry
CRTSRVREQ	Create a service request for a phone number
STRSRVMGR	Start the background service manager
ENDSRVMGR	End the service manager

16.3   Main Menu

From the main menu, the user should be able to:

- Start the main phone directory task manager
- Start and stop the background service manager program
- Sign off the system
- Perform regular system activities via a command line

Figure 16.1 shows how the main menu should appear.

```
PHONEDIR                    MAIN Menu

 Select one of the following:

     1. Work with phone directory
     2. Start service manager (batch)
     3. Terminate service manager

    90. Sign off




 Selection or command

 ===> _____
```

Figure 16.1 Phone directory main menu.

16.4 Messages

Table 16.3 lists the messages that are used in this project. Messages beginning with PHN are used with the interactive modules. REQ

TABLE 16.3 Message Definitions

Message ID	Description
PHN0001	Specified option "&1" is invalid
PHN0002	Specified state abbreviation is invalid
PHN0003	Service request submitted for account &1
PHN0004	Phone entry "&1" successfully removed
PHN0005	Name cannot be blank
PHN0006	Number already exists in the phone directory
PHN0007	Phone number is required
PHN0008	Requested number "&1" was not found
PHN0009	Requested program was not found
REQ0001	No dial tone
REQ0002	Can hear neighbor
REQ0003	Disconnect request
REQ0004	Horrible static
SVC0001	Service manager is not active—end request ignored
SVC0002	Service manager is already active—start request ignored
SVC0003	Service manager invoked
SVC9999	Terminate service manager

messages define the service requests that are supported by the CRTSRVREQ command. SVC messages are used by the service manager which runs in batch.

16.5   Work with Phone Directory (Main Task Manager)

This module acts as the main dispatcher for actions that can be performed against individual phone entries, as well as the directory as a whole. Each function that can be performed against an individual phone entry should be assigned an option number. The user will be able to perform an action against an entry by putting the option number in the option column next to the desired phone entry. Actions performed against the entire directory (adding, refreshing) will have an assigned function key.

16.5.1   Requirements

The user should have the ability to:

- Quickly reposition the list to any name within the directory
- Request to change a directory entry.
- Request to delete a directory entry.
- Request to view a directory entry.
- Log a service request against a directory entry.
- Request to add a single entry to the directory. When an entry is made, the list should be repositioned to the newly added entry.
- Request to add multiple entries to the directory. When multiple entries are made, the list should be positioned to the last entry added to the directory.
- Refresh the directory list to show changes that were possibly made by another user by pressing a designated function key.

16.5.2   Command definition   The syntax for the work with phone directory command is

```
WRKPHNDIR POSITION(position-to-name)
```

Optional parameters.   Position-to-name can be specified to start the list at a particular name. The default value is blanks (first name in the directory).

16.5.3 Messages

The messages used by this module are given in Table 16.4.

TABLE 16.4 Messages Used by the WRKPHNDIR Module

Message file	Message ID	Description
PHONEMSGS	PHN0001	Specified option "&1" is not valid
PHONEMSGS	PHN0009	Requested program was not found

16.5.4 Screen image

The Work with Phone Directory screen should appear as shown in Fig. 16.2.

```
                    Work with Phone Directory

Position to . . . . .  _____

Type options, press Enter.
   2=Change     4=Delete     5=View     8=Service request

Opt  Name                              Phone number           City
___  XXXXXXXXXXXXXXXXXXXXXXXXXXXXXXXX  XXXXXXXXXXXXXXXXXXXX   XXXXXXXXXXXXXXX
___  XXXXXXXXXXXXXXXXXXXXXXXXXXXXXXXX  XXXXXXXXXXXXXXXXXXXX   XXXXXXXXXXXXXXX
___  XXXXXXXXXXXXXXXXXXXXXXXXXXXXXXXX  XXXXXXXXXXXXXXXXXXXX   XXXXXXXXXXXXXXX
___  XXXXXXXXXXXXXXXXXXXXXXXXXXXXXXXX  XXXXXXXXXXXXXXXXXXXX   XXXXXXXXXXXXXXX
___  XXXXXXXXXXXXXXXXXXXXXXXXXXXXXXXX  XXXXXXXXXXXXXXXXXXXX   XXXXXXXXXXXXXXX
___  XXXXXXXXXXXXXXXXXXXXXXXXXXXXXXXX  XXXXXXXXXXXXXXXXXXXX   XXXXXXXXXXXXXXX
___  XXXXXXXXXXXXXXXXXXXXXXXXXXXXXXXX  XXXXXXXXXXXXXXXXXXXX   XXXXXXXXXXXXXXX
___  XXXXXXXXXXXXXXXXXXXXXXXXXXXXXXXX  XXXXXXXXXXXXXXXXXXXX   XXXXXXXXXXXXXXX
___  XXXXXXXXXXXXXXXXXXXXXXXXXXXXXXXX  XXXXXXXXXXXXXXXXXXXX   XXXXXXXXXXXXXXX
___  XXXXXXXXXXXXXXXXXXXXXXXXXXXXXXXX  XXXXXXXXXXXXXXXXXXXX   XXXXXXXXXXXXXXX
___  XXXXXXXXXXXXXXXXXXXXXXXXXXXXXXXX  XXXXXXXXXXXXXXXXXXXX   XXXXXXXXXXXXXXX
___  XXXXXXXXXXXXXXXXXXXXXXXXXXXXXXXX  XXXXXXXXXXXXXXXXXXXX   XXXXXXXXXXXXXXX
                                                              More...

F3=Exit    F5=Refresh    F6=Add name    F7=Add multiple names    F12=Cancel
```

Figure 16.2 Work with Phone Directory screen layout.

16.6 Add Phone Entry

This module allows the user to add a new entry to the phone directory.

16.6.1 Requirements

The user should have the ability to:

- Enter either a single directory entry or multiple repetitive entries. If the single-entry function is requested, the program will return after adding the entry. If multiple entries are requested, the user can continue to add entries until they are finished, at which time they can press the designated exit function key.
- Use a function key to reset all fields to blanks.

The following validation tests must be made:

- Phone number may not be blank
- Phone number cannot be a duplicate of a preexisting number
- Name may not be blank
- State code must be valid

16.6.2 Command definition

The syntax for the add phone entry command is

```
ADDPHNE ENTRIES(*SINGLE | *MULTIPLE) CLOSEDISP (*CLOSE | *LEAVE)
```

Optional parameters.

- ENTRIES specifies either *SINGLE for a single entry or *MULTIPLE for multiple phone entries. The default is *SINGLE.
- CLOSEDISP specifies either *CLOSE to close the display file after all entries are completed, or *LEAVE to leave the display file open for future invocations. The default is *CLOSE.

16.6.3 Messages

The messages given in Table 16.5 are used by this module.

TABLE 16.5 Messages Used by the ADDPHNE Module

Message file	Message ID	Description
PHONEMSGS	PHN0002	Specified state abbreviation is invalid
PHONEMSGS	PHN0005	Name cannot be blank
PHONEMSGS	PHN0006	Number already exists in the phone directory
PHONEMSGS	PHN0007	Phone number is required

16.6.4 Additional notes

The CLOSEDISP parameter is used to improve performance. Since this command may be executed many times from the main task manager, performance can be improved by leaving the display file open. The display file can be closed from outside the program by issuing the reclaim resources (RCLRSC) command.

16.6.5 Screen image

The Add Phone Entry screen should appear, as shown in Fig. 16.3.

```
                        Add Phone Number


Type choices, press Enter.

Phone number . . . . . . . .    BBBBBBBBBBBBBBBBBBBB

Name . . . . . . . . . . .      BBBBBBBBBBBBBBBBBBBBBBBBBBBBBBBBBBB
    Address1 . . . . . . . .     BBBBBBBBBBBBBBBBBBBBBBBBBBBBBBBBBBBBBBBB
    Address2 . . . . . . . .     BBBBBBBBBBBBBBBBBBBBBBBBBBBBBBBBBBBBBBBB
    City, State, Zip . . . . .   BBBBBBBBBBBBB  BB  99999

Company  . . . . . . . . .      BBBBBBBBBBBBBBBBBBBBBBBBBBBBBBBBBBB




F3=Exit     F5=Clear fields     F12=Cancel
```

Figure 16.3 Add Phone Number screen layout.

16.7 Display Phone Entry

This module allows the user to display a single entry in the phone directory.

16.7.1 Requirements

The user should have the ability to display the associated information pertaining to a single directory entry. The user can leave the screen by pressing either Enter or the designated exit function key.

16.7.2 Command definition

The syntax for the display phone entry command is

```
DSPPHNE PHNUMBER(phone-number-to-display) CLOSEDISP(*CLOSE | *LEAVE)
```

Required parameters. Phone-number-to-display must be specified.

Optional parameters. CLOSEDISP specifies either *CLOSE to close the display file after all entries are completed, or *LEAVE to leave the display file open for future invocations. The default is *CLOSE. See Sec. 16.6.4 for more information on this parameter.

16.7.3 Messages

The message given in Table 16.6 is used by this module.

TABLE 16.6   Messages Used by the DSPPHNE Module

Message file	Message ID	Description
PHONEMSGS	PHN0008	Requested number "&1" was not found

16.7.4 Screen Image

The Display Phone Entry screen should appear as shown in Fig. 16.4.

```
                         Display Phone Entry

     Phone number . . . . . . . :  OOOOOOOOOOOOOOOOOOOO

     Name . . . . . . . . . . . :  OOOOOOOOOOOOOOOOOOOOOOOOOOOOOOOO
         Address1 . . . . . . . :  OOOOOOOOOOOOOOOOOOOOOOOOOOOOOOOOOOOOOOOOO
         Address2 . . . . . . . :  OOOOOOOOOOOOOOOOOOOOOOOOOOOOOOOOOOOOOOOOO
         City, State, Zip . . . :  OOOOOOOOOOOOOOO  OO  OOOOO

     Company  . . . . . . . . . :  OOOOOOOOOOOOOOOOOOOOOOOOOOOOOOOOOOOOOOOOO

     Last updated by  . . . . . :  OOOOOOOOOO




     Press Enter to continue.

     F3=Exit     F12=Cancel
```

Figure 16.4 Display Phone Entry screen layout.

16.8   Change Phone Entry

This module allows the user to make changes to a phone directory entry. The user may not modify the phone number.

16.8.1 The user should have the ability to:

- Change information pertaining to a single phone directory entry.
- Use a function key to reset the fields to their original values (refresh).

The following validation tests must be made:

- Name may not be blank
- State code must be valid

16.8.2 Command Definition

The syntax for the change phone entry command is

```
CHGPHNE PHNUMBER(number-to-change) CLOSEDISP(*CLOSE | *LEAVE)
```

Required parameters. Number-to-change must be specified.

Optional parameters. CLOSEDISP specifies either *CLOSE to close the display file after all entries are completed, or *LEAVE to leave the display file open for future invocations. The default is *CLOSE.

16.8.3 Messages

The messages shown in Table 16.7 are used by this module.

TABLE 16.7 Messages Used by the CHGPHNE Module

Message file	Message ID	Description
PHONEMSGS	PHN0002	Specified state abbreviation is invalid
PHONEMSGS	PHN0005	Name cannot be blank
PHONEMSGS	PHN0008	Requested number "&1" was not found

16.8.4 Screen image

The Change Phone Entry screen should appear as shown in Fig. 16.5.

16.9 Delete Phone Entry

This command will delete an entry from the phone directory.

```
                         Change Phone Entry

Phone number . . . . . . . :   OOOOOOOOOOOOOOOOOOOOO

Type choices, press Enter.

Name . . . . . . . . . . .    BBBBBBBBBBBBBBBBBBBBBBBBBBBBBBBBBBBB
    Address1 . . . . . . . .    BBBBBBBBBBBBBBBBBBBBBBBBBBBBBBBBBBBBBBBBBB
    Address2 . . . . . . . .    BBBBBBBBBBBBBBBBBBBBBBBBBBBBBBBBBBBBBBBBBB
    City, State, Zip . . . . .  BBBBBBBBBBBBBBB  BB  99999

Company  . . . . . . . . .    BBBBBBBBBBBBBBBBBBBBBBBBBBBBBBBBBBBB




F3=Exit    F5=Refresh    F12=Cancel
```

Figure 16.5 Change Phone Entry screen layout.

16.9.1   Command definition

The syntax for the delete phone entry command is

```
DLTPHNE PHNUMBER(number-to-be-deleted)
```

Required parameters.   number-to-be-deleted must be specified.

16.9.2   Messages

The messages in Table 16.8 are used by this module.

TABLE 16.8   Messages Used by the DLTPHNE Module

Message file	Message ID	Description
PHONEMSGS	PHN0008	Requested number "&1" was not found
PHONEMSGS	PHN0004	Phone entry "&1" successfully removed

16.10   Add Service Request

This function should display a window to allow the user to select the type of service request necessary for the specified phone number. Once selected, the request should be sent to the service manager, which will run in the background.

16.10.1 Requirements

The user should be able to select from the following choices for a service request:

1. No dial tone
2. Can hear neighbor
3. Disconnect request
4. Horrible static

16.10.2 Command definition

The syntax for the create service request command is

```
CRTSRVREQ PHNUMBER(phone-number)
```

Required parameters. Phone-number must be specified.

16.10.3 Messages

The messages shown in Table 16.9 are used by this module.

TABLE 16.9 Messages Used by the CRTSRVREQ Module

Message file	Message ID	Description
PHONEMSGS	PHN0003	Service request submitted for account &1
PHONEMSGS	REQ0001	No dial tone
PHONEMSGS	REQ0002	Can hear neighbor
PHONEMSGS	REQ0003	Disconnect request
PHONEMSGS	REQ0004	Horrible static

16.10.4 Dependencies

Message queue SERVICEREQ must be present.

16.10.5 Window definition

The create service request function will pop up a Select Service Problem window. This window appears as shown in Fig. 16.6.

```
                    Work with Phone Directory

Position to  ........................................
             :         Select Service Problem        :
Type options :                                       :
   2=Change  :  Phone nbr:  0000000000000000000       :
             :                                       :
Opt  Name    :  Type choices, press Enter.           :  City
8_   xxxxxxx :                                       :  xxxxxxxxxxxxxxx
___  xxxxxxx :  Symptom . . :  _ 1. No dial tone      :  xxxxxxxxxxxxxxx
___  xxxxxxx :                 2. Can hear neighbors :  xxxxxxxxxxxxxxx
___  xxxxxxx :                 3. Disconnect request :  xxxxxxxxxxxxxxx
___  xxxxxxx :                 4. Horrible static     :  xxxxxxxxxxxxxxx
___  xxxxxxx :                                       :  xxxxxxxxxxxxxxx
___  xxxxxxx :  F12=Cancel                           :  xxxxxxxxxxxxxxx
___  xxxxxxx :                                       :  xxxxxxxxxxxxxxx
___  xxxxxxx :........................................:  xxxxxxxxxxxxxxx
___  xxxxxxxxxxxxxxxxxxxxxxxxxxxxxxxx xxxxxxxxxxxxxxxxxxxxxxxx  xxxxxxxxxxxxxxx
___  xxxxxxxxxxxxxxxxxxxxxxxxxxxxxxxx xxxxxxxxxxxxxxxxxxxxxxxx  xxxxxxxxxxxxxxx
___  xxxxxxxxxxxxxxxxxxxxxxxxxxxxxxxx xxxxxxxxxxxxxxxxxxxxxxxx  xxxxxxxxxxxxxxx
                                                             More...

F3=Exit    F5=Refresh    F6=Add name    F7=Add multiple names    F12=Cancel
```

Figure 16.6 Change Phone Entry screen layout.

16.11   Service Manager Functions

The service manager is a program that runs as a submitted batch job and monitors the status of message queue SERVICREQ. As service requests are received from the message queue, a line is printed in the report indicating which number requested the service and what the problem is. The date and time are also printed.

16.11.1   Commands

Start service manager command syntax:

```
STRSRVMGR JOBQ(library-name/jobq-name)
```

- If library-name is not specified, it is defaulted to *LIBL.
- If jobq-name is not specified, it will default to SERVICEREQ.

End service manager command syntax:

```
EMDSRVMGR
```

16.11.2 Messages

The messages given in Table 16.10 are used by this module.

TABLE 16.10   Messages Used by the Service Manager Module

Message file	Message ID	Description
PHONEMSGS	SVC0001	Service manager is not active—end request ignored
PHONEMSGS	SVC0002	Service manager is already active—start request ignored
PHONEMSGS	SVC0003	Service manager invoked
PHONEMSGS	SVC9999	Terminate service manager

16.11.3 Reports

A service request log will be printed when the service manager terminates. While the service manager is operating, service requests will be logged into the service request log (see Fig. 16.7).

```
SERVICE REQUEST LOG                                    PAGE:  0001
Date       Time      Phone number              Request details
--------   --------  ------------------------  ------------------------------
99/99/99   99/99/99  XXXXXXXXXXXXXXXXXXXXXXXX  XXXXXXXXXXXXXXXXXXXXXXXXXXXXXX
```

Figure 16.7   Report layout for service log.

16.11.4 Dependencies

If no parameters are specified on the STRSRVMGR command, the default job queue of SERVICEREQ is used. Steps to create a test subsystem as well as this job queue will be provided in Chap. 23.

17

Setting Up the Environment

In this chapter, you will prepare the environment necessary to enter and execute the phone directory program detailed in Chap. 16. You will be exposed to the following:

- Creating a menu
- Creating a field reference file
- Creating a database file
- OS/400 message-handling application program interfaces (APIs)
- Using the retrieve job attributes (RTVJOBA) command to determine the current workstation user

There are several ways of initiating the tools used during development. For example, if you are using PDM, you can put a "2" in front of a source member name to invoke the source utility entry (SEU) for that member. You can also use the STRSEU command to start SEU and request a list of members to select from. Since the focus of this book is not on the usage of the development tools (such as SEU, PDM, RLU, etc.), the commands used for starting the various programming tools will be via the command line. A brief introduction to using PDM and SEU can be found in Chap. 2.

The F9=Retrieve key is useful when entering the same command several times. This key will retrieve the last command executed and place it on the command line. You can then make any changes necessary and reexecute the command just by pressing Enter.

Finally, all commands throughout the remainder of this book will not specify a library name when the command defaults to either *LIBL or *CURLIB. For example, when compiling COBOL programs, the library name will not be specified. Thus, it is important that you make sure your current library is correct (as discussed in the Chap. 0).

17.1 Creating the Source Physical Files

This project consists of a variety of programs and objects written and described in different languages. Therefore, several source physical files will be required to hold the source for these objects. If you followed the instructions in Chap. 0, you should have created the source physical files shown in Table 17.1.

TABLE 17.1 Source Files Used by This Project

Source file	Contents
QCLSRC	Command language (CL) source programs
QCMDSRC	Command (CMD) source
QDDSSRC	Data description specifications (DDS) for physical, logical, and printer files
QLBLSRC	COBOL/400 source programs
QMNUSRC	Source for menus

17.2 Creating a Field Reference File

The field reference for this project contains a list of fields that are used in physical, logical, display, and printer files. The source for the field reference file is given in Listing 17.1.

Listing 17.1 Field-reference file.

```
MEMBER NAME: FIELDREF     FILE: QDDSSRC
.....A..........T.Name++++++RLen++TDpB......Functions++++++++++++++
      A* FIELD REFERENCE FILE
      A*
      A           R FIELDREF
      A             PHONENUM       20        COLHDG('PHONE')
      A             NAME           35        COLHDG('NAME')
      A             COMPANY        35        COLHDG('COMPANY')
      A             ADDRESS        40        COLHDG('ADDRESS')
      A             CITY           15        COLHDG('CITY')
      A             STATE           2        COLHDG('STATE')
      A             ZIP             5  0     COLHDG('POSTAL CODE')
      A                                      EDTCDE(X)
      A             COUNTRY         3        COLHDG('COUNTRY')
      A             LASTUSER       10        COLHDG('LAST UPD BY')
```

Use the following command to start SEU and enter this DDS source:

```
STRSEU QDDSSRC FIELDREF TYPE(PF) TEXT('Field reference file')
```

Use the create physical file (CRTPF) command to compile and create the field reference file:

```
CRTPF FILE(FIELDREF)
```

17.3   Creating the Database Files

This project requires two related database files:

- A physical file containing all telephone entries. Since the phone numbers are to be unique within the file, the phone number appears to be a good candidate for the primary key.

- A logical file that views the above-mentioned physical file in alphabetical order by name. This file will be used in the Work with Phone Directory program to allow the user to look-up phone entries by name rather than by number.

17.3.1   Creating the PHONEFILE physical file

PHONEFILE is a physical file that will contain most of the fields defined in the field-reference file. Listing 17.2 contains the DDS source member for physical file PHONEFILE.

Listing 17.2   DDS for the PHONEFILE physical file.

```
MEMBER NAME: PHONEFILE        FILE: QDDSSRC
.....A..........T.Name+++++++RLen++TDpB.....Functions++++++++++++++++
     A                                       REF(FIELDREF)
     A                                       UNIQUE
     A          R PHONEREC
     A            PHONENUM  R
     A            NAME      R
     A            COMPANY   R
     A            ADDRESS1  R                 REFFLD(ADDRESS)
     A            ADDRESS2  R                 REFFLD(ADDRESS)
     A            CITY      R
     A            STATE     R
     A            ZIP       R
     A            COUNTRY   R
     A            LASTUSER  R
     A          K PHONENUM
```

There are two areas that are highlighted in this listing. First, the REF function specifies that any fields in the source that have an "R" in the reference column are to reference file FIELDREF. Since no library name is specified, the library list will be searched to find the FIELDREF file when this source is compiled. Also, ADDRESS1 and ADDRESS2 are names that do not appear in the field reference file, yet they should be based on the standard definition of an address. The REFFLD function explicitly names a field in the referenced file. Both ADDRESS1 and ADDRESS2 take their attributes from the same field in the field-reference file; therefore they will both be defined the same. Additionally, the UNIQUE keyword indicates that duplicate keys are not permitted in the file.

To enter the source in Listing 17.2, use the following command:

```
STRSEU QDDSSRC PHONEFILE TYPE(PF) TEXT('Phone listings')
```

Use the create physical file command to compile and create the phone listings file:

```
CRTPF FILE(PHONEFILE)
```

17.3.2 Creating the NAMEFILE logical file

NAMEFILE is a logical file that will provide an access path to PHONE-FILE ordered by the customer's name. This file is used by the Work with Phone Directory program. Listing 17.3 contains the source for logical file NAMEFILE. The PFILE function indicates that the defined record format shall obtain its data from physical file PHONEFILE. The FORMAT function indicates that it should share the same field layout as that found in the physical file PHONEFILE. If the FORMAT function was not specified, any desired fields from the physical file would need to be declared in the record layout.

Listing 17.3 DDS for the NAMEFILE logical file.

```
MEMBER NAME: NAMEFILE        FILE: QDDSSRC
.....A...........T.Name+++++RLen++TDpB......Functions+++++++++++++++
  A           R PHONEREC          PFILE(PHONEFILE)
  A                               FORMAT(PHONEFILE)
  A           K NAME
```

To enter the source in Listing 17.3, use the following command:

```
STRSEU QDDSSRC NAMEFILE TYPE(LF) TEXT('Name listings')
```

Use the create logical file (CRTLF) command to compile and create this logical file:

```
CRTLF FILE(NAMEFILE)
```

17.4   Creating the Main Menu using the Screen Design Aid (SDA)

This section will take you through the necessary steps to create the main menu for the phone directory system. Menus are created using screen design aid (SDA). To start SDA, enter the following command:

```
STRSDA
```

From SDA's main menu, choose the option "Design Menus." Specify the following parameters when requested:

Source file	QMNUSRC
Library	*CURLIB (or YOURLIB)
Menu	PHONEDIR

After pressing Enter, the Specify Menu Functions menu will be displayed. Select "Work with menu image and commands" by putting a "Y" in the choice field, then press Enter (the choice may have already been made for you).

After pressing Enter, the screen in Fig. 17.1 will be displayed.

```
PHONEDIR                    PHONEDIR Menu

Select one of the following:

    1.
    2.
    3.
    4.
    5.
    6.
    7.
    8.
    9.
   10.


Selection or command                    _
F3=Exit                   F10=Work with commands      F12=Cancel
F13=Command area          F20=Reverse                 F24=More keys
```

Figure 17.1 Empty menu shell.

If you would like to explore the various commands available when designing menus, press the Help key. If your workstation does not have a Help key, you can use the F1=Help key.

The phone directory system requires four menu items. Each item listed below contains the menu text (italicized) and its underlying command.

- *1. Work with phone directory.* Command: WRKPHNDIR.
- *2. Start service manager (batch).* Command: STRSRVMGR.
- *3. End service manager.* Command: ENDSRVMGR.
- *90. Sign off.* Command: SIGNOFF

17.4.1 Adding the menu items.

Using the cursor keys, position the cursor on the same line as selection 1, exactly to the right of the period (if your workstation has a line and column indicator, it should be on line 5, column 9. Start by typing a single quote and then type the words

```
Work with phone directory
```

followed by another single quote. When you have finished this line, your display should look the same as that in Fig. 17.2.

After you have typed the text, press the Enter key. You will notice

```
PHONEDIR                        PHONEDIR Menu

Select one of the following:

    1.'Work with phone directory'█
    2.
    3.
    4.
```

Figure 17.2 Defining the menu text.

that the single quotes will disappear. The quotes are important because they keep all the words together as a single group. If you do not use the quotes, SDA will treat each word as a separate field. If you then try to delete the text, you would have to delete each word separately rather than a single delete for the entire group.

Continue by typing options 2 and 3 the same way. After you have pressed enter, your screen should look like the one in Fig. 17.3. You can now remove the unnecessary menu selections 4 through 10. Put the letter "d" in front of each option number, then press Enter. "d" is the code for delete.

Now you can place the last menu option below option 3. Sign off is

```
PHONEDIR                      PHONEDIR Menu

Select one of the following:

   1. Work with phone directory
   2. Start service manager (batch)
   3. Terminate service manager
   4.
   5.
```

Figure 17.3 Defining the menu text.

usually option 90, so we will continue with this AS/400 tradition. Move the cursor to line 9, column 6, and type '90. Sign off' (do not forget to type the quotes) and then press Enter. Your screen should now appear as shown in Fig. 17.4.

```
PHONEDIR                      PHONEDIR Menu

Select one of the following:

   1. Work with phone directory
   2. Start service manager (batch)
   3. Terminate service manager

  90. Sign off
```

Figure 17.4 The completed menu image.

17.4.2 Specifying the commands behind the menu items

Now that the menu image is complete, you can specify the commands that are to be processed when the user selects one of the menu items. Press the "Work with commands" function key. This is usually F10. You will see the display given in Fig. 17.5.

With the cursor on the first command line (next to option 01), type the command related to menu option 1. Since menu option 1 is "Work with phone directory," the command should be WRKPHNDIR. The command for option 2 is STRSRVMG. The command for option 3 is ENDSRVMGR. After specifying these commands, your display should look like that shown in Fig. 17.6.

Finally, scroll through the list (or use the "Position to" field at the top of the display) to reposition the list to option 90. For this command,

```
                        Define Menu Commands

Menu . . . . . . :     PHONEDIR          Position to menu option . . . . .    __

Type commands, press Enter.

Option    Command
  01      _____

  02      _____

  03      _____

  04      _____

  05      _____

  06      _____

  07      _____


                                                                     More...
F3=Exit       F11=Defined only options      F12=Cancel      F24=More keys
```

Figure 17.5 Defining underlying menu commands.


```
                        Define Menu Commands

Menu . . . . . . :     PHONEDIR          Position to menu option . . . . .    __

Type commands, press Enter.

Option    Command
  01      WRKPHNDIR_____

  02      STRSRVMGR_____

  03      ENDSRVMGR_____

  04      _____

  05      _____

  06      _____

  07      _____


                                                                     More...
F3=Exit       F11=Defined only options      F12=Cancel      F24=More keys
```

Figure 17.6 Defining the menu commands.

specify SIGNOFF. Then press Enter (you will be returned to the menu image screen).

You have now finished defining the menu and its commands. To exit, press the F3=Exit key. The Specify Menu Functions display will be shown. Leave the fields with their default values and press Enter.

The Exit SDA Menus display should be shown. Verify that the object library specified in the "Create menu objects" parameters specifies *CURLIB. If it is correct, press Enter to create the menu. The menu will be created and the display will return to the SDA "Design menus" screen. Use F3=Exit to exit SDA.

You can now test your menu by typing GO PHONEDIR. The GO command causes OS/400 to display the PHONEDIR menu. When OS/400 displays a menu, it automatically pushes the previous menu onto a "menu stack," thus keeping track of all of the menus previously displayed. You can always exit from the current menu by pressing F3 or F12, which will pop the previous menu from the stack and redisplay it.

17.5   Creating a Message File

The phone directory application defines a group of messages that are used by many of the programs. These predefined messages will be kept in an OS/400 message file.

To create the message file for the phone directory application, use the following command:

```
CRTMSGF PHONEMSGS
```

17.5.1   Adding messages to the message file

There are several types of messages that will be used by the phone directory application:

- Date entry messages describe when the user has entered something incorrectly. These messages will be preceded by the identifier PHN.

- Request messages send service requests to the service manager. These messages will be preceded by the identifier REQ.

- Service messages report the status of the service manager. Service messages are identified by the letters SVC.

Table 17.2 lists all of the messages used in the phone directory application. There are two ways of adding messages to a message file. The first is by using the add message description (ADDMSGD) command, and the other is by using the work with message descriptions

TABLE 17.2 Message Definitions

Message ID	Description
PHN0001	Specified option "&1" is invalid
PHN0002	Specified state abbreviation is invalid
PHN0003	Service request submitted for account &1
PNH0004	Phone entry "&1" successfully removed
PHN0005	Name cannot be blank
PHN0006	Number already exists in the phone directory
PHN0007	Phone number is required
PHN0008	Requested number "&1" was not found
PHN0009	Requested program was not found
REQ0001	No dial tone
REQ0002	Can hear neighbor
REQ0003	Disconnect request
REQ0004	Horrible static
SVC0001	Service manager is not active—end request ignored
SVC0002	Service manager is already active—start request ignored
SVC0003	Service manager invoked
SVC9999	Terminate service manager

(WRKMSGD) command. The ADDMSGD command will be used to quickly populate the message file (see Fig. 17.7). If you would like to

```
ADDMSGD PHN0001 PHONEMSGS MSG('Specified option "&1" is invalid.') FMT((*CHAR 25))
ADDMSGD PHN0002 PHONEMSGS MSG('Specified state abbreviation is invalid')
ADDMSGD PHN0003 PHONEMSGS MSG('Service request submitted for account &1') FMT((*CHAR 25))
ADDMSGD PHN0004 PHONEMSGS MSG('Phone entry "&1" successfully removed') FMT((*CHAR 25))
ADDMSGD PHN0005 PHONEMSGS MSG('Name cannot be blank.')
ADDMSGD PHN0006 PHONEMSGS MSG('Number already exists in the phone directory.')
ADDMSGD PHN0007 PHONEMSGS MSG('Phone number is required.')
ADDMSGD PHN0008 PHONEMSGS MSG('Requested number "&1" was not found.') FMT((*CHAR 25))
ADDMSGD PHN0009 PHONEMSGS MSG('Requested program was not found.')

ADDMSGD REQ0001 PHONEMSGS MSG('No dial tone')
ADDMSGD REQ0002 PHONEMSGS MSG('Can hear neighbors')
ADDMSGD REQ0003 PHONEMSGS MSG('Disconnect request')
ADDMSGD REQ0004 PHONEMSGS MSG('Horrible static')

ADDMSGD SVC0001 PHONEMSGS MSG('Service manager is not active - end request ignored.')
ADDMSGD SVC0002 PHONEMSGS MSG('Service manager is already active - start request ignored.')
ADDMSGD SVC0003 PHONEMSGS MSG('Service manager invoked.')
ADDMSGD SVC9999 PHONEMSGS MSG('Terminate program')
```

Figure 17.7 Adding messages to the message file.

print a listing of the messages that you entered, you can use the DSPMSGD command.

```
DSPMSGD RANGE(*FIRST *LAST) MSGF(PHONEMSGS) DETAIL(*BASIC) OUTPUT(*PRINT)
```

or to display the messages:

```
DSPMSGD RANGE(*FIRST *LAST) MSGF(PHONEMSGS) DETAIL(*BASIC)
```

17.6 Creating the COBOL Data Definition Copy Book

The copy book in Listing 17.4 contains the definitions of the most commonly used data types, program flags, and indicator definitions used throughout the application.

Listing 17.4 Common data definitions COPY book.

```
MEMBER NAME: DATADEFS      FILE: QLBLSRC
....-..A...B..-....2....-....3....-....4....-....5....-....6....-....7..
************************************************************************
* COMMON DATE DEFINITIONS
************************************************************************
01  USERID               PIC X(10)
01  SFL-RECNUM           PIC 9(7).
01  VALIDATE-FLAG        PIC 9 VALUE 0.
    88 NO-ENTRY-ERRORS         VALUE 0.
    88 ENTRY-ERRORS            VALUE 1.
01  PGM-STATUS           PIC 9 VALUE 0.
    88 PGM-ACTIVE              VALUE 0.
    88 PGM-EXIT                VALUE 1.
01  FILE-STATUS          PIC X VALUE "C".
    88 FILES-OPEN              VALUE "O".
    88 FILES-CLOSED            VALUE "C".

01  INDIC-AREA.
    03 EACH-IND OCCURS 99 TIMES PIC 1 INDICATOR 1.
       88 IND-OFF VALUE B"0".
       88 IND-ON  VALUE B"1".
01  INDIC-USAGE.
    03 F03-EXIT          PIC 99 VALUE 03.
    03 F05-REFRESH       PIC 99 VALUE 05.
    03 F06-CREATE        PIC 99 VALUE 06.
    03 F12-CANCEL        PIC 99 VALUE 12.
    03 I-OPT-ERROR       PIC 99 VALUE 30.
    03 I-SFLDSP          PIC 99 VALUE 41.
    03 I-SFLCLR          PIC 99 VALUE 42.
    03 I-SFLEND          PIC 99 VALUE 43.
    03 I-SFLNXTCHG       PIC 99 VALUE 44.
    03 I-SFLINZ          PIC 99 VALUE 45.
    03 I-MSGSFLEND       PIC 99 VALUE 46.
    03 I-OVERLAY         PIC 99 VALUE 47.
    03 I-ERASEINP        PIC 99 VALUE 48.
    03 I-PAGEDN          PIC 99 VALUE 52.
    03 I-PAGEUP          PIC 99 VALUE 51.
```

To enter the copy book in listing 17.4, use the following command to start SEU:

```
STRSEU QLBLSRC SRCMBR(DATADEFS) TYPE(CBL) TEXT('Data Definitions')
```

17.7   Using OS/400 APIs

It is occasionally necessary to execute OS/400 APIs from within a CO-BOL program. This is most often the case when a system service (such as sending a message or reading a data area) is required and COBOL does not support the desired service. Generally, you should avoid using APIs when writing COBOL programs that will require portability to other platforms.

If code portability is not important, you can take advantage of a variety of APIs that are defined in the *AS/400 System Programmer's Interface Reference*. APIs were included in this book because it may become necessary at some point to interface to OS/400 for functionality that is not directly available from COBOL/400. The brief introduction to the APIs provided will help form a better understanding of how to use the OS/400 APIs.

The phone directory application will use two OS/400 APIs:

- QMHSNDPM *(Send program message):* This API is used to send program messages from within a COBOL program. Several of the applications use this API to send a message back to the workstation indicating that the user has requested an invalid phone number. It is also used in the WRKPHNDIR program to indicate when the user has made an invalid choice.

- QMHRMVPM *(Remove the program messages):* This API is used by the Work with Phone Directory (WRKPHNDIR) program to clear the message subfile each time the user presses the enter key.

This chapter will not go into details about the parameters defined in the COPY book for these APIs. For more information on how the API works, please see Appendix A.

17.7.1   Data division copy books

There are three copy books that you must define in order to use the QMHSNDPM and QMHRMVPM APIs.

- The first defines the parameters for the QMHSNDM, QMHSNDPM, and QMHRMVPM. This will be named QMHDATADIV (MH stands for message handling) and will be included in the WORKING-STOR-AGE SECTION in the data division.

- The second defines any arguments necessary by all OS/400 APIs (including error structures). The name of this copy book is API.
- The third defines two PROCEDURE DIVISION paragraphs used to call the APIs and is named QMHPROCDIV.

In QMHDATADIV, all identifier names are made of two parts—the first is the name of the API that it is used in, and the second is a brief description of the parameter. The VALUE clause has been used to default some of the identifiers to the most commonly used choices. Use the following command to start SEU and enter the source in Listing 17.5.

```
STRSEU QLBLSRC QMHDATADIV TYPE(CBL) TEXT('Message handling API
structures')
```

Listing 17.5 QMHDATADIV copy book.

```
MEMBER NAME: QMHDATADIV     FILE: QLBLSRC
....-..A...B..-....2....-....3....-....4....-....5....-....6....-....7..
   01  QMHSNDM-PARMS
       03 QMHSNDM-MSGID          PIC X(7).
       03 QMHSNDM-MSGF.
          05 QMHSNDM-MSGFNAME     PIC X(10).
          05 QMHSNDM-MSGFLIB      PIC X(10) VALUE "*LIBL".
       03 QMHSNDM-MSGDTA          PIC X(100) VALUE SPACES.
       03 QMHSNDM-MSGDTALEN       LIKE BIN4 VALUE 100.
       03 QMHSNDM-MSGTYPE         PIC X(10).
          88 QMHSNDM-COMP            VALUE "*COMP".
          88 QMHSNDM-DIAG            VALUE "*DIAG".
          88 QMHSNDM-INFO            VALUE "*INFO".
          88 QMHSNDM-INQ             VALUE "*INQ".
       03 QMHSNDM-TOMSGQ.
          05 QMHSNDM-MSGQNAMES OCCURS 50 TIMES.
             07 QMHSNDM-MSGQNAME  PIC X(10).
                88 QMHSNDM-ALLACCT   VALUE "*ALLACT".
                88 QMHSNDM-REQUESTER VALUE "*REQUESTER".
                88 QMHSNDM-SYSOPR    VALUE "*SYSOPR".
             07 QMHSNDM-MSGQLIB   PIC X(10).
                88 QMHSNDM-LIBL      VALUE "*LIBL".
       03 QMHSNDM-NUMMSGQ         LIKE BIN4 VALUE 1.
       03 QMHSNDM-REPLYQ.
          05 QMHSNDM-RPYQNAME     PIC X(10).
             88 QMHSNDM-PGMQ         VALUE "*PGMQ".
             88 QMHSNDM-WRKSTN       VALUE "*WRKSTN".
          05 QMHSNDM-RPYQLIB      PIC X(10) VALUE "*LIBL".
       03 QMHSNDM-MSGKEY          PIC X(4).

   01  QMHSNDPM-PARMS
       03 QMHSNDPM-MSGID          PIC X(7).
       03 QMHSNDPM-MSGF.
          05 QMHSNDPM-MSGFNAME    PIC X(10).
          05 QMHSNDPM-MSGFLIB     PIC X(10) VALUE "*LIBL".
       03 QMHSNDPM-MSGDTA         PIC X(100) VALUE SPACES.
       03 QMHSNDPM-MSGDTALEN      LIKE BIN4 VALUE 100.
       03 QMHSNDPM-MSGTYPE        PIC X(10).
          88 QMHSNDPM-COMP           VALUE "*COMP".
```

```
      88 QMHSNDPM-DIAG                    VALUE "*DIAG".
      88 QMHSNDPM-ESCAPE                  VALUE "*ESCAPE".
      88 QMHSNDPM-INFO                    VALUE "*INFO".
      88 QMHSNDPM-INQ                     VALUE "*INQ".
      88 QMHSNDPM-NOTIFY                  VALUE "*NOTIFY".
      88 QMHSNDPM-RQS                     VALUE "*RQS".
      88 QMHSNDPM-STATUS                  VALUE "*STATUS".
   03 QMHSNDPM-CALLQ          PIC X(10) VALUE "*".
      88 QMHSNDPM-THISPGM                 VALUE "*".
      88 QMHSNDPM-EXT                     VALUE "*EXT".
   03 QMHSNDPM-STAKCNTR       LIKE BIN4 VALUE 0.
      88 QMHSNDPM-TOTHISPGM               VALUE 0.
      88 QMHSNDPM-TOCALLER                VALUE 1.
   03 QMHSNDPM-MSGKEY         PIC X(4).


01 QMHRMVPM-PARMS.
   03 QMHRMVPM-CALLQ          PIC X(10) VALUE "*".
      88 QMHRMVPM-THISPGM                 VALUE "*".
      88 QMHRMVPM-ALLINACT                VALUE "*ALLINACT".
      88 QMHRMVPM-EXT                     VALUE "*EXT".
   03 QMHRMVPM-STAKCNTR       LIKE BIN4 VALUE 0.
      88 QMHRMVPM-TOTHISPGM               VALUE 0.
      88 QMHRMVPM-TOCALLER                VALUE 1.
   03 QMHRMVPM-MSGKEY         PIC X(4).
   03 QMHRMVPM-MSGTORMV       PIC X(10).
      88 QMHRMVPM-ALL                     VALUE "*ALL".
      88 QMHRMVPM-BYKEY                   VALUE "*BYKEY".
      88 QMHRMVPM-KEEPRQS                 VALUE "*KEEPRQS".
      88 QMHRMVPM-NEW                     VALUE "*NEW".
      88 QMHRMVPM-OLD                     VALUE "*OLD".
```

The copy book in Listing 17.6 defines the layout of the API error structure. It is kept in a file separate from the message handling parameters because it is a common structure used by most callable APIs. Consequently, it must be included *before* any other copy books since it defines the binary-4 data type that is used by the APIs. Use the following command to start SEU and enter the source in Listing 17.6.

```
STRSEU QLBLSRC API TYPE(CBL) TEXT('API Data types and structures')
```

Listing 17.6 API error message structure.

```
MEMBER NAME: API             FILE: QLBLSRC
....-..A...B..-....2....-....3....-....4....-....5....-....6....-....7..
   01 BIN4                     PIC S9(9) BINARY.

   01 API-ERROR.
      03 ERR-BYTES-PROVIDED    LIKE BIN4 VALUE 116.
      03 ERR-BYTES-AVAILABLE   LIKE BIN4 VALUE 0.
      03 ERR-EXCEPTION-ID      PIC X(7) VALUE SPACES.
      03 FILLER                PIC X.
      03 ERR-EXCEPTION-DATA    PIC X(100) VALUE SPACES.
```

17.7.2 Procedure division copy book

The copy book in Listing 17.7 contains two paragraphs that are used in conjunction with the message APIs defined in QMHDATADIV (in Listing 17.5). Use the following command to enter the source in Listing 17.7:

```
STRSEU QLBLSRC QMHPROCDIV TYPE(CBL) TEXT('Message handling paragraphs')
```

Listing 17.7 QMHPROCDIV copy book.

```
MEMBER NAME: QMHPROCDIV      FILE: QLBLSRC
....-..A...B..-....2....-....3....-....4....-....5....-....6....-....7..
          CALL-QMHRMVPM.
              CALL "QMHRMVPM" USING  QMHRMVPM-CALLQ
                                     QMHRMVPM-STAKCNTR
                                     QMHRMVPM-MSGKEY
                                     QMHRMVPM-MSGTORMV
                                     API-ERROR.

          CALL-QMHSNDM.
              CALL "QMHSNDM" USING   QMHSNDM-MSGID
                                     QMHSNDM-MSGF
                                     QMHSNDM-MSGDTA
                                     QMHSNDM-MSGDTALEN
                                     QMHSNDM-MSGTYPE
                                     QMHSNDM-TOMSGQ
                                     QMHSNDM-NUMMSGQ
                                     QMHSNDM-REPLYQ
                                     QMHSNDM-MSGKEY
                                     API-ERROR.

          CALL-QMHSNDPM.
              CALL "QMHSNDPM" USING  QMHSNDPM-MSGID
                                     QMHSNDPM-MSGF
                                     QMHSNDPM-MSGDTA
                                     QMHSNDPM-MSGDTALEN
                                     QMHSNDPM-MSGTYPE
                                     QMHSNDPM-CALLQ
                                     QMHSNDPM-STAKCNTR
                                     QMHSNDPM-MSGKEY
                                     API-ERROR.
```

17.8 Creating the Retrieve Current User (RTVCURUSR) Program

Several programs within the application will need to be able to obtain the current user's identification (ID) at run time. In particular, the change phone entry and add phone entry programs both record the user profile ID of the last user to change a phone directory entry. Listing 17.8 defines a CL program that will obtain the current user's ID.

Listing 17.8 RTVCURUSR program.

```
MEMBER NAME: RTVCURUSR        FILE: QCLSRC
....-....1....-....2....-....3....-....4....-....5....-....6....-....7..
          PGM        PARM(&CURUSR)
          DCL        VAR(&CURUSR) TYPE(*CHAR) LEN(10)
          RTVJOBA    USER(&CURUSR)
```

```
RETURN
ENDPGM
```

To enter the source in this listing, type the following command:

```
STRSEU QCLSRC RTVCURUSR TYPE(CLP) TEXT ('Retrieve current user')
```

To compile this program, use the following command:

```
CRTCLPGM RTVCURUSR
```

The RTVJOBA command retrieves the job's current user ID and places it in the command language variable &CURUSR. This value is then returned to the caller.

18

Create the
"Add Phone Entry"
Module

In this chapter, you will create the module that adds phone directory entries to the phone database. The components that you will create in this chapter are as follows:

- Command ADDPHNE—A command to initiate the process of adding records.
- Display file ADDPHNE.
- COBOL program ADDPHNE.
- Linkage Copy book ADDPHNEL—this copy book contains the parameter definition for other programs that call ADDPHNE.

18.1 Creating the Command

The add phone entry (ADDPHNE) command has two parameters, outlined in Table 18.1.

Listing 18.1 Command definition for ADDPHNE.

```
MEMBER NAME:  ADDPHNE        FILE: QCMDSRC
....-....1....-....2....-....3....-....4....-....5....-....6....-....7
        CMD         PROMPT('Add Phone Entry')
        PARM        KWD(ENTRIES) TYPE(*CHAR) LEN(1) RSTD(*YES) +
                    DFT(*SINGLE) SPCVAL((*SINGLE 'S') +
                    (*MULTIPLE 'M')) PROMPT('Entry type')
        PARM        KWD(CLOSEDISP) TYPE(*CHAR) LEN(1) RSTD(*YES) +
                    DFT(*CLOSE) SPCVAL((*CLOSE 'C') (*LEAVE +
                    'L')) PROMPT('Leave display open?')
```

TABLE 18.1 Command Parameters for the ADDPHNE Command

Keyword	Description
ENTRIES	Specifies whether the program should allow only a single entry to be made, or whether to allow the user to continuously enter listings until the user presses F3 to exit. Possible values are as follows. *SINGLE: The program will allow the user to enter a single name into the directory, and then it will exit. *MULTIPLE: The program will continue to allow the user to enter names into the directory until the user presses the exit key.
CLOSEDISP	Specifies whether the display file should be closed when the program ends. Leaving the display open will result in a faster response time to the user when the ADDPHNE program is called again. Possible values are as follows. *YES: The display is to be left open. *NO: The display is to be closed upon exiting.

The source in Listing 18.1 defines the command. On the highlighted line, the SPCVAL keyword defines the special values that the user may choose from for the ENTRIES parameter. Replacement values are set up so that if the user types *SINGLE, the command will translate the user's choice to the letter S; if the user types *MULTIPLE, the command will translate the choice to the letter M. When the command processing program (in this case, a COBOL program named ADDPHNE) is called, it will receive either M or S for the first parameter, not the original text *MULTIPLE or *SINGLE. The same type of replacements will occur in the CLOSEDISP keyword: if the user chooses *CLOSE, the command will send the value C; likewise if the user types *LEAVE, the command will send the value L.

If the user does not specify a selection for the ENTRIES parameter, it will default to *SINGLE. The restricted values (RSTD) keyword specifies *YES, which prevents the user from typing anything other than *SINGLE or *MULTIPLE.

To enter the source code in Listing 18.1, use the following command:

```
STRSEU QCMDSRC ADDPHNE TEXT('Add phone entry')
```

To compile and create the command, use the following command:

```
CRTCMD CMD(ADDPHNE) PGM(ADDPHNE)
```

The CRTCMD command specifies the name of the command to create (ADDPHNE) as well as the name of the command processing program (ADDPHNE). The command processing program will be defined in Sec. 18.4.

18.2 Creating the Linkage Copy Book

The COBOL program that will process the command from Sec. 18.1 receives two parameters when it is called. These parameters will need to be defined in the LINKAGE SECTION (see Listing 18.2). The COBOL program is not limited to only being used by the previously defined command. In fact, it will be callable by any other program (despite what language it was written in). For this reason, it is good practice to include a copy book that contains the definition of the linkage section so that other programs may include it in their WORKING-STORAGE sections. This will be illustrated in the Work with Phone Directory program, which is defined later in this book.

There are two parameters to the COBOL program. The first defines whether the user should be allowed to enter only a single directory entry, or whether the entry screen should be displayed repetitively until the user chooses to exit. The second parameter specifies whether or not to leave the display file open when the program exits.

Listing 18.2 Linkage section for the COBOL program ADDPHNE.

```
MEMBER NAME:  ADDPHNEL        FILE: QLBLSRC
....-..A...B..-....2....-....3....-....4....-....5....-....6....-....7
     01  ADDPHNE-REPEAT            PIC X.
         88 ADDPHNE-MULTI-ENTRY              VALUE "M".
         88 ADDPHNE-SINGLE-ENTRY             VALUE "S".
     01  ADDPHNE-FILE-PROCESSING   PIC X.
         88 ADDPHNE-CLOSE-FILES              VALUE "C".
         88 ADDPHNE-LEAVE-FILES-OPEN         VALUE "L".
```

Use the following command to start the source entry utility (SEU) to enter the source in Listing 18.2:

```
STRSEU QLBLSRC ADDPHNEL TYPE(CBL) TEXT('Linkage to ADDPHNE')
```

The 88-level entries allow COBOL programs to easily set and test the values of the two parameters. For instance, a program may use

```
IF ADDPHNE-SINGLE-ENTRY PERFORM ...
```

Likewise, it may set a parameter as in the following example:

```
SET ADDPHNE-CLOSE-FILES TO TRUE.
```

18.3   Creating the Display File

The ADDPHNE COBOL program uses a single display file to communicate with the user. When run, it will appear as shown in Fig. 18.1.

```
                              Add Phone Number

Type choices, press Enter.

Phone number . . . . . . . .  BBBBBBBBBBBBBBBBBBBB

Name . . . . . . . . . . .    BBBBBBBBBBBBBBBBBBBBBBBBBBBBBBBBBBBB
  Address1 . . . . . . . .    BBBBBBBBBBBBBBBBBBBBBBBBBBBBBBBBBBBBBBBBBB
  Address2 . . . . . . . .    BBBBBBBBBBBBBBBBBBBBBBBBBBBBBBBBBBBBBBBBBB
  City, State, Zip . . . . .  BBBBBBBBBBBBBBB  BB  99999

Company  . . . . . . . . .    BBBBBBBBBBBBBBBBBBBBBBBBBBBBBBBBBBBBBB




F3=Exit    F5=Clear fields     F12=Cancel
```

Figure 18.1 The ADDPHNE display layout.

The source code to create the ADDPHNE display file is in Listing
18.3.

Listing 18.3 Data description specification source for the ADDPHNE display file.

```
MEMBER NAME: ADDPHNE        FILE: QDDSSRC
.....AAN01N02N03T.NAME++++++RLEN++TDPBLINPOSFUNCTIONS+++++++++++++++++++
     A                                REF (*LIBL/PHONEFILE)
     A                                INDARA
     A                                ERRSFL
     A*******************************************************************
     A          R ENTRY
     A                                CA03(03 'EXIT')
     A                                CA12(12 'CANCEL')
     A                                CA05(05 'CLEAR')
     A                                OVERLAY
     A    48                          ERASEINP(*ALL)
     A                                PRINT
     A                           1 33'ADD PHONE NUMBER'
     A                                DSPATR(HI)
     A                           3  2'TYPE CHOICES, PRESS ENTER.'
     A                                DSPATR(HI) COLOR(BLU)
     A                           7  2'NAME . . . . . . . . . . .'
     A                           5  2'PHONE NUMBER . . . . . . .'
     A                          13  2'COMPANY . . . . . . . . .'
     A                           8  4'ADDRESS1 . . . . . . . .'
```

```
A                               9  4'ADDRESS2 . . . . . . . . '
A                              10  4'CITY, STATE, ZIP
A                              11  4'COUNTRY . . . . . . . . '
A                              23  2'F3=EXIT'
A                                     DSPATR(HI) COLOR(BLU)
A                              23 13'F5=CLEAR FIELDS'
A                                     DSPATR(HI) COLOR(BLU)
A           PHONENUM    R       I  5 32
A  90                                 ERRMSGID(PHN0007 *LIBL/PHONEMSGS 90)
A  92                                 ERRMSGID(PHN0006 *LIBL/PHONEMSGS 92)
A           NAME        R       I  7 32
A  91                                 ERRMSGID(PHN0005 *LIBL/PHONEMSGS 91)
A           ADDRESS1    R       I  8 32
A           ADDRESS2    R       I  9 32
A           CITY        R       I 10 32
A           STATE       R       I 10 49VALUES ('AL''AK''AZ''AR''CA''CO-
A                                     ' 'CT' 'DE' 'DC' 'FL' 'GA' 'HI' 'ID-
A                                     ' 'IL' 'IN' 'IA' 'KS' 'KY' 'LA' 'ME-
A                                     ' 'MD' 'MA' 'MI' 'MN' 'MS' 'MO' 'MT-
A                                     ' 'NE' 'NV' 'NH' 'NJ' 'NM' 'NY' 'NC-
A                                     ' 'ND' 'OH' 'OK' 'OR' 'PA' 'RI' 'SC-
A                                     ' 'SD' 'TN' 'TX' 'UT' 'VT' 'VA' 'WA-
A                                     ' 'WV' 'WI' 'WY' ' ' ')
A                                     CHKMSGID(PHN0002 *LIBL/PHONEMSGS)
A           ZIP         R       I 10 53
A           COUNTRY     R       I 11 32
A           COMPANY     R       I 13 32
```

To enter the source in Listing 18.3, start SEU with the following command:

```
STRSEU QDDSSRC ADDPHNE TYPE(DSPF) TEXT('ADDPHNE Display File')
```

To create the display file, use the following command:

```
CRTDSPF FILE(ADDPHNE) SRCFILE(QDDSSRC)
```

18.4   Creating the COBOL Program

The final piece to the ADDPHNE puzzle is the COBOL program. Use the following command to start SEU and enter the COBOL program in Listing 18.4.

```
STRSEU QLBLSRC ADDPHNE TYPE(CBL) TEXT('ADDPHNE COBOL program')
```

Listing 18.4 COBOL source for the ADDPHNE program. See program notes in text for an explanation of numbered areas.

```
MEMBER NAME: ADDPHNEL        FILE: QLBLSRC
....-..A...B..-....2.....-....3....-....4....-....5....-....6....-....7
           IDENTIFICATION DIVISION.
           PROGRAM-ID. ADDPHNE.

           ENVIRONMENT DIVISION.
           CONFIGURATION SECTION.
[1]        SPECIAL-NAMES. LOCAL-DATA IS LDA.
```

```
        INPUT-OUTPUT SECTION.
        FILE-CONTROL.
            SELECT DISPFILE ASSIGN TO WORKSTATION-ADDPHNE-SI
                ORGANIZATION IS TRANSACTION.
            SELECT PHONEFILE ASSIGN TO DATABASE-PHONEFILE
                ORGANIZATION IS INDEXED
                ACCESS MODE IS DYNAMIC
                RECORD KEY IS EXTERNALLY-DESCRIBED-KEY.

        DATA DIVISION.
        FILE SECTION.
        FD  DISPFILE.
        01  DISP-REC                       PIC X(2000).

        FD  PHONEFILE.
        01  PHONE-REC.
            COPY DDS-ALL-FORMATS OF PHONEFILE.

        WORKING-STORAGE SECTION.
        01  ENTRY-IN.
[2]         COPY DDS-ENTRY-I OF ADDPHNE.

        COPY DATADEFS.
            03 FK-CLEAR-FIELDS             PIC 99 VALUE 05.
[3]         03 ERR-PHONENUM-REQUIRED       PIC 99 VALUE 90.
            03 ERR-NAME-BLANK              PIC 99 VALUE 91.
            03 ERR-PHONENUM-EXISTS         PIC 99 VALUE 92.

        LINKAGE SECTION.
        COPY ADDPHNEL.
[4]
        PROCEDURE DIVISION USING ADDPHNE-REPEAT ADDPHNE-FILE-PROCESSING.
        MAIN-PARA.
            PERFORM INIT-PROGRAM.
            PERFORM PROCESS-REQUESTS UNTIL PGM-EXIT.
            PERFORM SHUT-DOWN.
            GOBACK.

        INIT-PROGRAM.
[5]         CALL "RTVCURUSR" USING USERID.
            MOVE ZEROS TO INDIC-AREA.
            SET IND-ON(I-MSGSFLEND) TO TRUE.
            SET PGM-ACTIVE TO TRUE.
            IF FILES-CLOSED
                OPEN I-O DISPFILE PHONEFILE
                SET FILES-OPEN TO TRUE
            END-IF.

            IF ADDPHNE-LEAVE-FILES-OPEN
[6]             INITIALIZE PHONEREC
                DISPLAY NAME OF PHONEREC UPON LDA
            END-IF.

        SHUT-DOWN.
            IF ADDPHNE-CLOSE-FILES
                CLOSE PHONEFILE DISPFILE
                SET FILES-CLOSED TO TRUE
            END-IF.

        PROCESS-REQUESTS.
            WRITE DISP-REC FORMAT "ENTRY" INDICATORS ARE INDIC-AREA.
            READ DISPFILE INTO ENTRY-IN FORMAT "ENTRY"
                INDICATORS ARE INDIC-AREA.
```

```
      EVALUATE TRUE
          WHEN IND-ON(F03-EXIT)
              SET PGM-EXIT TO TRUE
          WHEN IND-ON(FK-CLEAR-FIELDS)
              SET IND-ON(I-ERASEINP) TO TRUE
              SET IND-OFF(ERR-PHONENUM-REQUIRED) TO TRUE
          WHEN IND-ON(F12-CANCEL)
              SET PGM-EXIT TO TRUE
          WHEN OTHER
              PERFORM VALIDATE-CHOICES
              IF NO-ENTRY-ERRORS
                  PERFORM SAVE-DATA
                  IF ADDPHNE-MULTI-ENTRY
                      SET IND-ON(I-ERASEINP) TO TRUE
                  ELSE
                      SET PGM-EXIT TO TRUE
                  END-IF
              ELSE
                      SET IND-OFF(I-ERASEINP) TO TRUE
              END-IF
      END-EVALUATE.

      VALIDATE-CHOICES.
          SET NO-ENTRY-ERRORS TO TRUE.
[7]       SET IND-OFF(ERR-PHONENUM-REQUIRED)
              IND-OFF(ERR-PHONENUM-EXISTS)
              IND-OFF(ERR-NAME-BLANK) TO TRUE.

          IF PHONENUM OF ENTRY-IN EQUAL SPACES
              SET IND-ON(ERR-PHONENUM-REQUIRED) TO TRUE
              SET ENTRY-ERRORS TO TRUE
          ELSE
              MOVE PHONENUM OF ENTRY-IN TO PHONENUM OF PHONEREC
              READ PHONEFILE WITH NO LOCK
                  INVALID KEY
                      CONTINUE
[8]               NOT INVALID KEY
                      SET IND-ON(ERR-PHONENUM-EXISTS) TO TRUE
                      SET ENTRY-ERRORS TO TRUE
              END-READ
          END-IF.
          IF NAME OF ENTRY-IN EQUAL SPACES
              SET IND-ON(ERR-NAME-BLANK) TO TRUE
              SET ENTRY-ERRORS TO TRUE
          END-IF.

      SAVE-DATA.
          MOVE CORRESPONDING ENTRY-I TO PHONEREC.
          MOVE USERID TO LASTUSER.
          WRITE PHONE-REC.
          IF ADDPHNE-LEAVE-FILES-OPEN
[9]               DISPLAY NAME OF PHONE-REC UPON LDA
          END-IF.
```

To compile the ADDPHNE program, use the following command:

```
CRTCBLPGM ADDPHNE
```

Program notes

1. The SPECIAL-NAMES clause gives the program accessibility to the job's local data area. The COBOL defined LOCAL-DATA is associated with the program-defined local data area (LDA). Statements that access the LDA will do so through the program-defined LDA. Commands will occur through the program-defined LDA.

2. The COPY DDS-ENTRY-I OF ADDPHNE will locate the display file named ADDPHNE (in the library list) and extract the definition of record format ENTRY. The -I part specifies that input-only fields should be copied from the record format (output fields will not be copied).

3. Several additional indicator assignments are defined to make the program easier to read and understand.

4. The COPY ADDPHNEL will include the copy book defined in Sec. 18.3. Notice that it is included in the LINKAGE SECTION and not the WORKING-STORAGE section.

5. The RTVCURUSR program is the command language (CL) program defined in Chapter 17. When the CL program returns control to the COBOL program, the variable USERID will contain the current user's profile identification (ID).

6. If the files are to be left open, it is usually a sign that another program has called the ADDPHNE program, rather than it being executed from the command line by the user. When this is the case, the last name entered by the user should be put into the job's LDA so that the previous program can be aware of the last name added. This piece of code clears the LDA in the event that the user presses the exit or cancel key without adding any entries.

7. This section illustrates how to use meaningful names instead of arbitrary numbers, to set indicators on.

8. If the READ statement fails, then the specified number does not exist in the database, which proves it to be unique. If the test does not fail, the number already exists (therefore it is invalid since it is a duplicate). The NOT INVALID KEY is an ideal way of determining whether the READ was successful or not. The CONTINUE statement is provided with the INVALID KEY for documentation purposes only—it also helps reduce the number of compiler warnings.

9. After saving an entry to the phone directory database, the name is put into the LDA for any other programs that may need it.

18.5 Testing the ADDPHNE Program

You can easily test the program by entering the ADDPHNE command from the command line. Optionally, you can type ADDPHNE and then press the F4=Prompt key to get the full set of parameters and choices.

The following command will start the ADDPHNE program:

```
ADDPHNE
```

To add repetitive entries to the phone directory, use the following command:

```
ADDPHNE ENTRIES(*MULTIPLE)
```

18.6   Using the Debugger

If you are coming from the IBM System/36, you will appreciate the debugging facilities available under OS/400. If you are coming from a visual development and debugging environment on a PC, please refrain from whining and complaining until the end of the book.

The OS/400 debugger is a command-oriented debugger that is capable of setting breakpoints, modifying variables, and tracing a program's execution. It does not provide an easy way of stepping through source code.

When debugging, it is relatively important to have a recent compiler listing of the program to debug (dual session terminals are particularly good for this). When debugging COBOL programs, you will refer to line numbers that are generated by the compiler, not in your source.

For this reason, the compiler listing to the ADDPHNE is shown in Listing 18.5 for line number references. If you changed any source code or reworked the example, your compiler listing will differ.

Listing 18.5   Compiler listing for ADDPHNE.

```
STMT SEQNBR -A 1 B..+....2....+....3....+....4....+....5....+....6....+....7..IDENTFCN  S COPYNAME
   1 000100 IDENTIFICATION DIVISION.
   2 000200 PROGRAM-ID. ADDPHNE.
     000300
  .3 000400 ENVIRONMENT DIVISION.
   4 000500 CONFIGURATION SECTION.
   5 000600 SPECIAL-NAMES.  LOCAL-DATA IS LDA.
   6 000700 INPUT-OUTPUT SECTION.
   7 000800 FILE-CONTROL.
   8 000900     SELECT DISPFILE ASSIGN TO WORKSTATION-ADDPHNE-SI
   9 001000        ORGANIZATION IS TRANSACTION.
  10 001100     SELECT PHONEFILE ASSIGN TO DATABASE-PHONEFILE
  11 001200        ORGANIZATION IS INDEXED
  12 001300        ACCESS MODE IS DYNAMIC
  13 001400        RECORD KEY IS EXTERNALLY-DESCRIBED-KEY.
  14 001500 DATA DIVISION.
  15 001600 FILE SECTION.
  16 001700 FD  DISPFILE.
  17 001800 01  DISP-REC PIC X(500).
     001900
  18 002000 FD  PHONEFILE.
  19 002100 01  PHONE-REC.
  20 002200     COPY DDS-ALL-FORMATS OF PHONEFILE.
```

```
21 +000001      05  PHONEFILE-RECORD PIC X(203).                                    <-ALL-FMTS
   +000002*    I-O FORMAT:PHONEREC    FROM FILE PHONEFILE  OF LIBRARY PHONEDIR       <-ALL-FMTS
   +000003*                                                                         <-ALL-FMTS
   +000004*THE KEY DEFINITIONS FOR RECORD FORMAT  PHONEREC                          <-ALL-FMTS
   +000005* NUMBER                NAME               RETRIEVAL    TYPE    ALTSEQ     <-ALL-FMTS
   +000006*  0001   PHONENUM                          ASCENDING    AN      NO        <-ALL-FMTS
22 +000007      05  PHONEREC    REDEFINES PHONEFILE-RECORD.                          <-ALL-FMTS
23 +000008          06 PHONENUM          PIC X(20).                                  <-ALL-FMTS
   +000009*            PHONE                                                         <-ALL-FMTS
24 +000010          06 NAME              PIC X(35).                                  <-ALL-FMTS
   +000011*            NAME                                                          <-ALL-FMTS
25 +000012          06 COMPANY           PIC X(35).                                  <-ALL-FMTS
   +000013*            COMPANY                                                       <-ALL-FMTS
26 +000014          06 ADDRESS1          PIC X(40).                                  <-ALL-FMTS
   +000015*            ADDRESS                                                       <-ALL-FMTS
27 +000016          06 ADDRESS2          PIC X(40).                                  <-ALL-FMTS
   +000017*            ADDRESS                                                       <-ALL-FMTS
28 +000018          06 CITY              PIC X(15).                                  <-ALL-FMTS
   +000019*            CITY                                                          <-ALL-FMTS
29 +000020          06 STATE             PIC X(2).                                   <-ALL-FMTS
   +000021*            STATE                                                         <-ALL-FMTS
30 +000022          06 ZIP               PIC S9(5)      COMP-3.                      <-ALL-FMTS
   +000023*            POSTAL CODE                                                   <-ALL-FMTS
31 +000024          06 COUNTRY           PIC X(3).                                   <-ALL-FMTS
   +000025*            COUNTRY                                                       <-ALL-FMTS
32 +000026          06 LASTUSER          PIC X(10).                                  <-ALL-FMTS
   +000027*            LAST UPD BY                                                   <-ALL-FMTS
   002300
33 002400 WORKING-STORAGE SECTION.
34 002500 01  ENTRY-IN.
35 002600     COPY DDS-ENTRY-I OF ADDPHNE.
   +000001* INPUT FORMAT:ENTRY      FROM FILE ADDPHNE   OF LIBRARY PHONEDIR          ENTRY
   +000002*                                                                         ENTRY
36 +000003      05  ENTRY-I.                                                         ENTRY
37 +000004          06 PHONENUM          PIC X(20).                                  ENTRY
   +000005*            PHONE                                                         ENTRY
38 +000006          06 NAME              PIC X(35).                                  ENTRY
   +000007*            NAME                                                          ENTRY
39 +000008          06 ADDRESS1          PIC X(40).                                  ENTRY
   +000009*            ADDRESS                                                       ENTRY
40 +000010          06 ADDRESS2          PIC X(40).                                  ENTRY
   +000011*            ADDRESS                                                       ENTRY
41 +000012          06 CITY              PIC X(15).                                  ENTRY
   +000013*            CITY                                                          ENTRY
42 +000014          06 STATE             PIC X(2).                                   ENTRY
   +000015*            STATE                                                         ENTRY
43 +000016          06 ZIP               PIC S9(5).                                  ENTRY
   +000017*            POSTAL CODE                                                   ENTRY
44 +000018          06 COUNTRY           PIC X(3).                                   ENTRY
   +000019*            COUNTRY                                                       ENTRY
45 +000020          06 COMPANY           PIC X(35).                                  ENTRY
   +000021*            COMPANY                                                       ENTRY
   002700
46 002800 COPY DATADEFS.
   +000100*********************************************************************
   +000200* COMMON DATA DEFSINITIONS
   +000300*********************************************************************
47 +000400 01  USERID               PIC X(10).                                      DATADEFS
48 +000500 01  SFL-RECNUM           PIC 9(7).                                       DATADEFS
49 +000600 01  VALIDATE-FLAG        PIC 9 VALUE 0.                                  DATADEFS
50 +000700     88 NO-ENTRY-ERRORS         VALUE 0.                                  DATADEFS
51 +000800     88 ENTRY-ERRORS            VALUE 1.                                  DATADEFS
52 +000900 01  PGM-STATUS           PIC 9 VALUE 0.                                  DATADEFS
53 +001000     88 PGM-ACTIVE              VALUE 0.                                  DATADEFS
54 +001100     88 PGM-EXIT                VALUE 1.                                  DATADEFS
55 +001200 01  FILE-STATUS          PIC X VALUE 'C'.                                DATADEFS
56 +001300     88 FILES-OPEN              VALUE 'O'.                                DATADEFS
57 +001400     88 FILES-CLOSED            VALUE 'C'.                                DATADEFS
   +001500                                                                          DATADEFS
58 +001600 01  INDIC-AREA.                                                          DATADEFS
59 +001700     03 EACH-IND OCCURS 99 TIMES PIC 1 INDICATOR 1.                       DATADEFS
60 +001800        88 IND-OFF VALUE B'0'.                                            DATADEFS
```

```
 61 +001900           88 IND-ON  VALUE B"1".                           DATADEFS
 62 +002000 01 INDIC-USAGE.                                            DATADEFS
 63 +002100     03 F03-EXIT             PIC 99 VALUE 03.               DATADEFS
 64 +002200     03 F05-REFRESH          PIC 99 VALUE 05.               DATADEFS
 65 +002300     03 F06-CREATE           PIC 99 VALUE 06.               DATADEFS
 66 +002400     03 F12-CANCEL           PIC 99 VALUE 12.               DATADEFS
 67 +002500     03 I-OPT-ERROR          PIC 99 VALUE 30.               DATADEFS
 68 +002600     03 I-SFLDSP             PIC 99 VALUE 41.               DATADEFS
 69 +002700     03 I-SFLCLR             PIC 99 VALUE 42.               DATADEFS
 70 +002800     03 I-SFLEND             PIC 99 VALUE 43.               DATADEFS
 71 +002900     03 I-SFLNXTCHG          PIC 99 VALUE 44.               DATADEFS
 72 +003000     03 I-SFLINZ             PIC 99 VALUE 45.               DATADEFS
 73 +003100     03 I-MSGSFLEND          PIC 99 VALUE 46.               DATADEFS
 74 +003200     03 I-OVERLAY            PIC 99 VALUE 47.               DATADEFS
 75 +003300     03 I-PAGEDN             PIC 99 VALUE 52.               DATADEFS
 76 +003400     03 I-PAGEUP             PIC 99 VALUE 51.               DATADEFS
 77 +003500     03 I-ERASEINP           PIC 99 VALUE 68.               DATADEFS
    +003600******************************************************      DATADEFS
 78 +002900     03 FK-CLEAR-FIELDS      PIC 99 VALUE 05.
 79 +003000     03 ERR-PHONENUM-REQUIRED PIC 99 VALUE 90.
 80 +003100     03 ERR-NAME-BLANK       PIC 99 VALUE 91.
 81 +003200     03 ERR-PHONENUM-EXISTS  PIC 99 VALUE 92.
    003300
 82 003400 LINKAGE SECTION.
 83 003500 COPY ADDPHNEL.
    +000001******************************************************      ADDPHNEL
    +000002* LINKAGE PARMS FOR ADDPHNE - ADD PHONE ENTRY               ADDPHNEL
    +000003******************************************************      ADDPHNEL
 84 +004403 01 ADDPHNE-REPEAT           PIC X.                         ADDPHNEL
 85 +004404     88 ADDPHNE-MULTI-ENTRY       VALUE "M".                ADDPHNEL
 86 +004405     88 ADDPHNE-SINGLE-ENTRY      VALUE "S".                ADDPHNEL
 87 +004406 01 ADDPHNE-FILE-PROCESSING  PIC X.                         ADDPHNEL
 88 +004407     88 ADDPHNE-CLOSE-FILES       VALUE "C".                ADDPHNEL
 89 +004408     88 ADDPHNE-LEAVE-FILES-OPEN  VALUE "L".                ADDPHNEL
    003600                                                             ADDPHNEL
 90 003700 PROCEDURE DIVISION USING ADDPHNE-REPEAT ADDPHNE-FILE-PROCESSING.
    003800 MAIN-PARA.
 91 003900     PERFORM INIT-PROGRAM.
 92 004000     PERFORM PROCESS-REQUESTS UNTIL PGM-EXIT.
 93 004100     PERFORM SHUT-DOWN.
    004200     GOBACK.
    004300
 94 004400 INIT-PROGRAM.
 95 004500     CALL "RTVCURUSR" USING USERID.
 96 004600     MOVE ZEROS TO INDIC-AREA.
 97 004700     SET IND-ON(I-MSGSFLEND) TO TRUE.
 98 004800     SET PGM-ACTIVE TO TRUE.
 99 004900     IF FILES-CLOSED
100 005000         SET IND-ON(I-OVERLAY) TO TRUE
101 005100         OPEN I-O DISPFILE PHONEFILE
102 005200         SET FILES-OPEN TO TRUE
    005300     ELSE
103 005400         SET IND-OFF(I-OVERLAY) TO TRUE
    005500     END-IF.
    005600
    005700***  INITIALIZE LOCAL DATA AREA ***
104 005800     IF ADDPHNE-LEAVE-FILES-OPEN
105 005900         INITIALIZE PHONEREC
106 006000         DISPLAY NAME OF PHONEREC UPON LDA
    006100     END-IF.
    006200
    006300 SHUT-DOWN.
107 006400     IF ADDPHNE-CLOSE-FILES
108 006500         CLOSE PHONEFILE DISPFILE
109 006600         SET FILES-CLOSED TO TRUE
    006700     END-IF.
    006800
    006900 PROCESS-REQUESTS.
110 007000     WRITE DISP-REC FORMAT "ENTRY" INDICATORS ARE INDIC-AREA.
111 007100     READ DISPFILE INTO ENTRY-IN FORMAT "ENTRY"
    007200         INDICATORS ARE INDIC-AREA.
112 007300     EVALUATE TRUE
```

```
        007400        WHEN IND-ON(F03-EXIT)
113     007500            SET PGM-EXIT TO TRUE
        007600        WHEN IND-ON(FK-CLEAR-FIELDS)
114     007700            SET IND-ON(I-ERASEINP) TO TRUE
115     007800            SET IND-OFF(ERR-PHONENUM-REQUIRED) TO TRUE
        007900        WHEN IND-ON(F12-CANCEL)
116     008000            SET PGM-EXIT TO TRUE
        008100        WHEN OTHER
117     008200            PERFORM VALIDATE-CHOICES
118     008300            IF NO-ENTRY-ERRORS
119     008400              PERFORM SAVE-DATA
120     008500              IF ADDPHNE-MULTI-ENTRY
121     008600                  SET IND-ON(I-ERASEINP) TO TRUE
        008700              ELSE
122     008800                  SET PGM-EXIT TO TRUE
        008900              END-IF
        009000            ELSE
123     009100              SET IND-OFF(I-ERASEINP) TO TRUE
        009200            END-IF
        009300        END-EVALUATE.
        009400
        009500 VALIDATE-CHOICES.
124     009600        SET NO-ENTRY-ERRORS TO TRUE.
125     009700        SET IND-OFF(ERR-PHONENUM-REQUIRED)
        009800            IND-OFF(ERR-PHONENUM-EXISTS)
        009900            IND-OFF(ERR-NAME-BLANK) TO TRUE.
        010000
126     010100        IF PHONENUM OF ENTRY-IN EQUAL SPACES
127     010200            SET IND-ON(ERR-PHONENUM-REQUIRED) TO TRUE
128     010300            SET ENTRY-ERRORS TO TRUE
        010400        ELSE
129     010500            MOVE PHONENUM OF ENTRY-IN TO PHONENUM OF PHONEREC
130     010600            READ PHONEFILE WITH NO LOCK
        010700              INVALID KEY
        010800                CONTINUE
131     010900              NOT INVALID KEY
132     011000                SET IND-ON(ERR-PHONENUM-EXISTS) TO TRUE
133     011100                SET ENTRY-ERRORS TO TRUE
        011200            END-READ
        011300        END-IF.
134     011400        IF NAME OF ENTRY-IN EQUAL SPACES
135     011500            SET IND-ON(ERR-NAME-BLANK) TO TRUE
136     011600            SET ENTRY-ERRORS TO TRUE
        011700        END-IF.
        011800
        011900 SAVE-DATA.
137     012000        MOVE CORRESPONDING ENTRY-I TO PHONEREC.
        *         ** CORRESPONDING items for statement 137:
        *         **    PHONENUM
        *         **    NAME
        *         **    ADDRESS1
        *         **    ADDRESS2
        *         **    CITY
        *         **    STATE
        *         **    ZIP
        *         **    COUNTRY
        *         **    COMPANY
        *         ** End of CORRESPONDING items for statement 137
138     012100        MOVE USERID TO LASTUSER.
139     012200        WRITE PHONE-REC.
140     012300        IF ADDPHNE-LEAVE-FILES-OPEN
141     012400            DISPLAY NAME OF PHONE-REC UPON LDA
        012500        END-IF.
```

```
              * * * * * E N D   O F   S O U R C E   * * * * *
```

18.6.1   Starting the debugger

To start the OS/400 debugger, you will use the start debug (STRDBG) command. There is one parameter on the start debug command that you should be aware of. The UPDPROD parameter specifies whether or not your program will be able to update data files if the data files are located in a production library. The default behavior is to prevent updating production data files. When you created your personal development library (in the Preface of this book), you used the CRTLIB command and specified a type of *TEST. If your library is of type *PROD, the debugger will prevent you from updating any of the files from within debug mode unless you specify UPDPROD(*YES). It is recommended that you *not* use this option as it can be disastrous to update production data. If your test library is not of type *TEST, you can change it by using the CHGLIB command: CHGLIB LIB(YOURLIB) TYPE(*TEST). The remainder of this chapter will assume your library is a *TEST library. Start the debugger with the following command.

```
STRDBG ADDPHNE
```

18.6.2   Adding breakpoints

You will add two breakpoints to the program (they are shown in gray in compiler Listing 18.5).

- The first breakpoint will be on line 96. Upon entry, the program first calls a CL program to obtain the current user's ID. You will set a breakpoint to inspect the ID to make sure that the subprogram worked properly.
- The second breakpoint will be on line 112, immediately after the READ of the display. You will want to see the phone number entered by the user, as well as the status of all the indicators in the program.

To set the first breakpoint, use the following command:

```
ADDBKP 96 USERID
```

The variable name USERID does not need to be put in single quotes because it does not contain any hyphens or special characters (when debugging CL programs, you must put variable names in quotes because they contain the ampersand character, e.g., ADDBKP 100 '&USER'). The next breakpoint will require the use of quotes because you are interested in seeing the value of all 99 indicators, and the variable name for the indicators is INDIC-AREA. Also, because there are several PHONENUM variables in the program, you will need to qualify PHONENUM with the OF clause:

```
ADDBKP 112 ('PHONENUM OF ENTRY-IN' 'INDIC-AREA')
```

18.6.3 Running the program

You can now execute the ADDPHNE command from the command line as you did earlier in this chapter. Use the following command to start ADDPHNE:

```
ADDPHNE
```

When the program starts, you should see the screen shown in Fig. 18.2.

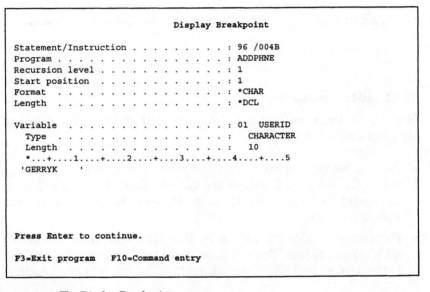

```
                        Display Breakpoint

Statement/Instruction . . . . . . . . . : 96 /004B
Program . . . . . . . . . . . . . . . . : ADDPHNE
Recursion level . . . . . . . . . . . . : 1
Start position . . . . . . . . . . . . : 1
Format  . . . . . . . . . . . . . . . . : *CHAR
Length  . . . . . . . . . . . . . . . . : *DCL

Variable  . . . . . . . . . . . . . . . : 01  USERID
  Type  . . . . . . . . . . . . . . . . :     CHARACTER
  Length  . . . . . . . . . . . . . . . :     10
  *...+....1....+....2....+....3....+....4....+....5
  'GERRYK    '




Press Enter to continue.

F3=Exit program    F10=Command entry
```

Figure 18.2 The Display Breakpoint screen.

Under the character ruler, you can see the user ID 'GERRYK'. From this display, you can set additional breakpoints by pressing the F10 key and issuing more ADDBKP commands. For now, press Enter to continue.

The display for the ADDPHNE program should be displayed. Enter some information into the display. Make sure to put something in the phone number field. When you are done, press Enter. Your display should look like that in Fig. 18.3. The first variable shows

```
                           Display Breakpoint

Statement/Instruction . . . . . . . . . : 112 /0118
Program . . . . . . . . . . . . . . . . : ADDPHNE
Recursion level . . . . . . . . . . . . : 1
Start position . . . . . . . . . . . . : 1
Format  . . . . . . . . . . . . . . . . : *CHAR
Length  . . . . . . . . . . . . . . . . : *DCL


Variable  . . . . . . . . . . . . . . . : 06  PHONENUM OF ENTRY-IN
  Type  . . . . . . . . . . . . . . . . :     CHARACTER
  Length  . . . . . . . . . . . . . . . :     20
  *...+....1....+....2....+....3....+....4....+....5
  '407-555-1212       '

Variable  . . . . . . . . . . . . . . . : 01  INDIC-AREA
  Type  . . . . . . . . . . . . . . . . :     CHARACTER
  Length  . . . . . . . . . . . . . . . :     99
  *...+....1....+....2....+....3....+....4....+....5

Press Enter to continue.

F3=Exit program    F10=Command entry
```

Figure 18.3 Displaying two variables in a breakpoint.

PHONENUM OF ENTRY-IN, and the second shows INDIC-AREA. You cannot see INDIC-AREA yet, so you will have to press the Page-up key on your keyboard, after which your display should look like that in Fig. 18.4.

```
                           Display Breakpoint

Statement/Instruction . . . . . . . . . : 112 /0118
Program . . . . . . . . . . . . . . . . : ADDPHNE
Recursion level . . . . . . . . . . . . : 1
Start position . . . . . . . . . . . . : 1
Format  . . . . . . . . . . . . . . . . : *CHAR
Length  . . . . . . . . . . . . . . . . : *DCL

  '00000000000000000000000000000000000000000011000'
  '00000000000000000000000000000000000000000000000'




Press Enter to continue.

F3=Exit program    F10=Command entry
```

Figure 18.4 Second page of the breakpoint display.

There are a total of 99 digits in the displayed output. Each digit corresponds to one of the indicators in the INDIC-AREA array. Since there are 50 indicators per line, you can quickly figure out that indicators 46 and 47 are turned on and all the rest are off.

18.6.4   Ending the debugger

When you are finished debugging, you can end it with the end debug (ENDDBG) command.

19

Create the
"Change Phone Entry"
Module

In this chapter, you will create the module that allows the user to change phone directory entries. You will see how to:

- Create a command to allow the user to change a specific phone directory entry (CHGPHNE)
- Create a display file (CHGPHNE)
- Create a COBOL program that updates a file
- Use a refresh key to refresh data on the display

19.1 Creating the Command

The change phone entry (CHGPHNE) command has two parameters, as shown in Table 19.1. The source in Listing 19.1 defines the command. There are two parameters defined in this command. Parameter PHNUMBER is defined as length 20 and CLOSEDISP is defined as character of length 1. The CLOSEDISP parameter is identical to that

TABLE 19.1 Command Parameters for the CHGPHNE Command

Keyword	Description
PHNUMBER	The phone number to be changed.
CLOSEDISP	Specifies whether the display file should be closed when the program ends. Possible values are as follows. *YES: The display is to be left open. *NO: The display is to be closed upon exiting.

of the ADDPHNE command. For more details on how the CLOSEDISP
parameter works, see Chap. 18.

Listing 19.1 Command definition for CHGPHNE.

```
MEMBER NAME: CHGPHNE          FILE: QCMDSRC
....-....1....-....2....-....3....-....4....-....5....-....6....-....7
            CMD       PROMPT ('Change Phone Entry')
            PARM      KWD (PHNUMBER) TYPE(*CHAR) LEN(20) +
                        PROMPT('Phone number')
            PARM      KWD(CLOSEDISP) TYPE(*CHAR) LEN(1) RSTD (*YES) +
                        DFT(*CLOSE) SPCVAL((*CLOSE 'C') (*LEAVE +
                        'L')) PROMPT('Leave display open?')
```

To enter the source code in Listing 19.1, use the following command:

```
STRSEU QCMDSRC CHGPHNE TEXT('Change phone entry')
```

To compile and create the command, use the following command:

```
CRTCMD CMD (CHGPHNE) PGM(CHGPHNE)
```

Both the command and the command processing program have the
same name (CHGPHNE). The command processing program will be
defined in Sec. 19.3.

```
                         Change Phone Entry

 Phone number . . . . . . . :   OOOOOOOOOOOOOOOOOOOO

 Type choices, press Enter.

 Name . . . . . . . . . . .   BBBBBBBBBBBBBBBBBBBBBBBBBBBBBBBB
    Address1 . . . . . . . .   BBBBBBBBBBBBBBBBBBBBBBBBBBBBBBBBBBBBBBBB
    Address2 . . . . . . . .   BBBBBBBBBBBBBBBBBBBBBBBBBBBBBBBBBBBBBBBB
    City, State, Zip . . . . .   BBBBBBBBBBBBBB BB 99999

 Company  . . . . . . . . .   BBBBBBBBBBBBBBBBBBBBBBBBBBBBBBBB




 F3=Exit     F5=Refresh     F12=Cancel
```

Figure 19.1 The CHGPHNE display layout.

19.2   Creating the Display File

The CHGPHNE program uses a single display file to communicate with the user. When run, it will appear as shown in Fig. 19.1. The source code that defines the CHGPHNE display file is given in Listing 19.2. The CHGPHNE display differs from the ADDPHNE display file in that it contains fields that are both input and output (the ADDPHNE display file contained only input capable fields).

Listing 19.2 Data description specification source for CHGPHNE display file.

```
MEMBER NAME: CHGPHNE        FILE: QDDSSRC
.....AAN01N02N03T.NAME+++++RLEN++TDPBLINPOSFUNCTIONS++++++++++++++++++++
     A                                REF(*LIBL/PHONEFILE)
     A                                INDARA
     A                                ERRSFL
     A************************************************************************
     A           R CHANGE
     A                                CA03(03 'Exit')
     A                                CA12(12 'Cancel')
     A                                CA05(05 'REFRESH')
     A                                OVERLAY
     A                                PRINT
     A                             1 32'Change Phone Entry'
     A                                DSPATR(HI)
     A                             5  2'Type choices, press Enter.'
     A                                DSPATR(HI) COLOR(BLU)
     A                             3  2'Phone number . . . . . . :'
     A                             7  2'Name . . . . . . . . . .'
     A                             8  4'Address1 . . . . . . . .'
     A                             9  4'Address2 . . . . . . . .'
     A                            10  4'City, State, Zip . . . . .'
     A                            11  4'Country . . . . . . . . .'
     A                            13  2'Company . . . . . . . . .'
     A                            23  2'F3=Exit'
     A                                DSPATR(HI) COLOR(BLU)
     A                            23 13'F5=Refresh'
     A                                DSPATR(HI) COLOR(BLU)
     A                            23 27'F12=Cancel'
     A                                DSPATR(HI) COLOR(BLU)
     A           PHONENUM R       O  3 32
     A           NAME     R       B  7 32
     A 91                             ERRMSGID(PHN0005 *LIBL/PHONEMSGS 91)
     A           ADDRESS1 R       B  8 32
     A           ADDRESS2 R       B  9 32
     A           CITY     R       B 10 32
     A           STATE        R   B 10 49VALUES('AL''AK''AZ''AR''CA''CO-
     A                                    ''CT''DE''DC''FL''GA''HI''ID-
     A                                    ''IL''IN''IA''KS''KY''LA''ME-
     A                                    ''MD''MA''MI''MN''MS''MO''MT-
     A                                    ''NE''NV''NH''NJ''NM''NY''NC-
     A                                    ''ND''OH''OK''OR''PA''RI''SC-
     A                                    ''SD''TN''TX''UT''VT''VA''WA-
     A                                    ''WV''WI''WY''  ')
     A                                CHKMSGID(PHN0002 *LIBL/PHONEMSGS)
     A           ZIP      R       B 10 53
     A           COUNTRY  R       B 11 32
     A           COMPANY  R       B 13 32
```

To enter the source in Listing 19.2, start the source entry utility (SEU) with the following command:

```
STRSEU QDDSSRC CHGPHNE TYPE(DSPF) TEXT('CHGPHNE Display File')
```

To create the display file, use the following command:

```
CRTDSPF FILE(CHGPHNE) SRCFILE(QDDSSRC)
```

19.3   Creating the COBOL Program

Use the following command to start SEU and enter the COBOL program in Listing 19.3.

```
STRSEU QLBLSRC CHGPHNE TYPE(CBL) TEXT('CHGPHNE COBOL program')
```

Listing 19.3   COBOL source for the CHGPHNE program. See program notes in text for an explanation of numbered regions.

```
MEMBER NAME: CHGPHNE          FILE: QLBLSRC
....-..A...B..-....2....-....3...-....4....-....5....-....6....-....7
          IDENTIFICATION DIVISION.
          PROGRAM-ID.  CHGPHNE.

          ENVIRONMENT DIVISION.
          CONFIGURATION SECTION.
          SPECIAL-NAMES. LOCAL-DATA IS LDA.
          INPUT-OUTPUT SECTION.
          FILE-CONTROL.
              SELECT DISPFILE ASSIGN TO WORKSTATION-CHGPHNE-SI
                  ORGANIZATION IS TRANSACTION.
              SELECT PHONEFILE ASSIGN TO DATABASE-PHONEFILE
                  ORGANIZATION IS INDEXED
                  ACCESS MODE IS DYNAMIC
                  RECORD KEY IS EXTERNALLY-DESCRIBED-KEY.

          DATA DIVISION.
          FILE SECTION.
          FD  DISPFILE.
          01  DISP-REC                    PIC X(2000).

          FD  PHONEFILE.
          01  PHONE-REC.
              COPY DDS-ALL-FORMATS OF PHONEFILE.

          WORKING-STORAGE SECTION.
          01  CHANGE-IN.
[1]           COPY DDS-CHANGE-I OF CHGPHNE.
          01  CHANGE-OUT.
              COPY DDS-CHANGE-O OF CHGPHNE.

          COPY DATADEFS.
              03  FK-REFRESH              PIC 99 VALUE 05.
              03  ERR-NAME-BLANK          PIC 99 VALUE 90.

[2]    COPY API.
```

```
COPY QMHDATADIV.

        LINKAGE SECTION.
        01  CHGPHNE-PHONENUM                 PIC X(20).
[3]     01  CHGPHNE-FILE-PROCESSING          PIC X.
            88  CHGPHNE-CLOSE-FILES               VALUE "C".
            88  CHGPHNE-LEAVE-FILES-OPEN          VALUE "L".
        PROCEDURE DIVISION USING CHGPHNE-PHONENUM
                                 CHGPHNE-FILE-PROCESSING.
        MAIN-PARA.
            PERFORM INIT-PROGRAM.

            MOVE CHGPHNE-PHONENUM TO PHONENUM OF PHONEREC.
            READ PHONEFILE
                INVALID KEY
                    MOVE "PHN0008" TO QMHSNDPM-MSGID
                    MOVE "CHGPHNE-PHONENUM TO QMHSNDPM-MSGDTA
[4]                 MOVE 25 TO QMHSNDPM-MSGDTALEN
                    SET QMHSNDPM-TOCALLER TO TRUE
                    PERFORM CALL-QMHSNDPM
                NOT INVALID KEY
[5]                 MOVE CORRESPONDING PHONEREC TO CHANGE-O
                    PERFORM PROCESS-REQUESTS UNITL PGM-EXIT
            END READ.

            PERFORM SHUT-DOWN.
            GOBACK.

        INIT-PROGRAM.
            CALL "RTVCURUSR" USING USERID.
            MOVE ZEROS TO INDIC-AREA.
            SET PGM-ACTIVE TO TRUE.
            IF FILES-CLOSED
                OPEN I-O DISPFILE PHONEFILE
                SET FILES-OPEN TO TRUE
            END-IF.

            IF CHGPHNE-LEAVE-FILES-OPEN
                INITIALIZE PHONEREC
                DISPLAY NAME OF PHONEREC UPON LDA
            END-IF.

        SHUT-DOWN.
            IF CHGPHNE-CLOSE-FILES
                CLOSE PHONEFILE DISPFILE
                SET FILES-CLOSED TO TRUE
            ELSE
                DISPLAY NAME OF PHONE-REC UPON LDA
            END-IF.

        PROCESS-REQUESTS.
            WRITE DISP-REC FROM CHANGE-O FORMAT "CHANGE"
                INDICATORS ARE INDIC-AREA.
            READ DISPFILE INTO CHANGE-IN FORMAT "CHANGE"
                INDICATORS ARE INDIC-AREA.
[6]         MOVE CORRESPONDING CHANGE-I TO CHANGE-O.
            EVALUATE TRUE
                WHEN IND-ON(F03-EXIT) OR IND-ON(FK-CANCEL)
                    SET PGM-EXIT TO TRUE
[7]                 REWRITE PHONE-REC
                WHEN IND-ON(FK-REFRESH)
[8]                 MOVE CORRESPONDING PHONEREC TO CHANGE-O
                    SET IND-OFF(ERR-NAME-BLANK) TO TRUE
```

```
                    WHEN OTHER
                        PERFORM VALIDATE-CHOICES
                        IF NO-ENTRY ERRORS
                            PERFORM SAVE-DATA
                            SET PGM-EXIT TO TRUE
                        END-IF
                END EVALUATE.

            VALIDATE-CHOICES.
                SET NO-ENTRY-ERRORS TO TRUE.
                SET IND-OFF(ERR-NAME-BLANK) TO TRUE.

                IF NAME OF CHANGE-IN EQUAL SPACES
                    SET IND-ON(ERR-NAME-BLANK) TO TRUE
                    SET ENTRY-ERRORS TO TRUE
                END-IF.
            SAVE DATA.
                MOVE CORRESPONDING CHANGE-I TO PHONEREC.
                MOVE USERID TO LASTUSER.
                REWRITE PHONE-REC.

            COPY QMHPROCDIV.
```

To compile the CHGPHNE program, use the following command:

```
CRTCBLPGM CHGPHNE
```

Program notes

1. Two display buffers are used in this program. When the user presses Enter, the READ statement will read the display into CHANGE-IN; thus any validation should be performed on the variables in CHANGE-IN. Before writing the display on the next cycle, the contents of CHANGE-IN will be moved to CHANGE-OUT by using the MOVE CORRESPONDING statement. *Note:* When the COBOL compiler creates the subordinate data items to CHANGE-IN, it will create another record named CHANGE-I. Likewise, when the compiler creates the subordinate data items to CHANGE-OUT, it will create a structure named CHANGE-O. When you move the contents of CHANGE-IN to CHANGE-OUT, by move corresponding, you must specify the lower level structures, as otherwise the variable names will not match.

2. This program sends a message back to its caller if a nonexistent phone number is requested. The program will utilize the OS/400 message application program interfaces (APIs) for this purpose. These two lines include the copy books necessary to use the message APIs.

3. The two parameters that are expected are defined in this section.

4. If it is detected that the user requested to change a phone number that does not exist, the program will send a message that indicates the problem and then terminate. This piece of code is executed if the number is not found. Variables are set up and the QMHSNDPM API will be

called to send the error message to the caller. (The caller may be either the user or another program. If it is another program, that program's message queue will receive the message. This is shown in the Work with Phone Directory example in the last chapter.)

5. If the user requested a valid phone number, the data from the database record will be moved to the output buffer of the display record. Then main program loop is then executed. Both notes 4 and 5 show the power of using the successful and unsuccessful completion clauses of the READ statement.

6. After the user presses the Enter key, the fields are moved from the screen input buffer to the screen output buffer. This is so the new data will be displayed on the next output operation.

7. The REWRITE statement is used here to release the locked record from the initial READ statement. This program is not using the WITH NO LOCK clause; therefore this statement is necessary.

If the user pressed the Refresh key, the original contents of the data file are copied back into the display output buffer for the next output operation. Any error indicators are also turned off.

19.4   Testing the Change Phone Entry Module

You can test this program from the command line by entering the CHGPHNE command and specifying a phone number. You will have to put the phone number in quotation marks if you enter the command from the command line. You can also prompt the command by typing CHGPHNE and pressing the F4=Prompt key. Specify a phone number that you entered in Chap. 18. If you forgot what phone numbers you entered, you can view the phone database file by typing the display physical file member command DSPPFM PHONEFILE.

20

Create the
"Display Phone Entry"
Module

In this chapter, you will create the module that displays individual phone entries. The components that you will create are the following:

- A command to allow the user to display a specific phone directory entry (DSPPHNE)
- A display file (DSPPHNE)
- A COBOL program that displays the selected phone entry

20.1 Creating the Command

The display phone entry (DSPPHNE) command has two parameters, as shown in Table 20.1. The source in Listing 20.1 defines the command. Since this command is almost identical to that of the CHGPHNE, no additional explanation will be given in this chapter.

TABLE 20.1 Command Parameters for the DSPPHNE Command

Keyword	Description
PHNUMBER	The phone number to be displayed.
CLOSEDISP	Specifies whether the display file should be closed when the program ends. Possible values are as follows. *YES: The display is to be left open. *NO: The display is to be closed upon exiting.

Listing 20.1 Command definition for DSPPHNE.

```
MEMBER NAME: DSPPHNE          FILE: QCMDSRC
....-....1....-....2....-....3....-....4....-....5....-....6....-....7
        CMD       PROMPT('Display Phone Entry')
        PARM      KWD(PHNUMBER) TYPE(*CHAR) LEN(20) +
                  PROMPT('Phone number')
        PARM      KWD(CLOSEDISP) TYPE(*CHAR) LEN(1) RSTD(*YES) +
                  DFT(*CLOSE) SPCVAL((*CLOSE 'C') (*LEAVE +
                  'L')) PROMPT('Leave display open?')
```

To enter the source code in Listing 20.1, use the following command:

```
STRSEU QCMDSRC DSPPHNE TEXT('Display phone entry')
```

To compile and create the command, use the following command:

```
CRTCMD CMD(DSPPHNE) PGM(DSPPHNE)
```

Both the command and the command processing program have the same name (DSPPHNE). The command processing program will be defined later in this chapter.

20.2   Creating the Display File

The DSPPHNE COBOL program uses a single display file to communicate with the user. When run, it will appear as shown in Fig. 20.1.

```
                        Display Phone Entry

Phone number . . . . . . . :  OOOOOOOOOOOOOOOOOOOO

Name . . . . . . . . . . . :  OOOOOOOOOOOOOOOOOOOOOOOOOOOOOO
   Address1 . . . . . . . . :  OOOOOOOOOOOOOOOOOOOOOOOOOOOOOOOOOOOOOOOOOO
   Address2 . . . . . . . . :  OOOOOOOOOOOOOOOOOOOOOOOOOOOOOOOOOOOOOOOOOO
   City, State, Zip . . . . :  OOOOOOOOOOOOOOO  OO   OOOOO

Company . . . . . . . . . :  OOOOOOOOOOOOOOOOOOOOOOOOOOOOOOOOOOOOOOOOOO

Last updated by  . . . . . :  OOOOOOOOOO




Press Enter to continue.

F3=Exit     F12=Cancel
```

Figure 20.1 The DSPPHNE display layout.

Listing 20.2 Data description specification source for the DSPPHNE display file.

```
MEMBER NAME: DSPPHNE          FILE: QDDSSRC
.....AAN01N02N03T.NAME++++++RLEN++TDPBLINPOSFUNCTIONS+++++++++++++++++++++
     A                                    REF(*LIBL/PHONEFILE)
     A                                    INDARA
     A*****************************************************************
     A           R VIEW
     A                                    CA03 CA12 PRINT
     A                                  1 31'Display Phone Entry'
     A                                    DSPATR(HI)
     A                                  3  2'Phone number . . . . . . . :'
     A                                  5  2'Name . . . . . . . . . . :'
     A                                  6  4'Address1 . . . . . . . . :'
     A                                  7  4'Address2 . . . . . . . . :'
     A                                  8  4'City, State, Zip . . . . :'
     A                                  9  4'Country  . . . . . . . . :'
     A                                 11  2'Company  . . . . . . . . :'
     A                                 21  2'Press Enter to continue.'
     A                                    DSPATR(HI) COLOR(BLU)
     A                                 23  2'F3=Exit'
     A                                    DSPATR(HI)  COLOR(BLU)
     A                                 23 13'F12=Cancel'
     A                                    DSPATR(HI) COLOR(BLU)
     A           PHONENUM  R          O  3 32
     A           NAME      R          O  5 32
     A           ADDRESS1  R          O  6 32
     A           ADDRESS2  R          O  7 32
     A           CITY      R          O  8 32
     A           STATE     R          O  8 49
     A           ZIP       R          O  8 53
     A           COUNTRY   R          O  9 32
     A           COMPANY   R          O 11 32
     A           LASTUSER  R          O 13 32
```

The source code that defines the DSPPHNE display file is given in Listing 20.2. The DSPPHNE display is an example of a display with no input fields. After it is displayed, the user can either press Enter, F3, or F12 to exit. To enter the source in Listing 20.2, start the source entry utility (SEU) with the following command:

```
STRSEU QDDSSRC DSPPHNE TYPE(DSPF) TEXT('DSPPHNE Display File')
```

To create the display file, use the following command:

```
CRTDSPF FILE(DSPPHNE) SRCFILE(QDDSSRC)
```

20.3 Creating the COBOL Program

Use the following command to start SEU and enter the COBOL program in Listing 20.3.

```
STRSEU QLBLSRC DSPPHNE TYPE(CBL) TEXT('DSPPHNE COBOL program')
```

Listing 20.3   COBOL source for the DSPPHNE program.

```
MEMBER NAME: CHGPHNE           FILE: QLBLSRC
....-..A...B..-....2....-....3...-....4....-....5....-....6....-....7
      IDENTIFICATION DIVISION.
      PROGRAM-ID. DSPPHNE.

      ENVIRONMENT DIVISION.
      CONFIGURATION SECTION.
      INPUT-OUTPUT SECTION.
      FILE-CONTROL.
          SELECT DISPFILE ASSIGN TO WORKSTATION-DSPPHNE-SI
              ORGANIZATION IS TRANSACTION.
          SELECT PHONEFILE ASSIGN TO DATABASE-PHONEFILE
              ORGANIZATION IS INDEXED
              ACCESS MODE IS DYNAMIC
              RECORD KEY IS EXTERNALLY-DESCRIBED-KEY.

      DATA DIVISION.
      FILE SECTION.
      FD  DISPFILE.
      01  DISP-REC                         PIC X(2000).

      FD  PHONEFILE.
      01  PHONE-REC.
          COPY DDS-ALL-FORMATS OF PHONEFILE.

      WORKING-STORAGE SECTION.
      01  VIEW-OUT.
          COPY DDS-VIEW-I-O OF DSPPHNE.

      COPY DATADEFS.

      COPY API.
      COPY QMHDATADIV.

      LINKAGE SECTION.
      01  DSPPHNE-PHONENUM                 PIC X(20).
      01  DSPPHNE-FILE-PROCESSING          PIC X.
          88 DSPPHNE-CLOSE-FILES               VALUE "C".
          88 DSPPHNE-LEAVE-FILES-OPEN          VALUE "L".

      PROCEDURE DIVISION USING DSPPHNE-PHONENUM
                               DSPPHNE-FILE-PROCESSING.
      MAIN-PARA.
          PERFORM INIT-PROGRAM.
          MOVE DSPPHNE-PHONENUM TO PHONENUM OF PHONEREC.
          READ PHONEFILE
              INVALID KEY
                  MOVE "PHN0008" TO QMHSNDPM-MSGID
                  MOVE "PHONEMSGS" TO QMHSNDPM-MSGFNAME
                  MOVE DSPPHNE-PHONENUM TO QMHSNDPM-MSGDTA
[1]               MOVE LENGH OF DSPPHNE-PHONENUM TO QMHSNDPM-MSGDTALEN
                  SET QMHSNDPM-TOCALLER TO TRUE
                  SET QMHSNDPM-INFO TO TRUE
                  PERFORM CALL-QMHSNDPM
              NOT INVALID KEY
                  MOVE CORRESPONDING PHONEREC TO VIEW-O
[2]               WRITE DISP-REC FROM VIEW-O FORMAT "VIEW"
                  READ DISPFILE
          END-READ.
```

```
    PERFORM SHUT-DOWN.
    GOBACK.

INIT-PROGRAM.
    IF FILES-CLOSED
        OPEN I-O DISPFILE
            INPUT PHONEFILE
        SET FILES-OPEN TO TRUE
    END-IF.

SHUT-DOWN.
    IF DSPPHNE-CLOSE-FILES
        CLOSE PHONEFILE DISPFILE
        SET FILES-CLOSED TO TRUE
    END-IF.

    COPY QMHPROCDIV.
```

To compile the DSPPHNE program, use the following command:

```
CRTCBLPGM DSPPHNE
```

Program notes

1. If the user requested to display a phone number that does not exist, the program will send a message indicating the problem and then terminate. This piece of code is executed if the number is not found. Variables are set up and the QMHSNDPM application program interface (API) will be called to send the error message to the caller. (The caller may be either the user or another program. If it is another program, that program's message queue will receive the message.)

2. If the user requested a valid phone number, the data from the file will be moved to the output buffer of the display and then shown.

20.4   Testing the Display Phone Entry Module

To test this program, enter the DSPPHNE command for one of the phone numbers entered in Chap. 18. You can enter the entire command from the command line in the form of DSPPHNE 'phone number' or you can type the DSPPHNE command and then press the F4=Prompt key.

21

Create the "Delete Phone Entry" Module

In this chapter, you will create the module that removes directory entries from the phone database. The components that you will create in this chapter are the following:

- Command DLTPHNE
- COBOL program DLTPHNE

21.1 Creating the Command

The delete phone entry (DLTPHNE) command has one parameter, as given in Table 21.1.

TABLE 21.1 Command Parameter for the DLTPHNE Command

Keyword	Description
PHNUMBER	The phone number to be deleted

The source in Listing 21.1 defines the command.

Listing 21.1 Command definition for DLTPHNE.

```
MEMBER NAME: DLTPHNE         FILE: QCMDSRC
....-....1....-....2....-....3....-....4....-....5....-....6....-....7
          CMD         PROMPT('Delete Phone Entry')
          PARM        KWD(PHNUMBER) TYPE(*CHAR) LEN(20) +
                      PROMPT('Phone number')
```

To enter the source code in this listing, use the following command:

```
STRSEU QCMDSRC DLTPHNE TEXT('Delete phone entry')
```

To compile and create the command, use the following command:

```
CRTCMD CMD(DLTPHNE) PGM(DLTPHNE)
```

21.2 Creating the COBOL Program

Use the following command to start SEU and enter the COBOL program in Listing 21.2.

```
STRSEU QLBLSRC DLTPHNE TYPE(CBL) TEXT('DLTPHNE COBOL program')
```

Enter the source code in Listing 21.2. To compile the DLTPHNE program, use the following command:

```
CRTCBLPGM DLTPHNE
```

Listing 21.2 COBOL source for the DLTPHNE program.

```
MEMBER NAME: DLTPHNE          FILE: QLBLSRC
....-..A...B..-....2....-....3....-....4....-....5....-....6....-....7
      IDENTIFICATION DIVISION.
      PROGRAM-ID.  DLTPHNE.

      ENVIRONMENT DIVISION.
      CONFIGURATION SECTION.
      SPECIAL-NAMES.  LOCAL-DATA IS LDA.
      INPUT-OUTPUT SECTION.
      FILE-CONTROL.
          SELECT PHONEFILE ASSIGN TO DATABASE-PHONEFILE
              ORGANIZATION IS INDEXED
              ACCESS MODE IS DYNAMIC
              RECORD KEY IS EXTERNALLY-DESCRIBED-KEY.

      DATA DIVISION.
      FILE SECTION.
      FD  DISPFILE.
      01  DISP-REC                        PIC X(500).

      FD  PHONEFILE.
      01  PHONE-REC.
          COPY DDS-ALL-FORMATS OF PHONEFILE.

      WORKING-STORAGE SECTION.

      COPY DATADEFS.

      COPY API.
      COPY QMHDATADIV.

      LINKAGE SECTION.
      01  DLTPHNE-PHONENUM                 PIC X(20).
```

```
       PROCEDURE DIVISION USING DLTPHNE-PHONENUM.
       MAIN-PARA.
           OPEN I-O PHONEFILE.
           MOVE DLTPHNE-PHONENUM TO PHONENUM OF PHONEREC.
           MOVE "PHONEMSGS" TO QMHSNDPM-MSGFNAME.
           SET QMHSNDPM-INFO TO TRUE.
[1]        SET QMHSNDPM-TOCALLER TO TRUE.
           MOVE DLTPHNE-PHONENUM TO QMHSNDPM-MSGDTA.
           MOVE LENGTH OF DLTPHNE-PHONENUM TO QMHSNDPM-MSGDTALEN.
           READ PHONEFILE
               INVALID KEY
                   MOVE "PHN0008" TO QMHSNDPM-MSGID
               NOT INVALID KEY
                   DISPLAY NAME OF PHONEREC UPON LDA
                   MOVE "PHN0004" TO QMHSNDPM-MSGID
                   DELETE PHONEFILE RECORD
           END READ.
           PERFORM CALL-QMHSNDPM.
[2]        CLOSE PHONEFILE.
           GOBACK.

       COPY QMHPROCDIV.
```

Program notes

1. This program always sends a message back to the caller that indicates whether the delete request was successful or unsuccessful. The message will contain the requested phone number as a substitution variable; therefore the length of the requested phone number is moved to QMHSNDPM-MSGDTALEN.

2. This program is not optimized to leave the files open; therefore each time a phone number is deleted, the file will be opened and closed. If this program were going to have heavy usage (hundreds of deletions at a time), this would be unacceptable.

21.3   Testing the Delete Phone Entry Module

To test this module, enter the DLTPHNE command for one of the phone numbers entered in Chap. 18. The command will take the form

```
DLTPHNE 'phone-number'
```

Optionally, you can type DLTPHNE and press the F4=Prompt key.

22

Create the "Work with Phone Directory" Module

In this chapter, you will create the Work with Phone Directory module. This module ties all of the other modules together into a single display. From the Work with Phone Directory screen, the user can add, delete, and change phone directory entries, as well as add a service request. The service request function has not been defined yet, but will be defined in Chap. 23.

In this chapter, you will:

- Create a display file that uses both a regular subfile and a message subfile.

- Create a program that manages a subfile where the page size is equal to the subfile size.

- See how to handle a "position to" request.

- Create the WRKPHNDIR command.

- Use the reclaim resources (RCLRSC) command.

- Manage the local data area (LDA) from a command language (CL) program and a COBOL program.

- Use QCMDEXC to execute commands from within a COBOL program.

22.1 Creating the Command

The work with phone directory (WRKPHNDIR) command has one parameter, given in Table 22.1. The source in Listing 22.1 defines the

TABLE 22.1   Command Parameter for the WRKPHNDIR Command

Keyword	Description
POSITION	The name (or partial name) that should appear first in the list. Possible values are as follows: value: the name to use for positioning the list *FIRST: the list will be positioned to the first name in the database (this is the default)

command. The POSITION parameters allows the user (or other programs that call the WRKPHNDIR command) to specify where to position the list when the display is first shown. For example, if the user enters WRKPHNDIR KAP, the list will initially be positioned to any names that begin with KAP.

Listing 22.1 Command definition for WRKPHNDIR.

```
MEMBER NAME: WRKPHNDIR         FILE: QCLSRC
....-....1....-....2....-....3....-....4....-....5....-....6....-....7
          CMD       PROMPT('Work with Phone Directory')
          PARM      KWD(POSITION) TYPE(*CHAR) LEN(35) +
                    DFT(*FIRST) SPCVAL((*FIRST ' ')) +
                    PROMPT('Position to')
```

If the parameter is not specified, the default value of *FIRST will be chosen. Since there is a special value *FIRST associated with blanks, the command will pass blanks to the command processing program.

To enter the source code in Listing 22.1, use the following command:

```
STRSEU QCMDSRC WRKPHNDIR TEXT('Work with Phone Directory')
```

To compile and create the command, use the following command:

```
CRTCMD CMD(WRKPHNDIR) PGM(WRKPHNDIR)
```

22.2 Creating the Command Language Program

Unlike the other modules in this project, the WRKPHNDIR command will first call a command language (CL) program instead of a COBOL program. The CL program will do some initial housekeeping before the COBOL program is called. The responsibilities of the CL program are the following:

- Put the name specified in the POSITION parameter into the LDA (the COBOL program will read the LDA to determine the starting name for the list)

- Call the WRKPHNDIR0 program (COBOL)
- Close any files that have been left open while the WRKPHNDIR0 program was running (this will be discussed in more detail shortly)

Listing 22.2 CL command processing program for the WRKPHNDIR command. See program notes in text for an explanation of numbered areas.

```
MEMBER NAME: WRKPHNDIR        FILE: QCLSRC
....-....1....-....2....-....3....-....4....-....5....-....6....-....7
            PGM       PARM(&POSNTO)
            DCL       VAR(&POSNTO) TYPE(*CHAR) LEN(35)
[1]         CHGDTAARA DTAARA (*LDA (1 35)) VALUE(&POSNTO)
            CALL      PGM(WRKPHNDIR0)
[2]         RCLRSC    LVL(*)
            RETURN
            ENDPGM
```

To enter the source in Listing 22.2, start the source entry utility (SEU) with the following command:

```
STRSEU QCLSRC WRKPHNDIR TYPE(CLP) TEXT('WRKPHNDIR command proc program')
```

To compile the program, use the following command: CRTCLPGM WRKPHNDIR.

Listing 22.2 program notes

1. The COBOL program first reads the LDA to determine where to start the phone directory file. This command takes the value sent from the command and puts it in the first 35 positions of the LDA.

2. When the WRKPHNDIR0 program executes the various functions (i.e., DSPPHNE, DLTPHNE, CHGPHNE, ADDPHNE), it requests that each program leave the display, and database files open for faster response time. This is accomplished by specifying the *LEAVE option for the CLOSEDISP parameter. Each of the programs therefore do not close the database files when they exit. When the WRKPHNDIR0 program ends, it is likely that there are still files that have not been closed. The RCLRSC command reclaims any resources held by programs, including files. After the RCLRSC command is executed, all files in the job will be closed.

22.3 Creating the Display File

The display for the WRKPHNDIR application will appear as shown in Fig. 22.1. The shaded portion of the display is a subfile. At the top of the display, the user will be able to specify a name in order to reposition the subfile list. For instance, if the user specifies KAP, the subfile will be cleared and reloaded starting with any names that begin with KAP from the database.

The user can exit the display with F3 and F12. F5 will refresh the list to reflect any additions or changes made by other users. F6 will invoke the ADDPHNE program for a single entry and F7 will call it for multiple entries.

By placing an option number next to a phone entry in the subfile, the user can change, delete, or view it. The user can also log a service request in the same manner.

The source code to create the display file in Fig. 22.1 is shown in Listing 22.3.

```
                        Work with Phone Directory

     Position to . . . . .    _____

     Type options, press Enter.
        2=Change      4=Delete      5=View      8=Service request

     Opt  Name                                  Phone number          City
      __  XXXXXXXXXXXXXXXXXXXXXXXXXXXXXXXXX     XXXXXXXXXXXXXXXXXXX    XXXXXXXXXXXXXXX
      __  XXXXXXXXXXXXXXXXXXXXXXXXXXXXXXXXX     XXXXXXXXXXXXXXXXXXX    XXXXXXXXXXXXXXX
      __  XXXXXXXXXXXXXXXXXXXXXXXXXXXXXXXXX     XXXXXXXXXXXXXXXXXXX    XXXXXXXXXXXXXXX
      __  XXXXXXXXXXXXXXXXXXXXXXXXXXXXXXXXX     XXXXXXXXXXXXXXXXXXX    XXXXXXXXXXXXXXX
      __  XXXXXXXXXXXXXXXXXXXXXXXXXXXXXXXXX     XXXXXXXXXXXXXXXXXXX    XXXXXXXXXXXXXXX
      __  XXXXXXXXXXXXXXXXXXXXXXXXXXXXXXXXX     XXXXXXXXXXXXXXXXXXX    XXXXXXXXXXXXXXX
      __  XXXXXXXXXXXXXXXXXXXXXXXXXXXXXXXXX     XXXXXXXXXXXXXXXXXXX    XXXXXXXXXXXXXXX
      __  XXXXXXXXXXXXXXXXXXXXXXXXXXXXXXXXX     XXXXXXXXXXXXXXXXXXX    XXXXXXXXXXXXXXX
      __  XXXXXXXXXXXXXXXXXXXXXXXXXXXXXXXXX     XXXXXXXXXXXXXXXXXXX    XXXXXXXXXXXXXXX
      __  XXXXXXXXXXXXXXXXXXXXXXXXXXXXXXXXX     XXXXXXXXXXXXXXXXXXX    XXXXXXXXXXXXXXX
      __  XXXXXXXXXXXXXXXXXXXXXXXXXXXXXXXXX     XXXXXXXXXXXXXXXXXXX    XXXXXXXXXXXXXXX
      __  XXXXXXXXXXXXXXXXXXXXXXXXXXXXXXXXX     XXXXXXXXXXXXXXXXXXX    XXXXXXXXXXXXXXX
                                                                          More...

     F3=Exit    F5=Refresh    F6=Add name     F7=Add multiple names    F12=Cancel
```

Figure 22.1 The CHGPHNE display layout.

Figure 22.3 Data description specification source for the WRKPHNDIR display file. See program notes in text for an explanation of numbered areas.

```
MEMBER NAME: WRKPHNDIR          FILE: QDDSSRC
.....AAN01N02N03T.Name++++++RLen++TDpBLinPosFunctions++++++++++++++++++++
     A                                           PRINT
     A                                           INDARA
[1]  A                                           REF(*LIBL/PHONEFILE)
     A**********************************************************************
     A          R LIST                           SFL
     A 44                                         SFLNXTCHG
     A            OPT            2A B  9 2
     A 30                                         DSPATR(RI PC MDT)
     A            NAME      R      -5 O  9 7
     A            PHONENUM  R         O  9 39
```

```
     A             CITY      R        O 9 61
     A****************************************
     A             R LISTCTL               SFLCTL(LIST)
     A                                     CF03(03 'Exit')
[2]  A                                     CF12(03 'Cancel')
     A                                     CF06(06 'Add')
     A                                     CF05(05 'Refresh')
     A                                     CF07(07 'Add multiple')
[3]  A                                     PAGEDOWN(52 'Next page')
     A                                     PAGEUP(51 'Prev page')
     A                                     OVERLAY
     A                                     SFLCSRRRN(&CSRPSN)
     A   41                                SFLDSP
     A                                     SFLDSPCTL
     A   42                                SFLCLR
[4]  A   43                                SFLEND(*MORE)
[5]  A                                     SFLSIZ(0012)
     A                                     SFLPAG(0012)
     A                          22  2'F3=Exit'
     A                                     DSPATR(HI) COLOR(BLU)
     A                          22 14'F5=Refresh'
     A                                     DSPATR(HI) COLOR(BLU)
     A                          22 69'F12=Cancel'
     A                                     DSPATR(HI) COLOR(BLU)
     A             CRSR      4S 0H         SFLRCDNBR(CRSR)
     A             CSRPSN    5  0H
     A                          22 29'F6=Add name'
     A                                     COLOR(BLU) DSPATR(HI)
     A                          22 44'F7=Add multiple names'
     A                                     COLOR(BLU) DSPATR(HI)
     A****************************************************************
     A             R MSGSFL                SFL
     A                                     SFLMSGRCD(24)
[6]  A             MSGKEY                  SFLMSGKEY
     A             MSGQ                    SFLPGMQ
     A****************************************
     A             R MSGSFLCTL             SFLCTL(MSGSFL)
     A                                     OVERLAY SFLDSP SFLINZ
     A   43                                SFLEND
     A                                     SFLSIZ(0002)
     A                                     SFLPAG(0001)
[7]  A             PGMQ                    SFLPGMQ
     A****************************************************************
     A             R HEADER
     A                           1 28'Work with Phone Directory'
     A                                     DSPATR(HI)
     A                           3  2'Position to . . . . .'
     A             POSNTO   15A  I  3 25
     A                           5  2'Type options press Enter
     A                                     DSPATR(HI) COLOR(BLU)
     A                           6  5'2=Change'
     A                                     COLOR(BLU)
     A                           6 18'4=Delete'
     A                                     COLOR(BLU)
     A                           6 31'5=View'
     A                                     COLOR(BLU)
     A                           6 42'8=Service request'
     A                                     COLOR(BLU) DSPATR(HI)
     A                           8  2'Opt'
     A                                     DSPATR(HI)
     A                           8  7'Name'
     A                                     DSPATR(HI)
```

```
A                            8 39'Phone number'
A                              DSPATR(HI)
A                            8 61'City'
A                              DSPATR(HI)
A*****************************************************************
A               R EMPTY
[8]  A                                  OVERLAY
A                                 10 15'(No directory entries -
A                                     have been entered yet)'
```

To enter the source in Listing 22.3, start SEU with the following command:

```
STRSEU QDDSSRC WRKPHNDIR TYPE(DSPF) TEXT('WRKPHNDIR display file')
```

To create the display file, use the following command:

```
CRTDSPF FILE(WRKPHNDIR) SRCFILE(QDDSSRC)
```

Listing 22.3 program notes

1. The fields found in the subfile record are referenced from file PHONEFILE; therefore the sizes and attributes of the fields will not need to be defined in this display file.

2. Notice that both F3 and F12 have the same resultant indicator (03). Since the program performs the same action for exiting and canceling, there is no need to differentiate between the two. Therefore, whether the user presses F3 or F12, indicator 03 will be turned on.

3. Since both PAGEDOWN and PAGEUP are specified, the COBOL program will be responsible for all scrolling of the subfile. Indicator 52 will be on if the user presses Page down, and 51 will be on if the user presses Page up.

4. Coding the *MORE option on the SFLEND keyword will cause the word "More . . . " to appear at the bottom of the display rather than the standard plus sign. If you do not specify *MORE, a plus sign will be shown, indicating that there are more records in the file (if the user scrolls to the end, the word "Bottom" will appear if the *MORE option is specified).

5. Both the subfile size and subfile page size are defined to be the same (12 records).

6. A message subfile is used to display error messages on the last line of the display.

7. The SFLPGMQ keyword specifies that the messages should come from the program's message queue; therefore the program will have to send a message to itself in order to display a message on the subfile. Remember that in the other programs, if the user requested an invalid phone number, a message would be sent to the caller of the function (i.e., if the work with phone directory program calls the change phone

entry program with an invalid phone number, the change phone entry program would send a message to the work with phone directory program). Therefore, the message will show up in the program message queue and ultimately be displayed in the message subfile.

8. This record format will be displayed if the PHONEFILE is empty.

22.4 Creating the COBOL Program

Use the command in Listing 22.4 to start SEU and enter the COBOL program in listing:

```
STRSEU QLBLSRC WRKPHNDIR0 TYPE(CBL) TEXT('WRKPHNDIR0 main program')
```

Listing 22.4 COBOL source for the WRKPHNDIR0 program.

```
MEMBER NAME: WRKPHNDIR0        FILE: QLBLSRC
....-..A...B..-....2....-....3....-....4....-....5....-....6....-....7
[1]     PROCESS FS9MTO0M.
        IDENTIFICATION DIVISION.
        PROGRAM-ID. WRKPHNDIR0.
        ENVIRONMENT DIVISION.
        CONFIGURATION SECTION.
[2]     SPECIAL-NAMES. LOCAL-DATA IS LDA.
        INPUT-OUTPUT SECTION.
        FILE-CONTROL.
            SELECT DISPFILE ASSIGN TO WORKSTATION-WRKPHNDIR-SI
            ORGANIZATION IS TRANSACTION
            ACCESS MODE IS DYNAMIC
            RELATIVE KEY IS SFL-RECNUM.
[3]         SELECT NAMEFILE ASSIGN TO DATABASE-NAMEFILE
            ORGANIZATION IS INDEXED
            ACCESS MODE IS DYNAMIC
            RECORD KEY IS EXTERNALLY-DESCRIBED-KEY WITH DUPLICATES.

        DATA DIVISION.
        FILE SECTION.
        FD  DISPFILE.
        01  DISP-REC                    PIC X(200).

        FD  NAMEFILE.
        01  NAME-REC.
            COPY DDS-ALL-FORMATS OF NAMEFILE.

        WORKING-STORAGE SECTION.
        77  SFL-SIZE                     PIC 99 VALUE 12.
        77  TWO-PAGES                    PIC 99.
        77  INDX                         PIC 9(5).
[4]     77  PGMNAME                      PIC X(10) VALUE "*".

        01  OPTIONS-FLAG                 PIC X.
            88  MORE-OPTIONS                 VALUE "M".
            88  NO-MORE-OPTIONS              VALUE "X".
        01  OPTION-ERROR-FLAG            PIC X.
            88  OPT-ERRORS                   VALUE "E".
            88  NO-OPTION-ERRORS             VALUE " ".
```

```
01  START-KEY LIKE NAME OF PHONEREC.

01  FILE-CONTENTS-FLAG              PIC X.
    88 FILE-IS-EMPTY                          VALUE "1".
    88 END-OF-FILE                            VALUE "2".
    88 MID-OF-FILE                            VALUE "3".
    88 BEG-OF-FILE                            VALUE "4".

01  SUBFILE-STATUS                  PIC X.
    88 SUBFILE-OK                             VALUE "1".
    88 SUBFILE-FULL                           VALUE "2".
```

[5]   `01  CMD-LENGTH                      PIC 9(10)V9(5) COMP-3.`

```
01  ADDPHNE-CMD PIC X(24) VALUE "ADDPHNE *MULTIPLE *LEAVE".
01  ADDPHNE-CMD-LENGTH LIKE CMD-LENGTH.

01  DSPPHNE-CMD.
    03 PIC X(18) VALUE "DSPPHNE PHNUMBER ('".
    03 DSPPHNE-NBR LIKE PHONENUM OF PHONEREC.
    03 PIC X(20) VALUE "') CLOSEDISP(*LEAVE)".
01  DSPPHNE-CMD-LENGTH LIKE CMD-LENGTH.

01  CHGPHNE-CMD.
    03 PIC X(18) VALUE "CHGPHNE PHNUMBER ('".
    03 CHGPHNE-NBR LIKE PHONENUM OF PHONEREC.
    03 PIC X(20) VALUE "') CLOSEDISP(*LEAVE)".
01  CHGPHNE-CMD-LENGTH LIKE CMD-LENGTH.

01  DLTPHNE-CMD.
    03 PIC X(18) VALUE "DLTPHNE PHNUMBER ('".
    03 DLTPHNE-NBR LIKE PHONENUM OF PHONEREC.
    03 PIC x(2) VALUE "')".
01  DLTPHNE-CMD-LENGTH LIKE CMD-LENGTH.
```

[6]   `COPY ADDPHNEL.`

```
01  LISTCTL-IN.
    COPY DDS-LISTCTL-I OF WRKPHNDIR.
01  LISTCTL-OUT.
    COPY DDS-LISTCTL-O OF WRKPHNDIR.
01  LIST-IN.
```
[7]   `    COPY DDS-LIST-I OF WRKPHNDIR.`
```
01  LIST-OUT.
    COPY DDS-LIST-O OF WRKPHNDIR.
01  MSGSFL-DATA.
    COPY DDS-MSGSFL-I-O OF WRKPHNDIR.
01  HEADER-IN.
    COPY DDS-HEADER-I OF WRKPHNDIR.
```

```
COPY DATADEFS.
    03 FK-ADD-MULTIPLE              PIC 99 VALUE 07.

COPY API.
COPY QMHDATADIV.

PROCEDURE DIVISION.
MAIN-PARA.
    PERFORM INIT-PROGRAM.
    PERFORM PROCESS-REQUESTS UNTIL PGM-EXIT.
    CLOSE DISPFILE NAMEFILE.
    GOBACK.
```

```
      INIT-PROGRAM.
          OPEN I-O DISPFILE INPUT NAMEFILE.
          MOVE ZEROS TO INDIC-AREA.
          MOVE LENGTH OF DSPPHNE-CMD TO DSPPHNE-CMD-LENGTH.
          MOVE LENGTH OF CHGPHNE-CMD TO CHGPHNE-CMD-LENGTH.
[8]       MOVE LENGTH OF ADDPHNE-CMD TO ADDPHNE-CMD-LENGTH.
          MOVE LENGTH OF DLTPHNE-CMD TO DLTPHNE-CMD-LENGTH.
          SET IND-ON (I-MSGSFLEND) TO TRUE.

[9]       ACCEPT START-KEY FROM LDA.
          PERFORM REFRESH-LIST.

          MOVE "PHONEMSGS" TO QMHSNDPM-MSGFNAME.
[10]      MOVE 2 TO QMHSNDPM-MSGDTALEN.
          SET QMHSNDPM-INFO TO TRUE.
          MOVE "PHN0001" TO QMHSNDPM-MSGID.

[11]      SET QMHRMVPM-ALL TO TRUE.

      POSITION-FILE.
          SET BEG-OF-FILE TO TRUE.
          MOVE START-KEY TO NAME OF NAME-REC.
[12]      START NAMEFILE KEY NOT LESS THAN EXTERNALLY-DESCRIBED-KEY
              INVALID KEY
                  MOVE LOW VALUES TO NAME OF NAME-REC
                  START NAMEFILE KEY NOT < EXTERNALLY-DESCRIBED-KEY
                      INVALID KEY
[13]                      SET FILE-IS-EMPTY TO TRUE
                      NOT INVALID KEY
                          PERFORM READ-NEXT-RECORD
                  END-START
              NOT INVALID KEY
[12]              PERFORM READ-NEXT-RECORD
          END-START.

      READ-NEXT-RECORD.
          READ NAMEFILE NEXT RECORD
              AT END
                  SET END-OF-FILE TO TRUE
[14]              SET IND-ON(I-SFLEND) TO TRUE
          END-READ.

      READ-PREV-PAGE.
          COMPUTE TWO-PAGES = SFL-RECNUM + SFL-SIZE - 1.
          IF END-OF-FILE
              SUBTRACT 1 FROM TWO-PAGES
[15]          MOVE HIGH-VALUES TO START-KEY
              START NAMEFILE KEY NOT < EXTERNALLY-DESCRIBED-KEY
                  INVALID KEY CONTINUE
              END-START
          END-IF.
          SET MID-OF-FILE TO TRUE.
          PERFORM VARYING INDX FROM 1 BY 1 UNTIL INDX > TWO-PAGES
          OR BEG-OF-FILE
              READ NAMEFILE PRIOR RECORD
[16]              AT END
                      SET BEG-OF-FILE TO TRUE
                      MOVE LOW-VALUES TO START-KEY
                      PERFORM POSITION-FILE
              END-READ
```

```
        END-PERFORM.

        IF NOT FILE-IS-EMPTY
[17]        PERFORM READ-NEXT-PAGE
        END-IF.


    READ-NEXT-PAGE.
        PERFORM CLEAR-SUBFILE.
[18]    PERFORM VARYING SFL-RECNUM FROM 1 BY 1
            UNTIL SFL-RECNUM > SFL-SIZE OR END-OF-FILE
            MOVE CORRESPONDING PHONEREC TO LIST-O
            MOVE SPACES TO OPT OF LIST-O
            WRITE SUBFILE DISP-REC FROM LIST-OUT
                FORMAT "LIST"
                INDICATORS ARE INDIC-AREA
                INVALID KEY
[19]                SET SUBFILE-FULL TO TRUE
            END-WRITE
            PERFORM READ-NEXT-RECORD
        END-PERFORM.


    CLEAR-SUBFILE.
        MOVE 1 TO CRSR OF LISTCTL-O.
        SET IND-ON(I-SFLCLR) TO TRUE.
        WRITE DISP-REC FORMAT "LISTCTL" INDICATORS INDIC-AREA.
        SET IND-OFF(I-SFLCLR) TO TRUE.
        MOVE ZERO TO SFL-RECNUM.
        SET SUBFILE-OK TO TRUE.


    PROCESS-REQUESTS.
        PERFORM DISPLAY-SCREEN.
        READ DISPFILE INTO LISTCTL-IN FORMAT "LISTCTL"
            INDICATORS ARE INDIC-AREA.

[20]    MOVE SPACES TO START-KEY.
        DISPLAY START-KEY UPON LDA.

[21]    PERFORM CALL-QMHRMVPM.
[22]    MOVE CSRPSN OF LISTCTL-I TO CRSR OF LISTCTL-O.
        EVALUATE TRUE
            WHEN IND-ON(I-PAGEDN)
                IF NOT END-OF-FILE
                    PERFORM READ-NEXT-PAGE
                END-IF
            WHEN IND-ON(I-PAGEUP)
                PERFORM READ-PREV-PAGE
            WHEN IND-ON(F03-EXIT)
                SET PGM-EXIT TO TRUE
            WHEN IND-ON(F05-REFRESH)
                MOVE LOW-VALUES TO START-KEY
                PERFORM REFRESH-LIST
            WHEN IND-ON(F06-CREATE)
                SET ADDPHNE-SINGLE-ENTRY TO TRUE
                SET ADDPHNE-LEAVE-FILES-OPEN TO TRUE
                CALL "ADDPHNE"
                    USING
                        ADDPHNE-REPEAT
[23]                    ADDPHNE-FILE-PROCESSING
                    ON EXCEPTION
                        PERFORM LINKAGE-ERROR
                END-CALL
```

```
[24]              ACCEPT START-KEY FROM LDA
                  IF START-KEY NOT EQUAL SPACES
                      PERFORM REFRESH-LIST
                  END-IF
              WHEN IND-ON(FK-ADD-MULTIPLE)
[25]              CALL "QCMDEXC" USING ADDPHNE-CMD ADDPHNE-CMD-LENGTH
                  ACCEPT START-KEY FROM LDA
                  IF START-KEY NOT EQUAL SPACES
                      PERFORM REFRESH-LIST
                  END-IF
              WHEN IND-ON(F12-CANCEL)
                  SET PGM-EXIT TO TRUE
              WHEN OTHER
                  READ DISPFILE INTO HEADER-IN FORMAT "HEADER"
                      INDICATORS ARE INDIC-AREA
                  IF POSNTO EQUAL SPACES
                      PERFORM PROCESS-OPTIONS
                  ELSE
                      MOVE POSNTO TO START-KEY
                      PERFORM REFRESH-LIST
                  END-IF
              END-EVALUATE.


          DISPLAY-SCREEN.
              SET IND-OFF(I-SFLDSP) TO TRUE.
              WRITE DISP-REC FORMAT "HEADER".
              IF SFL-RECNUM NOT EQUAL ZERO
                  SET IND-ON(I-SFLDSP) TO TRUE
[26]          ELSE
                  WRITE DISP-REC FORMAT IS "EMPTY"
              END-IF.


[27]          WRITE DISP-REC FROM PGMNAME FORMAT IS "MSGSFLCTL"
                  INDICATORS ARE INDIC-AREA.


[28]          WRITE DISP-REC FROM LISTCTL-OUT FORMAT IS "LISTCTL"
                  INDICATORS ARE INDIC-AREA.


          REFRESH-LIST.
              PERFORM POSITION-FILE.
              IF NOT FILE-IS-EMPTY
                  PERFORM READ-NEXT-PAGE
              END-IF.


          PROCESS-OPTIONS.
              SET MORE-OPTIONS NO-OPTION-ERRORS TO TRUE.
              PERFORM WITH TEST AFTER UNTIL NO-MORE-OPTIONS OR OPT-ERRORS
[29]              READ SUBFILE DISPFILE NEXT MODIFIED RECORD
                      INTO LIST-I FORMAT IS "LIST"
                      AT END
                          SET NO-MORE-OPTIONS TO TRUE
                      NOT AT END
[30]                      MOVE CORRESPONDING LIST-I TO LIST-O
                          EVALUATE OPT OF LIST-I
                              WHEN "2"  PERFORM OPTION-CHANGE
                              WHEN "5"  PERFORM OPTION-DISPLAY
                              WHEN "4"  PERFORM OPTION-DELETE
                              WHEN "8"  PERFORM OPTION-SERVICE
                              WHEN " "  PERFORM OPTION-RESET
                              WHEN OTHER PERFORM OPTION-ERROR
                          END-EVALUATE
                  END-READ
```

```
                 END-PERFORM.
[31]             IF NO-OPTION-ERRORS
                     ACCEPT START-KEY FROM LDA
                     IF START-KEY NOT EQUAL SPACES
                         PERFORM REFRESH-LIST
                     END-IF
                 END-IF.

[32]         OPTION-RESET.
                 MOVE SPACES TO OPT OF LIST-O.
                 REWRITE SUBFILE DISP-REC FROM LIST-OUT
                     FORMAT "LIST" INDICATORS ARE INDIC-AREA
                         INVALID KEY
                             SET SUBFILE-FULL TO TRUE
                 END-REWRITE.

             OPTION-ERROR.
                 SET IND-ON(I-OPT-ERROR) TO TRUE.
                 REWRITE SUBFILE DISP-REC FROM LIST-OUT
                     FORMAT "LIST" INDICATORS ARE INDIC-AREA
[33]                     INVALID KEY
                             SET SUBFILE-FULL TO TRUE
                 END-REWRITE.
                 SET IND-OFF(I-OPT-ERROR)
                 OPT-ERRORS TO TRUE.
                 MOVE OPT OF LIST-O TO QMHSNDPM-MSGDTA.
[34]             PERFORM CALL-QMHSNDPM.

             OPTION-CHANGE.
                 MOVE PHONENUM OF LIST-I TO CHGPHNE-NBR.
                 CALL "QCMDEXC" USING CHGPHNE-CMD DSPPHNE-CMD-LENGTH.
                 PERFORM OPTION-RESET.

             OPTION-DISPLAY.
                 MOVE PHONENUM OF LIST-I TO DSPPHNE-NBR.
                 CALL "QCMDEXC" USING DSPPHNE-CMD DSPPHNE-CMD-LENGTH.
                 PERFORM OPTION-RESET.

             OPTION-DELETE.
                 MOVE PHONENUM OF LIST-I TO DLTPHNE-NBR.
                 CALL "QCMDEXC" USING DLTPHNE-CMD DLTPHNE-CMD-LENGTH.
                 PERFORM OPTION-RESET.

             OPTION-SERVICE.
                 CALL "CRTSRVREQ"
                     USING
                         PHONENUM OF LIST-I
                     ON EXCEPTION
[35]                         PERFORM LINKAGE-ERROR
                 END-CALL.
                 PERFORM OPTION-RESET.

             LINKAGE-ERROR.
[36]             MOVE "PHN0009" TO QMHSNDPM-MSGID.
                 PERFORM CALL-QMHSNDPM.
                 MOVE "PHN0001" TO QMHSNDPM-MSGID.

             COPY QMHPROCDIV.
```

To compile the WRKPHNDIR0 program in Listing 22.4, use the following command:

```
CRTCBLPGM WRKPHNDIR0
```

Listing 22.4 program notes

1. The PROCESS FS9MTO0M statement translates a file status of 9M to 0M. File status 9M is sent to a program (by OS/400) when the program writes the last record in a subfile. (For example, if the subfile is defined with a size of 12 records and you write the 12th record, OS/400 will raise this error.) File status 9M is considered a critical error, and thus a break message will be displayed on the workstation. Using this process statement converts status 9M to 0M, which is not critical; thus the program will not be interrupted. You can experiment to see what will happen by removing this statement. You will need to add at least 12 records to the database to see the problem occur.

2. The program name LDA is assigned to the local data area; therefore any input/output (I/O) to the LDA will occur through this mnemonic.

3. This program reads from NAMEFILE instead of PHONEFILE. NAMEFILE is a logical file that orders PHONEFILE by customer name instead of by phone number.

4. The display file for this program contains a message subfile. The message subfile for this program specifies that the messages to display in the subfile should come from a program message queue. This variable will be used to indicate the name of the message queue to use. The asterisk is a special value that indicates "this" program. This field will be sent to the message subfile control record—this will direct the message subfile to get its message from "this" program's message queue.

5. CMD-LENGTH is defined here as a data type for later reference. Variables ADDPHNE-CMD-LENGTH, DSPPHNE-CMD-LENGTH, ADDPHNE-CMD-LENGTH, and DLTPHNE-CMD-LENGTH use CMD-LENGTH as a prototype for their definitions.

6. The ADDPHNEL copy book is included here—note 22 shows how the ADDPHNE program is CALLED instead of executed as a command using QCMDEXC.

7. Each of the display record formats are copied into WORKING-STORAGE. Separate buffers are maintained for input and output buffers.

8. The special LENGTH OF register is used to set up the lengths of the four commands used in this program. When calling QCMDEXC, the actual command length must be specified (for an example, see OPTION-CHANGE paragraph).

9. The program retrieves the "Position to" name from the local data

area in this step. This value was placed in the LDA by the initial CL program.

10. The OS/400 send program message (QMHSNDPM) and remove program message (QMHRMVPM) application program interfaces (APIs) are used in this program to send messages to the user when they have made an invalid choice. This step initializes the variables or the QMHSNDPM API.

11. Setting QMHRMVPM-ALL to true will cause the QMHRMVPM API to remove all messages from the destination message queue. The QMHRMVPM API will be called each time the user presses the Enter key. This will remove any error messages generated during the prior cycle.

12. When using an externally described database file, you must use the EXTERNALLY-DESCRIBED-KEY phrase in the START command. Prior to issuing the START command, move the appropriate values into the record's fields. When the START statement is executed, it will reference the values in the record buffer's fields. This is necessary because files may contain key fields that are not contiguous. This note also shows a good example of the benefits of scope terminators—note how there is another START statement nested within the INVALID KEY phrase of this START statement. By using the END-START scope terminator, the START statement can be treated as an imperative statement and therefore can be used in this case without any problems. If the START fails, the INVALID KEY clause will be executed (described in note 13). If it does not fail, the first record will be fetched into the buffer (this is seen in the NOT INVALID KEY phrase).

13. The inner START statement is executed if the requested position-to name is not found (if it is greater than the highest key value in the file). If this condition occurs, the inner START will attempt to position to the beginning of the file. If this fails, the file is empty.

14. When the last record in the file is read, the SFLEND indicator is turned on. This will cause the word "Bottom" to appear on the display. If SFLEND is not on, the word "More . . ." will appear.

15. When reading a previous page, you must first determine if the current file position is valid. If the END-OF-FILE flag is TRUE, the file position is undefined (meaning that the file has been read past the end); therefore the file must be repositioned to the last record in the file. This START statement positions the file to the last record in the file. The variable TWO-PAGES is used to determine how many records to back up. The number will not always be a full page (maybe the last subfile page only had three records displayed). SFL-RECNUM contains one more than the last number of records displayed in the subfile (if three records were displayed, SFL-RECNUM will equal 4). Thus, to determine the number of records to back up, add one full page size to the SFL-RECNUM and then subtract 1. However, if the file is at the

end, then one more record must be read since the previous calculation assumes that the file position is on a valid record.

16. The READ PRIOR statement will continue to repeat until either two pages of records have been read (TWO-pages is defined in note 15) or until the beginning of the file is reached. When finished, the file position will be ready to start reading forward.

17. When this entire back-up process is complete, the READ-NEXT-PAGE paragraph will be executed to fill the subfile with the next page of records.

18. This paragraph assumes that there is already a record in the record buffer. The inner PERFORM will cycle enough times to fill the subfile with records, or until the end of file is reached. A subfile record will be written (from the database file's input buffer) and then the next record will be read. If the subfile becomes full, the last record read will be the first record added to the next subfile page (it will remain in the buffer).

19. This line may never be executed since we are assuring that we write no more records than the size of the subfile. This line is included for documentation purposes only.

20. After each read, spaces are moved into START-KEY and then displayed upon the LDA. If this was not done and a program put a start key value in the LDA, it would remain there until another program changes it.

21. The message subfile is cleared in this step.

22. When the user presses Enter, the position of the cursor (in the subfile) is put into variable CSRPSN. When the subfile is redisplayed, the cursor should remain in the same location; therefore the CSRPSN value is moved to the output buffer for the next WRITE operation.

23. This shows the use of the ON EXCEPTION phrase of the CALL statement. If the ADDPHNE program is not found, the paragraph named LINKAGE-ERROR will be executed. The ADDPHNE program could have been executed as a command by using QCMDEXC instead of using the CALL statement. This is shown in line 25.

24. The ADDPHNE program will place the last name added to the database into the LDA. This program retrieves this name and uses it to reposition the list so that the newly added name appears first on the screen.

25. QCMDEXC is used to execute the ADDPHNE command as opposed to using the CALL statement as in step 23.

26. This step ensures that you do not try and display a subfile when there are no records in it. If the subfile record number is zero, this block of code will display the EMPTY record, otherwise it will turn on the SFLDSP indicator.

27. This step writes the message subfile to the display. The MSGSFLCTL record format is not defined in this program; however,

that does not prevent you from using it. The MSGSFLCTL record expects the name of the program message queue to display on the last line. This program uses the special * value directing the message subfile to take the message from this program's message queue.

28. The subfile and the subfile control record are both written to the display in this step.

29. The NEXT MODIFIED phrase causes the OS/400 to read only subfile records that were modified by the user. If the user types an option number in the OPT (Option) field of a subfile record, that record will be considered modified. This prevents the program from having to read every record in the subfile.

30. Since separate buffers are used for input and output, the values read from the subfile must be moved to the output buffer before writing the output buffer back to the subfile.

31. After all of the user's entries are processed, this block checks to see if there were any errors, and if not, gets the next start key from the LDA and repositions the list.

32. This paragraph is executed in the event that the user keyed spaces into the option. It could be that in the prior cycle, the user made a keying error—after pressing Enter, the invalid option number was highlighted. To rectify the problem, the user would type spaces over the incorrect option or press the Field exit key to clear the field. When the program reads this record, it will receive spaces. This paragraph will reset the error indicator for the field so that the reverse image will be turned off.

33. If an option error is detected, this paragraph will be performed. The option indicator for reverse image will be turned on and the subfile record is rewritten to the subfile. On the next display of the subfile, the erroneous option will appear in reverse image.

34. To complete the error processing, the QMHSNDPM API is called to send a message back to this program, causing the message to show up in the message subfile.

35. If the CRTSRVREQ program is not found when it is called, a paragraph called LINKAGE-ERROR will be called.

36. Message PHN0009 is moved to the message ID before the error message is sent. After sending it, the original message (PHN0001) is restored.

22.5 Taking a Test Drive

To start the Work with Phone Directory programs, enter the WRKPHNDIR command and then press Enter. Try out the various functions against the names entered in previous chapters. You can add more names to the list by using the F6 or F7 (add) functions.

23

Creating the
Service Manager

In this chapter, you will be exposed to:

- Using a qualified name in a command
- Creating a job queue entry
- Creating a subsystem description
- Starting and stopping a subsystem
- Receiving messages in a command language (CL) program
- A display file that displays a pop-up window
- Using the data description specification (DDS) CHOICE keyword
- Submitting a job to a job queue
- An externally described printer file
- Using the allocate object (ALCOBJ) command to lock an object
- Using the deallocate object (DLCOBJ) command to unlock an object

The service manager is a program that monitors a message queue for incoming service requests and upon receiving a request, prints a log entry in a special "service request log."

The service manager is actually a small set of programs that are used to:

- Start the service manager
- End the service manager
- Create a service request

- Get the next request from the service request queue and print it
- Submit a service request

The service manager is designed to run as a batch job. Because of this, care should be taken not to submit this program into a production environment's batch job queue, especially if the queue only allows for one job to run at a time. Running this program may result in other jobs being clogged behind it. For this reason, it is recommended that a separate subsystem and job queue be created for these examples.

23.1   Creating a Learning Subsystem

Because the service manager program runs as a background job, it will need to be submitted into a job queue. The system you are working on may only have a single batch job queue, and that queue may be set up to allow only a single job to run at any given time. If the service manager is submitted into this job queue, no other jobs will be able to run until it is terminated. Furthermore, since this job must be terminated either manually (by canceling the job) or by sending it an end-request message, it will never terminate by itself.

As a solution to this problem, you can create your own subsystem and job queue to use for the service manager. You may not have authority to create the subsystem and job queue, so it may be necessary to contact a security administrator who can create them for you. Also, it is beyond the scope of this book to explain the details of subsystems and job queues; therefore only brief descriptions of the commands will be provided. For more information on subsystems and job queues, see the *AS/400 Work Management Guide*.

23.1.1   Creating the subsystem description

The command in Fig. 23.1 will create a subsystem named CBLBOOKSBS.

```
CRTSBSD SBSD(CBLBOOKSBS) POOLS((1 *BASE)) TEXT('Used for learning')
```

Figure 23.1 Command to create the test subsystem.

23.1.2   Adding a routing entry to the subsystem

Routing entries are used by a subsystem to determine how to process a command when one arrives into the subsystem. The command in Fig.

23.2 will add a routing entry that will handle requests coming from the job queue that you will create in the next step.

```
ADDRTGE SBSD(CBLBOOKSBS) SEQNBR(10) CMPVAL('QCMDB') PGM(QCMD) +
    CLS(QGPL/QBATCH)
```

Figure 23.2 Command to add a routing entry to the subsystem.

23.1.3 Creating a job queue

Use the command in Fig. 23.3 to create a job queue named SERV-ICEMGR. This job queue will be used for the service manager. Once created, the job queue must be added to the subsystem as a job queue entry. The command in Fig. 23.4 will add job queue SERVICEMGR to subsystem CBLBOOKSBS.

```
CRTJOBQ JOBQ(SERVICEMGR) TEXT('Phone directory job queue')
```

Figure 23.3 Command to create the job queue SERVICEMGR.

```
ADDJOBQE SBSD(CBLBOOKSBS) JOBQ(SERVICEMGR)
```

Figure 23.4 Command to add the job queue entry to the subsystem.

23.1.4 Starting the subsystem

Once the subsystem has been created and the job queue has been added to it, it must be started in order to become active. The following command will start the CBLBOOKSBS subsystem: STRSBS CBLBOOKSBS.

You can verify that the subsystem is active by using the work with active jobs (WRKACTJOB) command. The job queue will not show up under the subsystem name until a job has been submitted into the queue.

23.1.5 Ending the subsystem

Once started, the subsystem will remain active until it is manually ended or when the system is shut down. Leaving the subsystem active may not be desirable in some environments; therefore you should know how to end your subsystem. When you are finished doing the examples in this book, make sure to end the subsystem. To end the CBLBOOKSBS subsystem, type the command in Fig. 23.5.

```
ENDSBS CBLBOOKSBS *IMMED
```

Figure 23.5 Command to end the CBLBOOKSBS subsystem.

23.2 Creating the Service Request Message Queue

Programs will communicate with the service manager by sending messages to it and receiving messages from it. A message queue will be set up and dedicated exclusively to the service manager. Use the command in Fig. 23.6 to create a message queue names SERVICEREQ.

```
CRTMSGQ MSGQ(SERVICEREQ) TEXT('Service request queue')
```

Figure 23.6 Command to create the message queue for this project.

23.3 Creating the Start and End Modules

You will define two commands to control the service manager. The start service manager (STRSRVMGR) command will submit the service manager program into the job queue created earlier. The end service manager (ENDSRVMGR) command sends a message to the service manager requesting it to terminate itself.

23.3.1 The start service manager command

The source code in Listing 23.1 defines the start service manager (STRSRVMGR) command.

Listing 23.1 Command definition for the start service manager (STRSRVMGR).

```
MEMBER NAME: STRSRVMGR        FILE: QCMDSRC
....-....1....-....2....-....3....-....4....-....5....-....6....-....7
            CMD          PROMPT('Start Service Manager')
            PARM         KWD(JOBQ) TYPE(JOBQNAME) PROMPT('JobQ')
JOBQNAME:   QUAL         TYPE(*NAME) LEN(10) DFT(SERVICEREQ)
            QUAL         TYPE(*NAME) LEN(10) DFT(*LIBL) +
                         SPCVAL((*LIBL)) PROMPT('Library')
```

The PARM statement declares a keyword called JOBQ that is declared as type JOBQNAME. This data type is not a standard OS/400 type (such as *NAME or *CHAR); therefore it must be defined. The highlighted area defines the data type JOBQNAME as a qualified name containing two parts: a job queue name and a library name. If the user does not specify a job queue name, the default SERVICEREQ job queue (created in Sec. 23.1.3) will be used. If the library name is not specified, the default of *LIBL will be used.

When the command passes the JOBQ parameter (which is defined as a JOBQNAME), it will concatenate both of the qualified parts together, forming a single character string of length 20—the first 10 characters of the string will be the job queue name, the second ten characters will be the library name. To enter the source code in Listing 23.1, use the following command:

```
STRSEU QCMDSRC STRSRVMGR TYPE(CMD) TEXT ('Start Service Manager')
```

To compile the command, use

```
CRTCMD STRSRVMGR STRSRVMGR
```

The command processing program will receive the single parameter containing both the job queue's name and its library. It will first parse the name into two separate variables (&JOBQ and &LIB) using the %SST function.

Listing 23.2 Command processing program for STRSRVMGR. See program notes in text for an explanation of numbered areas.

```
MEMBER NAME: STRSRVMGR        FILE: QCLSRC
....-....1....-....2....-....3....-....4....-....5....-....6....-....7
             PGM      PARM(&JOBQNAME)
             DCL      VAR(&JOBQNAME) TYPE(*CHAR) LEN(20)
             DCL      VAR(&JOBQ) TYPE(*CHAR) LEN(10)
             DCL      VAR(&LIB) TYPE(*CHAR) LEN(10)

[1]          ALCOBJ   OBJ((SERVICE *PGM *EXCL)) WAIT(0)
             MONMSG    MSGID(CPF1002) EXEC(DO)
                   SNDPGMMSG MSGID(SVC0002) MSGF(PHONEMSGS +
                             TOPGMQ(*PRV) MSGTYPE(*INFO)
                       GOTO END
             ENDDO

[2]          CHGVAR   VAR(&JOBQ) VALUE(%SST(&JOBQNAME 1 10))
[2]          CHGVAR   VAR(&LIB) VALUE(%SST(&JOBQNAME 11 10))
[3]          SBMJOB   CMD(CALL PGM(SERVICE)) JOB(SERVICEMGR) +
                             JOBQ(&LIB/&JOBQ)
[4]          DLCOBJ   OBJ((SERVICE *PGM *EXCL)
             MONMSG    MSGID(CPF1005)

[5]          SNDPGMMSG MSGID(SVC0003) MSGF(PHONEMSGS) MSGDTA(*NONE) +
                             TOPGMQ(*PRV) MSGTYPE(*INFO)
END:
             ENDPGM
```

Listing 23.2 is the command processing program for the STRSRVMGR command. To enter the source code in Listing 23.2, use the following command:

```
STRSEU QCLSRC STRSRVMGR TYPE(CLP) TEXT('Start Service Manager')
```

To compile the command use

```
CRTCLPGM STRSRVMGR
```

Listing 23.2 program notes

1. The allocate object (ALCOBJ) command is being used in this program to prevent multiple copies of the service manager from being submitted to the batch queue. When the service manager is submitted to the batch queue, it obtains an exclusive lock on itself, preventing any other jobs from being able to use it. In this step, the STRSRVMGR program is testing whether it can obtain a lock on the SERVICE program—if it successfully obtains a lock, the SERVICE program is *not* active and therefore it can be invoked. If the ALCOBJ command returns with a CPF1002 message, then the SERVICE program has already obtained a lock on itself, indicating that it is already running. If the MONMSG command does trap message CPF1002, a message will be forwarded to the user that the service manager is already active, and the STRSRVMGR program will end.

2. In this step, the qualified name is being parsed into a job queue name and a library name.

3. The submit job (SBMJOB) command submits a command into a specified job queue. In this case, the command is CALL PGM(SERVICE). The JOB parameter is a textual identifier that will appear in the Work with Active Jobs (WRKACTJOB) display.

4. Once the command has been submitted to the job queue, the exclusive lock that was obtained in note 1 is deallocated. If you do not deallocate that lock, the SERVICE program just submitted in note 3 will fail, since the first thing it will try and do is obtain an exclusive lock on itself. If the DLCOBJ command fails because there is no allocation on the specified object, it will receive message CPF1005. In this example, it is pointless to include this MONMSG since if the original ALCOBJ command had failed, the program would skip to the end—therefore the mere fact that the program reaches this line would indicate that it successfully allocated the SERVICE program in note 1.

5. Once the program has been submitted to the batch queue and the lock has been removed from the SERVICE program, a message is sent to the user indicating that the service manager was started.

23.3.2   The end service manager command

The end service manager (ENDSRVMGR) command first checks to see whether the SERVICE program is active, and if so, sends a request for termination. The command in Listing 23.3 defines the ENDSRVMGR command. Notice that there are no keywords for this command.

Listing 23.3 Command definition for the end service manager (ENDSRVMGR).

```
MEMBER NAME: ENDSRVMGR        FILE: QCMDSRC
....-....1....-....2....-....3....-....4....-....5....-....6....-....7
                 CMD        PROMPT('End Service Manager')
```

To enter the source code for this listing, use the following command:

```
STRSEU QCMDSRC ENDSRVMGR TYPE(CMD) TEXT('End Service Manager')
```

To compile the command use

```
CRTCMD ENDSRVMGR ENDSRVMGR
```

The command processing program in Listing 23.4 will first attempt to obtain an exclusive lock on the SERVICE program. If the SERVICE program is active, it will have already obtained a lock on itself; therefore the ALCOBJ command will fail. If the command fails, the program will send a message to the service manager, requesting it to terminate itself. If the ALCOBJ command does not fail, the program will release the lock just obtained and send a message to the user indicating that the service manager is not active, and thus cannot be terminated.

Listing 23.4 Command processing program for ENDSRVMGR.

```
MEMBER NAME: ENDSRVMGR        FILE: QCLSRC     LIBRARY: PHONEDIR
....-....1....-....2....-....3....-....4....-....5....-....6....-....7....
          PGM

          ALCOBJ     OBJ((SERVICE *PGM *EXCL)) WAIT(0)
          MONMSG     MSGID(CPF1002) EXEC(DO)
           SNDPGMMSG MSGID(SVC9999) MSGF(PHONEMSGS) TOMSGQ(SERVICEREQ)
           GOTO END
          ENDDO
          DLCOBJ     OBJ((SERVICE *PGM *EXCL))
          MONMSG     MSGID(CPF1005)
          SNDPGMMSG  MSGID(SVC0001) MSGF(PHONEMSGS)
END:
          RETURN
          ENDPGM
```

To enter the source code in Listing 23.4, use the following command:

```
STRSEU QCLSRC ENDSRVMGR TYPE(CLP) TEXT('End Service Manager')
```

To compile the command use

```
CRTCLPGM ENDSRVMGR
```

23.4 Creating the Service Manager

This section describes the actual service manager program. There are three programs that comprise the service manager:

- SERVICE: A CL program that is initially submitted to the job queue by the STRSRVMGR command. This program will first obtain an exclusive lock on itself that will indicate to other programs that it is active. It will then call the COBOL program SERVICEMGR. When the COBOL program returns control back to this program, it will release the lock that it placed on itself, then end.

- SERVICEMGR: A COBOL program that will monitor the SERVICEREQ message queue for incoming requests. Each time a request arrives, it will be printed in the service log. This program uses a CL program to receive the messages from the message queue.

- GETNXTMSG: A CL program that uses the RCVMSG command to receive a message from the message queue. Once a message has been received, the CL program returns the message information to the SERVICEMGR COBOL program.

23.4.1 The SERVICE invocation program

The SERVICE invocation program is a CL program that first obtains a lock on itself, and then calls the main SERVICEMGR COBOL program. The source code for the SERVICE program is given in Listing 23.5.

Listing 23.5 Service manager invocation program (SERVICE).

```
MEMBER NAME: Service          FILE: QCLSRC
....-....1....-....2....-....3....-....4....-....5....-....6....-....7
          PGM

          ALCOBJ      OBJ((SERVICE *PGM *EXCL)) WAIT(5)
          MONMSG      MSGID(CPF1002) EXEC(GOTO CMDLBL(ABORT))

          CALL        SERVICEMGR

          DLCOBJ      OBJ((SERVICE *PGM *EXCL))
          MONMSG      MSGID(CPF1005)

ABORT:
          RETURN
          ENDPGM
```

If the ALCOBJ command fails, it indicates that the job is already running, and thus control transfers to the end where the program is aborted. The WAIT parameter tells the ALCOBJ command to wait for the lock for five seconds. If after five seconds it cannot obtain the lock, the allocate request will fail and message CPF1002 will be sent (which will cause control to transfer to the ABORT label).

To enter the source code in Listing 23.5, use the following command:

```
STRSEU QCLSRC SERVICE TYPE(CLP) TEXT ('Service Manager Invocation pgm')
```

To compile the command use

```
CRTCLPGM SERVICE
```

23.4.2 Creating the service request log (printed report)

As the service manager program receives service requests, they are logged in a printed report. The DDS in Listing 23.6 defines the report. For a detailed description of this printer file, see the sample in Sec. 9.5.2.

Listing 23.6 External printer file for service request log.

```
MEMBER NAME: SRVREQLOG        FILE: QDDSSRC
.....AAN01N02N03T.NAME+++++RLen++TDPBLINPOSFUNCTIONS+++++++++++++++++++
     A          R HEADER
     A                                    SKIPB(002)
     A                                    2
     A                                    'SERVICE REQUEST LOG'
     A                                    +48
     A                                    'Page:'
     A                                    +2
     A                                    PAGNBR
     A                                    2
     A                                    'Date:'
     A                                    SPACEB(002)
     A                                    +6
     A                                    'Time'
     A                                    +6
     A                                    'Phone number'
     A                                    +15
     A                                    'Request details'
     A                                    2
     A                                    '--------'
     A                                    SPACEB(001)
     A                                    +2
     A                                    '--------'
     A                                    +2
     A                                    '-----------------------'
     A                                    +2
     A                                    '------------------------
                                          ------'
```

```
A           R DETAIL
A                                    SPACEB(001)
A             REQDAT       6S  O     2
A                                    EDTCDE(Y)
A             REQTIM       6S  00    12
A                                    EDTWRD('  :   :   ')
A             REQNBR      25A  O     22
A             REQDTL      31A  O     +2
```

To enter the source code in Listing 23.6, use the following command:

```
STRSEU QDDSSRC SRVREQLOG TYPE(PRTF) TEXT('Service Request Log')
```

To compile the command use

```
CRTPRTF SRVREQLOG
```

When the report is printed, it will appear as shown in Fig. 23.7.

```
SERVICE REQUEST LOG                              Page:  0001

Date      Time      Phone number          Request details
--------  --------  --------------------  --------------------
95/03/01  10:05:20  555-1212              NO DIAL TONE
95/03/28  13:02:33  555-1213              BROKEN PHONESET
95/05/07  23:10:00  555-1214              NO RINGER
95/06/15   8:00:00  555-1215              BAD STATIC
95/07/26  17:33:21  555-1216              NO DIAL TONE
```

Figure 23.7 Sample service request log output.

23.4.3   Creating the service manager program

The source code in Listing 23.7 defines the service manager COBOL program. Its primary function is to receive messages from the service request message queue and process them.

Listing 23.7 Main service manager program. See program notes in text for an explanation of numbered areas.

```
MEMBER NAME: SERVICEMGR        FILE: QLBLSRC
....-..A...B..-....2....-....3....-....4....-....5....-....6....-....7
        IDENTIFICATION DIVISION.
        PROGRAM-ID.  SERVICEMGR.

        ENVIRONMENT DIVISION.
        CONFIGURATION SECTION.
        INPUT-OUTPUT SECTION.
        FILE-CONTROL.
[1]        SELECT PRINT-FILE ASSIGN TO FORMATFILE-SRVREQLOG
              ORGANIZATION IS SEQUENTIAL.
```

```
DATA DIVISION.
FILE SECTION.
FD  PRINT-FILE.
01  PRINT-LINE              PIC X(132).

WORKING-STORAGE SECTION.
77  MSGID                   PIC X(7).
77  MSGQUEUE                PIC X(10) VALUE "SERVICEREQ".
77  SENDER                  PIC X(10).
77  MSGTEXT                 PIC X(256).
77  DATESENT                PIC X(6).
77  TIMESENT                PIC X(6).
77  MSGDATA                 PIC X(100).

01  DETAIL-REC.
    COPY DDS-DETAIL-O OF SRVREQLOG.
    PROCEDURE DIVISION.
    MAIN-PARA.
        OPEN OUTPUT PRINT-FILE.
        PERFORM PRINT-HEADER.
        PERFORM UNTIL MSGID = "SVC9999"
[2]         CALL "GETNXTMSG" USING MSGQUEUE MSGID SENDER DATESENT
                TIMESENT MSGTEXT MSGDATA
            EVALUATE MSGID
[3]             WHEN "SVC9999"
                    CLOSE PRINT-FILE
                WHEN OTHER
                    PERFORM PRINT-DETAIL
            END-EVALUATE
        END-PERFORM.
        STOP RUN.

    PRINT-HEADER.
        WRITE PRINT-LINE FORMAT "HEADER".

    PRINT-DETAIL.
        MOVE DATESENT TO REQDAT.
        MOVE TIMESENT TO REQTIM.
        MOVE MSGTEXT TO REQDTL.
        MOVE MSGDATA TO REQNBR.
        WRITE PRINT-LINE FROM DETAIL-REC FORMAT "DETAIL"
            AT EOP PERFORM PRINT-HEADER.
```

This program calls GETNXTMSG (a CL program), which receives a message from the service request message queue and returns it to the COBOL program. An alternative method would have been to use the OS/400 API QMHRTVM to receive the message directly into the COBOL program without having to call a CL program.

Listing 23.7 program notes

1. The printer file must be declared as a FORMATFILE since it is an externally described printer file.

2. The call to GETNXTMSG illustrates a call to a CL program. Upon return, the parameters will contain information pertaining to the most recent message received from the message queue. Calls to CL pro-

grams are done in exactly the same way as calls to other COBOL and RPG programs.

3. If the service manager receives message SVC9999, it will prepare to terminate itself.

To enter the source code in Listing 23.7, use the following command:

```
STRSEU QLBLSRC SERVICEMGR TYPE(CBL) TEXT('Service Manager')
```

To compile the command use

```
CRTCBLPGM SERVICEMGR
```

23.4.4   Creating the get next message CL program

Since COBOL does not support the manipulation of messages (without using an OS/400 API), it has been decided to use a CL subprogram to perform the receive message (RCVMSG) action (see Listing 23.8).

Listing 23.8   Get next message (GETNXTMSG) CL program. See program notes in text for an explanation of numbered areas.

```
MEMBER NAME: GETNXTMSG              FILE: QCLSRC
....-....1....-....2....-....3....-....4....-....5....-....6....-....7
            PGM         PARM(&QUEUE &MSGID &FROMUSR &DATESENT +
                          &TIMESENT &MESSAGE &MSGDTA)
            DCL         VAR(&QUEUE) TYPE(*CHAR) LEN(10)
            DCL         VAR(&MESSAGE) TYPE(*CHAR) LEN(256)
            DCL         VAR(&MSGID) TYPE(*CHAR) LEN(7)
            DCL         VAR(&SENDER) TYPE(*CHAR) LEN(80)
            DCL         VAR(&DATESENT) TYPE(*CHAR) LEN(6)
            DCL         VAR(&TIMESENT) TYPE(*CHAR) LEN(6)
            DCL         VAR(&FROMUSR) TYPE(*CHAR) LEN(10)
            DCL         VAR(&MSGDTA) TYPE(*CHAR) LEN(100)

[1]         RCVMSG      MSGQ(&QUEUE) WAIT(*MAX) RMV(*NO) MSG(&MESSAGE) +
                          MSGDTA(&MSGDTA) MSGID(&MSGID) SENDER(&SENDER)

            CHGVAR      VAR(&DATESENT) VALUE(%SST(&SENDER 44 6))
[2]         CHGVAR      VAR(&TIMESENT) VALUE(%SST(&SENDER 50 6))
            CHGVAR      VAR(&FROMUSR) VALUE(%SST(&SENDER 11 10))

            RETURN
            ENDPGM
```

Listing 23.8 program notes

1. The receive message (RCVMSG) command is used to obtain the next message from the message queue. This command can be used against any message queue, since the &QUEUE parameter (provided by the COBOL program) contains the name of the message queue to use. The WAIT keyword specifies *MAX, which will cause the com-

mand to wait indefinitely for a message if one does not exist. The SENDER keyword specifies a variable to place information pertaining to the job that sent the message. This value is later parsed to determine who sent the message and the time and date the message was sent.

2. The &SENDER variable is parsed to obtain the date (positions 44 to 49), the time (positions 50 to 55), and the user ID (positions 11 to 20).

To enter the source code in Listing 23.8, use the following command:

```
STRSEU QCLSRC GETNXTMSG TYPE(CLP) TEXT('Get Next Message')
```

To compile the command use

```
CRTCLPGM GETNXTMSG
```

23.5   The Create Service Request Module

The create service request (CRTSRVREQ) module is used to allow the user to create a service request. When called, the program displays a pop-up window and allows the user to select from a list of four different service problems.

23.5.1   Defining the create service request command

The source in Listing 23.9 defines the create service request (CRTSRVREQ) command.

Listing 23.9 Command definition for CRTSRVREQ.

```
MEMBER NAME: CRTSRVREQ        FILE: QCMDSRC
....-....1....-....2....-....3....-....4....-....5....-....6....-....7
            CMD       PROMPT('Create Service Request')
            PARM      KWD(PHNUMBER) TYPE(*CHAR) LEN(20) MIN(1) +
                      PROMPT('Phone number')
```

To enter the source code in this listing, use the following command:

```
STRSEU QCMDSRC CRTSRVREQ TYPE(CMD) TEXT('Create Service Request')
```

To compile the command use

```
CRTCMD CRTSRVREQ CRTSRVREQ
```

23.5.2   Defining the create service request
pop-up window

When the create service request program is executed, it displays a pop-up window without erasing the current contents of the display. The DDS source code in Listing 23.10 defines the pop-up window used by the create service request program.

Listing 23.10 Display file for the create service request program. See program notes in text for an explanation of numbered areas.

```
MEMBER NAME: CRTSRVREQ        FILE: QDDSSRC
.....AAN01N02N03T.Name++++++RLen++TDpBLinPosFunctions++++++++++++++++++++
     A                                       PRINT
     A                                       INDARA
     A******************************************************************
     A           R BORDERS
[1]  A                                       WINDOW(3 15 13 40)
     A******************************************************************
     A           R SRVREQ
[2]  A                                       WINDOW(BORDERS)
     A                                       CA12(12 'Cancel')
     A                                       OVERLAY
     A                                     1 10'Select Service Problem'
     A                                       DSPATR(HI)
[3]  A             CHOICE        2Y 0B   7 17SNGCHCFLD
     A                                       CHOICE(1 'No dial tone')
     A                                       CHOICE(2 'Can hear -
     A                                       neighbors')
     A                                       CHOICE(3 'Disconnect -
     A                                       request')
     A                                       CHOICE(4 'Horrible static')
     A                                     5  2'Type choice, press Enter.
     A                                       COLOR(BLU)
     A                                    12  2'F12=Cancel'
     A                                       COLOR(BLU) DSPATR(HI)
     A                                     7  2'Symptom . . :'
     A                                     3  2'Phone nbr:'
     A             PHONENUM   R        O   3 14REFFLD(PHONEREC/PHONENUM -
     A                                       *LIBL/PHONEFILE)
     A******************************************************************
[4]  A           R DUMMY1                     CLRL(*NO) OVERLAY FRCDTA
     A******************************************************************
[5]  A           R DUMMY2                     ASSUME
     A                                    11  1' '
```

Listing 23.10 program notes

1. The WINDOW keyword defines the location (in row and column coordinates) where the window is to appear. This is the record that will actually open a window on the display. Other record formats within this file will refer to this window record.

2. The WINDOW keyword in this case references the window defined in line 1. All of the fields will be placed into the window defined in record format BORDERS.

3. The SNGCHCFLD keyword specifies that this field is a single-choice field and that the following CHOICE keywords will define the

available choices for the user. Each CHOICE keyword specifies the choice number along with the text to be displayed for the choice. You can control whether an option is available or not by using an option indicator. If the indicator is off, the choice will not be available to the user.

4. This record is used to restore the display to its original condition before the window was displayed. The CLRL(*NO) specifies that no lines are to be cleared before this record format is displayed.

5. When the ASSUME keyword is associated with at least one record in the display file, the screen will not be erased when the display file is opened.

To enter the source code in Listing 23.10, use the following command:

```
STRSEU QDDSSRC CRTSRVREQ TYPE(DSPF) TEXT('Create Service Request
DSPF')
```

To create the display file use

```
CRTDSPF CRTSRVREQ
```

23.5.3 Defining the create service request COBOL program

The create service request program displays a pop-up window, enabling the user to select a service problem (see Listing 23.11). Once a problem has been selected, the program calls the OS/400 QMHSNDM API to send a message to the service request message queue (SERVICEREQ).

Listing 23.11 Program to create a service request.

```
MEMBER NAME: CRTSRVREQ         FILE: QLBLSRC
....-..A...B..-....2.....-....3....-....4....-....5....-....6....-....7
      IDENTIFICATION DIVISION.
      PROGRAM-ID.  CRTSRVREQ.

      ENVIRONMENT DIVISION.
      CONFIGURATION SECTION.
      INPUT-OUTPUT SECTION.
      FILE-CONTROL.
          SELECT DISPFILE ASSIGN TO WORKSTATION-CRTSRVREQ-SI
              ORGANIZATION IS TRANSACTION.

      DATA DIVISION.
      FILE SECTION.
      FD  DISPFILE.
      01  DISP-REC                      PIC X(200).

      WORKING-STORAGE SECTION.
      01  CHOICE-IN.
          COPY DDS-SRVREQ-I OF CRTSRVREQ.
      01  CHOICE-OUT.
          COPY DDS-SRVREQ-O OF CRTSRVREQ.
```

```
       01  PROBLEMS-TABLE.
           03 CONSTANTS.
               05 PIC X(7) VALUE "REQ0001".
               05 PIC X(7) VALUE "REQ0002".
               05 PIC X(7) VALUE "REQ0003".
               05 PIC X(7) VALUE "REQ0004".
           03  MSGIDS REDEFINES CONSTANTS OCCURS 4 TIMES PIC X(7).

       01  MSGDTA PIC X(100).

       COPY DATADEFS.

       COPY API.
       COPY QMHDATADIV.

       LINKAGE SECTION.
       01  REQ-PHONENUM                           PIC X(20).

       PROCEDURE DIVISION USING REQ-PHONENUM.
       MAIN-PARA.
           IF FILES-CLOSED
               OPEN I-O DISPFILE
               SET FILES-OPEN TO TRUE
           END-IF.
           PERFORM GET-CHOICE.
[1]        WRITE DISP-REC FORMAT "DUMMY1".
           GOBACK.
           GET-CHOICE.
              MOVE REQ-PHONENUM TO PHONENUM OF CHOICE-OUT.
[2]           WRITE DISP-REC FORMAT "BORDERS".
              MOVE ZERO TO CHOICE OF CHOICE-OUT.
[3]           WRITE DISP-REC FROM CHOICE-OUT FORMAT "SRVREQ".
              READ DISPFILE INTO CHOICE-IN FORMAT "SRVREQ"
              IF CHOICE OF CHOICE-IN NOT EQUAL ZERO
[4]               MOVE MSGIDS(CHOICE OF CHOICE-IN) TO QMHSNDM-MSGID
[5]               MOVE "PHONEMSGS" TO QMHSNDM-MSGFNAME
[6]               MOVE REQ-PHONENUM TO QMHSNDM-MSGDTA
[7]               MOVE LENGTH OF REQ-PHONENUM TO QMHSNDM-MSGDTALEN
[8]               SET QMHSNDM-INFO TO TRUE
[9]               MOVE "SERVICEREQ" TO QMHSNDM-MSGQNAME(1)
[10]              SET QMHSNDM-LIBL(1) TO TRUE
                  PERFORM CALL-QMHSNDM
              END-IF.
           COPY QMHPROCDIV.
```

Listing 23.11 program notes

1. Before the program terminates, it writes record format DUMMY1 to remove the pop-up window from the display.
2. The "BORDERS" record format is written to the display first. This causes the window frame to be drawn.
3. This WRITE will fill the window with the choices for the user.
4. The user's choice will be in identifier CHOICE. It is used as an index to determine the appropriate request ID (defined in PROBLEMS-TABLE in the WORKING-STORAGE section). This message ID is moved into the MSGID field for the QMHSNDM API.
5. The name of the message file where the message being sent is defined. In this case, the message definition is found in message file PHONEMSGS.

6. The phone number that is defined in the program's linkage section will be sent as the message data. The recipient of the message will be able to inspect the message's data to determine any necessary details regarding the request.

7. The special LENGTH OF register is used to set the length of the message data.

8. The message being sent will be of type *INFO (informational).

9. In this statement, the destination message queue is specified. Since the QMHSNDM API uses an array of message queue names, the name is put into an array element rather than an elementary data item. The default number of message queues to send to is 1.

10. This statement sets the library name to *LIBL as defined in the API copy book.

To enter the source code in Listing 23.11, use the following command:

```
STRSEU QLBLSRC CRTSRVREQ TYPE(CBL) TEXT('Create Service Request')
```

To create the program use

```
CRTCBLPGM CRTSRVREQ
```

23.6   Testing the Service Manager

First, you must start the subsystem that you created earlier in this chapter, if you have not already. You can start it with the STRSBS command as follows:

```
STRSBS CBLBOOKSBS
```

Next, display the menu the main phone directory menu. To do this, type

```
GO PHONEDIR
```

To start the service manager, choose option 2, "Start Service Manager". Once started, you can see if it is running by typing the work with active jobs (WRKACTJOB) command and look for your subsystem (CBLBOOKSBS). You should see the display in Fig. 23.8 (the CBLBOOKSBS subsystem and the SERVICEMGR job are highlighted).

If you received an error or the SERVICE program is not showing up, something went wrong and you should inspect your job log (DSPJOBLOG) as well as any job logs that may have been printed by the batch job. You can see job logs by using the WRKSPLF and look for files with names that contain the word JOBLOG in them.

```
                         Work with Active Jobs                    S1011514
                                              02/21/95  12:07:29
CPU %:      .0    Elapsed time:   00:00:00    Active jobs:  17

Type options, press Enter.
  2=Change   3=Hold   4=End    5=Work with   6=Release   7=Display message
  8=Work with spooled files   13=Disconnect ...

Opt  Subsystem/Job  User       Type  CPU %  Function        Status
  __   CBLBOOKSBS   QSYS        SBS    .0                    DEQW
  __     SERVICEMGR GERRYK      BCH    .0    PGM-SERVICE     MSGW
  __   QBASE        QSYS        SBS    .0                    DEQW
  __     DSP01      GERRYK      INT    .0    CMD-WRKACTJOB   RUN
  __   QSPL         QSYS        SBS    .0                    DEQW
  __     PRT01      QSPLJOB     WTR    .0                    MSGW
  __   QSYSWRK      QSYS        SBS    .0                    DEQW
  __     QECS       QSYS        BCH    .0    PGM-QNMECSJB    DEQW
  __   QALERT       QSYS        SYS    .0                    DEQW
                                                              More...

Parameters or command
===> _____
F3=Exit      F5=Refresh    F10=Restart statistics   F11=Display elapsed data
F12=Cancel   F23=More options    F24=More keys
```

Figure 23.8 Work with the subsystems.

If everything is working, you should now be able to log service requests against phone numbers. Start the Work with Phone Directory program (you can choose option 1 from the PHONEDIR menu).

If you have not added any names to the phone directory database, you should add one now using F6=Add. Type the number 8 in front of one of the names in the list and press Enter. You should see a pop-up window asking for more information about the service request.

Select one of the available service options and press Enter. After pressing Enter, the service request will be sent to the SERVICEREQ message queue which is being monitored by the service manager. The service manager will receive the service request and print it in the service log.

Exit the Work with Phone Directory program (F3) to return to the main phone directory menu. Choose option 3 to end the service manager.

When you end the service manager, the printer file (service log) will be closed and will be ready to view or print. You can see the service log by using the WRKSPLF command. If your profile or workstation is set up to print directly to a printer, the service log will automatically be printed.

Message-Handling
Application Program
Interfaces

Because COBOL does not have statements that support the use of OS/400 messages, an alternative method must be used to send, receive, and remove messages. There are two ways of doing this from within a COBOL program:

- Call a command language (CL) program and have the CL program execute the appropriate CL message command. For example, when a COBOL program needs to send a message, it can call a CL program, which will execute the SNDPGMMSG command.
- Call an OS/400 API to perform the message function directly from the COBOL program.

A.1 Sending Messages with QMHSNDM
Application Program Interface

The send nonprogram message (QMHSNDM) application program interface (API) sends a message to a nonprogram message queue so your program can communicate with another job or user. The QMHSNDM API differs from the QMHSNDPM API (described in Sec. 17.7) in that it sends a message to a user or a regular message queue, whereas the QMHSNDPM API sends messages between active programs within the current job.

A.2   QMHSNDM Parameter List

There are 10 required parameters for the QMHSNDM API (see Table A.1).

TABLE A.1   QMHSNDM Required Parameters

#	Parameter Description	In/Out	Length	COBOL PIC
1	Message Identifier	Input	Char(7)	PIC X(7)
2	Qualified message file name	Input	Char(20)	PIC X(20)
3	Message data or immediate text	Input	Char(*)	PIC X(nn) where nn may be any length
4	Length of message data or immediate text	Input	Binary(4)	PIC S9(9) BINARY
5	Message type	Input	Char(10)	PIC X(10)
6	List of qualified message queue names	Input	Array of Char(20)	Array of PIC X(20)
7	Number of message queues	Input	Binary(4)	PIC S9(9) BINARY
8	Qualified name of the reply message queue	Input	Char (20)	PIC X(20)
8	Message key	Output	Char(4)	PIC X(4)
9	Error code	I/O	Char(*)	See A.2.10

A.2.1   Message identifier

The message identifier for the predefined message being sent, or blanks for an immediate message. If you specify a message identifier, you must specify a qualified message file name. If you do not specify a message identifier, the API ignores the qualified message file name parameter.

A.2.2   Qualified message file name

For a predefined message, the name of the message file and the library in which it resides. The first 10 characters specify the file name, and the second 10 characters specify the library. You can use these special values for the library name:

*CURLIB	The job's current library
*LIBL	The library list

For an immediate message, use blanks for this parameter. If you specify a name, the API ignores it and does not return an error.

A.2.3 Message data or immediate text

If a message identifier is specified, this parameter specifies the data to insert in the predefined message's substitution variables. If blanks are used for the message identifier, this parameter specifies the complete text of an immediate message.

A.2.4 Length of message data or immediate text

The length (in bytes) of the message data or immediate text. Valid values for each are as follows:

Message data	0 to 32767
Immediate text	1 to 6000

A.2.5 Message type

You must specify one of these values for the type of the message:

*COMP	Completion
*DIAG	Diagnostic
*INFO	Informational
*INQ	Inquiry

For more information on these message types, see Chap. 12.

A.2.6 List of qualified message queues

A list of 1 through 50 message queues to which the message is being sent and the libraries in which they reside. When sending an inquiry message or using the special value *ALLACT, you can list only one queue. In all other cases, you can list up to 50 message queues.

You can specify user profile message queues or other nonprogram message queues, or you can use several special values. To specify the default message queue associated with a user profile, use the first 10 characters for the user profile name. In the second ten characters, use the special value *USER. To specify other nonprogram message queues, use the first 10 characters for the message queue name and the second 10 characters for the library name. You can also use *CURLIB or *LIBL. You can also specify *ALLACT (for all accounts), *REQUESTER (for the interactive job's user), or *SYSOPR (the system operator's message queue). If you use any of these values, you should leave the second 10 characters blank.

A.2.7 Number of message queue

The number of message queues specified in the list of qualified message queue names parameter. Valid values are 1 through 50. When sending an inquiry message or using the special value *ALLACT for the message queue, you must specify 1.

A.2.8 Qualified name of the reply message queue

For an inquiry message only, the name of the message queue to receive the reply message, and the library in which it resides. The first 10 characters specify the message queue, and the second 10 characters specify the library.

You can also use the values *PGMQ (for the current program's message queue) or *WRKSTN (for the current work station message queue). If you use either of these values, you should leave the library name blank.

A.2.9 Message key

For an inquiry message only, the key to the sender's copy of the message in the reply message queue. This API assigns the key when it sends the message. For all other message types, no key is returned.

A.2.10 Error code

The structure in which to return error information. The COBOL data structure for error messages is defined in Listing 17.6.

A.3 Sending Messages with QMHSNDPM API

The send program message (QMHSNDPM) API sends a message to a call message queue or the external message queue. (The external message queue is the part of the job message queue that handles messages between an interactive job and the workstation user. It is not associated with a specific program within the call stack.) This API allows the current call stack entry (in this case, the COBOL program) to send a message to its caller, a previous caller, or itself. The QMHSNDPM can perform many of the same functions available with the CL send program message (SNDPGMMSG) command.

A.4   QMHSNDPM Parameter List

There are nine required parameters for the QMHSNDPM API (see Table A.2).

TABLE A.2   QMHSNDPM Required Parameters

#	Parameter Description	In/Out	Length	COBOL PIC
1	Message Identifier	Input	Char(7)	PIC X(7)
2	Qualified message file name	Input	Char(20)	PIC X(20)
3	Message data or immediate text	Input	Char(*)	PIC X(nn) where nn may be any length
4	Length of message data or immediate text	Input	Binary(4)	PIC S9(9) BINARY
5	Message type	Input	Char(10)	PIC X(10)
6	Call message queue	Input	Char(*)	PIC X(nn) - See below for details
7	Call stack counter	Input	Binary(4)	PIC S9(9) BINARY
8	Message key	Output	Char(4)	PIC X(4)
9	Error code	I/O	Char(*)	See A.4.9

A.4.1   Message identifier

The message identifier for the predefined message being sent, or blanks for an immediate message. When sending an escape, notify, or status message, you must specify blanks. When sending other types of messages, you can use either a message identifier or blanks.

If you specify a message identifier, you must specify a qualified message file name. If you do not specify a message identifier, the API ignores the qualified message file name parameter.

A.4.2   Qualified message file name

For a predefined message, the name of the message file and the library in which it resides. The first 10 characters specify the file name, and the second 10 characters specify the library. You can use these special values for the library name:

*CURLIB	The job's current library
*LIBL	The library list

For an immediate message, use blanks for this parameter. If you specify a name, the API ignores it and does not return an error.

A.4.3   Message data or immediate text

If a message identifier is specified, this parameter specifies the data to insert in the predefined message's substitution variables. If blanks are used for the message identifier, this parameter specifies the complete text of an immediate message.

A.4.4   Length of message data or immediate text

The length of the message data or immediate text, in bytes. Valid values for each are

Message data   0 to 32767
Immediate text   1 to 6000

A.4.5   Message type

The type of message. You must specify one of these values:

*COMP	Completion
*DIAG	Diagnostic
*ESCAPE	Escape
*INFO	Informational
*INQ	Inquiry—you can send inquiry messages only to the external message queue
*NOTIFY	Notify
*RQS	Request
*STATUS	Status

For more information on these message types, see Chap. 12.

A.4.6   Call message queue

The name of the call message queue to send the messages to, or the name of the call stack entry to start counting from when using a value other than 0 for the call stack counter parameter. The call stack entry you specify must be in the call stack. You can specify a call stack entry by name or use one of these special values:

*	The message queue of the current call stack entry (that is, the call stack entry of the program sending the message).
*EXT	The external message queue. The call stack counter parameter is ignored. You cannot send escape messages to this message queue. If you are sending an inquiry message, you must specify this message queue.

A.4.7 Call stack counter

A number identifying the location in the call stack of the call message queue receiving the messages. The number is relative to the name specified in the call message queue parameter. It indicates how may calls up the call stack this call message queue is from the one specified in the call message queue parameter.

Valid values for this parameter are as follows:

0   Send the message to the queue of the call stack entry specified in the call message queue parameter.

1   Send the message to the queue of the caller of the call stack entry specified in the call message queue parameter.

n Send the message to the queue of the nth caller up the stack from the call stack entry specified in the call message queue.

You can use any positive number that does not exceed the actual number of call stack entries in the call stack, excluding the external message queue.

A.4.7.1 Using the call stack The call stack represents the programs that are currently active and the order in which they were called. For example, if program A calls program B, and program B calls program C, the program stack may look like that in Fig. A.1.

```
┌─────────────────┐
│ User  (*EXT)    │
├─────────────────┤
│ PROGA           │
├─────────────────┤
│ PROGB           │
├─────────────────┤
│ PROGC    *      │
└─────────────────┘
```

Figure A.1 Call stack with three programs.

The *EXT program message queue is associated with the workstation. The most recently executed program in the stack is the current program, identified by an asterisk (*). A combination of the call message queue and the call stack counter parameters identifies which program in the call stack will receive the message.

For example, if program C sends a message and specifies the call message queue parameter as an asterisk and zero for the call stack counter, the message will be sent back to itself (PROGC). The zero in the call stack counter entry indicates that the message should go to the program identified in the call message queue (which is an asterisk indicating the current program).

If program C sends a message and specifies the call message queue parameter as an asterisk and 2 for the call stack counter, the message will be sent to PROGA's program message queue. A stack counter of 2 indicates two programs above the program specified in the program message queue (which again is an asterisk indicating the current program).

Finally, if program C sends a message and specifies the call message queue parameter as PROGB and a 1 for the call stack counter, the message will be sent to PROGA's program message queue, since the call stack counter is a relative number based on the message queue specified in the call message queue parameter.

A common use of sending program messages is when a program wants to send a message to its own program message queue, which should then be displayed in a message subfile. In this case, the message queue is specified as * for the current program, and the call stack counter is specified as 0.

A.4.8   Message key

The key to the message being sent. This API assigns the key when it sends a message of any type except status. For a status message, no key is returned and this parameter is not changed. For inquiry and notify messages, this is the key to the sender's copy of the message in the sending program's message queue.

A.4.9   Error code

The structure in which to return error information. The COBOL data structure for error messages is defined in Listing 17.6.

A.5   Removing Messages with the QMHRMVPM API

The remove program messages (QMHRMVPM) API removes messages from call message queues and the external message queue. The removed instances of the messages are no longer available for you to work with. However, other instances of the messages might still exist in other message queues, and the definitions of predefined messages are still in the message files.

The remove program messages API is particularly useful when working with a message subfile such as that used in the Work with Phone Directory program. If a message is sent to the program message queue of the work with phone directory program, the message will automatically show up on the bottom line of the workstation. However, after the user presses Enter, it is desirable to have the messages removed. The remove program message API is an ideal way to clear the program's message queue.

A.6 QMHRMVPM Parameter List

There are five required parameters for the QMHRMVPM API (shown in Table A.3).

TABLE A.3 QMHRMVPM Required Parameters

#	Parameter Description	In/Out	Length	COBOL PIC
1	Call message queue	Input	Char(*)	PIC X(10)
2	Call stack counter	Input	Binary(4)	PIC S9(9) BINARY
3	Message key	Input	Char(4)	PIC X(4)
4	Messages to remove	Input	Char(10)	PIC X(10)
5	Error code	In/Out	Char(*)	See A.6.5

A.6.1 Call message queue

The name of the call message queue from which to remove messages, or the name of the call stack entry to start counting from when using the call stack counter parameter. The call stack entry you specify must be in the call stack. You can specify a call stack entry by name or use of these special values:

*	The message queue of the current call stack entry (that is, the call stack entry of the program sending the message).
*ALLINACT	All message queues for inactive call stack entries. The messages to remove parameters must specify *ALL. The call stack counter parameter is ignored.
*EXT	The external message queue. The call stack counter parameter is ignored. You cannot send escape messages to this message queue. If you are sending an inquiry message, you must specify this message queue.

If you specify a message key and the messages to remove parameter specifies *BYKEY, this parameter is ignored.

A.6.2 Call stack counter

A number identifying the location in the call stack of the call message queue from which to remove messages. The number is relative to the call stack entry specified in the call message queue parameter. It indicates how many calls up the call stack the targeted call message queue is from the one specified in the call message queue parameter.

Valid values for this parameter are as follows:

0   Remove the messages from the queue of the call stack entry specified in the call message queue parameter.

1   Remove the messages from the queue of the call stack entry that called the call stack entry specified in the call message queue parameter.

n Remove the messages from the queue of the nth call stack entry up the stack from the call stack entry specified in the call message queue parameter. You can use any positive number that does not exceed the actual number of call stack entries in the call stack, excluding the external message queue.

This parameter is ignored in these cases:

- When the program message queue parameter specifies all queues for inactive call stack entries (*ALLINACT) or the external message queue (*EXT).
- When you specify a message key and the messages to remove parameter specifies *BYKEY.

A.6.3   Message key

If the messages to remove parameter specifies *BYKEY, the key to the single message being removed. (The key is assigned by the command or API that sends the message.) The call message queue and call stack counter parameters are ignored. If the messages to remove parameter does not specify *BYKEY, you must use blanks for this parameter.

A.6.4   Messages to remove

The message or group of messages being removed. Valid values are the following:

*ALL	All messages in the call message queue.
*BYKEY	The single message specified in the message key parameter.
*KEEPRQS	All messages in the call message queue except requests.
*NEW	All new messages in the call message queue. New messages are those that have not been received.
*OLD	All old messages in the call message queue. Old messages are those that have already been received.

A.6.5   Error code

The structure in which to return error information. The COBOL data structure for error messages will be defined in Listing 17.6.

Summary of IBM Extensions

This appendix contains a brief summary of the COBOL/400 extensions. All references in this appendix refer to the *COBOL / 400 User's Guide.*

B.1 Character-String Considerations

The apostrophe can be used in place of the quotation mark. See "Characters" in Part 1.

Boolean literals can be used. See "Boolean Literals" in Part 1.

Hexadecimal notation can be used for nonnumeric literals. See "Nonnumeric Literals" in Part 1.

B.2 Identification Division

The system uses the first 10 characters of the program name specified in the PROGRAM-ID paragraph. See "PROGRAM-ID Paragraph" in Part 2.

The abbreviation ID DIVISION may be substituted for the standard division header. See "Identification Division" in Part 2.

B.3 Environment Division

The CONSOLE IS CRT clause, the CURSOR IS clause, and the CRT STATUS IS clause may be used in the SPECIAL-NAMES paragraph for extended ACCEPT or DISPLAY statements.

The CONSOLE IS CRT clause changes the default interpretation of ACCEPT or DISPLAY statements from the American National Standards Institute (ANSI) defined format to extend ACCEPT or DISPLAY statements for work station I/O.

The CURSOR IS clause specifies the data item to contain the cursor address used by the ACCEPT statement.

The CRT STATUS IS clause specifies a data item into which a status value is moved after an ACCEPT statement.

See the "SPECIAL-NAMES' Paragraph" in Part 2.

The device that a file will use can be changed at run time with the OVRxxxF CL command. See "FILE-CONTROL Paragraph, ASSIGN Clause" in Part 2.

COBOL programs can process database files. The ORGANIZATION of the file indicates the current program usage. See "File Processing Summary" and "FILE-CONTROL Paragraph, ORGANIZATION Clause" in Part 2.

If the data description specification (DDS) keyword DESCEND is used when the field is specified as a key, the records are accessed in the sequence of descending record key values within the index. The OVRDBF command can set the file position indicator when the file is opened. See "FILE-CONTROL Paragraph, ACCESS MODE Clause" in Part 2.

The RECORD KEY data item, data-name-2, can be numeric when the file is assigned to a DATABASE device type. EXTERNALLY-DE-SCRIBED-KEY can be specified in the RECORD KEY clause. See "FILE-CONTROL Paragraph, RECORD KEY Clause" in Part 2.

The DUPLICATES phrase can only be specified for files assigned to DATABASE. See "FILE-CONTROL Paragraph, RECORD KEY Clause" in Part 2. Additional information is given in discussions of the READ, REWRITE, DELETE, and WRITE statements in Part 3.

The keywords specified for the data item in DDS can modify the record sequence. See "FILE-CONTROL Paragraph, RECORD KEY Clause" in Part 2.

The COMMITMENT CONTROL clause can be specified to enable the synchronizing or canceling of database changes and to provide additional record locking for records being changed. See "COMMITMENT CONTROL Clause" in Part 2 and the section on Commitment Control in the *COBOL/400 User's Guide*.

B.4   Data Division

A Boolean data type has been provided as a means of modifying and passing the values of the indicators associated with the display screen formats. See "Data Description Entry—Boolean Data" in Part 2.

The Boolean symbol 1 is allowed once in the PICTURE clause. See "PICTURE Clause" in Part 2.

Elementary items or group items immediately subordinate to one group item can have unequal level numbers. See "Data Relationships" in Part 2.

If the CODE-SET clause is omitted, the CODE parameter of the CRTDKTF or CRTTAPF command is used. The OVRDKTF or the OVRTAPF command can change the CODE-SET clause at run time. See "File Description Entry, CODE-SET Clause" in Part 2.

COMPUTATIONAL-3 (internal decimal) and COMPUTATIONAL-4 (binary) can be specified for the USAGE clause of numeric items. See "USAGE Clause" in Part 2.

The key specified for an OCCURS clause can have USAGE of COMPUTATIONAL-3 or COMPUTATIONAL-4. See "USAGE Clause" in Part 2.

The JUSTIFIED clause can be specified for alphanumeric edited items. See "JUSTIFIED Clause" in Part 2.

The LIKE clause can be used to copy characteristics from a previously defined data item. See "LIKE Clause" in Part 2.

Pointer data items allow easier migration of COBOL code from other SAA (System Application Architecture) platforms, and allow access to APIs and languages that require pointers. See "POINTER Phrase" in Part 2.

B.5   Procedure Division

Workstation input/output (I/O) may be performed through the extended ACCEPT or DISPLAY statements. See "ACCEPT Statement— Format 7" and "DISPLAY Statement—Format 3" in Part 3.

The mnemonic names OPEN-FEEDBACK and I-O-FEEDBACK are used for file information and are accessed through an ACCEPT statement format. See "ACCEPT Statement" in Part 3.

The GOBACK statement can be used to specify the logical end of a called program. See "GOBACK Statement" in Part 3.

The FORMAT phrase is valid for DELETE, READ, REWRITE, START, and WRITE statements. See "DELETE Statement," "READ Statement" < "REWRITE Statement," "START Statement," and "WRITE Statement" in Part 3.

The special register DB-FORMAT-NAME contains information about the processing of a file input/output statements. See "DB-FORMAT-NAME Special Register" in Part 3.

The identifier in a Format 2 ACCEPT statement can be an internal decimal item. See "ACCEPT Statement" in Part 3.

The ACCEPT statement can be used to transfer data from a job's local data area to a specified data item. See "ACCEPT Statement" in

Part 3 and the section on the local data area in the *COBOL/400 User's Guide*.

The ACCEPT statement can be used to transfer data from a program initialization parameter (PIP) data area into an identifier item. See "ACCEPT Statement" in Part 3 and the section on the PIP data area in the *COBOL/400 User's Guide*.

The system always rewinds and unloads the tape when REEL/UNIT is specified in the CLOSE statement. See "CLOSE Statement" in Part 3.

The INHWRT parameter of the OVRDBF command can inhibit the DELETE, READ <, and WRITE statements. See DELETE Statement," "READ Statement," and "WRITE Statement" in Part 3.

For a file with duplicate primary keys allowed, a successfully completed READ statement must immediately precede a DELETE or REWRITE statement to ensure proper deletion. See "DELETE Statement" and "REWRITE Statement" in Part 3.

For the DISPLAY statement, signed noninteger numeric literals are allowed. See "DISPLAY Statement" in Part 3. In a format 1 DISPLAY statement, environment-name may be specified in place of the mnemonic-name. See "DISPLAY Statement" in Part 3.

The DISPLAY statement can be used to transfer data to a job's local data area. See "DISPLAY Statement" in Part 3 and the section on the local data area in the *COBOL/400 User's Guide*.

A logical file opened for OUTPUT does not remove all records in the physical file on which it is based; the records are added to the end of the file. The OVRDBF command can specify the first record to be made available to the program at run time. See "OPEN Statement" in Part 3.

FIRST, PRIOR, and LAST can be specified in the READ statement for indexed files with dynamic access. See "READ Statement" in Part 3.

NO LOCK can be specified in the READ statement for files opened in I-O (update) mode. See "READ Statement" in Part 3.

EXTERNALLY-DESCRIBED-KEY can be specified through the KEY phrase of the START statement. A comparison can be affected by the type of key fields in the record area defined for the file. See "START Statement" in Part 3.

The composite of all operands in an arithmetic statement can have a maximum of 30 digits. See "Arithmetic Statement Operands" in Part 2.

In the CORRESPONDING phrase of an ADD or SUBTRACT statement, the identifiers d1 and d2 can be subordinate to a FILLER item. See "ADD Statement" and "SUBTRACT Statement" in Part 3.

Two active PERFORM statements can have a common exit point. See "PERFORM Statement" in Part 3.

Input files do not need to be sequenced before a sort or merge operation. See "MERGE Statement" and "SORT Statement" in Part 3.

The COMMIT statement can be used to synchronize changes to records in database files under commitment control, while preventing other jobs from accessing or modifying those records until the COMMIT is complete. See "COMMIT Statement" in Part 3.

The ROLLBACK statement can be used to cancel database changes from files under commitment control when the changes should not remain permanent. See "ROLLBACK Statement" in Part 3.

The CALL GDDM statement lets you access the OS/400 graphics routines, graphical data display manager (GDDM), and presentation graphics routines (PGR). See "OS/400 Graphics Support" in Part 3.

The WHEN-COMPILED special register (a 16-character alphanumeric data item) makes available to the object program the date and time compiled constant in the object module at the start of compilation; it is valid only as the sending item in a MOVE statement. See "MOVE Statement" in Part 3.

The ADDRESS OF phrase can be used to refer to the calculated address of a data item. See "ADDRESS OF" in Part 2.

The ADDRESS OF special register returns a pointer containing the address of an item in the Linkage Section of a program. See "ADDRESS OF Special Register" in Part 2.

The LENGTH OF special register eliminates the need to refer to the exact length of a data item. See "LENGTH OF Special Register" in Part 1.

The NULL figurative constant returns a pointer whose address is not valid. See "VALUE Clause" in Part 2.

B.6   COPY Statement—All Divisions

The filename is optional for the format 1 COPY statement. The default filename is QLBLSRC. See "Qualification Rules" in Part 4.

The COPY statement (DD, DDR, DDS, or DDSR option) is used to specify record description entries so that field descriptions for a record format are exactly as defined in DDS. See "Data Division" in Part 2 and "Compiler Directing Statements" in Part 4.

B.7   Transaction Files

The data organization for workstations, programs, devices on a remote system, or any combination of the above, is TRANSACTION. Transaction files have special formats for the file-control entry, file description entry, and the input/output statements. Transaction file considerations are covered in the *COBOL/400 User's Guide*.

Considerations for the TRANSACTION file-control entry include those for:

- The ASSIGN clause
- The ORGANIZATION clause
- The ACCESS MODE clause
- The FILE STATUS clause
- The CONTROL-AREA clause

Considerations for the TRANSACTION file description entry are the same as those for other file description entries.

The ACCEPT statement provides a way of accessing information about a program device when the function name is associated with a mnemonic name of ATTRIBUTE-DATA in the SPECIAL-NAMES paragraph. See "ACCEPT Statement, Format 5 Considerations" in Part 3.

TRANSACTION file considerations for OPEN, CLOSE, READ, WRITE, REWRITE, and USE statements are given under the discussions for the respective statements. A section on transaction files is provided in the *COBOL/400 User's Guide*.

The ACQUIRE statement can be used to acquire a program device for a transaction file. See "ACQUIRE Statement" in Part 3.

The DROP statement can be used to release a program device acquired by a transaction file. See "DROP Statement" in Part 3.

B.8   Compiler-Directing Statements

The *CONTROL or *CBL statement can be used to selectively display or suppress the listing of source code throughout the source program.

The SUPPRESS phrase can be used in the COPY statement to suppress the listing of source statements. See "COPY Statement" in Part 4.

The Format 2 COPY statement can be used to create COBOL data division statements that describe an existing file in the system. See "COPY Statement" in Part 4.

The EJECT, SKIP1, SKIP2, SKIP3, and TITLE statements have been provided to allow formatting control over program listings. See "EJECT Statement," "SKIP/1/2/3 Statements," and "TITLE Statement" in Part 4.

Comment entry may contain the EJECT, SKIP1, SKIP2, SKIP3, or TITLE statement anywhere on the line. See "Optional Paragraphs" in Part 1.

COBOL/400
Compiler Limits

Table C.1 lists the compiler limits supported by the COBOL/400 compiler.

TABLE C.1 Compiler Limits

Language element	COBOL/400 limit
General	
Number of	
Files	99*
REPLACING operands in one COPY	Not defined†
Total length of literal objects	Not defined†
Total storage available for VALUE clauses	Not defined†
Number of characters to identify	
Library name	10
Program name	10
Text name	10
Environment division	
Number of SELECT filenames	99*
Maximum number of buffers (areas) specified in the RESERVE clause	Not defined†
Length of RECORD KEY in one file	2000 bytes
Data Division	
Length of	
Working-storage section group item	3,000,000 bytes‡
Linkage section group item	3,000,000 bytes‡
Elementary item	3,000,000 bytes‡
Maximum block size	32,766 bytes
Maximum record length	32,766 bytes

Language element	COBOL/400 limit
Number of	
FDs (File definition)	99^2
OCCURS levels	7
Levels in data hierarchy	49
SD (Sort definition) filenames	99^2
Number of	
Numeric-edited (data items) character positions	127
Picture character strings	30
Picture replications	3,000,000
OCCURS	
Table size (fixed length)	3,000,000 bytes
Table size (variable length)	32,767 bytes
Table element size	32,767 bytes
Number of ASC/DESC KEY clauses in one table	Not defined†
Total length of ASC/DESC keys in one table	Not defined†
INDEXED BY clauses (per table)	
Pointers in one table	Not defined†
Procedure Division	
Number of	
GO TO procedure name DEPENDING ON	255
IF nesting levels	30
CALL parameters	30
SORT-MERGE input files	31
SORT-MERGE keys	30
SEARCH ALL . . . WHEN relation conditions	Not defined†
UNSTRING delimiters	Not defined†
INSPECT TALLYING identifiers	Not defined†
INSPECT REPLACING identifiers	Not defined†
Length of SORT-MERGE keys	256 bytes

*Limit is 98 if extended ACCEPT or extended DISPLAY statements are coded.

†Limit is determined by system constraints.

‡Limit is 32 767 bytes for the ACCEPT, CANCEL, DISPLAY, EVALUATE, IF, INSPECT, PERFORM, STRING, UNSTRING, and USE statements.

COBOL/400
Syntax Reference

Procedure Division Header

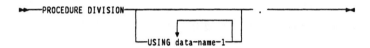

```
►►──PROCEDURE DIVISION──┬─────────────────────────┬──.──────────►◄
                        │      ┌───────────────┐   │
                        └──USING data-name-1────┘
```

Procedure Division — Format 1 — Declaratives Section

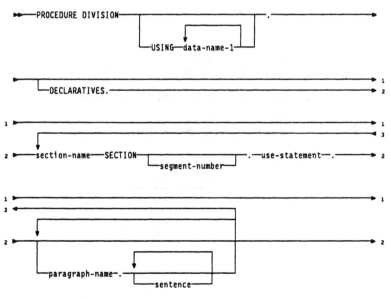

```
►►──PROCEDURE DIVISION──┬─────────────────────────┬──.───────────►
                        │      ┌──────────────┐    │
                        └──USING──data-name-1───┘

►──────────────────────────────────────────────────────────► 1
  └──DECLARATIVES.──────────────────────────────────────────► 2

1 ►────────────────────────────────────────────────────────► 1
  ┌────────────────────────────────────────────────────────◄ 3
2 ►──section-name──SECTION──┬──────────────────┬──.──use-statement──.──► 2
                            └──segment-number──┘

1 ►────────────────────────────────────────────────────────► 1
3 ◄────────────────────────────────────────────┐
         ┌───────────────────────────────────┐ │
2 ►──────┴────────────────────────────────────┘──────────────► 2
         └──paragraph-name──.──┬──────────────┐
                               └──sentence────┘
```

(continued on next page)

413

(continued from previous page)

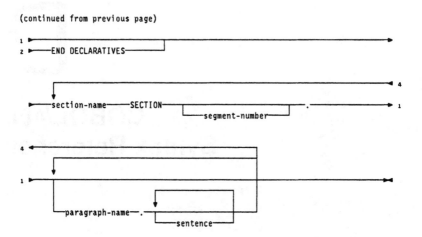

For the syntax of the USE statement, see Chapter 9, "Compiler-Directing Statements" on page 81.

Procedure Division — Format 2

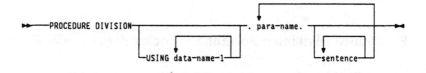

Procedure Division Statements

These statements are presented in alphabetical order.

ACCEPT Statement — Format 1 — Data Transfer

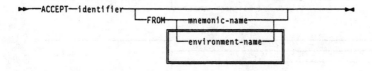

ACCEPT Statement — Format 2 — System Information Transfer

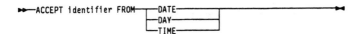

ACCEPT Statement — Format 3 — Feedback

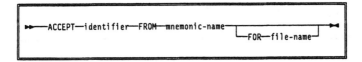

ACCEPT Statement — Format 4 — Local Data Area

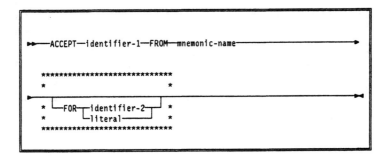

ACCEPT Statement — Format 5 — PIP Data Area

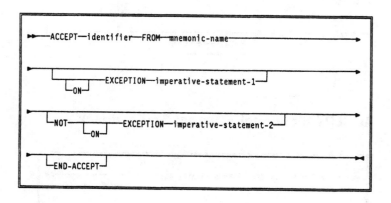

ACCEPT Statement — Format 6 — Attribute Data

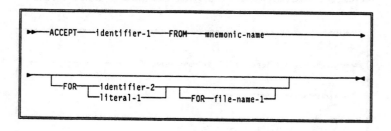

ACCEPT Statement — Format 7 — Work Station I/O

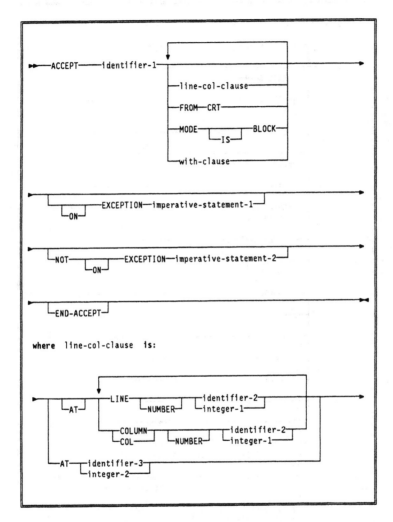

where line-col-clause is:

(continued on next page)

(continued from previous page)

where with-clause **is:**

```
►─WITH─┬─┬─┬─AUTO──────┬──────────────────────────────────────────►
       │ │ └─AUTO-SKIP─┘
       │ │
       │ ├─┬─BELL─┬───────────────────────
       │ │ └─BEEP─┘
       │ │
       │ ├─BLINK───────────────────────────
       │ │
       │ ├─┬─FULL─────────┬────────────────
       │ │ └─LENGTH-CHECK─┘
       │ │
       │ ├─HIGHLIGHT───────────────────────
       │ │
       │ ├─┬─REQUIRED────┬─────────────────
       │ │ └─EMPTY-CHECK─┘
       │ │
       │ ├─REVERSE-VIDEO───────────────────
       │ │
       │ ├─┬─SECURE──┬────────────────────
       │ │ └─NO-ECHO─┘
       │ │
       │ ├─UNDERLINE───────────────────────
       │ │
       │ ├─RIGHT-JUSTIFY───────────────────
       │ │
       │ ├─SPACE-FILL──────────────────────
       │ │
       │ ├─TRAILING-SIGN───────────────────
       │ │
       │ ├─UPDATE──────────────────────────
       │ │
       │ ├─ZERO-FILL───────────────────────
       │ │
       │ │  ***********************************************
       │ │  *                                             *
       │ ├─SIZE─┬────┬─┬─identifier-4─┬────
       │ │  *   └─IS─┘ └─integer-3────┘    *
       │ │  *                                             *
       │ ├─PROMPT─┬──────────────┬─┬─identifier-5─┬─
       │ │  *     └─CHARACTER IS─┘ └─literal──────┘ *
       │ │  *                                             *
       │ ├─┬─FOREGROUND-COLOR──┬─┬────┬─integer-4──
       │ │ *└─FOREGROUND-COLOUR─┘ └─IS─┘            *
       │ │  *                                             *
       │ ├─┬─BACKGROUND-COLOR──┬─┬────┬─integer-5──
       │ │ *└─BACKGROUND-COLOUR─┘ └─IS─┘            *
       │ │  *                                             *
       │ └─LEFT-JUSTIFY───────────────────
       │    *                                             *
       │    ***********************************************
```

ACQUIRE Statement – TRANSACTION File

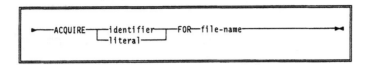

ADD Statement – Format 1

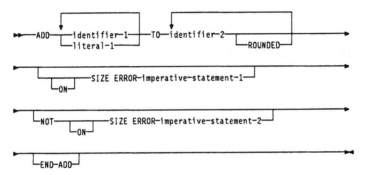

ADD Statement – Format 2 – Giving

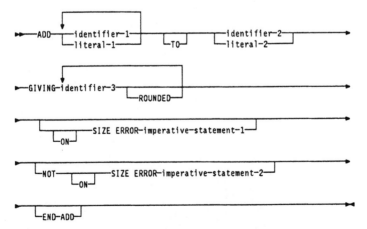

ADD Statement – Format 3 – Corresponding

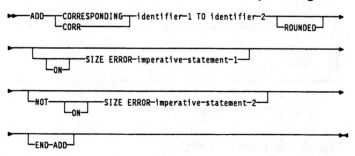

ALTER Statement

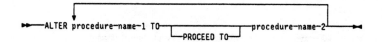

CALL Statement — Format 1

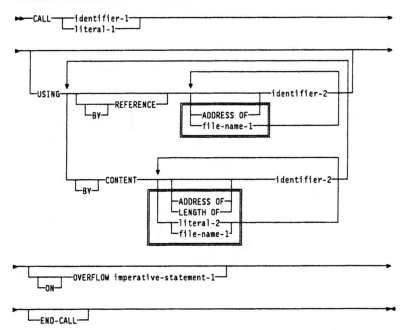

CALL Statement — Format 2

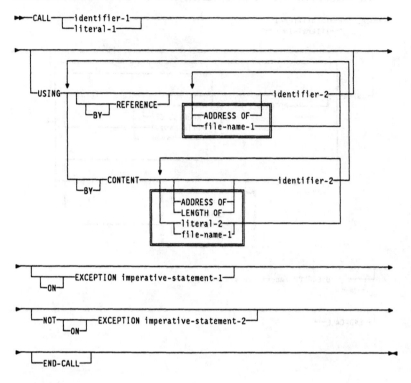

CANCEL Statement

CLOSE Statement — Format 1 — Sequential

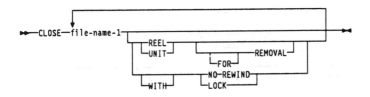

CLOSE Statement — Format 2 — INDEXED and RELATIVE

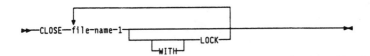

CLOSE Statement — Format 3 — TRANSACTION

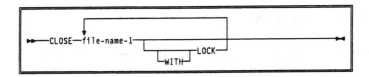

COMMIT Statement

```
►►─COMMIT──────────────────────────────────►◄
```

COMPUTE Statement

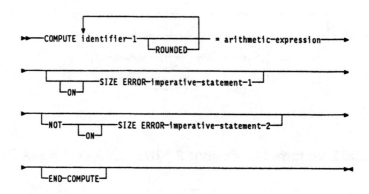

CONTINUE Statement

DELETE Statement

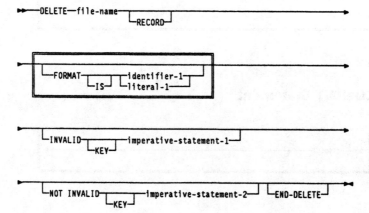

DISPLAY Statement – Format 1

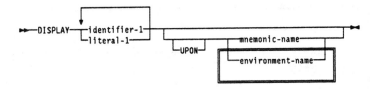

DISPLAY Statement – Format 2 – Local Data Area

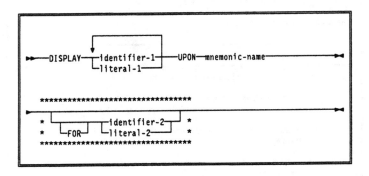

DISPLAY Statement — Format 3 — Work Station I/O

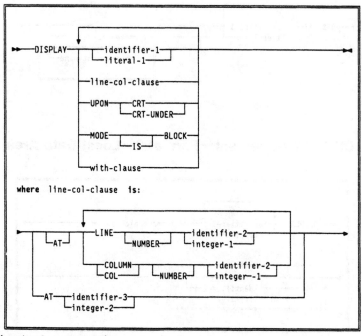

where line-col-clause is:

(continued on next page)

(continued from previous page)

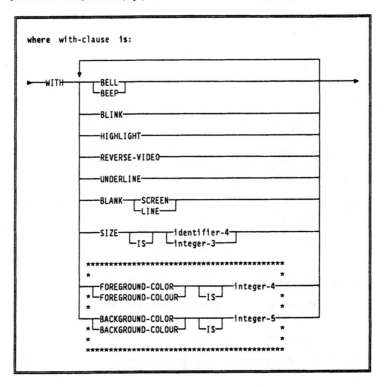

DIVIDE Statement — Format 1

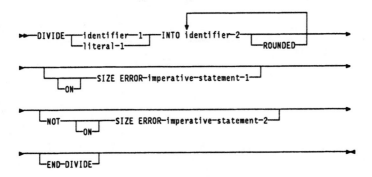

DIVIDE Statement — Format 2 — Giving

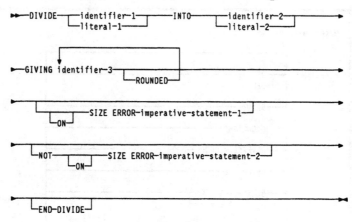

DIVIDE Statement — Format 3 — Giving

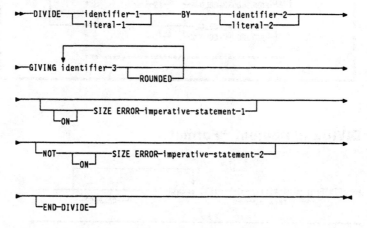

DIVIDE Statement — Format 4 — Giving, Remainder

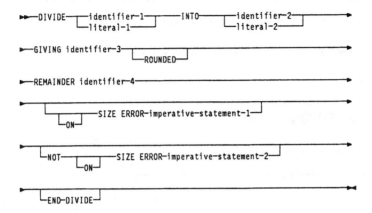

DIVIDE Statement — Format 5 — Giving, Remainder

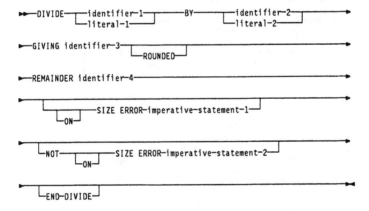

DROP Statement

ENTER Statement

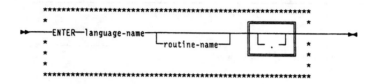

EVALUATE Statement

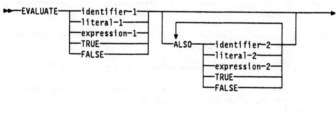

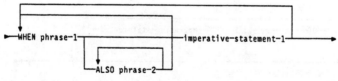

(continued on next page)

(continued from previous page)

```
►─────────────────────────────────────────────────────────────────────◄
  └─WHEN OTHER imperative-statement-2─┘  └─END-EVALUATE─┘
```

where phrase-1 is:

```
►┬─ANY──────────────────────────────────────────────────────────────►
 ├─condition-1──────────────────────────────────────────────────────
 ├─TRUE─────────────────────────────────────────────────────────────
 ├─FALSE────────────────────────────────────────────────────────────
 └─NOT─┬─identifier-3─┬──────────────────────────────────────────────
       ├─literal-3────┤  ┌─THROUGH─┐ ┌─identifier-4─┐
       └─arith-exp-1──┘  └─THRU────┘ ├─literal-4────┤
                                     └─arith-exp-2──┘
```

where phrase-2 is:

```
►┬─ANY──────────────────────────────────────────────────────────────►
 ├─condition-2──────────────────────────────────────────────────────
 ├─TRUE─────────────────────────────────────────────────────────────
 ├─FALSE────────────────────────────────────────────────────────────
 └─NOT─┬─identifier-5─┬──────────────────────────────────────────────
       ├─literal-5────┤  ┌─THROUGH─┐ ┌─identifier-6─┐
       └─arith-exp-3──┘  └─THRU────┘ ├─literal-6────┤
                                     └─arith-exp-4──┘
```

EXIT Statement

```
►►──EXIT───────────────────────────────────────────────────────────◄
```

Note: The EXIT statement must be in a sentence by itself, and that sentence must be the only one in the paragraph.

EXIT PROGRAM Statement

```
►►──EXIT PROGRAM──────────────────────────────────────────────────◄
```

GOBACK Statement

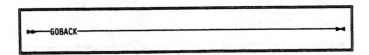

GO TO Statement — Format 1 — Unconditional

GO TO Statement — Format 2 — Conditional

GO TO Statement — Format 3 — Altered

IF Statement

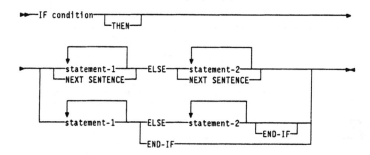

INITIALIZE Statement

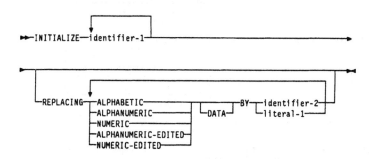

INSPECT Statement – Format 1 – Tallying

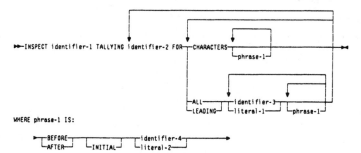

INSPECT Statement — Format 2 — Replacing

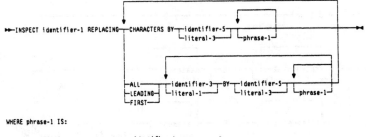

WHERE phrase-1 IS:

INSPECT Statement — Format 3 — Tallying and Replacing

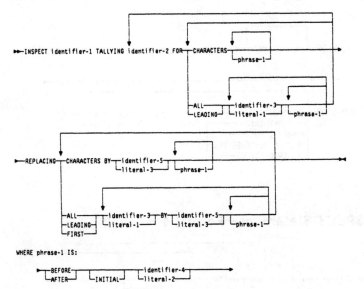

WHERE phrase-1 IS:

INSPECT Statement — Format 4 — Converting

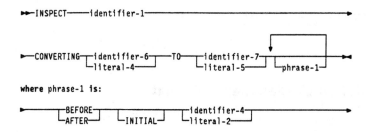

where phrase-1 **is:**

MERGE Statement

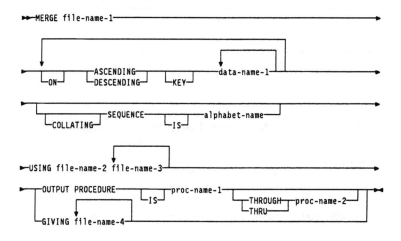

MOVE Statement — Format 1

MOVE Statement — Format 2 — Corresponding

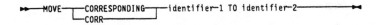

MULTIPLY Statement — Format 1

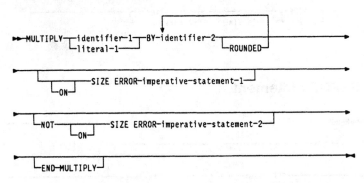

MULTIPLY Statement — Format 2 — Giving

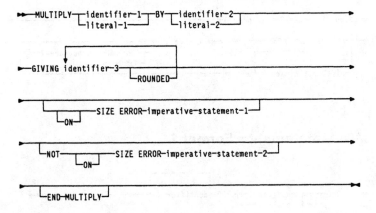

OPEN Statement — Format 1 — Sequential

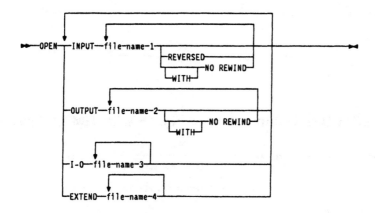

OPEN Statement — Format 2 — Indexed, Relative

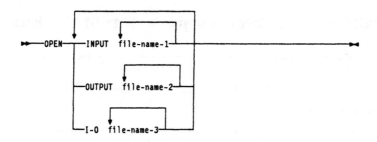

OPEN Statement — Format 3 — TRANSACTION

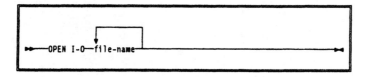

PERFORM Statement — Format 1 — Basic PERFORM

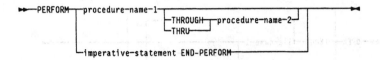

PERFORM Statement — Format 2 — With TIMES Phrase

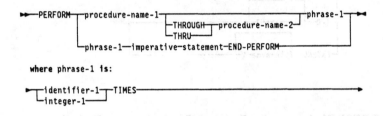

PERFORM Statement — Format 3 — With UNTIL Phrase

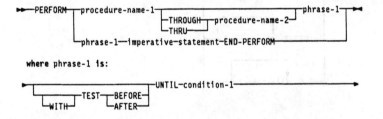

PERFORM Statement – Format 4 – Varying Index or Identifier

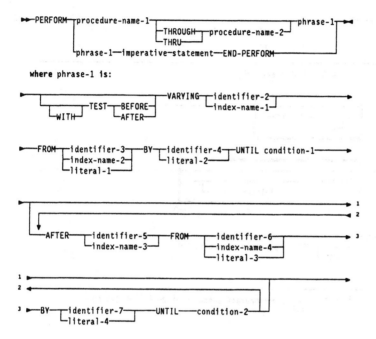

where phrase-1 is:

READ Statement — Format 1 — Sequential Retrieval using SEQUENTIAL Access

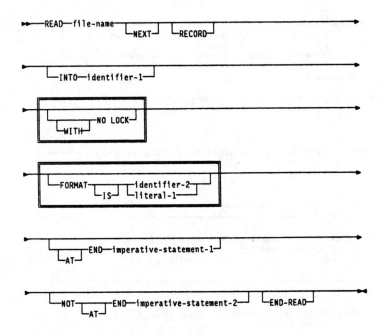

READ Statement — Format 2 — Sequential Retrieval using DYNAMIC Access

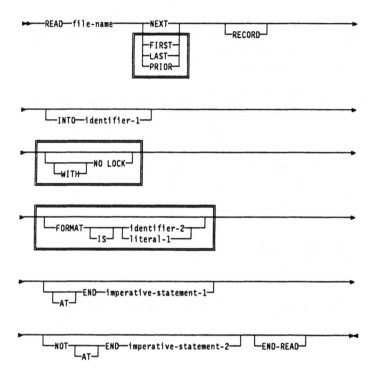

READ Statement — Format 3 — Random Retrieval

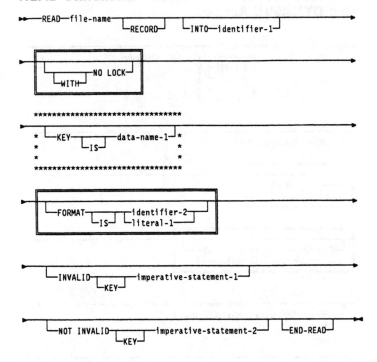

READ Statement — Format 4 — TRANSACTION (Nonsubfile)

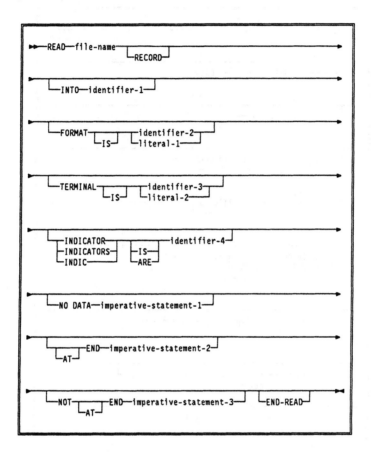

READ Statement – Format 5 – TRANSACTION (Subfile)

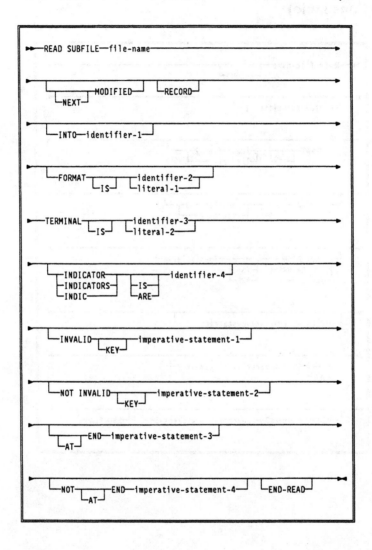

RELEASE Statement

```
►►──RELEASE─record─name──┬──────────────────────┬──────────────────────►◄
                         └─FROM identifier──────┘
```

RETURN Statement

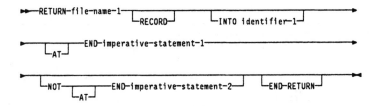

```
►►──RETURN─file─name─1──┬──────────┬──────┬─────────────────────┬───────►
                        └─RECORD───┘      └─INTO identifier─1────┘

►──┬──────┬──END─imperative─statement─1──────────────────────────────────►
   └─AT──┘

►──┬─────────────────────────────────────────────┬──┬──────────────┬──►◄
   └─NOT──┬──────┬──END─imperative─statement─2────┘  └─END─RETURN───┘
          └─AT──┘
```

REWRITE Statement ─ Format 1

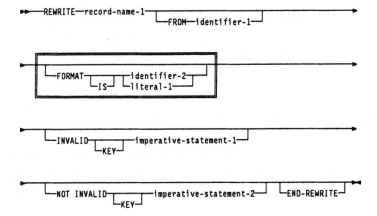

```
►►──REWRITE─record─name─1──┬────────────────────────┬──────────────────►
                          └─FROM─identifier─1───────┘

►──┌─────────────────────────────────────────┐──────────────────────────►
   │  ┌─FORMAT─┬──────┬──┬─identifier─2─┬───┐ │
   │  │        └─IS───┘  └─literal─1────┘   │ │
   └──┴───────────────────────────────────────┘

►──┬──────────────────────────────────────────────┬─────────────────────►
   └─INVALID─┬──────┬──imperative─statement─1──────┘
             └─KEY──┘

►──┬──────────────────────────────────────────────────┬──┬──────────────┬──►◄
   └─NOT INVALID─┬──────┬──imperative─statement─2──────┘  └─END─REWRITE──┘
                 └─KEY──┘
```

REWRITE Statement – Format 2 – TRANSACTION (Subfile)

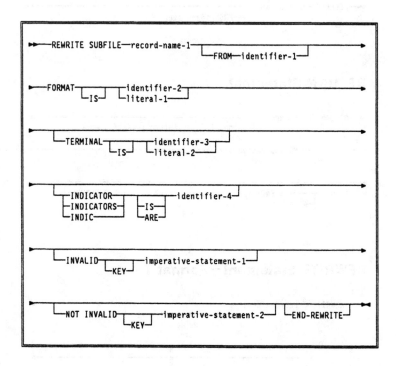

ROLLBACK Statement

SEARCH Statement — Format 1 — Serial Search

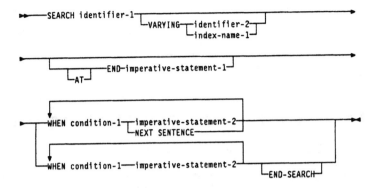

SEARCH Statement — Format 2 — Binary Search

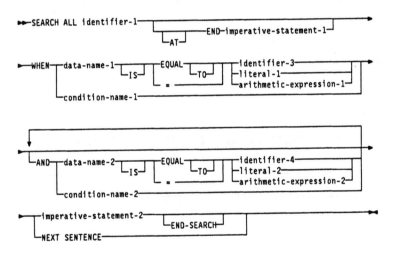

SET Statement — Format 1 — TO Phrase

SET Statement — Format 2 — UP BY/DOWN BY Phrase

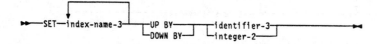

SET Statement — Format 3 — ON/OFF Phrase

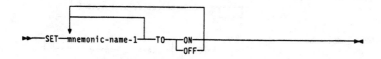

SET Statement — Format 4 — TO TRUE Phrase

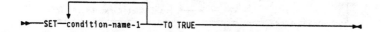

SET Statement — Format 5 — Pointer Data Item Phrase

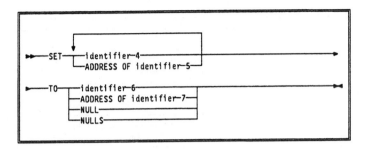

SORT Statement

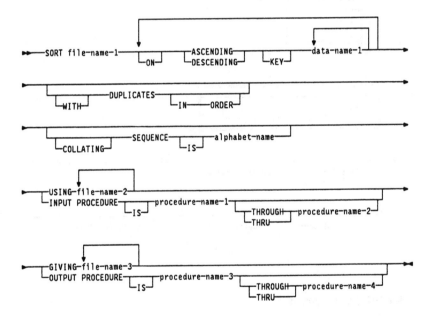

START Statement

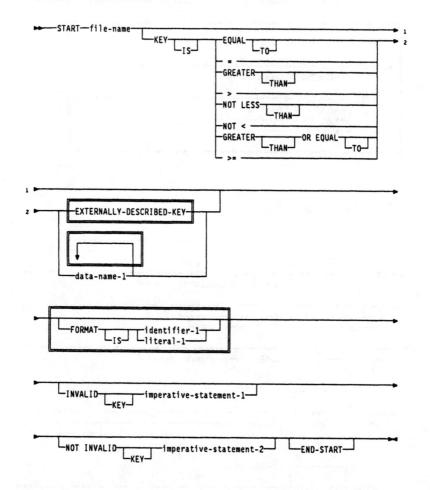

STOP Statement

STRING Statement

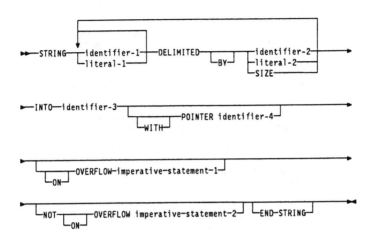

SUBTRACT Statement — Format 1

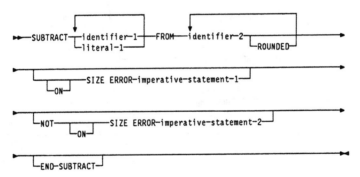

SUBTRACT Statement – Format 2 – Giving

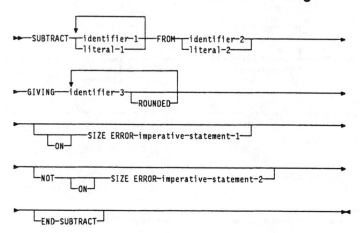

SUBTRACT Statement – Format 3 – Corresponding

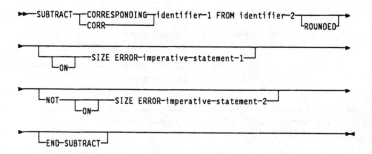

UNSTRING Statement

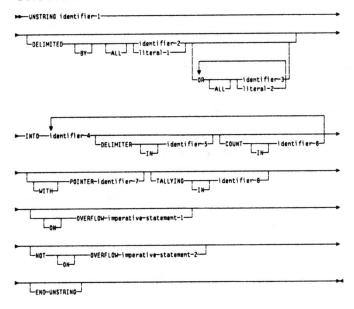

WRITE Statement — Format 1 — Sequential

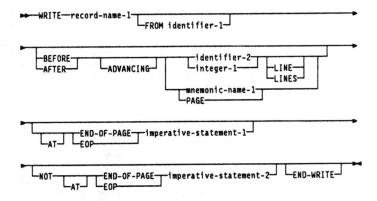

WRITE Statement — Format 2 — Indexed, and Relative

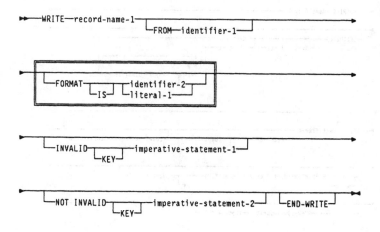

WRITE Statement — Format 3 — FORMATFILE

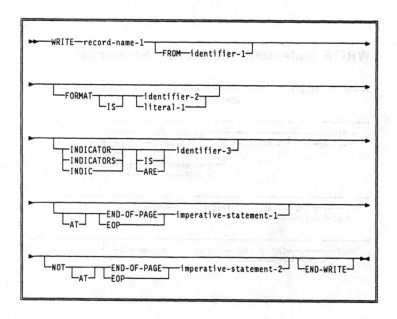

WRITE Statement — Format 4 — TRANSACTION (Nonsubfile)

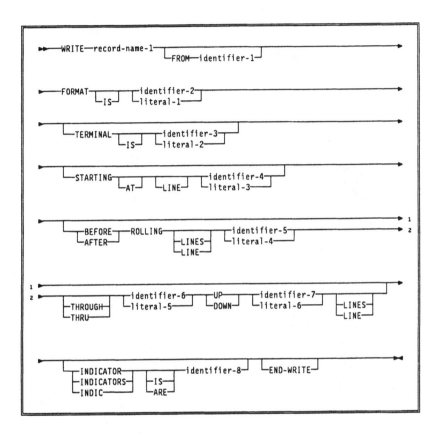

EBCDIC and ASCII
Collating Sequences

The ascending collating sequences for both the Extended Binary Coded Decimal Interchange Code (EBCDIC) and American National Standard Code for Information Interchange (ASCII) character sets are shown in this appendix. In addition to the symbol and meaning for each character, the ordinal number (beginning with 1), decimal representation, and hexadecimal representation are given.

E.1 EBCDIC Collating Sequence

TABLE E.1

Ordinal number	Symbol	Meaning	Decimal representation	Hex representation
65	ƀ	Space	64	40
.				
.				
.				
75	¢	Cent sign	74	4A
76	.	Period, decimal point	75	4B
77	<	Less than sign	76	4C
78	(	Left parenthesis	77	4D
79	+	Plus sign	78	4E
80	|	Vertical bar, logical OR	79	4F
81	&	Ampersand	80	50
.				
.				
.				
91	!	Exclamation point	90	5A
92	$	Dollar sign	91	5B
93	*	Asterisk	92	5C

Ordinal number	Symbol	Meaning	Decimal representation	Hex representation
94	)	Right parenthesis	93	5D
95	;	Semicolon	94	5E
96	¬	Logical NOT	95	5F
97	–	Minus, hyphen	96	60
98	/	Slash	97	61
.				
.				
.				
108	, Comma	107	6B	
109	%	Percent sign	108	6C
110	_	Underscore	109	6D
111	>	Greater than sign	110	6E
112	?	Question mark	111	6F
.				
.				
.				
123	:	Colon	122	7A
124	#	Number sign, pound sign	123	7B
125	@	At sign, circa sign	124	7C
126	'	Apostrophe, prime sign	125	7D
127	=	Equal sign	126	7E
128	"	Quotation marks	127	7F
.				
.				
.				
130	a		129	81
131	b		130	82
132	c		131	83
133	d		132	84
134	e		133	85
135	f		134	86
136	g		135	87
137	h		136	88
138	i		137	89
.				
.				
.				
146	j		145	91
147	k		146	92
148	l		147	93
149	m		148	94
150	n		149	95
151	o		150	96
152	p		151	97
153	q		152	98
154	r		153	99
.				
.				
.				
163	s		162	A2
164	t		163	A3
165	u		164	A4
166	v		165	A5

Ordinal number	Symbol	Meaning	Decimal representation	Hex representation
167	w		166	A6
168	x		167	A7
169	y		168	A8
170	z		169	A9
.				
.				
.				
194	A		193	C1
195	B		194	C2
196	C		195	C3
197	D		196	C4
198	E		197	C5
199	F		198	C6
200	G		199	C7
201	H		200	C8
202	I		201	C9
.				
.				
.				
210	J		209	D1
211	K		210	D2
212	L		211	D3
213	M		212	D4
214	N		213	D5
215	O		214	D6
216	P		215	D7
217	Q		216	D8
218	R		217	D9
.				
.				
.				
227	S		226	E2
228	T		227	E3
229	U		228	E4
230	V		229	E5
231	W		230	E6
232	X		231	E7
233	Y		232	E8
234	Z		233	E9
.				
.				
.				
241	0		240	F0
242	1		241	F1
243	2		242	F2
244	3		243	F3
245	4		244	F4
246	5		245	F5
247	6		246	F6
248	7		247	F7
249	8		248	F8
250	9		249	F9

E.2 ASCII Collating Sequence

TABLE E.2

Ordinal number	Symbol	Meaning	Decimal representation	Hex representation
1		Null	0	0
.				
.				
.				
33	ƀ	Space	32	20
34	!	Exclamation point	33	21
35	"	Quotation mark	34	22
36	#	Number sign	35	23
37	$	Dollar sign	36	24
38	%	Percent sign	37	25
39	&	Ampersand	38	26
40	'	Apostrophe, prime sign	39	27
41	(	Left parenthesis	40	28
42	)	Right parenthesis	41	29
43	*	Asterisk	42	2A
44	+	Plus sign	43	2B
45	, Comma	44		2C
46	-	Hyphen, minus	45	2D
47	.	Period, decimal point	46	2E
48	/	Slash	47	2F
49	0		48	30
50	1		49	31
51	2		50	32
52	3		51	33
53	4		52	34
54	5		53	35
55	6		54	36
56	7		55	37
57	8		56	38
58	9		57	39
59	:	Colon	58	3A
60	;	Semicolon	59	3B
61	<	Less than sign	60	3C
62	=	Equal sign	61	3D
63	>	Greater than sign	62	3E
64	?	Question mark	63	3F
65	@	At sign, circa sign	64	40
66	A		65	41
67	B		66	42
68	C		67	43
69	D		68	44
70	E		69	45
71	F		70	46
72	G		71	47
73	H		72	48
74	I		73	49
75	J		74	4A
76	K		75	4B

Ordinal number	Symbol	Meaning	Decimal representation	Hex representation
77	L		76	4C
78	M		77	4D
79	N		78	4E
80	O		79	4F
81	P		80	50
82	Q		81	51
83	R		82	52
84	S		83	53
85	T		84	54
86	U		85	55
87	V		86	56
88	W		87	57
89	X		88	58
90	Y		89	59
91	Z		90	5A
92	[	Left bracket	91	5B
93	\	Reverse slash	92	5C
94	]	Right bracket	93	5D
95	^	Circumflex accent, caret	94	5E
96	_	Underscore	95	5F
97	`	Grave accent, right prime	96	60
98	a		97	61
99	b		98	62
100	c		99	63
101	d		100	64
102	e		101	65
103	f		102	66
104	g		103	67
105	h		104	68
106	i		105	69
107	j		106	6A
108	k		107	6B
109	l		108	6C
110	m		109	6D
111	n		110	6E
112	o		111	6F
113	p		112	70
114	q		113	71
115	r		114	72
116	s		115	73
117	t		116	74
118	u		117	75
119	v		118	76
120	w		119	77
121	x		120	78
122	y		121	79
123	z		122	7A
124	{	Left brace	123	7B
125			Split vertical bar	124	7C
126	}	Right brace	125	7D
127	~	Tilde	126	7E

COBOL/400 Reserved Words

The following key identifies the reserved words in Version 2 Release 2 of the COBOL/400 language:

Blank A COBOL/400 reserved word from the 1985 ANSI Standards.

(1) A COBOL/400 reserved word that is an IBM extension of the 1985 ANSI Standard.

(2) A COBOL reserved word from the 1985 (revised 1989) ANSI Standard that is not used by the COBOL/400 compiler. These words should not be used if compatibility is important to an installation. If used, a diagnostic message will be issued.

(3) A CODASYL COBOL reserved word that is not in the 1985 ANSI Standard and is not supported by the COBOL/400 compiler. If used, a diagnostic message will be issued.

(4) An SAA COBOL reserved word that is not in the 1985 ANSI Standard and is not supported by the COBOL/400 compiler. If used, a diagnostic message will be issued.

(5) A COBOL reserved word that is supported by the COBOL/400 compiler when *EXTACCDSP is specified in the CRTCBLPGM CL command, or when EXTACCDSP is used in the PROCESS statement.

(6) A COBOL reserved word from the 1985 ANSI standard that is not used by the COBOL/400 compiler unless *EXTACCDSP or EXTACCDSP is specified. If the word is used in the absence of these options, a diagnostic message will be issued.

ACCEPT

ACCESS

ACQUIRE (1)

ADD

ADDRESS (1)

ADVANCING

AFTER

ALL

ALPHABET

ALPHABETIC

ALPHABETIC-LOWER

ALPHABETIC-UPPER

ALPHANUMERIC

ALPHANUMERIC-EDITED

ALSO

ALTER

ALTERNATE

AND

ANY (2)

ARE

AREA

AREAS

ARITHMETIC (3)

ASCENDING

ASSIGN

AT

AUTHOR

AUTO (5)

AUTO-SKIP (5)

BACKGROUND-COLOR (5)

BACKGROUND-COLOUR (5)

B-AND (3)

BEEP (5)

BEFORE

BELL (5)

B-EXOR (3)

BINARY

BIT (3)

BITS (3)

BLANK

B-LESS (3)

BLINK (5)

BLOCK

B-NOT (3)

BOOLEAN (3)

B-OR (3)

BOTTOM

BY

CALL

CANCEL

CD (2)

CF (2)

CH (2)

CHARACTER

CHARACTERS

CLASS

CLOCK-UNITS (2)

CLOSE

COBOL (2)

CODE (2)

CODE-SET

COL (5)

COLLATING

COLUMN (5) (6)

COMMA

COMMIT (1)

COMMITMENT (1)

COMMON (2)

COMMUNICATION (2)

COMP

COMP-3

COMP-4

COMPUTATIONAL

COMPUTATIONAL-3

COMPUTATIONAL-4

COMPUTE

CONFIGURATION

CONNECT (3)

CONTAINED (3)

CONTAINS

CONTENT

CONTINUE

CONTROL

CONTROL-AREA (1)

CONTROLS

CONVERSION (3)

CONVERTING

COPY

CORR

CORRESPONDING

COUNT

CRT (5)

CRT-UNDER (5)

CURRENCY

CURRENT (3)

CURSOR (5)

DATA

DATE

DATE-COMPILED

DATE-WRITTEN

DAY

DAY-OF-WEEK (2)

DB (3)

DB-ACCESS-CONTROL-KEY (3)

DB-DATA-NAME (3)

DB-EXCEPTION (3)

DB-FORMAT-NAME (1)

DB-RECORD-NAME (3)

DB-SET-NAME (3)

DB-STATUS (3)

DBCS (4)

DE (2)

DEBUG-CONTENTS

DEBUG-ITEM

DEBUG-LINE

DEBUG-NAME

DEBUG-SUB-1

DEBUG-SUB-2

DEBUG-SUB-3

DEBUGGING

DECIMAL-POINT

DECLARATIVES

DEFAULT (3)

DELETE

DELIMITED

DELIMITER

DEPENDING

DESCENDING

DESTINATION (2)

DETAIL (2)

DISABLE (2)

DISCONNECT (3)

DISPLAY

DISPLAY-1 (3)

DISPLAY-n (3)

DIVIDE

DIVISION

DOWN

DROP (1)

DUPLICATE (3)

DUPLICATES

DYNAMIC

EGI (2)

EJECT (1)

ELSE

EMI (2)

EMPTY-CHECK (5)

ENABLE (2)

END

END-ACCEPT (1)

END-ADD

END-CALL

END-COMPUTE

END-DELETE

END-DIVIDE

END-EVALUATE

END-IF

END-MULTIPLY

END-OF-PAGE

END-PERFORM

END-READ

END-RECEIVE (2)

END-RETURN

END-REWRITE

END-SEARCH

END-START

END-STRING

END-SUBTRACT

END-UNSTRING

END-WRITE

ENTER

ENVIRONMENT

EOP

EQUAL

EQUALS (2)

ERASE (3)

ERROR

ESI (2)

EVALUATE

EVERY

EXCEEDS (3)

EXCEPTION

EXCLUSIVE (3)

EXIT

EXOR (3)

EXTEND

EXTERNAL (2)

EXTERNALLY-DESCRIBED-KEY(1)

FALSE (2)

FD

FETCH (3)

FILE

FILE-CONTROL

FILES (3)

FILLER

FINAL (2)

FIND (3)

FINISH (3)

FIRST

FOOTING

FOR

FOREGROUND-COLOR (5)

FOREGROUND-COLOUR (5)

FORMAT (1)

FREE (3)

FROM

FULL (5)

FUNCTION (2)

GENERATE

GET (3)

GIVING

GLOBAL (2)

GO

GOBACK (1)

GREATER

GROUP (2)

HEADING (2)

HIGHLIGHT (5)

HIGH VALUE

HIGH-VALUES

I-O

I-O-CONTROL

ID (1)

IDENTIFICATION

IF

IN

INDEX

INDEXED

INDEX-N (3)

INDIC (1)

INDICATE

INDICATOR

INDICATORS (1)

INITIAL

INITIALIZE

INITIATE

INPUT

INPUT-OUTPUT

INSPECT

INSTALLATION

INTO

INVALID

IS

JUST

JUSTIFIED

KEEP (3)

KEY

LABEL

LAST

LD (3)

LEADING

LEFT

LEFT-JUSTIFY (5)

LENGTH

LENGTH-CHECK (5)

LESS

LIKE (1)

LIMIT (2)

LIMITS (2)

LINAGE

LINAGE-COUNTER

LINE

LINE-COUNTER (2)

LINES

LINKAGE

LOCALLY (3)

LOCK

LOW-VALUE

LOW-VALUES

MEMBER (3)

MEMORY

MERGE

MESSAGE (2)

MODE

MODIFIED (1)

MODIFY (3)

MODULES

MOVE

MULTIPLE

MULTIPLY

NATIVE

NEGATIVE

NEXT

NO

NO-ECHO (5)

NONE (3)

NOT

NULL (1)

NULLS (1)

NUMBER (5) (6)

NUMERIC

NUMERIC-EDITED

OBJECT-COMPUTER

OCCURS

OF

OFF

OMITTED

ON

ONLY (3)

OPEN

OPTIONAL

OR

ORDER

ORGANIZATION

OTHER (2)

OUTPUT

OVERFLOW

OWNER (3)

PACKED-DECIMAL

PADDING (2)

PAGE

PAGE-COUNTER (2)

PERFORM

PF (2)

PH (2)

PIC

PICTURE

PLUS (2)

POINTER

POSITION

POSITIVE

PRESENT (3)

PRINTING

PRIOR (1)

PROCEDURE

PROCEDURES

PROCEED

PROCESS (1)

PROGRAM

PROGRAM-ID

PROMPT (5)

PROTECTED (3)

PURGE (2)

QUEUE (2)

QUOTE

QUOTES

RANDOM

RD (2)

READ

READY (3)

REALM (3)

RECEIVE (2)

RECONNECT (3)

RECORD

RECORD-NAME (3)

RECORDS

REDEFINES

REEL

REFERENCE

REFERENCE-MONITOR (3)

REFERENCES

RELATION (3)

RELATIVE

RELEASE

REMAINDER

REMOVAL

RENAMES

REPEATED (3)

REPLACE (2)

REPLACING

REPORT (2)

REPORTING (2)

REPORTS (2)

REQUIRED (5)

RERUN

RESERVE

RESET (2)

RETAINING (3)

RETRIEVAL (3)

RETURN

RETURN-CODE (4)

REVERSED

REVERSE-VIDEO (5)

REWIND

REWRITE

RD (2)

RF (2)

RH (2)

RIGHT

RIGHT-JUSTIFY (5)

ROLLBACK (1)

ROLLING (1)

ROUNDED

RUN

SAME

SCREEN (5)

SD

SEARCH

SECTION

SECURE (5)

SECURITY

SEGMENT (2)

SEGMENT-LIMIT

SELECT

SEND (2)

SENTENCE

SEPARATE

SEQUENCE

SEQUENTIAL

SET

SHARED (3)

SIGN

SIZE

SKIP1 (1)

SKIP2 (1)

SKIP3 (1)

SORT

SORT-MERGE

SORT-RETURN (4)

SOURCE (2)

SOURCE-COMPUTER

SPACE

SPACE-FILL (5)

SPACES

SPECIAL-NAMES

STANDARD

STANDARD-1

STANDARD-2

START

STARTING (1)

STATUS

STOP

STORE (3)

STRING

SUB-QUEUE-1 (2)

SUB-QUEUE-2 (2)

SUB-QUEUE-3 (2)

SUB-SCHEMA (3)

SUBFILE (1)

SUBTRACT

SUM (2)

SUPPRESS

SYMBOLIC (2)

SYNC

SYNCHRONIZED

TABLE (2)

TALLYING

TAPE

TENANT (3)

TERMINAL

TERMINATE (2)

TEST

TEXT (2)

THAN

THEN

THROUGH

THRU

TIME

TIMES

TITLE (1)

TO

TOP

TRAILING

TRAILING-SIGN (5)

TRANSACTION (1)

TRUE

TYPE (2)

UNDERLINE (5)

UNEQUAL (3)

UNIT

UNSTRING

UNTIL	WORDS
UP	WORKING-STORAGE
UPDATE (5)	WRITE
UPON	ZERO
USAGE	ZEROES
USAGE-MODE (3)	ZERO-FILL (5)
USE	ZEROS
USING	<
VALID (3)	<=
VALIDATE (3)	+
VALUE	*
VALUES	**
VARYING	-
WAIT (3)	/
WHEN-COMPILED (1)	>
WITH	>=
WITHIN (3)	=

File Status Key Values and Meanings

File Status Keys and their Corresponding Return Codes

Table 5. File Status Keys and their Corresponding Return Codes

File Status Key	Major Return Code	Minor Return Code	Explanation
00	00	XX	Normal completion (operation was successful).
	03	XX (except 09)	No data received.
	08	00	Acquire operation attempted to acquire an already active session or device.
	09	00	File has been dynamically created for OPEN OUTPUT. See the description of GENOPT(*CRTF) in the *COBOL/400 User's Guide*.
10	11	00	Read-from-invited-program-device rejected; no invites outstanding.
30	80	XX	Permanent system error. The session has been ended.
92	81	XX	Permanent device or session error.
9A	02	XX	Job being cancelled (controlled).
	03	09	
9C	82	XX	Open or acquire failed; session was not started.
9G	34	XX	Output exception to device or session.
9I	04	XX	Output exception to device or session.
9K	83	E0	Format not found.
9N	83	XX (except E0)	Session error. Session is still active.

File Status Key Values and Meanings

Table 6 (Page 1 of 10). File Status Key Values and Meanings

High Order Digit	Meaning	Low Order Digit	Meaning
0	Successful Completion	0	No further information
		2	The READ statement was successfully executed, but a duplicate key was detected. That is, the key value for the current key of reference was equal to the value of the key in the next record.
		4	A READ statement was successfully executed, but the length of the record being processed did not conform to the fixed file attributes for that file.
		5	An OPEN statement is successfully executed, but the referenced optional file is not present at the time the OPEN statement is executed. If the open mode is I-O or EXTEND, the file has been created.
		7	For a CLOSE statement with the NO REWIND, REEL/UNIT, or FOR REMOVAL phrase or for an OPEN statement with the NO REWIND phrase, the referenced file was on a non-reel/unit medium.
		M	Last record written to a subfile. CPF5003
		P	The file has been opened successfully, but it contains null-capable fields.
		Q	A CLOSE statement for a sequentially-processed relative file was successfully executed. The file was created with the *INZDLT and *NOMAX options, so its boundary has been set to the number of records written.

Table 6 (Page 2 of 10). File Status Key Values and Meanings

High Order Digit	Meaning	Low Order Digit	Meaning
1	At end conditions	0	A sequential READ statement was attempted and no next logical record existed in the file because the end of the file had been reached (no invites outstanding) CPF4740, CPF5001, CPF5025.
		2	⌐――― IBM Extension ―――⌐ No modified subfile record found. CPF5037 ∟― End of IBM Extension ―――⌟
		4	A sequential READ statement was attempted for a relative file and the number of significant digits in the relative record number was larger than the size of the relative key data item described for the file.

Table 6 (Page 3 of 10). File Status Key Values and Meanings

High Order Digit	Meaning	Low Order Digit	Meaning
2	Invalid Key	1	A sequence error exists for a sequentially accessed indexed file. The prime record key value has been changed by the program between the successful execution of a READ statement and the execution of the next REWRITE statement for that file, or the ascending requirements for successive record key values were violated. Alternatively, the program has changed the record key value between a successful READ and subsequent REWRITE or DELETE operation on a randomly or dynamically-accessed file with duplicate keys.
		2	An attempt was made to write a record that would create a duplicate key in a relative file; or an attempt was made to write or rewrite a record that would create a duplicate prime record key in an indexed file. CPF4759, CPF5008, CPF5026, CPF5034, CPF5084, CPF5085.
		3	An attempt was made to randomly access a record that does not exist in the file. CPF5001, CPF5006, CPF5013, CPF5020, CPF5025.
		4	An attempt was made to write beyond the externally defined boundaries of a relative or indexed file. Or, a sequential WRITE statement was attempted for a relative file and the number of significant digits in the relative record number was larger than the size of the relative record key data item described for the file. CPF5006, CPF5018, CPF5021, CPF5043, CPF5272.

Table 6 (Page 4 of 10). File Status Key Values and Meanings

High Order Digit	Meaning	Low Order Digit	Meaning
3	Permanent error condition	0	No further information CPF4192, CPF5101, CPF5102, CPF5129, CPF5030, CPF5143.
		4	A permanent error exists because of a boundary violation; an attempt was made to write beyond the externally-defined boundaries of a sequential file. CPF5116, CPF5018, CPF5272 if organization is sequential.
		5	An OPEN statement with the INPUT, I-O, or EXTEND phrase was attempted on a non-optional file that was not present. CPF4101, CPF4102, CPF4103, CPF4207, CPF9812.
		7	An OPEN statement was attempted on a file that would not support the open mode specified in the OPEN statement. Possible violations are: 1. The EXTEND or OUTPUT phrase was specified but the file would not support write operations. 2. The I-O phrase was specified but the file would not support the input and output operations permitted. 3. The INPUT phrase was specified but the file would not support read operations. CPF4194.
		8	An OPEN statement was attempted on a file previously closed with lock.
		9	The OPEN statement was unsuccessful because a conflict was detected between the fixed file attributes and the attributes specified for that file in the program. Level check error. CPF4131.

Table 6 (Page 5 of 10). File Status Key Values and Meanings

High Order Digit	Meaning	Low Order Digit	Meaning
4	Logic error condition	1	An OPEN statement was attempted for a file in the open mode.
		2	A CLOSE statement was attempted for a file not in the open mode.
		3	For a sequential file in the sequential access mode, the last input-output statement executed for the associated file prior to the execution of a REWRITE statement was not a successfully executed READ statement. For relative and indexed files in the sequential access mode, the last input-output statement executed for the file prior to the execution of a DELETE or REWRITE statement was not a successfully executed READ statement.
		4	A boundary violation exists because an attempt was made to rewrite a record to a file and the record was not the same size as the record being replaced.

High Order Digit	Meaning	Low Order Digit	Meaning
Table 6 (Page 6 of 10). File Status Key Values and Meanings			
4	Logic error condition	6	A sequential READ statement was attempted on a file open in the input or I-O mode and no valid next record had been established because the preceding START statement was unsuccessful, or the preceding READ statement was unsuccessful or caused an at end condition. CPF5001, CPF5025, CPF5183.
		7	The execution of a READ or START statement was attempted on a file not open in the input or I-O mode.
		8	The execution of a WRITE statement was attempted on a sequential file not open in the output, or extend mode. The execution of a WRITE statement was attempted on an indexed or relative file not open in the I-O, output, or extend mode.
		9	The execution of a DELETE or REWRITE statement was attempted on a file not open in the I-O mode.

Table 6 (Page 7 of 10). File Status Key Values and Meanings

High Order Digit	Meaning	Low Order Digit	Meaning
9	Other Errors	0	Other errors: • File not found • Member not found • Unexpected I-O exceptions CPF4101, CPF4102, CPF4103 if a USE is applicable for the file (on OPEN OUTPUT, non-optional file). The following exceptions are monitored generically: CPF4101 through CPF4399 CPF4501 through CPF4699 CPF4701 through CPF4899 CPF5001 through CPF5099 CPF5101 through CPF5399 CPF5501 through CPF5699 These exceptions are caught, and FILE STATUS is set to 90. **With Standard Error Handling:** If there is an applicable file status clause (but not an applicable USE procedure), the file status is updated, and control returns to the program. In the absence of a file status clause, USE procedure, AT END clause, or INVALID KEY clause to handle the error, a run-time message is issued, giving you the option to end or return to the program. **Without Standard Error Handling:** If a USE procedure applies, it runs. Otherwise, the program ends and gives the operator the exception and the option to cancel, take a partial dump, or take a full dump.
		1	Undefined or unauthorized access type CPF2207, CPF4104, CPF4236, CPF5057, CPF5109, CPF5134, CPF5279.

High Order Digit	Meaning	Low Order Digit	Meaning
9	Other errors	2	Logic error: • File locked • File already open • I-O to closed file • READ after end of file • CLOSE on unopened file CPF4106, CPF4132, CPF4740, CPF5013, CPF5067, CPF5070, CPF5119, CPF5145, CPF5146, CPF5149, CPF5176, CPF5209.
		4	No file position indicator REWRITE/DELETE when *not* sequential access, and last operation was not a successful READ.
		5	Invalid or incomplete file information (1) Duplicate keys specified in COBOL program. The file has been successfully OPENed, but indexed database file created with unique key; or (2) Duplicate keys not specified in COBOL program, and indexed database file created allowing duplicate keys.
		9	Undefined (display or ICF).

Table 6 (Page 8 of 10). File Status Key Values and Meanings

Table 6 (Page 9 of 10). File Status Key Values and Meanings

High Order Digit	Meaning	Low Order Digit	Meaning
9	Other Errors	A	Job ended in a controlled manner by CL command ENDJOB, PWRDWNSYS, ENDSYS, or ENDSBS CPF4741. Escape message sent during an accept input operation, READ from invited program device (multiple device listings only).
		C	Acquire failed; session was not started.
		D	Record is locked CPF5027, CPF5032.
		G	Output exception to device or session.
		H	ACQUIRE operation failed. Resource owned by another program, or unavailable. (9H is the result when an ACQUIRE operation causes any of the OS/400 exceptions monitored for 90, or 9N to occur.)
		I	WRITE operation failed CPF4702, CPF4737, CPF5052, CPF5076.
		K	Invalid format-name; format not found CPF5022, CPF5023, CPF5053, CPF5054, CPF5121, CPF5152, CPF5153, CPF5186, CPF5187.
		M	Last record written to subfile. CPF5003. To convert file status 9M to 0M, use PROCESS statement option FS9MTO0M.

Table 6 (Page 10 of 10). File Status Key Values and Meanings

High Order Digit	Meaning	Low Order Digit	Meaning
9	Other Errors	N	Temporary (potentially recoverable) hardware I-O error. (Error during communication session.) CPF4145, CPF4146, CPF4193, CPF4229, CPF4291, CPF4299, CPF4354, CPF4526, CPF4542, CPF4577, CPF4592, CPF4602, CPF4603, CPF4611, CPF4612, CPF4616, CPF4617, CPF4622, CPF4623, CPF4624, CPF4625, CPF4628, CPF4629, CPF4630, CPF4631, CPF4632, CPF4705, CPF5107, CPF5128, CPF5166, CPF5198, CPF5280, CPF5282, CPF5287, CPF5293, CPF5352, CPF5353, CPF5517, CPF5524, CPF5529, CPF5530, CPF5532, CPF5533.
		P	OPEN failed because file cannot be placed under commitment control CPF4293, CPF4326, CPF4327, CPF4328, CPF4329.
		Q	An OPEN statement for a randomly- or dynamically-accessed relative file failed because its size was *NOMAX. Change the file size (for example, using CHGPF) to the size you expect, and submit the program again.
		S	REWRITE or DELETE failed because last READ operation specified NO LOCK.
		U	Cannot complete READ PRIOR because records are left in block from READ NEXT, or vice versa. CPF5184 To clear records from block, perform random READ, START, or sequential READ FIRST or LAST.

Symbols Used in the PICTURE Clause

Symbol	Meaning
A	Alphabetic character or space
B	Space insertion character
P	Decimal scaling position (not counted in size of data item)
S	Operational sign (not counted in size of data item unless a SIGN clause with optional SEPARATE CHARACTER phrase is specified)
V	Assumed decimal point (not counted in size of data item)
X	Alphanumeric character (any from the EBCDIC set)
Z	Zero suppression character
9	Numeric character
1	Boolean character (IBM extension)
0	Zero insertion character
/	Slash insertion character
,	Comma insertion character
.	Decimal point or period editing control character
+	Plus sign insertion editing control character
-	Minus sign editing control character
CR	Credit editing control character
DB	Debit editing control character
*	Check protect insertion character
$	Currency symbol insertion character ($ is default)

Index

An *f.* or *t.* after a page number refers to a figure or table.

ABOUT THE AUTHOR

Gerry Kaplan, a graduate of the Florida State University, is currently a member of the Corporate Technology division at J.P. Morgan in Japan. He is also a contributing author to *News/400*, a key mid-range computing journal, and has written extensively for other PC-based publications.